Social Protection versus Economic Flexibility

NBER Comparative Labor Markets Series
A National Bureau of Economic Research Series
Edited by Richard B. Freeman

Also in the series

David Card and Richard B. Freeman, editors
Small Differences That Matter: Labor Markets and Income Maintenance in Canada and the United States

Lisa M. Lynch, editor
Training and the Private Sector: International Comparisons

Social Protection versus Economic Flexibility

Is There a Trade-off?

WITHDRAWN

Edited by   Rebecca M. Blank

 The University of Chicago Press

Chicago and London

REBECCA M. BLANK is professor of economics at Northwestern University, faculty affiliate at Northwestern's Center for Urban Affairs and Policy Research, and a research associate of the National Bureau of Economic Research.

The University of Chicago Press, Chicago 60637
The University of Chicago Press, Ltd., London

© 1994 by the National Bureau of Economic Research
All rights reserved. Published 1994
Printed in the United States of America
03 02 01 00 99 98 97 96 95 94   1 2 3 4 5
ISBN: 0–226–05678–3

Library of Congress Cataloging-in-Publication Data

Social protection versus economic flexibility : is there a trade-off? / edited
   by Rebecca M. Blank.
        p.   cm.—(NBER Comparative labor markets series)
     "These papers were first presented at a conference held at the Centre
   for Economic Performance (CEP) at the London School of
   Economics"—Pref.
     Includes bibliographical references and index.
     ISBN 0-226-05678-3 (cloth)
     1. Social security—Congresses.   2. Labor market—Congresses.
   I. Blank, Rebecca M.   II. Series.
   HD9975.U52L49   1994   94-5186
                                                                     CIP

♾ The paper used in this publication meets the minimum requirements of the American National Standard for Information Sciences—Permanence of Paper for Printed Library Materials, ANSI Z39.48–1984.

Relation of the Directors to the
Work and Publications of the
National Bureau of Economic Research

1. The object of the National Bureau of Economic Research is to ascertain and to present to the public important economic facts and their interpretation in a scientific and impartial manner. The Board of Directors is charged with the responsibility of ensuring that the work of the National Bureau is carried on in strict conformity with this object.

2. The President of the National Bureau shall submit to the Board of Directors, or to its Executive Committee, for their formal adoption all specific proposals for research to be instituted.

3. No research report shall be published by the National Bureau until the President has sent each member of the Board a notice that a manuscript is recommended for publication and that in the President's opinion it is suitable for publication in accordance with the principles of the National Bureau. Such notification will include an abstract or summary of the manuscript's content and a response form for use by those Directors who desire a copy of the manuscript for review. Each manuscript shall contain a summary drawing attention to the nature and treatment of the problem studied, the character of the data and their utilization in the report, and the main conclusions reached.

4. For each manuscript so submitted, a special committee of the Directors (including Directors Emeriti) shall be appointed by majority agreement of the President and Vice Presidents (or by the Executive Committee in case of inability to decide on the part of the President and Vice Presidents), consisting of three Directors selected as nearly as may be one from each general division of the Board. The names of the special manuscript committee shall be stated to each Director when notice of the proposed publication is submitted to him. It shall be the duty of each member of the special manuscript committee to read the manuscript. If each member of the manuscript committee signifies his approval within thirty days of the transmittal of the manuscript, the report may be published. If at the end of that period any member of the manuscript committee withholds his approval, the President shall then notify each member of the Board, requesting approval or disapproval of publication, and thirty days additional shall be granted for this purpose. The manuscript shall then not be published unless at least a majority of the entire Board who shall have voted on the proposal within the time fixed for the receipt of votes shall have approved.

5. No manuscript may be published, through approved by each member of the special manuscript committee, until forty-five days have elapsed from the transmittal of the report in manuscript form. The interval is allowed for the receipt of any memorandum of dissent or reservation, together with a brief statement of his reasons, that any member may wish to express; and such memorandum of dissent or reservation shall be published with the manuscript if he so desires. Publication does not, however, imply that each member of the Board has read the manuscript, or that either members of the Board in general or the special committee have passed on its validity in every detail.

6. Publications of the National Bureau issued for informational purposes concerning the work of the Bureau and its staff, or issued to inform the public of activities of Bureau staff, and volumes issued as a result of various conferences involving the National Bureau shall contain a specific disclaimer noting that such publication has not passed through the normal review procedures required in this resolution. The Executive Committee of the Board is charged with review of all such publications from time to time to ensure that they do not take on the character of formal research reports of the National Bureau, requiring formal Board approval.

7. Unless otherwise determined by the Board or exempted by the terms of paragraph 6, a copy of this resolution shall be printed in each National Bureau publication.

(Resolution adopted October 25, 1926, as revised through September 30, 1974)

Contents

Preface

This volume contains eleven papers that explore and compare the effects of social protection policies on the labor market in the United States with the effects of such policies in Japan and various western European countries. The papers are the result of a larger set of cross-national research papers funded jointly by the Ford Foundation and the National Bureau of Economic Research (NBER). I particularly thank Richard Freeman at NBER for his work in encouraging and supporting this project.

These papers were first presented at a conference held at the Centre for Economic Performance (CEP) at the London School of Economics. I thank CEP for sharing the cost of this conference and handling the organizational details, and I thank the many conference participants, particularly the nine discussants, for their valuable input into this project.

Introduction

Rebecca M. Blank

Starting in the mid-1970s, most western industrialized countries experienced a sharp decrease in growth and a corresponding rise in unemployment. In Europe these problems continued throughout the 1980s. In fact, growth in most European countries was slower from 1980 through 1990 than it had been from 1973 to 1979. Unemployment—particularly long-term unemployment—continued to rise in the 1980s to unprecedented rates. While the United States experienced similar trends between 1973 and 1983, over the late 1980s the United States saw a substantial decline in unemployment and an acceleration in growth. This generated a sustained discussion about what the United States was doing right that European countries were doing wrong. One answer to that question came to be widely accepted: the idea that the European growth difficulties were at least partially caused by their more extensive welfare states. The level of social protection provided through labor market regulation and income support programs limited the market response to high unemployment, it was argued, preventing workers from shifting rapidly from slower- to faster-growing segments of the economy. In other words, a trade-off was posited between social protection and economic flexibility. The United States, with lower levels of income or employment protection for workers, had an economy that adjusted more rapidly to the perilous economic environment of the past two decades.

This volume explores in more detail the relationship between social protection programs and labor market flexibility. As Rebecca Blank and Richard Freeman note in the first chapter, there is actually very little direct empirical evidence that measures the impact of social programs on the speed of labor

Rebecca M. Blank is professor of economics at Northwestern University, faculty affiliate at Northwestern's Center for Urban Affairs and Policy Research, and a research associate of the National Bureau of Economic Research.

market adjustment to a changing economic environment. The papers in this volume are designed to fill that gap, looking at cross-national comparisons over time between countries that demonstrate particularly interesting differences in the structure of their social protection systems and analyzing the effects of these differences on labor market adjustment.

What Can Cross-National Comparisons Contribute?

The divergent European and U.S. economic experiences of the 1980s have increased interest in cross-national research. This volume uses differences between countries, both across programs and over time, to study the impact of different tax, transfer, and regulatory programs on the degree of short-term price, wage, and mobility adjustment within labor markets. Cross-national comparisons are not perfect "natural experiments," however. Many significant differences in behavior among different countries, such as the greater work hours of Americans compared to Europeans, have developed over time and probably reflect responses to long-term differences in institutional structures and economic incentives. These national differences can create problems in making proper cross-national inferences, but this is no different than the problem that economists long have faced in drawing inferences by comparing different individuals within a country. It is the essential problem of all nonexperimental research: potential unmeasured heterogeneity or omitted variables may lead the analyst to draw mistaken causal conclusions.

There are several ways to deal with this problem in cross-national research. One way is to limit comparisons to countries with relatively similar economic, institutional, and demographic patterns. Thus, comparisons between the Swedish and the U.S. income transfer systems may have fewer useful policy implications than comparisons between the Canadian and the U.S. transfer systems. Meaningful comparisons require careful choice of the right countries. For some issues, it may be useful to compare the United States and the United Kingdom, since both have relatively unregulated private-sector labor markets. For other issues, it may be more useful to compare Germany and the United States, both of which have a well-developed federalist system, with strong state governments. But here, as elsewhere in economics, there is a trade-off. Countries that are similar in many respects are unlikely to have extremely different policies. The gain in similarity comes at the likely cost of less variation in the independent variable of concern.

A second way to deal with country heterogeneity in cross-national comparisons is to focus on changes in differences over time rather than on point-in-time differences in programs and outcomes. Looking at the changes in relative vacancy rates between two countries when one country implements stricter severance provisions is more convincing than comparing vacancy rates in a country with strict severance laws to those in a country with few severance restrictions. Fixed-effects models—difference in difference techniques—that contrast changes in country A before and after a program has been introduced with changes in country B (with no program) offer a way to control for long-term differences between countries.

Third, meaningful interpretation of statistical results requires an understanding of the institutional differences between countries. It is time consuming to learn about the institutional structure of any particular country and to become familiar with and gain access to its microdata sources. This means that good cross-national analysis will often involve comparisons between only a few countries at a time. A careful two-country analysis by a scholar who understands the history and structure of both countries and who has good microdata samples of individual behavior in each country should provide more information than a fifteen-country comparison based on aggregate data that necessarily ignores many of the most interesting institutional differences between the countries involved.

The papers in this volume are explicitly designed to meet these criteria. The authors have carefully selected countries whose comparison seems particularly appropriate for their topic; they limit their analysis to two or three countries, providing detailed information on the economic and institutional differences between these countries (many authors are writing about countries they know well); they use as many different sources of national data as are available, particularly seeking good microeconomic data; and when possible they focus on the effects of changes in programs over time rather than on point-in-time comparisons.

The next eleven sections of this introduction briefly summarize the main conclusions of each of the eleven chapters of the book. Readers interested in the overall conclusions of the volume should skip to the final section.

Evaluating the Connection between Social Protection and Economic Flexibility

Rebecca Blank and Richard Freeman set up the issues in this volume in chapter 1, summarizing the cross-Atlantic debate of the past decade over the question "Why are European unemployment rates so high?" and reviewing the evidence for the argument that a primary culprit was the larger welfare state in most European countries.

Blank and Freeman describe a variety of ways by which social protection was believed to promote high European unemployment, limiting both employers' and workers' economic adjustment to macroeconomic shocks. In general, these arguments rely on economic analysis showing that government interventions can cause inefficiencies by creating incentives for market participants to behave differently than they would in an unregulated economy. For instance, income transfer programs may lead a worker to stay out of the labor market longer, adding to the unemployment rate. Severance pay requirements may make employers less likely to hire workers who will be costly to fire.

Those who argue for strong social protection programs typically respond in several ways. Some admit that social programs have distortionary costs but argue that the benefits of these programs in terms of increased well-being, which critics rarely measure, exceed the costs. Others, skeptical about the "trade-off" argument, often point out that most analysts of the distortionary effects of social protection programs compare them to a situation of perfect competition, a rarity in most modern economies. In a world with many overlapping tax, regulation, and transfer programs, some social programs may offset the inefficiencies and distortions caused by others. Finally, many proponents of social protection programs deny the premise of a trade-off altogether, stressing the role of such programs in enhancing human capital and productivity in the labor market.

Evaluating the evidence for these arguments, Blank and Freeman conclude that there is little empirical evidence of large trade-offs between labor market flexibility and social protection programs in general. They argue that the best attitude toward the trade-off hypothesis should be one of open-minded skepticism and suggest a research agenda that might usefully expand our knowledge in this area.

Trends in Social Protection Programs and Expenditures

In the second chapter, Peter Scherer looks at trends in social protection programs within the Organization for Economic Cooperation and Development (OECD) countries. He uses just-released OECD data that provide consistent country-specific estimates of public expenditures on social protection programs from 1960 through 1988. Since the early 1980s, there has been little increase on average in the share of gross domestic product (GDP) spent on public social protection programs within OECD countries, a sharp contrast to the 1960s and 1970s. In addition, there appears to be relative stability in the share of the major components of social expenditure: health care, expenditure on elderly pensions, and expenditures on the non-aged. The United States, of course, is an exception to this, with a growing share of health care expenditures.

The stability in the OECD average hides a great deal of variance across countries, and Scherer discusses some of the different variance patterns. The general conclusion, however, is that social protection expenditures have not been increasing at a rate faster than GDP in most industrialized countries over the past decade. Scherer discusses some of the reasons common across countries for the slowdown in the growth rate of social spending.

After reviewing these data, Scherer discusses differences in how various social protection systems deal with the issues of individual risk. Countries whose legal history is Anglo-Saxon have different presumptions about the role of the state versus the role of the family than do countries whose legal history is based on the Napoleonic code. This creates somewhat different public tensions and debates in these different countries. Scherer also discusses the question of how social protection expenditures relate to labor force participation, noting the inherent tensions between greater income protection and work incentives.

Does Employment Protection Reduce Labor Market Flexibility?

Laws that restrict firms' ability to lay off workers should slow the employment decline that occurs during a downturn and may also limit employment growth in a boom, as firms are reluctant to hire workers who will be costly to fire. In chapter 3, Katharine Abraham and Susan Houseman investigate the extent to which job security regulations adversely affect labor market flexibility, particularly focusing on advance notice and severance pay requirements in West Germany, France, and Belgium. The result should be much less cyclicality in employment in countries with strong job security legislation. But Abraham and Houseman note that many of these countries also have policies that encourage firms to utilize hours adjustments, such as short-time benefits that provide partial wage replacement to workers whose hours have been reduced. If firms facing restrictions on employment adjustment make greater use of hours adjustment, total labor adjustment over the cycle may not be lower but may be differently distributed between employment and hours changes.

In the 1970s, to protect workers suddenly threatened by mass layoffs and plant closings, many European countries strengthened their requirements for advance notice and severance pay. As European unemployment problems continued, however, many countries subsequently loosened these regulations by the late 1980s. West Germany, France, and Belgium all experienced these changes, in sharp contrast to the United States, which had no advance-notice or severance pay requirements throughout most of this period.

Through both graphic and econometric analysis of the data, Abraham and Houseman investigate the speed of adjustment of employment and hours. The results indicate that the United States has much faster employment adjustment than does West Germany, France, or Belgium, consistent with its lower level of employment security legislation. In contrast, hours adjust at about the same speed in West Germany, Belgium, and the United States, indicating that hours adjustment is a far more important component in aggregate labor adjustment in these European countries.

To test the effect of employment security legislation on labor market adjustment, Abraham and Houseman compare the speed of employment and hours adjustments in West Germany, France, and Belgium before and after changes in the stringency of job protection laws. If, as many European employers claim, such regulations limit their ability to adapt flexibility to market changes, then the loosening of these laws in the mid-1980s should have accelerated the rate of employment adjustment in these three economies. Strikingly, they find virtually no evidence that the rate of adjustment over time changed in any of these countries after job security provisions were loosened.

Thus, this paper indicates that strong job security provisions may well be compatible with labor market flexibility. But it is flexibility of a different kind than we see in the United States, with more emphasis on hours adjustment and less emphasis on employment adjustment. One effect of this is to spread the costs of an economic downturn more broadly among workers. This is, of course, also consistent with the institutional structure of the Japanese labor market (although this paper does not look at that country), which provides substantial job security to its workers and yet seems able to respond quite flexibly to economic changes.

Is Regional Mobility Necessary for Flexible Labor Markets?

Labor mobility is often taken to be a necessary ingredient in economic flexibility. In chapter 4, Edward Montgomery looks at regional labor adjustments in the United States and Japan, investigating the persistence of regional wage and unemployment differentials in each country and the role of interregional migration in offsetting these differentials.

Both Japan and the United States experienced greater economic growth in the 1980s than did Europe, although Japan's growth outpaced the United States'. Many have suggested that Japan's greater growth is due at least in part to policies designed to enhance labor mobility. If Japan's policies to encourage labor mobility are more successful, this implies that interregional differences should be less persistent and interregional migration should be higher in Japan. Comparing equal-area migration rates, it turns out that regional migration in Japan is less than half that in the United States.

Montgomery investigates the persistence of regional levels of employment growth, unemployment rates, and earnings in the two countries, looking at Japanese prefectures and U.S. states. Unemployment rates and rates of economic growth show significant persistence within Japanese prefectures over time but are not persistent over time within U.S. states. Prefectural earnings seem to show little persistence over time, however, while higher wages do show some persistence within states.

To further investigate these differences, Montgomery explores the determinants of regional earnings and unemployment rates over time. He finds evidence in both countries that regional labor markets respond to regional demand factors. Regional migration rates in both countries are also responsive to economic forces. Because of the size of Japanese prefectures, it is quite possible to commute between them for work. Therefore, Montgomery investigates interprefectural commuting patterns as well as migration patterns and finds that commuting patterns are similar to migration patterns and affected in the same way by economic forces.

The overall conclusion of this paper is that regional adjustment appears to be somewhat slower and regional mobility lower in Japan. Both countries show evidence of substantial responsiveness within their regional labor markets. Regional wages, unemployment rates, and migration rates all vary as the economic environment within regions changes. But migration across equivalent regions is lower and regional employment growth and unemployment are more persistent over time in Japan than in the United States. Thus, there is little evidence that Japanese labor market policy creates greater regional economic flexibility or migration. While regional labor market flexibility might have been an important factor behind the relatively more successful U.S. and Japanese economies in the 1980s, this cannot explain the higher growth and lower unemployment experienced by Japan versus the United States over this decade.

Does Housing Market Policy Influence Labor Market Mobility?

Most governments intervene heavily in housing markets through tax laws, building codes, rent subsidies, subsidized housing construction, and tenant protection. To the extent that these policies tie people to particular locations, they may limit labor market flexibility by limiting mobility. In chapter 5, Axel Börsch-Supan compares the effects of housing policy in the United States, West Germany, and Japan. He focuses on the impact of tenant protection regulation and of homeownership subsidies across these countries.

German tenant protection laws make rent increases on sitting tenants difficult to obtain but do not regulate starting rents. Börsch-Supan investigates the effect of these laws on tenure discounts—that is, the tendency for there to be a growing difference over time between the rents of sitting tenants and the rents of new tenants in equivalent housing. He finds large tenure discounts in West Germany. Certain cities in the United States also have rent controls, and Börsch-Supan compares these cities to those without such laws. He finds tenure discounts in the United States that are as large or larger than in West Germany and that are virtually the same in cities without rent control as they are in cities with rent control. This indicates that tenure discounts are not caused by rent control laws. To the extent that worker mobility is limited by tenant discounts, this is not due to tenant protection legislation.

Börsch-Supan also compares mobility in West Germany before and after tenant protection laws were introduced in 1971 and after they were weakened in 1983 and 1987. There is no observable change in mobility rates in West Germany consistent with the claim that these legislative changes in tenant protection affected mobility. While mobility declined in the early 1970s, when the law was first being implemented, it declined even further in the 1980s, when the law was substantially weakened.

Homeownership subsidies, designed to improve households' well-being by fostering homeownership, are another major source of government intervention into the housing market. All three countries offer substantial subsidies to homeowners through tax and loan subsidy programs. Börsch-Supan presents evidence that these subsidies increase homeownership.

To the extent that homeownership subsidies encourage greater homeownership, this may decrease labor mobility. Homeowners have much lower rates of mobility in all three countries. Aggregate cross-national mobility rates, however, are clearly not dominated by this effect. Homeownership rates in Japan and the United States are at 61 percent and 64 percent respectively, while they are only half this in Germany, at 39 percent. Yet 18 percent of U.S. households move every year, while 10 percent of Japanese households move and only 7 percent of German households move. Thus, the country with the lowest homeownership level also has the lowest mobility rate.

The overall conclusion of this paper is that there is little evidence that housing market regulations substantially impact national labor mobility. While homeownership subsidies appear to increase homeownership, which is linked with lower mobility rates, these differences do not dominate cross-national patterns of mobility. Tenant protection laws also do not appear to impact mobility rates.

Does Tying Health Insurance to Employment Limit Job Mobility?

One of the many complaints about the U.S. health system of employer-provided care is that it may interfere with the smooth functioning of the labor market by creating "job lock": workers may be discouraged from changing jobs if they fear that such a change could produce an interruption or termination of health insurance. In chapter 6, Douglas Holtz-Eakin investigates this issue in the United States and West Germany. While Germany ensures health care, some German workers must change insurance funds when they change jobs, whereas others do not. Those who change funds can face a change in the price they pay. For these German workers, this could also limit job mobility.

The raw data in the United States are consistent with the hypothesis that those with health insurance on their job change jobs less often. Of married workers who are insured on their job, 26 percent will change jobs in the next three years; 37 percent of those who are uninsured will change jobs. The insured are a very different group from the uninsured, however, and it may be these differences rather than the availability of insurance that is causing differential job mobility. Holtz-Eakin investigates the possibility of job lock by looking at whether those with insurance on their own job or on their spouse's job are less likely to change jobs, controlling for all other characteristics of the individual and the job.

His conclusions for the United States are straightforward. There is no evidence of significant job lock among married or single workers, nor is there any evidence that this effect is any different over a three-year period than over a one-year period. Even workers in poorer health or with larger families show no evidence that they are less likely to change jobs if they are insured.

In the West German data, Holtz-Eakin estimates that about 50 percent of the work force may face a change in health insurance rates if they change jobs. Job changes in West Germany are quite infrequent compared to the United States, consistent with the evidence in the previous chapter that indicated migration rates in West Germany are well below those in the United States. Again, the raw data indicate that workers in national insurance funds are somewhat more likely to move than workers who face potential insurance price changes.

When the probability of job changes is estimated, controlling for individual and job characteristics, West German data provide somewhat more support for the job lock hypothesis than do U.S. data. For some groups, there is evidence of small effects that are weakly significant. Holtz-Eakin concludes that his evidence supports the possibility that the low rate of West German job mobility is reduced further by the institutional structure of the German health insurance system, but the evidence is relatively weak and the estimated effects are small.

The conclusion of this paper is that the health insurance systems of these two countries do not appear to have major effects on labor market mobility. This implies that these systems should not be judged by their secondary effects on labor mobility, which are small or nonexistent, but should be judged by their primary effects on access to health care and on the efficiency and quality of care they provide.

Do Public Pension Plans Limit Older Workers' Labor Market Responsiveness?

Publicly supported pension and early retirement plans exist in all industrialized countries. In times of high unemployment, these policies may, by providing alternative sources of income, encourage older workers to leave the labor market. Of course, this may mean older workers are less likely to enter the labor market in times of high demand, as well. In chapter 7, using data from the United States, Japan, and Sweden, Marcus Rebick investigates the effect of public pension plans on the responsiveness of older workers' labor market behavior.

In all three of these countries, there have been expansions in public pension benefits, coverage, and eligibility over time. At the same time, older men have substantially decreased their labor market participation, although older women's labor force participation has increased or (at higher ages) shown little change. The economic well-being of older persons has unambiguously improved in all three countries as the public pension system has expanded. For instance, poverty among the elderly has decreased. To the extent these public pensions are designed to improve the well-being of the elderly, they appear to be successful.

Rebick investigates the responsiveness of the share of older workers who are employed to cyclical changes in aggregate demand. The results indicate that the share of older men who are employed decreases significantly when unemployment rises. The response among both Japanese and Swedish men is larger than among U.S. men, primarily because men in these two countries have a larger propensity to drop out of the labor market when the unemployment rate rises. Among older women, the patterns are similar but not quite as strong. Rebick concludes that both Japan and Sweden rely heavily on their older workers to leave the labor force in economic downturns in order to maintain their reputation as countries with stable employment and low unemployment.

To investigate the effect of changes in public retirement laws, Rebick looks at differences in the responsiveness of older workers to economic changes during two periods, one with lower benefits and one with higher benefits, in the United States and Japan. If higher benefits make it more possible for older workers to leave the labor market in times of economic downturns, then the employment of these workers should be more responsive in the second period than in the first. If, however, higher benefits make it harder to induce older workers to reenter the labor market when labor demand rises, then the employment of workers should be less responsive in the second period. The results are very mixed, with greater responsiveness among some groups and less responsiveness among others. There appears to be little consistent pattern in the changes in labor market responsiveness to the macroeconomy among older workers as benefits expand.

Rebick concludes that the responsiveness of older workers to aggregate economic conditions is greater in Japan and Sweden than in the United States, indicating that, by leaving the labor market and using public assistance, they bear more of the burden of labor market adjustment to a recession. Although levels of labor force participation among older workers have clearly declined as public pensions have increased, there is little evidence that the responsiveness of older workers to aggregate economic demand has changed. Rebick concludes that the primary effects of these programs are on the economic well-being of the elderly, not on their labor market responsiveness.

Does the Size of the Public Sector Limit Labor Market Flexibility?

Expansions of social protection programs almost inevitably result in expansions of the public sector, as workers are needed to implement and oversee the operation of public programs. Exclusive of the effect of any particular welfare state program, the public sector expansion that it induces may limit labor market flexibility if the public sector labor market is less responsive to demand changes. Rebecca Blank investigates this question in chapter 8, using data from the United States and the United Kingdom, two countries whose leadership over the 1980s launched strong attacks on public sector bureaucracy.

Worker characteristics in the public sector are relatively similar in the United States and the United Kingdom. In both places, expansion in the public sector will create relative employment expansion among well-educated, white-collar, clerical and service workers, women, and minorities.

Both the United States and United Kingdom have positive aggregate public/ private wage differentials. Public sector workers earned 10.5 percent more than private workers in 1987 in the United Kingdom and 3.1 percent more than private workers in the United States in 1989. There is evidence in both countries over the 1980s that public sector wages came more into alignment with private sector wages, although these changes varied substantially among different groups of workers in both countries.

Over the 1980s the distribution of wages in both the United States and the United Kingdom has widened. In both countries, wages in the public sector are more compressed than in the private sector, but they have widened along with private sector wage distributions. This indicates that wage distributions in both sectors are responding in similar ways to the economic forces causing these distributional changes.

In addition, Blank looks at variability in employment and wages among public and private sector workers over time. In general, she finds that, in both countries, variation in employment and in wages is as great over time in the public sector as in the private sector, providing little indication that the public sector is less adaptable over time. The correlation between employment changes and the economic cycle is lower in the public sector, however, than in the private sector. But if public sector demands do not move cyclically, there is no reason for public sector employment to move cyclically. The more important question is how public employment responds to the demand for public services.

The last part of the paper estimates a series of models, relating changes in aggregate private and public sector demand to changes in private and public sector employment. In both the United States and the United Kingdom, increases in government demand appear to have little long-run effect on public or private sector employment. Increases in private demand, however, increase both public and private sector employment in the United States. In the United Kingdom, in contrast, increases in private demand increase private employment but have few effects on public employment.

Blank concludes that there is little evidence of substantial inflexibility in public sector labor markets. In both countries, public sector labor markets have shown substantial changes over the past decade, with wages coming closer to private sector wages and with similar distributional changes. In both countries, there is considerable variability in public and private sector employment and wages over time, although the patterns of variability in the public sector are less cyclical than those in the private sector. In the United States, both public and private sector labor markets expand when private demand grows. The main evidence of inflexibility occurs in the United Kingdom, where there appears to be less spillover in demand between the growth of the public and private sectors.

Does the Avoidance of Employment Mandates Increase Flexibility?

Most mandatory social protection legislation assumes that enforcement will be effective. If noncompliance is possible, however, an underground economy may emerge that allows those workers and firms who find these mandates most costly to avoid government regulations, thereby creating greater economic flexibility. In chapter 9, Sara de la Rica and Thomas Lemieux investigate the employer provision of health insurance in the United States, where health insurance is optional, with health insurance coverage in Spain, which levies mandatory taxes to pay for its nationalized health plan but where substantial noncompliance occurs.

Health, disability, and pension benefits in Spain are publicly provided and supported through a 24 percent mandatory social security tax per worker. These high tax rates create incentives for firms to hire workers off the books, especially since enforcement is weak and fines for noncompliance are not punitive. If workers are hired off the books, they will not receive a social security card, which they need to gain access to the national health care system. Since care is provided to all members of a worker's family, however, those who have working spouses can receive insurance through their spouse.

A survey in 1985 found that 12 percent of all Spanish workers reported they avoided social security taxes. This is in contrast to 32 percent of U.S. workers who report that they are not covered by health insurance through their employer. The well-being implications of these two systems are very different, however. Virtually 100 percent of uncovered Spanish workers have a working spouse who is covered by the system, but this is not true in the United States. For instance 13 percent of employed married women in the United States have no health insurance coverage.

De la Rica and Lemieux estimate the probability that a worker receives health insurance through his or her employer in the two countries. In both countries, similar factors determine the likelihood of receiving health insurance. Married males in full-time jobs with longer tenure, higher wages, and more education are most likely to get health insurance. Even after controlling for a substantial number of personal and job characteristics, however, there are big differences across industries in the propensity to provide health insurance to workers. The industries with higher tax avoidance in Spain are also less likely to provide health insurance in the United States.

De la Rica and Lemieux conclude that the provision of health insurance by both U.S. and Spanish firms is affected by labor demand and supply factors and that these factors are quite similar across the two countries. Thus, although the institutional systems governing health care are different, similar groups of workers remain uncovered. The possibility of noncompliance in Spain produces a market outcome relatively similar to the outcome in the United States. The primary difference in the systems is one of well-being; in the United States a substantial number of workers remain without access to health insurance.

While it would be wrong to conclude that a good policy is to pass mandatory laws and then be relatively lax about enforcing compliance, this paper does indicate that attention to compliance and underground economy questions are very important if the actual adaptability of the labor market is to be understood.

Do Limits on Income Assistance Payments Move Women into the Labor Market?

In the United States in particular, there has been an ongoing debate about the extent to which income transfer programs for low-income single mothers keep women out of the labor market. In chapter 10, Maria Hanratty compares U.S. income support programs for single mothers, which provide similar levels of support for a family until a child reaches age eighteen, with French income support programs, which are sharply curtailed after the youngest child in a family reaches age three.

Single parents in France receive assistance from a variety of programs with much higher total benefits than public support programs would provide to similar women in the United States. After the youngest child reaches age three, however, French mothers' benefits become less generous than those in the United States. In addition, public nursery school is available in France, substantially decreasing the cost of child care for mothers. Virtually 100 percent of children age three and over attend public nursery school, which is viewed not as child care but as the beginning of public education.

Hanratty compares the employment rates of single mothers with preschoolers over age 3 to those with preschoolers under age 3, in France and in the United States. She estimates the effect of decreased public transfers on labor supply through several methods. Even after controlling for the availability of public child care in France and the propensity for mothers to work more in general as their children age, she finds a significant net increase in employment among single women as a result of this program structure.

Hanratty tests this result further by looking at the effects of a similar change in income support for married mothers with three or more children who quit work for the birth of a child. These mothers receive a special allowance until their youngest child turns three or until they reenter the labor force, whichever occurs first. Using similar analysis, Hanratty demonstrates that these mothers also increase their labor force participation, but by a much smaller amount, when their income support is terminated.

The results of this paper indicate that single French mothers with preschool children increase their labor force participation when their public assistance income is cut back. The implication is that putting time limits on welfare programs in France seems to increase women's labor market involvement. It is important to recognize, however, that the magnitude of this effect may be dependent upon the network of social programs available in France for working single parents.

The effect of this policy on long-term labor market flexibility and family well-being is hard to predict. On the one hand, women are obtaining more labor market experience with this program, which should increase their wage and employment opportunities and thus increase the skill level and size of the labor force. On the other hand, the children may be receiving somewhat less parental attention, and any long-run effect of this is difficult to measure.

What Difference Do Childcare and Maternal Leave Policies Make?

Compared to the United States, many European countries have far more extensive maternity leave policies and more publicly available child care. The effect of these programs on labor market flexibility may be twofold. First, they may affect women's long-run productivity if they change women's level of labor market experience. Maternity leave programs may decrease experience, but childcare programs may increase labor market contact. Second, such programs may affect long-term productivity in an economy if they enhance the cognitive development of young children. The net effect of such programs on overall labor market flexibility is clearly uncertain. In chapter 11, Siv Gustafsson and Frank Stafford investigate the labor market effects of childcare policies in the United States, the Netherlands, and Sweden.

The United States provides little public support for women who have children, except among those with very low incomes. It has no paid maternity leave and little publicly funded care. In contrast, Sweden provides universally available and quite generous maternity leave and public day care. The Netherlands' childcare policy is similar to the U.S. policy, with little public day care or leave, but it emerged from a very different history in which opposing religious groups tried to foster fertility among their members by encouraging women to stay at home.

Gustafsson and Stafford indicate that these policy differences lead to substantial differences in family behavior. In the United States, there is high labor force participation by women, and mothers return to work almost immediately after a child is born. Sweden has high labor force participation rates among mothers of older preschoolers, but there is very low labor force participation among mothers with children under age one. The Netherlands has relatively low labor force participation rates among all young mothers, and work behavior is strongly affected by religious affiliation. While 72 to 82 percent of young married women work in the United States and in Sweden, only 49 percent of these women work in the Netherlands.

Estimates of the determinants of wages for younger women in these three countries indicate that the returns to education and experience, while positive in all countries, are much larger in the United States. While these returns are partly determined by the childcare policies in the United States that encourage women to work more, they in turn reinforce the U.S. system by giving larger returns to those women who return to work quickly and remain in the labor market more constantly over their lifetime.

The conclusions of this paper are twofold. First, long-term institutional forces within countries shape their childcare policy. These forces have resulted in very different institutional structures across countries and continue to shape women's behavior. Second, once these structures are created, they in turn reinforce behavior, so that the labor market participation patterns and wage patterns of U.S. and Swedish women are very different in ways determined by the vast differences in policy between the two countries.

Pulling It All Together: What Does This Volume Say?

Several main conclusions emerge from the empirical papers in this volume. Most important, these papers give little evidence that labor market flexibility is substantially affected by the presence of social protection programs, nor is there evidence that the speed of labor market adjustment can be enhanced by limiting these programs. Abraham and Houseman find little effect on labor adjustment in West Germany, France, or Belgium when advance notice and severance pay requirements are loosened. Montgomery finds that Japan has less interregional mobility and greater persistence of regional differentials than the United States, even though it (Japan) had greater economic growth over the past several decades. Börsch-Supan finds little evidence that differences in housing market regulations between West Germany, Japan, and the United States strongly affect country-specific mobility rates. Holtz-Eakin finds no evidence that tying health insurance to jobs in the United States prevents job mobility, and only weak evidence of such an effect in West Germany. Rebick finds little evidence that increases in pension benefits in Japan, Sweden, and the United States substantially changed the responsiveness of older workers to changes in labor market demands. Blank finds little evidence that public sector labor markets in the United States and the United Kingdom have been much less responsive to the overall economy over the past decade than the private sector has. De la Rica and Lemieux find that mandated fringe benefit taxes in Spain have had less impact on the labor market than might be predicted, because extensive noncompliance has occurred. Finally, both Hanratty and Gustafsson and Stafford find evidence that child-related policies definitely affect the labor market behavior of mothers of young children, but these authors are unable to conclude whether this substantially affects the flexibility of the labor market.

The consistency of this conclusion is particularly striking in this volume because it occurs across papers that use very different data sets to investigate the effects of different programs in different countries. When the authors of this volume came together to present their research to one another, all of us were struck by the correspondence in results and inferences across these papers.

This conclusion is consistent with other research that questions the hypothesis that social protection laws are the primary cause of economic inflexibility. *Labour and Society* (1987) devoted an entire issue to articles reviewing this hypothesis skeptically. Burtless (1987) indicates that the more-extensive unemployment benefits in European countries did not cause the relative rise in European versus U.S. unemployment rates over the 1970s and 1980s, because the estimated effects are far too small to generate the large observed unemployment changes. Blanchflower and Freeman (1993) find that even the most liberal estimates of the effects of Prime Minister Margaret Thatcher's programs on labor market flexibility were dwarfed by the effects of aggregate economic conditions. Buechtemann (1993) argues that mechanisms to limit labor market adjustment and protect workers arise because of failures in the labor market and that these "inflexibilities" would exist even in the absence of strong employment protection laws.

Rather than finding that more-extensive social protection systems seem to limit labor market adjustment, a second conclusion of this volume is that countries with more extensive social protection systems find other ways by which adjustment can occur. In other words, the entire *system* of interlocking programs and behavior in different countries is quite different. In comparison to the United States, Germany and Belgium rely more heavily on hours adjustment rather than employment adjustment when faced with an economic downturn. Even though Japan has less interregional mobility than the United States, it has high rates of interregional commuting. Sweden and Japan rely more heavily than does the United States on older workers leaving the labor market in an economic downturn to keep unemployment rates low. Young Swedish women have labor force participation rates very similar to young American women's, but a much higher fraction of the Swedish women take more than a year off work when they have a child.

Two important implications follow from the fact that there are many routes to economic adjustment. On the one hand, this means that simple measures of economic flexibility may say little about the overall economic adaptability of an economy. The speed of employment adjustment alone is not a good measure of labor market adjustment, without corresponding information on wage and hours adjustment. Mobility rates alone can vary for many reasons and are not a good measure of labor market flexibility. Information on the amount of movement between employment and unemployment is of limited usefulness without matching information on how many people are leaving the labor market entirely.

On the other hand, comparing single programs across countries can produce misleading inferences. It is important to understand how individual programs link into the web of rules and institutions in each country. High and mandatory per-employee taxes to pay for public health and pensions plans in Spain do not produce major disemployment of low-skilled workers, because of the prevalence of tax avoidance. Time-limited income support payments to single young mothers in France have strong labor market effects partly because free public child care is available just at the point when transfer payments drop. Higher homeownership subsidies in the United States than in Germany do not produce lower mobility rates in the United States, as many other factors influence mobility.

Finally, the third main conclusion of this volume is that it is hard to conclude anything about the net effect of social protection programs simply by observing that they cause behavioral changes. Virtually all of these papers confirm the classic economist's wisdom that the structure of government programs can affect the behavior of employers and workers. Germany, France, and Belgium do less employment adjustment in the face of significant restrictions on major layoffs. Homeownership subsidies in Germany, Japan, and the United States significantly affect homeownership rates in those countries. Rising public retirement benefits have produced a downward trend in the labor market participation of older men over time. Cutting off income transfers to young mothers increases their propensity to spend more time in the labor market. There is nothing in these papers that denies the standard conclusions about the potentially distortionary effects of government programs on behavior.

Yet, among the papers in this volume that study specific social protection programs, virtually all of them also point to changes in worker well-being provided by these programs. Higher public retirement benefits have increased the economic well-being of the elderly. The Spanish health insurance system provides health insurance to virtually 100 percent of Spanish workers, while the U.S. system leaves many uninsured. Extensive maternity leave programs in Sweden allow mothers to stay home with young children.

These papers were not written with the intention of trying to measure the aggregate costs and benefits of social protection programs; thus, they do not produce any answer to the question of whether the net costs and benefits of such programs are positive or negative. But they do serve as a reminder that these programs often have substantial positive social benefits associated with them, benefits too rarely discussed in the economics literature. The research agenda laid out by Blank and Freeman to look more carefully at these questions indicates some ways to begin more fully analyzing the effects of social protection programs.

There are some important caveats to these conclusions. First, the research in all of these papers focuses on particular programs in particular countries at particular points in time. The results in this volume indicate that the changes in social protection programs enacted by European countries in the 1980s in order to increase labor market flexibility had few effects. It is possible that programmatic changes in other countries at other time periods might have produced different effects.

Second, it could be claimed that many of the program changes studied in these papers are relatively small. Rather than the implementation or abolishment of programs, most of the changes studied here involve the expansion or contraction of existing programs. This sort of marginal change may be too minor to have big effects on aggregate labor market flexibility. Perhaps only major economic restructuring in European economies, involving the complete abolishment of collective bargaining systems or radical changes in the nature of the welfare state, will produce noticeable increases in the speed of labor market adjustment. The research here cannot reject such a hypothesis, but it is worth noting that such radical changes are rarely possible within stable political environments. The program changes studied here represent ones that are conceivable in the short run in most countries.

Third, all cross-national research is subject to the caution that there may be missing variables that are not adequately controlled for or considered in the analysis. The methodology in many of these papers, looking at changes in behavior before and after regime changes, will control for many of the fixed differences between countries and groups. Future availability of better data and new methodologies may make possible more effective comparisons than are presented here, and this may in turn lead to new and different conclusions.

If we accept the conclusion of this volume, it is perhaps worthwhile to speculate why analysts were wrong when they argued in the mid-1980s that substantial cutbacks in social protection programs would solve European unemployment problems. One possible reason is that the interlocking systems of legislation and labor market operation in the European economies, while different from those in the United States or Japan, nonetheless had their own internal consistency. Workers and employers were used to these systems and had adopted modes of behavior that minimized any distortionary effects (such as the tacit acceptance of limited employer tax avoidance in Italy or the more extensive use of hours adjustment in West Germany.) Given that this system was working, there was little incentive for employers or workers to substantially change their behavior even after legislative changes in some of these programs. This is the argument made by Abraham and Houseman in explaining the lack of response to loosening of job security regulations in West Germany, France, and Belgium, and it may well be applicable to other changes as well.

A second possible explanation is that the analysis of social protection programs as a primary cause of inflexibility and high unemployment in Europe was simply flawed from the beginning. The best counterexample here is Japan, a country with extensive job-security provisions and with less interregional mobility than the United States that has consistently outperformed the United States as well as its European competitors. Japan at least provides evidence that there is no inherent correlation between poor economic performance and the presence of welfare state programs and/or slower labor market adjustment in terms of employment or mobility. It is possible that the sluggish economies of Europe over the 1980s were due to quite different factors, such as a lack of useful cooperation and communication between the political system and the private sector or the increasing social alienation of growing groups of workers—particularly youth—from mainstream jobs.

Results in this volume and elsewhere also suggest that perhaps the entire focus of the past decade's discussion about "What did the United States do right with regard to labor market policy?" has been misconceived. As Blank and Freeman note, the growth of GDP per employee—one measure of productivity growth—has been as low in the United States as in Europe, while it has been substantially higher in Japan. Only the United States' success at employment creation over the past decade has made it appear more successful in the labor market. Viewed in terms of productivity measures, Japan is the outstanding country and the United States performs as poorly as most European economies.

It is true that the U.S. economy created far more jobs than the European economies in the past decade and therefore unemployment fell to much lower levels. The full reasons behind this "job miracle" in the United States are not fully understood, although it may well be at least partially due to the lower level of employment regulation and taxation in the United States. But the United States has also seen real wage declines among less-skilled workers and a much larger increase in wage inequality than any other nation over the past decade (Freeman and Katz 1994). In 1993, after several years of stagnant employment growth and growing concern about the problems of low-wage U.S. workers, it is increasingly unclear that the labor market of the United States over the 1980s should be either envied or emulated.

The evidence in this volume indicates that the differences in labor markets in the United States and in other economies over the 1980s cannot be simply ascribed to the United States' relatively lower level of social protection programs, which allowed the U.S. economy to adjust more rapidly to economic change. While there is evidence of higher worker mobility in U.S. labor markets and faster employment adjustment than in other countries, these factors are not easily correlated with the presence or absence of social protection programs in these countries, nor can greater flexibility—as measured by a variety of "speed of adjustment" measures—be seen as a necessary or sufficient condition for an adaptable and responsive labor market.

References

Blanchflower, D. G., and R. B. Freeman. 1993. Did the Thatcher reforms change British labor performance? NBER Working Paper no. 4384. Cambridge, Mass.: National Bureau of Economic Research.

Buechtemann, C. F. 1993. *Employment security and labor market behavior.* Ithaca, N.Y.: ILR Press.

Burtless, G. 1987. Jobless pay and high European unemployment. In *Barriers to European growth: A transatlantic view,* ed. R. Lawrence and C. Schultze. Washington, D.C.: Brookings Institution.

Freeman, R. B., and L. F. Katz. 1994. Rising wage inequality: The United States versus other advanced countries. In *Working under Different Rules,* ed. R. B. Freeman. New York: Russell Sage Foundation.

Labour and Society. 1987. Vol. 12. Special volume on labour market flexibility.

1   Evaluating the Connection Between Social Protection and Economic Flexibility

Rebecca M. Blank and Richard B. Freeman

From the mid-1970s through the early 1980s, most western industrialized countries suffered from slow economic growth and high or rising unemployment. While the United States was no exception, it had markedly better employment growth than western Europe. The United States added some 20 million jobs from 1975 to 1984, whereas employment was stagnant in Europe. European rates of unemployment, which had historically been below those in the United States, came to exceed the U.S. level. Many analysts and policymakers attributed the U.S. "job creation miracle" to that country's flexible and unregulated labor market. A consensus developed that the cure for Europe's employment problems required greater labor market flexibility, specifically including a reduction in social protection programs that impeded flexibility (OECD 1990). To speed up market adjustments and increase employment, many European countries tightened provisions for unemployment insurance benefits, loosened dismissal regulations, decentralized collective bargaining, and sought to increase worker mobility through government subsidies or training. Under Prime Minister Margaret Thatcher, the United Kingdom tried to revamp its entire set of labor market institutions to create a more flexible and market-driven economic system.

Developments in the late 1980s and early 1990s have called into question the 1980s analysis that welfare state programs and labor market rigidities were

Rebecca M. Blank is professor of economics at Northwestern University, faculty affiliate at Northwestern's Center for Urban Affairs and Policy Research, and research associate of the National Bureau of Economic Research. Richard B. Freeman is professor of economics at Harvard University and at the London School of Economics and directs the Labor Studies Program at the National Bureau of Economic Research.

The authors thank the Ford Foundation, the National Bureau of Economic Research, and the Center for Urban Affairs and Policy Research, Northwestern University, for their support for this project. Participants in the conference for this volume provided excellent suggestions and comments, and Rebecca London provided top-quality research assistance.

major causes of the decade's economic problems. The curative powers of labor market flexibility seem far more limited at this writing than they did a decade ago. The expansion in U.S. employment after the 1983 recession ended in several years of stagnant growth in the 1990s and was accompanied by rising inequality and falling real earnings for many workers. In the United Kingdom, the increase in unemployment in the early 1990s to over three million workers, rising inequality, and financial woes in many sectors raised serious doubts as to the efficacy of the Thatcher reforms. In both countries, the government began to back away from relying solely on market-oriented reforms. High U.S. unemployment in summer 1992 forced the Bush administration to extend unemployment benefits; in fall 1992, U.S. voters chose a new president who promised a more activist government economic policy. Devaluation of the pound forced the British government from a zero-inflation, noninterventionist economic policy to one more attuned to growth.

How valid was the 1980s belief that an extensive social protection system— defined broadly to include all governmentally sponsored programs that protect individuals or families from serious income declines or job loss[1]—contributes to economic problems? In what ways can social protection advance or retard economic progress? How strong is the empirical evidence on the effect of welfare state or social safety net programs on the functioning of economies?

We begin to examine these questions by reviewing the economic record that gave rise to the belief that social protection harms economic progress. Then we consider the argument that such protection has deleterious effects and the counterargument that it has positive economic effects and, finally, evaluate the empirical evidence on this debate.

1.1 Employment and Growth Woes: The 1980s Analysis

The belief that the extensive social welfare programs in the Organization for Economic Cooperation and Development countries in Europe (OECD-Europe) limited labor market flexibility is rooted in the economic developments of the late 1970s and 1980s, when virtually all major OECD countries suffered from high unemployment and reduced economic growth. Table 1.1 indicates the extent of these problems. Part A shows unemployment rates across a sample of countries. Although rates showed no secular change in the 1960s, during the 1970s they rose everywhere, in many cases to levels once considered highly

---

1. This includes income transfer programs that protect families against poverty, and in-kind programs such as housing or health insurance that ensure access to particular goods or services, as well as social insurance programs that cushion workers against unemployment, disability, or old age. It also includes employment regulation programs that provide greater job security and programs that mandate employer payments to support particular fringe benefits, such as social security or health care. We limit our discussion to government programs, though we recognize the Rein and Friedman (1992) point that social protection involves other sectors of the society as well.

Table 1.1   **Unemployment Rates and Rates of Growth of GDP, 1960–1990**

| Country | A. Rates of Unemployment | | | |
	1960	1968	1979	1990
United States	5.4%	3.5%	5.8%	5.4%
OECD-Europe	2.9	3.4	5.7	7.8
West Germany	1.0	1.2	3.3	6.2
France	1.4	2.7	5.9	9.0
United Kingdom	1.3	2.1	4.6	5.5
Italy	5.5	5.6	7.6	10.8
Smaller European	3.9	4.5	6.4	7.9
Country	B. Annual Rates of Real GDP Growth			
	1960–68	1968–73	1973–79	1979–90
United States	4.5%	3.2%	2.4%	2.6%
OECD-Europe	4.7	4.9	2.6	2.3
West Germany	4.1	4.9	2.3	2.0
France	5.4	5.4	2.8	2.1
United Kingdom	3.0	3.4	1.5	2.1
Italy	5.7	4.5	3.7	2.4
Smaller European	5.4	5.6	2.6	2.6

Sources: Organization for Economic Cooperation and Development 1992b, tables 2.15 and 3.1; Organization for Economic Cooperation and Development 1991, table 2.15.

recessionary. In the 1980s, unemployment in most European countries increased further. In contrast, after reaching a post–World War II peak in 1983, unemployment fell substantially in the United States. Japan was an exception throughout the period, with a low and stable unemployment rate.

Part B of table 1.1 shows rates of gross domestic product (GDP) growth over the same years. Economic growth slowed between the 1960s and the 1970s and in most countries decelerated further between the 1970s and 1980s. The United States is again an exception. U.S. economic growth was as strong (or weak) in the 1980s as in the 1970s. Much of the growth of U.S. GDP, however, took the form of growing employment per capita rather than growing output per worker (table 1.2). GDP per capita grew at the same rate in the United States as in Europe, whereas growth in GDP per worker in the United States was poor by OECD standards and by past U.S. standards as well. While the aggregate data thus give a mixed message about the U.S. experience—better employment growth but worse productivity growth—analysts of European problems focused largely on the output and employment success of the United States in their assessment of the virtue of deregulated labor markets.[2]

Table 1.3 explores one reason for this: differential U.S.-European performance in creating full-time jobs and in the duration of joblessness. Part A

2. This point is documented in Freeman (1988) for the first half of the 1980s.

Table 1.2   Rates of Growth of Employment per Capita, GDP per Capita, and
                   GDP per Employee, 1979–90

	United States	OECD-Europe	OECD–Smaller European
Growth of GDP per capita	1.6%	1.7%	1.5%
Growth of employment per capita	0.6	0.3	0.3
Growth of GDP per employee	1.0	1.4	1.2

Source: Organization for Economic Cooperation and Development 1992b, tables 3.2 and 3.7, with
employment per capita obtained by subtracting GDP per employee from GDP per capita.

Table 1.3   Part-Time Employment and Duration of Unemployment

| | A. Part-Time Employment as Share of Total | | |
Country	1979	1983	1990
United States	16.4%	18.4%	16.9%
OECD-Europe			
West Germany	11.4	12.6	13.2*
France	8.2	9.7	12.0
United Kingdom	16.4	19.4	21.8*
Italy	5.3	4.6	5.7*
Smaller European			
Belgium	6.0	8.1	10.2*
Netherlands	16.6	21.4	33.2
	B. Percentage Unemployed Twelve Months or More		
Country	1979	1983	1990
United States	4.3%†	13.3%	5.6%
OECD-Europe			
West Germany	28.7	39.3	46.3
France	32.6†	42.2	38.3
United Kingdom	29.5	47.0	36.0
Italy	51.2	57.7	71.1
Smaller European			
Belgium	61.5	66.3	69.9
Netherlands	35.9	50.5	48.4

*1989 statistic.
†1980 statistic.
Source: Organization for Economic Cooperation and Development 1991, tables 2.7, 2.9; 1992,
table N.

shows that the share of part-time employees in the labor force rose in most European economies, so that employment growth consisted largely of part-time rather than full-time jobs. Indeed, in many countries, full-time employment fell while part-time employment rose. In the United States, by contrast, while the share of part-time workers increased in the early 1980s recession, it then fell so that it stood at nearly the same level in 1990 as in 1979.[3] Part B of table 1.3 shows the large differential in duration of unemployment between Europe and the United States. Jobless spells in Europe were long and rising, whereas those in North America were relatively short, as might be expected in a flexible and adaptable market system. More than any other single fact, the lengthy duration of European joblessness led many to believe that European social policies supporting the unemployed or protecting the employed might be part of the problem of high joblessness rather than part of the solution.

At first, economists analyzing this problem stressed the potential adverse effect of social protection and labor institutions on short-run labor market flexibility, limiting wage adjustments in the face of macroeconomic shocks. As high unemployment persisted, however, and estimates of the nonaccelerating inflation rate of unemployment (NAIRU) indicated that the unemployment rate consistent with stable inflation had increased,[4] economists came to view labor market flexibility as a tool to reduce the NAIRU and long-term unemployment.[5] The notion grew that flexibility was necessary if not sufficient for any major reduction of unemployment and restoration of growth.

But what exactly is meant by labor market flexibility? The precise meaning of the term is often unclear, because of the many margins along which economic agents can be flexible.[6] The most common usage measures flexibility by the speed of price and quantity adjustment in a changing economic environment. The more flexible market has wages adjusting rapidly when unemployment or prices change; has employment or hours adjusting rapidly when labor demand changes; has greater mobility of labor between different sectors, firms, and geographic areas as demands shift; has more rapid transitions from unemployment to employment; and so on. For analysts addicted to Phillips curve regressions, flexibility means larger coefficients on unemployment variables in wage change regressions. For analysts concerned with mobility of labor,

---

3. Although more difficult to measure, temporary work increased in both the U.S. and the European economies.

4. For instance, the European Unemployment Program conferences reached this conclusion, as summarized in the papers in Bean, Layard, and Nickell (1987) and Drèze and Bean (1990). For a good summary of the changing discussion over the nature of the unemployment program in Europe, see Krugman (1987).

5. For an example of such a policy discussion on how to reduce the NAIRU, see Layard (1986).

6. Boyer (1988) has an excellent discussion of alternative definitions of flexibility and of some ways in which flexibility may or may not be to the long-run advantage of the economy. Metcalf (1987) also presents an extended discussion of various types of labor market flexibility.

flexibility means greater exit rates from unemployment (and presumably from employment as well).

More heterodox analysts, noting the success of Japan in adjusting to the shocks of the period, used flexibility to refer to a broader set of responses, such as adaptive corporate strategies, changeable production technologies, or multiskilled and adaptable workers. When flexibility is restricted to short-term, market-driven wage and employment responses, Japan's commitment to life-time employment contracts raises the possibility that "flexible rigidities," to use Ronald Dore's (1986) phrase, rather than unconstrained markets are the requisite for economic success. As arguments over labor market flexibility focus largely on the trade-off between European-style social protection and U.S.-style short-term flexibility, however, we will use the term *flexibility* to refer to the speed of short-term quantity and price adjustments in the labor market in the ensuing discussion.

What was Europe doing wrong in terms of labor market practices and social protection that the flexible United States was doing right? There is a diverse set of policies and institutions that, arguably, adversely affected labor market flexibility and thus economic progress:[7]

1. Labor relations practices that strengthen the position of workers within firms can limit employers' ability to adjust to the changing economic environment by creating sticky wages and slow reallocation of labor (within and between firms). Legislation regulating the hiring and firing of workers will reduce employer ability to reduce employment in the face of short-run shocks and can make them reluctant to hire workers in a boom if they fear it is temporary.[8] Centralized wage settlements, viewed as helpful in an era of inflationary pressures (Bruno and Sachs 1985) can similarly impair industry or firm wage adjustments to changing market conditions. Worker organizations inside firms can prevent wage adjustments that might increase new hires (Lindbeck and Snower 1990).

2. The size and nature of the welfare state can slow workers' responses to changing labor market signals. According to this view, generous unemployment benefit programs limit the incentives of workers to reenter the labor market upon becoming unemployed, while extensive income support programs make long-term unemployment or nonparticipation in the labor market more economically possible and socially acceptable.[9]

3. Inadequate skills or mobility can limit workers' ability to adjust to changing labor demands. "Skill mismatches" could result in high unemployment

7. A number of the papers in Jessop et al. (1991) summarize and critique these different causal theories. Lawrence and Schultze (1987) and Krugman (1987) also provide good summaries.

8. A variety of different articles discuss this problem, from Piore and Sabel's (1984) call for greater "flexible specialization" to Boyer's (1988) discussion of the failure of the Fordist system of industrial relations.

9. The argument against the welfare state is nicely summarized in Lawrence and Schultze (1987).

even when demand for new workers remains strong. Attempts to test the skill mismatch hypothesis, however, found little evidence that mismatches were a major factor in the rise of unemployment in the 1980s, leading this explanation to lose its attractiveness.[10] But the notion remains that low mobility of labor is one cause of high unemployment, despite the Japanese example of low mobility and low unemployment.

4. Excessively high wages and wage shares can limit long-term job creation. Failure by employers to invest in physical capital during the late 1970s and early 1980s was blamed for permanently lowering employment demand. For instance, Modigliani et al. (1987) estimated that by 1985 available production capacity was 15 percent below that needed for full employment, because of inadequate capital investment. To generate greater investment, wage reductions that raise profitability were viewed as necessary, making the decline in real wages in the United States seem the "right" adjustment and the maintenance of high real wages in Europe the "wrong" strategy.

5. Linking all of these arguments were a series of "hysteresis hypotheses" that tried to explain how a short-term rise in unemployment could permanently raise the NAIRU, so that adverse shocks in unemployment would not be self-correcting.[11] Insider/outsider models argued that the unemployed have little say in wage bargaining and thus little effect on wage levels.[12] Other models focused on behavioral changes among the long-term unemployed. As the human capital of the unemployed deteriorates and they adjust to unemployment, workers become less productive or stop seeking jobs.[13] In either case, a short-run rise in unemployment would lead to higher long-term unemployment in the future.

While different analysts stressed the adverse effects of different social protection policies, the broad message was the same: greater flexibility in the labor market and less social protection were the road to reducing unemployment and curing the economic woes of the 1980s. Decreased labor market regulation would permit reductions in wages and related costs of employment when demand fell. Having fewer social benefits would increase incentives for the unemployed and nonemployed to seek work. Targeted job training or related labor market programs might also be necessary to bring the unemployed (especially the long-term unemployed) back into the world of work.

10. For instance, the argument is dismissed by Layard and Nickell, using U.K. data, and by Franz and König, using data from West Germany (both articles are in Bean, Layard, and Nickell 1987), but Blanchard (in Dréze and Bean 1990) argues for possible mismatch effects that this empirical work would not have measured. Flanagan (1987) provides a nice summary of the evidence on occupational and spatial mismatch.

11. For instance, the empirical work of Oswald and Blanchflower (1990) indicates that unemployment has a strong effect on wages at low unemployment but little effect at high unemployment.

12. A summary of this approach is in Lindbeck and Snower (1990).

13. Blanchard (in Dréze and Bean 1990) summarizes this argument nicely. Franz (1987) provides empirical support for this hypothesis, using West German data.

1.2   Policy Reactions and Outcomes

Given the wisespread belief that flexible labor markets were part of the cure, if not *the* cure, to high unemployment and slow growth, many OECD countries sought to increase labor market flexibility over the 1980s (see table 1.4).[14] France tried increased work-sharing. It decentralized collective bargaining, as did the Netherlands and Spain. Italy got rid of automatic wage indexing, the Scala Mobile. Virtually all European countries expanded training measures targeted at unemployed workers. West Germany and Spain introduced short-term employment contracts. The United Kingdom changed its labor relations laws to weaken trade unions and sought to ensure that the unemployed were really seeking jobs. A wave of privatization reduced the governmental share of employment throughout Europe. Some countries cut unemployment benefits and other social protection programs, aiming to emulate the lower level of benefits in the United States. By the end of the 1980s, most European countries had less state involvement in labor market outcomes, less centralized labor relations, and more limited transfer programs than they had a decade earlier.

But the effort to increase labor market flexibility did not reduce aggregate unemployment. In the United Kingdom, policies for greater flexibility appeared to do little on the unemployment front.[15] Spain introduced new fixed-term contracts to increase employer flexibility. While unemployment dropped from 1985 to 1990, it never dropped below 15 percent, although nearly all new hires in the 1980s were on these temporary contracts. In some other countries, such as the Netherlands, there were only limited reductions in social programs, suggesting that policy changes large enough to create a U.S.-style flexible market were politically difficult to implement.

At the same time, the U.S. economy began to look less attractive. The benefits of growth within a flexible and decentralized labor market turned out to be uneven in the 1980s: the earnings and the income distributions widened, growth had less of a "trickle-down" effect than it had in previous decades, and poverty rates remained high throughout the decade.[16] Visitors to the country saw homeless people in the streets and the increasingly Third World appearance of many parts of the inner cities. Some European economies also experienced growing earnings inequality, but only the relatively decentralized and flexible United Kingdom had large rises in inequality.[17] In most European countries, moreover, increased earnings inequality did not translate into increased family income inequality, seemingly because these countries had more

---

14. Boyer (1988) and OECD (1990) discuss different European countries' policy responses to the economic problems of the 1980s.

15. They presumably did help in other ways. For instance the U.K. legislation that weakened unions seems to have spurred unionized firms to higher rates of productivity.

16. For a summary of U.S. inequality trends, see various articles in the *Quarterly Journal of Economics* 107 (February 1992), or Danziger and Gottschalk (1993). For a discussion of the changes in the effect of the macroeconomy on poverty, see Blank (1993).

17. For instance, see Davis (1992) or Katz, Loveman, and Blanchflower (1992).

Table 1.4   **Sample Policy Changes Implemented over the 1980s to Increase Labor Market Flexibility in Europe**

Country	Policy Change
Belgium	Established short-time unemployment benefits Created programs to assist temporary work placements Weakened dismissal laws
France	Increased decentralization in bargaining Weakened dismissal laws Increased training for long-term unemployed Decreased workweek
West Germany	Weakened dismissal laws Increased incentives for early retirement Increased limits on unemployment benefit receipt Decreased workweek
Italy	Eliminated automatic wage indexation
Netherlands	Decentralized wage agreements Lowered relative minimum wage Created programs to assist temporary work placements Increased limits on unemployment benefit receipt Increased training for long-term unemployed
Spain	Decentralized wage agreements Decreased workweek Increased training and job creation for long-term unemployed Increased availability of part-time and short-term work
Sweden	Increased training and job search requirements for those receiving unemployment benefits
United Kingdom	Implemented privatization of major government-owned industries Decentralized wage agreements Weakened dismissal laws Increased limits on unemployment benefit receipt Increased training for long-term unemployed

Source: Organization for Economic Cooperation and Development 1990.

extensive transfer systems. The rise of inequality in the United States, accompanied by a very visible urban homelessness problem, reminded analysts of the benefits of social protection and transfer programs.[18] In addition, the cyclical downturn in the U.S. economy in the early 1990s showed that flexibility did not guarantee permanently lower unemployment or an ongoing strong economy.

By the early 1990s the claim that weakening social protection systems

18. Another possible factor affecting thinking was the political and economic changes in eastern Europe. These changes made it clear that market capitalism is not easily or quickly transplanted to economies with a history of control and planning and that historical economic, political, and institutional differences shape the possibilities for economic reform.

would increase labor market flexibility and cure economic stagnation could not be made as strongly or convincingly as it had been at the height of Reaganomics and Thatcherism. Reforms to increase flexibility by weakening welfare state programs did not deliver what they had promised. The conventional wisdom of the 1980s—that social protection impairs flexibility in ways that harm economic performance—deserves a serious rethink.

1.3   The Case against Social Protection

> Every program that protects people from the consequences of unemployment provides an incentive not to work and is a drag on the economy.
> —Archetypal opponent of social protection

The argument that social protection harms economic outcomes is familiar to economists because it is derived from first principles about the effect of interventions in perfectly functioning markets. Most institutional interventions create incentives for market participants to behave differently than they otherwise would, implying some distortionary loss of social welfare from the competitive ideal.

In terms of labor supply, transfer programs drive a wedge between individual utility-maximizing outcomes and the socially efficient outcome. Unemployment assistance or welfare benefits may lead a worker to choose leisure instead of work until such benefits end. This maximizes the worker's well-being but lowers output and lengthens the spell of unemployment. Similar distortionary side effects are likely to accompany other social protection measures. Low-cost public housing in a particular city may limit workers' mobility, leading a worker to reject jobs in other areas of the country. Programs that mandate fringe benefit packages may constrain worker choices, producing nonoptimal and inefficient outcomes as well as high labor costs. Generous sick benefits may produce an epidemic of headaches, backaches, and related ills until all benefit days are used up.

In terms of labor demand, social assistance may also change employer decisions in socially inefficient ways. Laws that constrain employers' hiring or firing behavior, for instance, may distort market wage signals, reduce profitability due to "excess labor," or lead employers to hire fewer workers because of the additional expected future cost. Laws that levy taxes on employers to fund retirement or unemployment payments may induce firms to hide income or to hire off the books or may make it unprofitable to hire low-wage labor, depending on the incidence of those taxes. Socially determined minimum wages, such as the French SMIC or Italy's collectively bargained Scala Mobile adjustments, can lower employment in low-wage activities.

The case against social programs also stresses that there can be sizable investment opportunity costs and deadweight losses to raising the taxes necessary to support programs. Social assistance programs may divert capital from more fruitful alternative investments. If those opportunities have higher multipliers or greater job creation potential, money spent to support low-income families could permanently lower employment opportunities, leaving both the unemployed and the rest of society worse off in the long run. Most social protection policies create some "excess burden" through the tax system and expand public sector employment, which may further add to labor market rigidities.

Furthest from neoclassical analysis but of great importance in popular discussion is the possibility that income support programs may change individual preferences by creating "dependency." If labor-leisure preferences are malleable over the short run, programs that induce people to remain out of the labor market may permanently shift their preferences toward greater leisure and away from work, resulting in lower labor market involvement even after the transfer program comes to an end. Some of the discussion over hysteresis effects in unemployment evokes this argument, as the long-term unemployed become less and less attuned to work as their spells lengthen.

Finally, there is an additional potential negative impact in an open economy if social protection programs have any or all of the above negative effects. By burdening business, social programs may reduce trade competitiveness. This leads to falling exports, rising imports, currency devaluation, and deleterious effects on a country's long-term employment and economic growth. Whether an extensive welfare state can survive in an open economy that trades with countries that have less-extensive programs is a question that the Common Market and the North American Free Trade Agreement will put to the text.

1.4   The Case against the Case against Social Protection

> Social programs cost resources and may have some undesirable effects on market efficiency, but they generate benefits that are greater than their costs and may be viewed as investments that pay off in higher long-run productivity.
>
>   —Archetypal supporter of social programs

There are two ways to criticize the conventional criticism of social protection programs. The first "case against the case against"[19] admits that social programs have distortionary costs that impact labor markets but argues that the benefits of programs, which critics rarely measure, exceed the costs. The second argument denies that social programs have deleterious effects on markets

---

19. Making cases against cases is a tradition in economics fathered by Robert Solow, to whom we give full credit for this mode of argumentation about where the burden of proof lies in discussing a policy issue.

at all and claims instead that they are investments in a more productive work force that promise substantial economic returns.

The first defense of social programs begins with the observation that the case against them focuses almost exclusively on one side of the benefit-cost calculus: the losses in social well-being due to distortionary incentives. Haveman (1985, 17) may be right that "the gains [of welfare state programs] are relatively familiar and directly experienced," but the criticism of these programs rarely acknowledges these benefits. The standard 1980s economists' study of unemployment insurance or income support, for instance, is an exercise in estimating distortionary labor supply or related costs, not in assessing how well or poorly the program fulfills its purpose of reducing economic uncertainty through income and/or employment guarantees. A complete cost-benefit analysis of any program requires, of course, that the increase in economic well-being among citizens that is due to the program be set against its costs, direct and indirect, through lost growth or productivity. Simply showing that programs have distortionary effects or inefficiency costs does not make the case against them.

Many social insurance programs provide "goods" that competitive markets intrinsically cannot provide because of the presence of moral hazards, externalities, or other forms of market failure, which means these programs cannot be criticized for crowding out market alternatives. For instance, the competitive labor market is unlikely to offer socially optimal levels of workplace-related benefits such as sickness benefits or unemployment insurance, because of the adverse selection of workers into insurance schemes. If a firm offers particularly good sickness benefits, it will attract a disproportionate number of workers prone to illness, which will be costly. In contrast, if all firms offer identical (mandated) sickness packages, no single firm will bear the cost of attracting these more costly workers. The abortive effort by one major British bank to offer private unemployment insurance in the 1970s and the difficulties of unions in particular industries to provide private schemes support this point.

The claim that social programs reduce economic growth is, the case against the case against argues, weak even in terms of standard theory. Existing analyses of welfare triangle losses have no compelling predictions for investment or growth. They show that social protection creates a static efficiency loss— lower GDP—but not that it reduces growth rates. Programs that waste resources reduce the pie available for investment, but they may not alter the share of savings and investment in national output. Standard growth theory does not give a clear prediction about how static distortions alter growth, leading Mancur Olson (1982) and others who believe that those distortions have long-term growth effects to make more heterodox arguments for their position.

In a similar vein, conclusions about distortionary costs are typically derived from first-best models of economic equilibrium. But in a second-best (or third-best) world where other distortions already exist due to taxation, regulation, or institutional structures, it is unclear that social protection programs produce less-efficient outcomes. They may offset inefficiencies and distortions caused by other political or economic constraints. For instance, if union collective bargaining contracts require firms to lay off younger workers before older workers, raising unemployment among younger workers, employment protection laws that mandate all workers be given four months notification before layoff may produce an employment outcome for younger workers that is closer to the first-best equilibrium. The implication is that the effects of any program must be analyzed in the context of the entire economic system in which it fits rather than as an isolated change in an otherwise ideal competitive world.

In short, without denying that social protection programs cause some inefficiencies, one can still reject the claim that such programs are socially deleterious. Looking only at efficiency losses provides an incomplete analysis that fails to evaluate the benefits of the programs and ignores the broad context in which these programs work.

The second attack on the case against social protection stresses the role of programs in enhancing human capital and productivity in the labor market. This is the type of argument put forth by the Clinton administration in 1993 for expanding various government expenditure programs.

From a human capital perspective, social protection programs could create long-term incentives for employers and workers to invest in training. For instance, laws that limit dismissal might induce employers to invest more in worker training, since these laws create the long-term attachment that makes investment in specific skills profitable. Income protection programs might allow greater opportunities for returning to school or investing in retraining. For instance, maternity leave programs, that allow women to leave the labor market for several years when they have a child, such as Sweden's, provide a chance for women to acquire additional job training.

Greater employment and income security may increase workers' productivity in other ways as well. Japanese workers with lifetime contracts may be more productive because they concentrate better on the job and feel more committed to their firm. A worker whose job is protected may be more willing to look for ways to improve productivity and to accept new machines or technological changes. A generous income transfer program may make workers more likely to take risks, change jobs, or move locations.

Social assistance programs aimed at children and teenagers, such as health care programs, educational assistance, child allowances, or teen apprenticeships, are a particular favorite of those who look upon the welfare state as a productive investment. Programs that shift resources to children are a "capital investment" in a country's future labor resources. Assistance to families with small children may improve the health or emotional well-being of those children, resulting in lower future social expenditures and higher future productivity. Assistance to teens may expand their labor market knowledge and improve their skills.

If social protection and economic growth and flexibility complement each other in these ways, emphasis on short-term "speed of adjustment" trade-offs would be shortsighted and inaccurate. But a case can even be made that social programs are not harmful in the short run. First, there are potential counter-cyclical social benefits in programs that reduce cyclical fluctuations in consumption spending and provide employment protection. For instance, worker uncertainty about possible job losses arguably can reduce consumer confidence and expenditures on durables, delaying economic recovery, as in Britain in the early 1990s. Second, short-run flexibility can have negative social effects, so that a bit of inflexibility may be virtuous. Bubbles in financial markets and speculative swings or panics make it clear that rapid responses to economic changes are not always good; overshooting equilibria result from too much rather than too little flexibility.

1.5 Evaluating the Evidence

In reviewing the arguments about the relationship between social protection programs, labor market flexibility, and aggregate economic welfare, we are struck by how little evidence is available on many issues. The economics literature contains many studies that measure the static efficiency impacts of some social protection policies but few that deal with labor market *adjustment* per se or with effects on economic growth.

Probably the most-extensive literature on the efficiency costs of social programs attempts to measure the impact of income transfers on labor supply and of unemployment benefits on the duration of unemployment. The evidence shows behavioral responses to the incentives in these programs but has not yielded a definitive consensus over whether the magnitude of this response is large or small. If, as some studies suggest, two months of additional unemployment benefits increase the time a person is unemployed by one to two weeks (Katz and Meyer 1990), one analyst may regard this with horror while another may find it an acceptable cost of assisting the unemployed.[20] Moffitt (1992, 16) has summarized the literature on the effect of welfare support on the labor supply of recipients in the United States by stressing the "considerable uncertainty regarding the magnitude of the effects" even after twenty years of research.

Research on other routes by which programs may reduce efficiency is limited. The distortionary effects of social regulation on employers has been studied for some programs in some countries, but the results do not yield a simple generalization. When Sweden provided a highly generous sick-leave policy, this seemed to produce excessive use of sick leave (OECD 1991). But, to take another example, Houseman (1991) finds that European employment protection preserved jobs in steel compared to the loss of employment in the United

---

20. For a review of the literature on the effects of unemployment insurance, see Atkinson and Micklewright (1991).

Kingdom, and Abraham and Houseman (1993) find that West Germany's employment protection law did not reduce the long-run adjustment of labor to changes in shipments. Lazear (1990), by contrast, finds that such provisions reduce employment across countries but reports that this result was sensitive to specification. Because it is difficult to design empirical studies that separate the effect of social programs on export competitiveness, investment spending, and dynamic labor market behavior from other factors, there is relatively little work on these topics.

Even if estimated efficiency costs are viewed as substantial, there is limited evidence linking these costs directly to the difference in labor market outcomes between the United States and Europe that sparked belief in the virtues of flexibility. Burtless (1987) indicates that the more extensive unemployment benefits in European countries did not cause the relative rise in European versus U.S. unemployment rates over the 1970s and 1980s, because the estimated effects are far too small to generate the huge observed unemployment changes. The introduction of temporary contracts in Spain seemed to increase employment, but Spanish unemployment still remained the highest in Europe. Similarly, introduction of temporary contracts in West Germany appears to have had no great effect on employment practices.

The papers in this volume add to the research linking social protection programs to labor market developments within and across countries in the last decade. In most cases, the studies reject the existence of a substantial trade-off between these programs and market flexibility. Abraham and Houseman (chap. 3) find that loosening of dismissal law in West Germany, France, and Belgium had little effect on the speed of employment adjustment. Börsch-Supan (chap. 5) finds that implementing or loosening tenant protection laws in West Germany did not change mobility or housing construction rates. Blank (chap. 8) finds that employment and wages in the public sector are as variable as in the private sector in the United States and only slightly less variable in the United Kingdom. Holtz-Eakin (chap. 6) finds little evidence that inequitable health benefits between jobs limit worker mobility in the United States or West Germany. Rebick (chap. 7) finds little evidence that the implementation of early retirement programs in Japan induced elderly workers to leave the labor market. What is striking in all of these papers is the lack of evidence that the government programs had substantial effects on labor market adjustment.

Why has research failed to turn up the large trade-off that the 1980s conventional wisdom posited? One possible reason is that there is in fact no sizable trade-off between *specific* programs, flexibility, and efficiency. Program-induced inefficiency losses may have much more limited effects on labor market dynamics than economists would like to believe. This may be because the programs are embedded in a larger system of employment and family relations, so that changes in one program do not change incentives as much as might at first appear to be the case and thus do not induce large changes in behavior.

Another possibility is that the program changes are too modest and the time period covered by the studies too short to capture the "big" adverse effect of these welfare state programs on the overall operation of society. Behavior may change slowly as experience and information are acquired over time. The claim that social protection limits economic adjustment may not be well tested by looking at marginal changes in program parameters. Perhaps European nations have not achieved a substantial increase in labor market flexibility because they have not gone far enough in cutting back their degree of social protection. Only major changes, abolishing whole sets of programs, may produce the degree of market flexibility needed to bring down long-term unemployment.

Whatever the reason for the findings, our reading of the evidence in this volume and elsewhere is that there is little empirical evidence for large trade-offs between labor market flexibility and social protection programs in general. At the present state of knowledge, the best attitude toward the trade-off hypothesis is one of open-minded skepticism.

If there is little evidence of substantial trade-offs between social protection programs and labor market adjustment, however, estimates of the magnitude of purported benefits of such programs are almost nonexistent. Researchers have made only a few attempts to estimate the benefits of programs to individuals and thus to provide a fuller cost-benefit analysis.[21] Lampman's (1984) analysis of the full effects of changes in social welfare spending in the United States between 1950 and 1978 on economic and social well-being and Haveman's (1985) comparison of U.S. and Netherlands social welfare spending took a broad benefit-cost view but lacked the necessary microstudies of how citizens value benefits that would provide a definitive welfare accounting. Hansen and İmrohoroğlu's (1992) evaluation of the behavioral and social welfare effects of an unemployment insurance scheme relied on simulation rather than on detailed empirical analysis of these effects. Their finding that, with some plausible parameters, the social benefits of unemployment insurance can outweigh the efficiency costs supports the notion that a full accounting of this program may yield a different welfare assessment than is implicit in studies focused on its undesirable effects in lengthening spells of joblessness.

The claim that social protection should be viewed as an investment in future productivity is based upon even less solid evidence. We know of no studies that persuasively link labor market protection programs to worker productivity nor that definitively connect child and family assistance programs with labor market productivity in later life. Compensatory preschool programs have been linked with greater school achievement and more years of schooling, both of which are correlated with economic success in the labor market (Barnett 1992), but there is no evidence on whether income assistance for poor families

---

21. For instance, Haveman and Wolfe (1984) attempt to measure a wide variety of nonmarket effects from public education. Weisbrod (1983) tries to measure the net social benefits of alternative programs for the mentally ill. Kemper, Long, and Thornton (1984) estimate the net social benefit of a job-training program. Haveman (1985) discusses the full range of social benefits and costs that should be considered in evaluating income protection programs.

improves children's long-term economic outlook. On the contrary, some evidence suggests that parents' participation in welfare programs in the United States raises the probability of welfare participation among their children when grown (Gottschalk 1992).

Given the extensive public discussion of the value and costs of social programs, and the resources spent on different programs, it is unfortunate that we lack the studies that might provide the full benefit-cost assessment of the effects of the programs necessary to make a scientific case for reducing or increasing their scope.

1.6   Improving Analysis of Social Protection Programs

Our assessment of the arguments and evidence on the effects of social protection programs has implicitly suggested some directions for future research in this area. We conclude this essay by bringing these suggestions together.

First, the greatest immediate need is for detailed studies that measure the benefit side of social programs, in particular assessing the nonincome value of the income protection and job security of social insurance programs. Given the increasing recognition of the importance of risk and risk aversion in economic theory, this is an area in which empirical research has failed to keep pace with theory.[22] To evaluate social programs properly, we need to measure the value to individual workers and families of reducing the risk and ensuring incomes or employment. This may require more interaction between economists and other social scientists, such as social psychologists, who more routinely use nonincome measures of personal well-being.

Second, there is also a need to analyze the effects of specific programs within the general equilibrium of social and market institutions. The impact of any particular program depends on the environment of institutions and economic conditions in which it is located. For instance, the differential effect of weakening employment protection in Spain versus West Germany presumably reflects differences in labor market institutions and in the strength of unions or works councils in the two countries. Similarly, multiple and simultaneous programs can cause offsetting behavioral incentives or can reinforce each other in ways that create synergies, so that the effect of several programs together may be different from any individual program alone. For example, Hanratty's paper (chap. 10 in this volume) indicates that time-limited welfare in France moves women into the labor force, but shows that this occurs in part because France's educational system admits children to full-time schooling at exactly the point when women lose their benefits. On the one hand, programs that appear distortionary in isolation may not be distortionary when viewed in a broader systemic context. If a generous minimum-income support system is combined with job creation or skill training programs, the expected adverse

---

22. Best known, perhaps, is the literature measuring the effect of job-related risks on wage rates.

effects on labor supply may be muted or overwhelmed in importance by the positive effects of job training. On the other hand, it is also possible that a host of social protection programs may coalesce to produce an inflexible system, so that reforming a single program may fail to produce the benefits that reformers expect. Research that measures joint effects from multiple programs would provide insight into these issues and indicate the extent to which effective policy might be better conceptualized as a combination of interactive programs rather than as a list of separate program efforts.[23]

Third, greater attention should be given to the gap between a program's legal requirements and its implementation. Often research parameterizes programs by their legal definition, with only scant attention to implementation issues. For instance, according to law, welfare programs to single parents in the United States levy extremely high tax rates on earnings, between 67 and 100 percent. Many studies have used these legislated rates in their estimation of the impact of welfare on labor supply, generally concluding that high tax rates seem to have little effect on labor supply decisions of recipients. Yet the actual marginal tax rates on earnings faced by most women are much lower, because of a combination of work expense deductions and income underreporting. Perhaps the inference that labor supply is only modestly responsive to the tax rates in income support programs is correct because the effective tax rates are actually quite low.

Fourth, we should go beyond determining the immediate effects of a program on labor supply or mobility behavior to the multiple and possible long-term effects on a broader set of variables, including skill formation. This means looking at efficiency, flexibility, and well-being effects of programs over a time horizon greater than one or two years. At this stage we are not even sure whether effects increase or decrease over time. Economists normally expect long-run effects to exceed short-run effects (as the number of constraints on behavior is reduced, own partial derivatives increase by the Le Chatelier principle), but when one program changes, the use and purpose of a whole range of other programs may also change in an offsetting way. Changes in employee dismissal laws may lead to differences in the way unemployment benefits are paid out, with uncertain consequences. To assess more reliably the effects of specific program reforms, we need at least some understanding of how the entire interconnected system of programs adjusts.

Finally, the purported long-term investment effects of social programs should be analyzed. Do particular investments in children's education or health programs or transfers to families with children pay off in terms of future adult productivity? Is the claim valid that many social programs are investments in the future, or are these more properly viewed as consumption transfers? The availability of long-term longitudinal data makes studies of long-term effects

---

23. For an example of multiple-program analysis with respect to the U.S. income support system, see Blank and Ruggles (1992).

increasingly possible. The argument that social protection programs are investment- and productivity-enhancing policies needs to be seriously evaluated both by proponents and by skeptics.

In short, we believe that the research and policy community actually knows quite a bit less about the aggregate effect of social protection programs on individual behavior or on the aggregate economy than is typically claimed. Our reading of the debate over flexibility, social protection, and the labor market suggests that analyses more directly focused on the key points in that debate would enrich our understanding of how the welfare state and labor market interact in needed and useful ways.

References

Abraham, K., and S. N. Houseman. 1993. *Job security in America: Lessons from Germany.* Washington, D.C.: Brookings Institution.

Atkinson, A. B., and J. Micklewright. 1991. Unemployment compensation and labor market transitions: A critical review. *Journal of Economic Literature* 29:1679–727.

Barnett, W. S. 1992. Benefits of compensatory preschool education. *Journal of Human Resources* 27:279–312.

Bean, C. R., R. Layard, and S. Nickell. 1987. *The rise in unemployment.* Oxford: Basil Blackwell.

Blank, R. M. 1993. Why were poverty rates so high in the 1980s? In *Poverty and prosperity in the U.S. in the late twentieth century,* ed. D. Papadimitriou and E. Wolf. London: Macmillan.

Blank, R. M., and P. Ruggles. 1992. *Multiple program use in a dynamic context.* Report to the U.S. Bureau of the Census. Washington, D.C.

Boyer, R. 1988. *The search for labour market flexibility.* Oxford: Clarendon.

Bruno, M., and J. Sachs. 1985. *The economics of worldwide stagflation.* Cambridge: Harvard University Press.

Burtless, G. 1987. Jobless pay and high European unemployment. In *Barriers to European growth: A transatlantic view,* ed. R. Lawrence and C. Schultze. Washington, D.C.: Brookings Institution.

Danziger, S., and P. Gottschalk. 1993. *Uneven tides: Rising inequality in the 1980s.* New York: Russell Sage Foundation.

Davis, S. J. 1992. Cross-country patterns of changes in relative wages. NBER Working Paper no. 4085. Cambridge, Mass.: National Bureau of Economic Research.

Dore, R. 1986. *Flexible rigidities.* Stanford, Calif.: Stanford University Press.

Drèze, J. H., and C. R. Bean. 1990. *Europe's unemployment problem.* Cambridge: MIT Press.

Flanagan, R. J. 1987. Labor market behavior and European economic growth. In *Barriers to european growth: A transatlantic view,* ed. R. Lawrence and C. Schultze. Washington, D.C.: Brookings Institution.

Franz, W. 1987. Hysteresis, persistence, and the NAIRU: An empirical analysis for the Federal Republic of Germany. In *The fight against unemployment,* ed. R. Layard and L. Calmfors. Cambridge: MIT Press.

Freeman, R. B. 1988. Evaluating the European view that the United States has no unemployment problem. *American Economic Review* 78:294–99.

Gottschalk, P. 1992. Is the correlation in welfare participation across generations spurious? Boston College. Manuscript.

Hansen, G., and A. İmrohoroğlu. 1992. The role of unemployment insurance in an economy with liquidity constraints and moral hazard. *Journal of Political Economy* 100:118–42.

Haveman, R. H. 1985. *Does the welfare state increase welfare?* Leiden, The Netherlands: H. E. Stenfert Kroese.

Haveman, R. H. and B. L. Wolfe. 1984. Schooling and economic well-being: The role of nonmarket effects. *Journal of Human Resources* 19:377–407.

Houseman, S. N. 1991. *Industrial restructuring with job security: The case of European steel.* Cambridge: Harvard University Press.

Jessop, B., H. Kastendiek, K. Nielson, and O. K. Pederson. 1991. *The politics of flexibility: Restructuring state and industry in Britain, Germany, and Scandinavia.* Worcester, England: Billing and Sons.

Katz, L. F., G. W. Loveman, and D. G. Blanchflower. 1992. A comparison of changes in the structure of wages in four OECD countries. Working paper prepared for the NBER Comparative Labor Markets Project Conference on Differences and Changes in Wage Structures. Cambridge, Mass.: National Bureau of Economic Research. In *Differences and changes in wage structure,* ed. L. F. Katz and R. B. Freeman. Chicago: University of Chicago Press. Forthcoming.

Katz, L. F., and B. D. Meyer. 1990. The impact of the potential duration of unemployment benefits on the duration of unemployment. *Journal of Public Economics* 41:45–72.

Kemper, P., D. A. Long, and C. Thornton. 1984. A benefit-cost analysis of the supported work experiment. In *The national supported work demonstration,* ed. E. G. Hollister Jr., P. Kemper, and R. A. Maynard. Madison: University of Wisconsin Press.

Krugman, P. R. 1987. Slow growth in Europe: Conceptual issues. In *Barriers to European growth: A transatlantic view,* ed. R. Lawrence and C. Schultze. Washington, D.C.: Brookings Institution.

Lampman, R. J. 1984. *Social welfare spending: Accounting for changes from 1950 to 1978.* Orlando: Academic Press.

Lawrence, R. Z., and C. L. Schultze. 1987. Overview, in *Barriers to European growth: A transatlantic view,* ed. R. Lawrence and C. Schultze. Washington, D.C.: Brookings Institution.

Layard, R. 1986. *How to beat unemployment.* Oxford: Oxford University Press.

Lazear, E. P. 1990. Job security provisions and employment. *Quarterly Journal of Economics* 60:699–726.

Lindbeck, A., and D. Snower. 1990. Demand- and supply-side policies and unemployment: Policy implications of the insider-outsider approach. In *Unemployment and wage determination in Europe: Labour market policies for the 1990s,* ed. B. Holmlund and K-G. Loftgren. Oxford: Basil Blackwell.

Metcalf, D. 1987. Labour market flexibility and jobs: A survey of evidence from OECD countries with special reference to Europe. In *The fight against unemployment,* ed. R. Layard and L. Calmfors. Cambridge: MIT Press.

Modigliani, F., M. Monti, J. H. Drèze, H. Giersch, and R. Layard. 1987. Reducing unemployment in Europe: The role of capital formation. In *The fight against unemployment,* ed. R. Layard and L. Calmfors. Cambridge: MIT Press.

Moffitt, R. 1992. Incentive effects of the U.S. welfare system: A review. *Journal of Economic Literature* 30:1–61.

Olson, M. 1982. *The growth and decline of nations.* New Haven, Conn.: Yale University Press.

Organization for Economic Cooperation and Development (OECD). 1990. *Labor market policies for the 1990s.* Paris: OECD.

———. *Employment outlook: 1991.* Paris; OECD.

———. 1992a. *Employment outlook: 1992.* Paris: OECD.

———. 1992b. *Historical Statistics, 1960–1990.* Paris: OECD.

Oswald, A. J. and D. G. Blanchflower. 1990. The wage curve. In *Unemployment and wage determination in Europe: Labour market policies for the 1990s,* ed. B. Holmlund and K-G. Loftgren. Oxford: Basil Blackwell.

Piore, M. J., and C. F. Sabel. 1984. *The second industrial divide.* New York: Basic Books.

Rein, M., and B. L. Friedman. 1992. *Social protection and economic change.* Cambridge: MIT Press.

Weisbrod, B. A. 1983. Defining benefits of public programs: Some guidance for policy analysts. In *Public expenditure and policy analysis,* ed. R. H. Haveman and J. Margolis. Boston: Houghton Mifflin.

2   Trends in Social Protection Programs and Expenditures in the 1980s

Peter Scherer

In 1980, the Organisation for Economic Co-operation and Development (OECD) held a conference whose proceedings were subsequently published under the title *The Future of Social Protection* (OECD 1981). Emile van Lennep, who was then the secretary general of the OECD, specified in his opening speech what he considered to be "main principles" that should not be placed in jeopardy by the economic crisis then facing the OECD area (OECD 1981, 10):

1. We must surely continue to build on the principle that adequate income from work is the primary basis of well-being;
2. The State has a clear responsibility, in response to the common will in democratic societies, to achieve through the fiscal system a more equitable distribution of income than the market system would of itself provide;
3. The State must surely remain as the main guarantor against social risks such as unemployment, ill-health, disability, and old age—that is to say, "social security";
4. Transfers to the vulnerable groups in society can be achieved in a variety of ways: direct transfers involving states, provinces or municipalities; price subsidies leading to lower consumer prices, for example rents and transportation; and, of course, various forms of private solidarity.

However, the accompanying secretariat paper (OECD 1981, 73–83) warned that the inspiration of these ideals—the drive toward a more egalitarian distribution of income—had already started to break down. The "tax revolt" was calling the viability of some forms of social provision into question. Hence, it

Peter Scherer is head of the Social Affairs and Industrial Relations Division of the Organisation for Economic Co-operation and Development (OECD).

The opinions expressed in this chapter are the author's own and do not engage the OECD. He is grateful for comments and suggestions from Rebecca Blank, Patrick Hennessy, and Bettina Cass, although he remains responsible for any defects that remain.

appeared that some OECD countries were about to reject many of the principles which the organization's secretary general had identified as crucial. A decade later, this rejection has indeed occurred, but it has been less general than is often thought. Apart from the United States, only the United Kingdom and (since 1990) New Zealand have rejected the thrust of the principles van Lennep enunciated as public policy. Although there has been a general decline in trade union membership in all OECD countries (see OECD 1991), only in these three countries has collective bargaining been downplayed and even condemned in public-policy terms. These changes were related: collective determination of employment provisions was generally related to social arrangements. In fact, in many countries, this was, and is, institutionalized; many social protection measures, including workers' compensation, health insurance, and pension provision, are administered by tripartite institutions.[1]

2.1 Social Expenditures in the 1980s: The End of Growth

The crisis in the welfare state to which the OECD conference volume title referred was primarily a fiscal one. Social expenditures had grown at a faster rate than real national product during the period of rapid growth in per capita gross domestic product (GDP), which ended in the early 1970s. During the 1970s, the rate of increase in expenditure slowed but not as much as the decline in economic growth, so that social expenditures continued to rise as a percentage of GDP in most OECD countries.

The reasons for this were mixed. Pension systems instituted over the previous twenty years were maturing so that retirees had accrued more substantial pension entitlements. Some other items of expenditure, associated with education and transfers to families, could be expected to decline in the 1980s.[2]

However, other pressures seemed likely to continue. In particular, the cost of health care systems was increasing as a proportion of GDP in all countries and seemed unstoppable in the light of the development of medical technologies and the growth in expenditure on incomes of the medical profession. And the decline in the employment:population ratio in many countries was associated either with a growth in expenditure on benefits for the openly unemployed or a growth in other support for those without a job—in particular, disability pensions and various forms of early retirement pensions.

Public social protection expenditure did continue to increase as a proportion of GDP until 1983, but since then it has been relatively stable (see fig. 2.1,

---

1. Less often, but still frequently, they are provided through provisions in multiemployer collective bargains which are "extended" to all employers potentially covered by the negotiations and thus become subsidiary legislation. This is particularly significant for some supposedly "private" supplementary pension provision. See, for example, OECD (1992a, 1993) for discussions of such arrangements in the Netherlands and Finland.
2. For a discussion of these prospects as they appeared a decade ago, see OECD (1985).

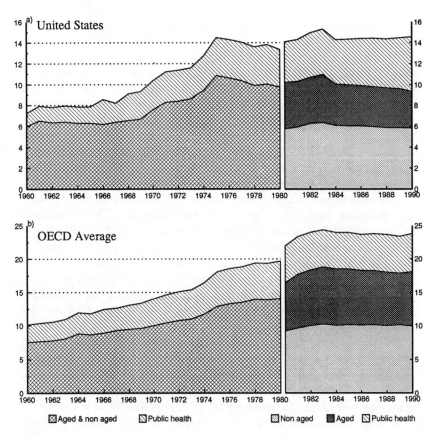

Fig. 2.1   Public expenditure on social protection as a percentage of GDP in the United States and the OECD
Source: OECD 1994.
Note: 1960–1980 excludes Iceland, Luxembourg, Portugal, Spain, and Turkey: 1980–1990 excludes Iceland, Switzerland, and Turkey.

which shows the trend in social expenditures over the past three decades as an unweighted average of twenty-one OECD countries). Furthermore, this stability applies to each of the three components of expenditure into which expenditure data can currently be disaggregated: health care, expenditure on the aged (predominantly public old-age pensions and related survivors' benefits), and transfers to the non-aged, which include family allowances and unemployment benefits, support for single parents, and disability and early retirement pensions.[3] In the case of the United States, a fall since 1983 in expenditure on the non-aged, associated with the improved labor market situation, was balanced

3. Work continues on developing comprehensive data series for each of these individual components of expenditure, but data on a comparative basis are not yet available.

by an increase in public expenditure on health care—an increase reflecting the general inflation in health care expenditures in the United States.[4]

However, this apparent stability in the OECD average is the result of a considerable variety in trends and levels across OECD countries (see appendix). In 1988 (the latest year for which data are available for all the twenty-one OECD countries included in the data base at the moment), social protection expenditures as a percentage of GDP range from 11.8 (Japan) and 12.2 (Australia) to 28.1 (Norway) and 33.3 (Sweden). The sources of this cross-country variation are too extensive to discuss in detail here. Variations in public expenditures on health—which range in percentage of GDP from 4.7 (United States) and 4.9 (Japan) to 7.4 (Norway) and 7.6 (Sweden)—are not the main cause. Differences in the extent and generosity of public old-age pensions are greater, and expenditure on the aged varies from 3.8 percent of GDP (Australia) to 14.1 percent (Italy). However, an equally important source of variation lies in public social protection expenditures for the non-aged, which vary from 2.1 percent of GDP in Japan and 3.2 percent in Australia, to 13.3 percent in Denmark and 13.9 percent in Sweden. In general, the countries of Europe fall between these extremes, with average expenditures in the European Community for these three components being 5.6, 9.7, and 7.7 percent of GDP, respectively.

The sources of the stability in the overall average since 1983 are mixed. With the exception of the United States, Iceland, and Finland, OECD countries generally stabilized public health expenditures as a percentage of GDP in the latter part of the 1980s. The maturation of generous public pension systems in Japan, Italy, and Greece led to a growth in the proportion of GDP transferred to the aged (particularly in Italy and Greece, where, in contrast to Japan, changes to the structure of public pensions also increased the expenditure levels). In some other countries, a tightening of means tests for pension provision (Australia) or a narrowing of entitlement (West Germany and Denmark) led to a slight reduction in this ratio. Hence, the overall average for this component increased only very slightly. Transfers to the non-aged were the most volatile, largely because unemployment benefit payments and other transfers to people without employment fell as labor market conditions improved during the decade, while other transfers (particularly various forms of assistance to families) increased faster than GDP in the Nordic countries.

Developments over the past decade have established that social protection expenditures are not, in general, out of control, in the sense that their previous tendency to increase at a rate greater than GDP has been controlled. However, this apparent equilibrium is an uneasy one; many countries are experiencing pressures, such as the following, that could well result in this apparent stability being only temporary:

---

4. Unlike all other OECD countries except Turkey, expenditure on health care in the United States is largely private.

- Slowdown in economic growth combined with continuing growth in demand for health care and a possible growth in income transfers to the unemployed and other jobless people can result in cyclical increases in expenditures that can easily become structural.
- Inflationary tendencies in medical services, familiar in the United States (where they are largely met by private insurance), are also evident in the rest of the OECD, where public systems bear the financing burden. Such tendencies are particularly intense in those systems (such as France's) that are based on fee-for-service reimbursement. Many countries are responding by introducing or expanding direct contracts between suppliers and public third-party payers, but others are shifting the burden of some payments to the private sector by requiring higher copayments for some services. Higher copayments have also been imposed for pharmaceutical products sold at prices higher than their generic equivalents.[5]
- The aging of populations in OECD countries as the postwar "baby boom" generation retires will threaten the apparent stability in old-age function expenditure. In particular, in a number of southern European countries (Greece, Italy, Spain, and Portugal), the net replacement rate (the ratio of pension received to final salary net of taxes and charges) is above 80 percent and is no lower for those with high salaries than for those with low ones (Eurostat 1993).

These public social protection provisions are, of course, additional to the systems of employment protection contained in employment laws or in collective agreements. However, they are closely related. While it is possible to build up a system of employment regulation without an employment-related social protection system,[6] this is unusual. Concern for security outside or after the employment relationship has in most cases led to public underwriting of various forms of social insurance—and in particular to the assurance of old-age pensions that guarantee the replacement of a substantial part of earnings after retirement.

2.2 Interpreting Differences in Social Protection Arrangements

Recent analytic work in this field (for a brief survey, see Mitchell 1992) has tried to analyze social protection policies and their outcomes by categorizing countries into groups: Mishra (1990) uses two ("social corporatist" as in Sweden and Austria and "neoconservative" as in the United States and the United Kingdom), while Esping-Anderson (Esping-Anderson and Micklewright

---

5. See OECD (1992c) for further discussion of the "internal" reforms of publicly funded health care systems in seven OECD countries.

6. Australia, with its means-tested approach to public income security, is one example—although the mandating of retirement provisions by employers since 1992 has modified even this case.

1991) suggests a three-way typology ("liberal residual" as in the United States, "conservative" as in West Germany, and "social democratic" as in Sweden). Lødemel and Schulte (1992) add a fourth—a "Latin" (i.e., Mediterranean) group—to complete the typology. This group approach has a certain attraction: the countries with the highest ratio of GDP to social expenditures fall in the "social democratic" group, with the "conservative" group intermediate and the "liberal residual" group the lowest, and "Latin" countries show high expenditure on the aged but not on other functions. However, closer examination of the patterns and trends suggests that these typologies are not very useful for explaining expenditure differentials and trends. Most of the significant differences are due to the presence or absence of particular types of transfers (notably family allowances), and some particular components of social expenditure in countries in the "liberal" economic camp (e.g., old-age pensions in the United States and Japan) are clearly not at all "residual." Social transfer patterns are the outcome of historical processes within each society, and there are considerable divergencies between countries in these processes from one type of expenditure to another.

However, an important part of social expenditures comprises what might broadly be called social insurance—coverage against particular risks for all persons in a particular category.[7] Social insurance is often analyzed as an alternative to private insurance markets. Its advocates argue that social insurance avoids the externalities inherent in private insurance markets (risk selection on the part of providers, moral hazard on the part of consumers) through universal provision (eliminating risk selection) and administrative controls (substituting for private litigation to ensure the insurance contract is not undermined). This perspective orients analysis toward the relative merits of universal public and voluntary private provision in achieving the satisfactory mechanism for dealing with *individual* risk.

In reviewing the relative merits of different systems of social protection against risks, it is important to recognize that the contingencies individuals might face are different on the Continent and in Japan than in Anglo-Saxon countries. The law in most of the non-Anglo-Saxon countries specifies that families are responsible for the upkeep of their indigent members. In English-speaking countries, this obligation is confined to the nuclear family: the spouse while the marriage is intact, children until age of majority (now generally 18). In the case of children, the recent emphasis on child support has led to attempts to enforce obligation on absent parents. But the obligation stops when children reach maturity and is not reciprocal. It is possible to regard these responsibilities as being absorbed into a production unit—the family—which is jointly managed and responds as a unit to market signals. It is therefore possible to envisage that such a unit should be able to manage its lifetime income stream

---

7. These categories can comprise all citizens (paying through taxation) but more usually comprise labor force participants who pay (or whose employers pay) compulsory levies.

and to assess social insurance arrangements in the light of alternative individual insurance arrangements and lifetime consumption patterns.

Elsewhere, however, the responsibility does not stop at the boundaries of the nuclear household. The Napoleonic Code—which formalizes legal obligations which existed previously and continues to influence contemporary legal codes throughout Europe—refers to an *obligation alimentaire:* a legal responsibility under which the obligation of parents to maintain their children is matched by an obligation by adults to maintain their aged parents. In Germany and Austria, this obligation goes further: children are jointly responsible for their indigent grandparents, and parents are liable for the maintenance of their indigent adult children. In Luxembourg, these responsibilities extend to further kin relationships. Similar provisions exist in Japanese law and in the laws of most other European countries—though they have been abolished in Nordic countries.

Historically, these responsibilities were exercised through cohabitation: the extended family was an extended household, which operated as a unit. However, today this is only true in Japan, and even there cohabitation between generations is in decline (OECD 1994). It is difficult to reconcile mutual family responsibility with separate living arrangements and personal autonomy. How does an individual insure against parents becoming indigent or children (or grandchildren) bankrupting themselves? The moral hazard and risk-shedding features of such a market would be insuperable.

A concrete instance of such concerns is currently the subject of intense public debate in Germany. Long-term care of the frail aged is not currently covered by social insurance in that country, and the German government has committed itself to extending statutory health insurance to cover this risk through a new levy of 1.7 percent of "insurable" earnings, to be shared equally between the insured and the employer. One of the authors of the law has noted that it is being proposed in part because "becoming dependent on long-term care puts the persons affected and their families in a precarious and often quite hopeless financial position" (Vollmer 1993).[8]

2.3   Working Life Reduction

Social insurance evens out income over the lifetime, reducing disposable incomes while in employment in order to ensure adequate incomes when not. This carries the risk that the relative price of leisure (sometimes enforced through layoffs) is reduced so much that significant withdrawal from the labor force occurs—resulting in a narrowing of the base for employment levies, forcing an increase in the rate of levy to keep budgetary balance, which in turn reduces further the relative price of leisure. . . . This sort of process has brought

---

8. At the time of writing, actual passage of this measure is blocked through debate on how to compensate employers for the cost of the levy: The government parties have proposed that payment for the first two days of sick leave should be dropped, but the unions oppose this.

pension systems in a number of European countries (notably France) to a point of crisis.[9]

A general symptom of this trend is the "leakage" of provision for old-age income into working life. This has been happening in a number of countries through public pension provisions. These generally provide for pensions for those who become disabled during their working life, on similar terms to old-age pensions. If ability to obtain employment is one of the criteria for assessing disability, eligibility for disability pensions will increase during recessions. This has happened in a number of countries. In general, the reduction in the cost of leisure in old age through very high rates of earnings replacement raises the individuals' perceived lifetime income and can lead to a desire to "spend" some of this wealth earlier in life. It can and does also lead employers (and unions) to single out those who are eligible for income support when layoffs are necessary. As a result, average productive life in most OECD countries is falling, as individuals (both males and females) leave the labor force earlier.[10]

Public social protection systems thus suffer from some of the same risks of moral hazard as workplace employment protection legislation: by driving a wedge between income from employment and total labor costs, they can lead to a level of overall employment lower than that implicitly assumed in their design. Unless this issue is addressed with care, these systems can add to the imbalances they were established to correct.

However, it would be incorrect to conclude that the idea of social protection is therefore unviable. Systems which emphasize labor force participation as a condition for social protection are associated with low rates of poverty (however measured) *before* social transfers in a number of European countries (Förster 1994). Thus, the risk of reduction in labor force participation has to be set against the encouragement of participation in order to take part in the system. To the extent that lifetime wealth has been augmented as a result, use of part of that wealth to consume more leisure should be welcomed, not condemned.

9. France has started to address this bias by shifting some of the burdens of financing social protection expenditures from payroll taxes to a "general social contribution" (GSG) levied on all incomes—including those of social security beneficiaries.

10. See OECD (1992b, 1994) for a further discussion of this trend and its causes.

Appendix

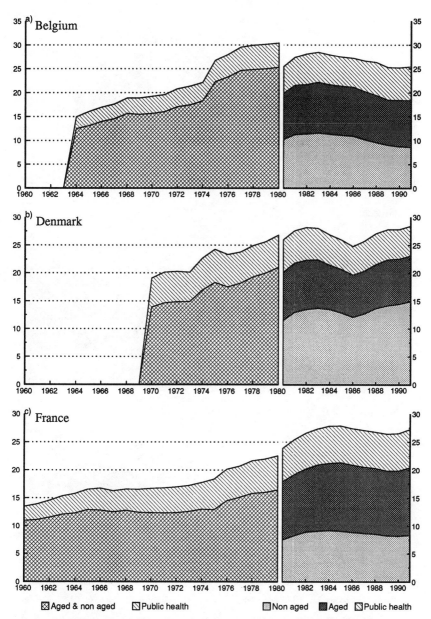

Fig. 2A.1   Public Expenditure on Social Protection as a Percentage of GDP in Other OECD Countries

Source: OECD 1994.

Note: OECD countries for which graphs are based on a mixture of old and new data from Eurostat. For reasons for differentiation, see cited source.

Fig. 2A.1 (continued)

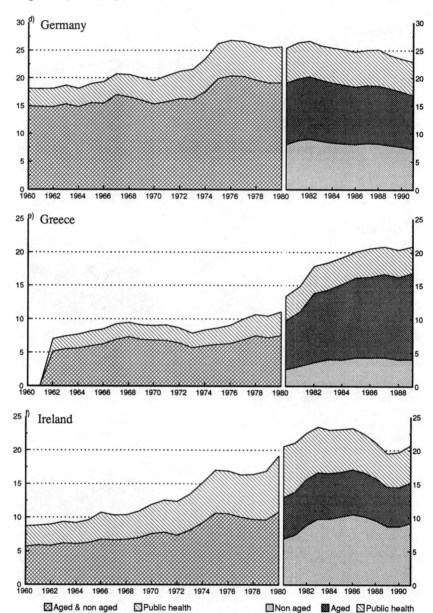

Fig. 2A.1 (continued)

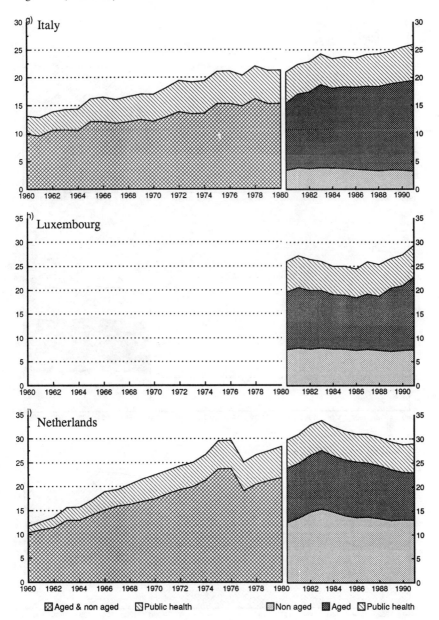

g) Italy

h) Luxembourg

i) Netherlands

⊠ Aged & non aged   ⊠ Public health   ▨ Non aged   ▨ Aged   ⊠ Public health

Fig. 2A.1 (continued)

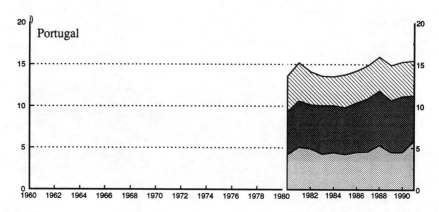

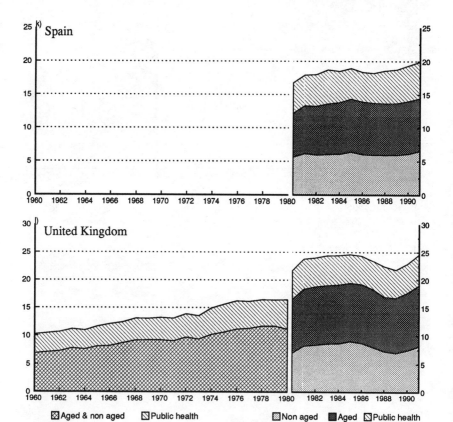

Fig. 2A.1 (continued)

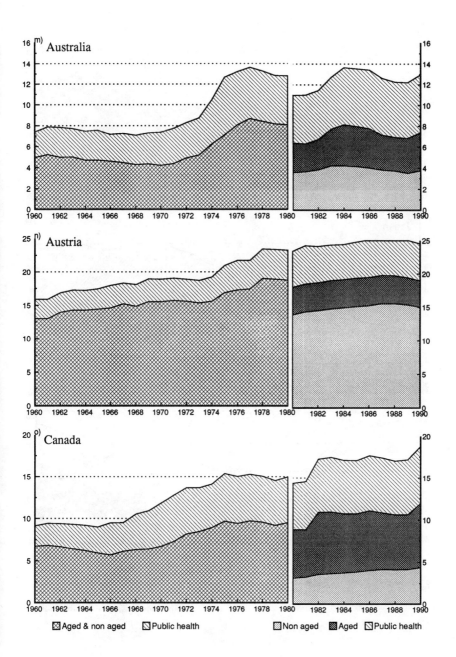

Fig. 2A.1 (continued)

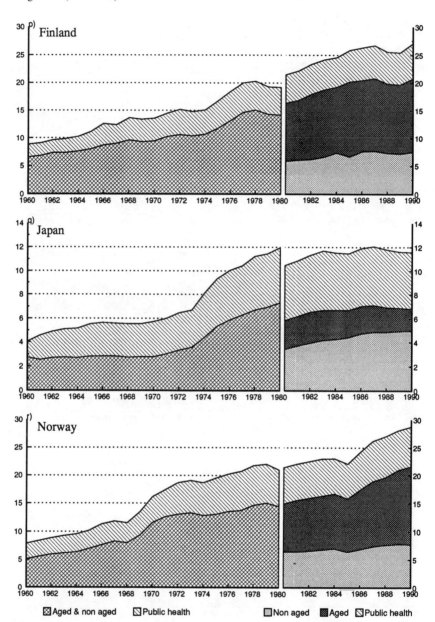

Fig. 2A.1 (continued)

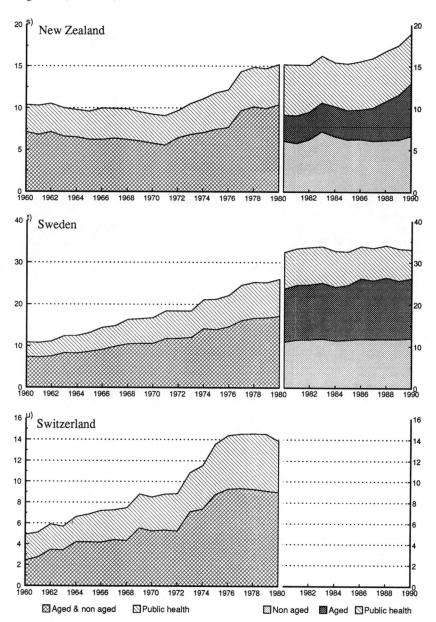

References

Esping-Anderson, G., and J. Micklewright. 1991. Welfare models in OECD countries: An analysis for the debate in central and eastern Europe. In *Children and the transition to the market economy,* ed. G. Cornia, A. Sándor, and S. Sándor, 35–68. Aldershot, U.K.: Avebury.

Eurostat (Statistical Office of the European Communities). 1993. *Old age replacement ratios. Vol. 1: Relation between pensions and income from employment at the moment of retirement.* Luxembourg: Office for Official Publications of the European Communities.

Förster, M. 1994. *Measurement of low incomes and poverty in a perspective of international comparisons.* Labour Market and Social Policy Occasional Paper. Paris: OECD.

Lødemel, I., and B. Schulte. 1992. Social assistance: A part of social security or the poor law in new disguise. In *Social security, five years after Beveridge. Vol. 2: Competing models of social security: A comparative analysis.* International Conference at University of York, 27–30 September.

Mishra, R. 1990. *The welfare state in capitalist society.* London: Harvester.

Mitchell, D. 1992. Welfare state and welfare outcomes in the 1990s. In *Social Security, five years after Beveridge. Vol. A: Plenary papers.* International Conference at University of York, 27–30 September.

Organization for Economic Cooperation and Development (OECD).
1981. *The welfare state in crisis.* Paris: OECD
1985. *Social expenditure 1960–1990: Problems of growth and control.* Paris: OECD
1990. *Employment outlook July 1990.* Paris: OECD.
1991. *Employment outlook July 1991.* Paris: OECD.
1992a. *Economic surveys—Finland.* Paris: OECD.
1992b. *Employment outlook July 1992.* Paris: OECD.
1992c. *The reform of health care: A comparative analysis of seven OECD countries.* Health Policy Studies no. 2. Paris: OECD.
1993. *The labour market in the Netherlands.* Paris: OECD.
1994. *New orientations for social policy.* Paris: OECD.

Vollmer, R. J. 1993. *Statutory care insurance: A challenge for Germany's hospitals.* Paper given at the twenty-eighth International Hospital Congress, Madrid, 21 April.

3 Does Employment Protection Inhibit Labor Market Flexibility? Lessons from Germany, France, and Belgium

Katharine G. Abraham and Susan N. Houseman

In most west European countries, workers historically have enjoyed strong job rights, including the right to advance notice of layoff and the right to severance pay or to negotiations over compensation for layoff. During the 1970s, on the eve of the first oil price shock, many of these countries significantly strengthened the notice and severance pay requirements imposed on employers who carried out collective dismissals. Particularly following the rapid growth in European unemployment during the late 1970s and early 1980s, these laws came under attack, and many were weakened over the course of the 1980s.

The question of whether and to what extent job-security regulations adversely affect labor market flexibility remains a matter of continuing controversy. Critics have claimed that strong job rights prevent employers from adjusting to economic fluctuations and secular changes in demand. It has also been alleged that, by inhibiting layoffs during downturns, strong job-security provisions reduce employers' willingness to hire during upturns and thereby contribute to unemployment.[1]

In fact, the effects of job-security regulations on labor market adjustment are poorly understood. Although such regulations would be expected to slow the adjustment of employment to an unexpected shock, the magnitude of this effect is debatable. Moreover, strong job-security regulations typically have been accompanied by measures intended to facilitate alternatives to layoffs, such as work-sharing. Whether and to what extent variation in working hours

Katharine G. Abraham is professor of economics at the University of Maryland and a research associate of the National Bureau of Economic Research. Susan N. Houseman is a senior economist at the W. E. Upjohn Institute for Employment Research.

Carolyn Thies provided research assistance and Claire Vogelsong provided secretarial support. The authors are grateful to Rebecca Blank, Alan Manning, and Bernd Reissert for their comments on an earlier draft of the paper. Helpful suggestions also were received from conference participants and from participants in a seminar at Columbia University.

1. For an elaboration of these arguments, see OECD (1986) and Soltwedel (1988).

offers employers a viable substitute to adjustment through layoffs remains an open question.

In this paper we provide new evidence on these issues. We compare the adjustment of employment to changing levels of demand in West Germany, France, and Belgium (all countries with strong job-security regulations) with that in the United States. Insofar as is possible with existing data, we also examine the responsiveness of hours worked to changes in the level of output in each of these countries. Finally, we ask whether changes in the strength of German, French, and Belgian job-security regulations during the 1970s and 1980s were associated with corresponding changes in the speed of employment or hours adjustment.

We begin in section 3.1 with a discussion of selected features of the West German, French, and Belgian industrial relations systems, focusing on job-security regulations and on measures intended to encourage work-sharing. For purposes of comparison, relevant U.S. institutions are also described. Our modeling strategy and data are briefly outlined in section 3.2. Section 3.3 documents the responsiveness of employment and, where possible, the responsiveness of hours to changes in output in the countries studied. Section 3.4 contains our tests of the effects of changes in job-security law on observed adjustment, and section 3.5 offers a few concluding observations.

3.1   Institutional Background

Many features of a country's industrial relations system may affect employers' adjustment decisions. Among the most noteworthy are regulations that impose notice and severance pay requirements on employers who dismiss workers, and measures that encourage hours adjustment in lieu of layoffs. Like most other west European countries, Germany, France, and Belgium all impose significant notice and severance pay requirements on employers who lay off workers. The most important features of these countries' job-security regulations are summarized in table 3.1. In addition, as outlined in table 3.2, all three countries have unemployment insurance systems that allow for prorated replacement of lost income for workers whose hours have been reduced as part of an approved short-time plan.

Like other west European countries, West Germany, France, and Belgium tightened their job-security regulations during the 1970s, then weakened them in one or more important ways during the 1980s. All three countries experienced substantial increases in unemployment during the late 1970s and early 1980s. Thus, tighter job-security regulations were associated with subsequent increases in unemployment. In each country, the relaxation of job-security regulations during the 1980s reflected pressure from employer groups who argued that existing regulations were unduly restrictive and that weakening those regulations would increase employment.

Below we briefly review the laws governing collective dismissals in Ger-

Table 3.1   Summary of Selected Provisions in German, French and Belgian Dismissal Law

	Germany	France	Belgium
Individual dismissal law			
Social or economic justification of dismissal required	Yes	Yes	No
Period of notice to affected individuals	Blue-collar: <5 years: 2 weeks >5 years: 1 month >20 years: 3 months White-collar: <5 years: 6 weeks >5 years: 3 months >12 years: 6 months	>6 months: 1 month >2 years: 2 months Middle management: 3 months	Blue-collar: <20 years: 28 days >20 years: 56 days White-collar: Since 1978, 3 months per new period of 5 years seniority and longer for highly paid employees
Compensation to affected individuals	None	1/10th of month's pay per year of service plus 1/15 of month's pay for each year over 10 years of service	None
Collective dismissal law			
Definition of collective dismissal	Approximately 20% of work force over 30-day period, depending on establishment size; thresholds raised in 1985	2 or more employees over 30-day period; more stringent regulations apply if 10 or more dismissed	Approximately 10% of work force over a 60-day period, depending on establishment size

(continued)

Table 3.1 (continued)

	Germany	France	Belgium
Additional notice and consulation requirements	Obligation to inform and consult with worker representatives; local employment office must be informed of dismissal and may delay dismissal for up to 2 months	Obligation to inform and consult with worker representatives; labor inspector must be informed of dismissal of 10 or more workers, and dismissal may take place only after specified waiting period	Obligation to inform and consult with worker representatives; government must be informed of dismissal; 30-day waiting period following notification to government may be extended to 60 days
Additional compensation to affected individuals	Social plan must be negotiated between works council and management; provision for binding arbitration if agreement cannot be reached	None	Workers entitled to receive 50% of difference between previous pay and unemployment benefit for up to four months, depending on length of notice; special payments in the event of a plant closing
Other requirements	None	Administrative authorization of all economic dismissals of 2 or more persons required from 1975 through 1986	None

Table 3.2 Selected Features of German, French, and Belgian Short-Time Compensation Systems

Feature	Germany	France	Belgium
Benefit amount	63–68% of net pay for hours not worked	1. Public payment of 65% of minimum wage for reductions below 39 hours per week 2. Employer payment to raise short-time benefit to 50% of gross wages for reduction below 36 hours per week, subject to a ceiling; state may reimburse employers for 50–80% of this payment	55–60% of net pay for hours not worked
Noteworthy limitations	Works council and local employment office must approve plan	No benefits paid to strikers; employer benefit not paid to any worker idled by an industrial dispute; labor inspector must approve plan	Usually available only for blue-collar workers; white-collar workers guaranteed full pay during slack periods
Allowable period of benefit receipt	6–24 months, depending on industry, regional, or national economic conditions; allowable periods extended by 1969 and 1975 laws; special provisions for steel	Up to a maximum of 500 hours per year (600 hours per year July 1981–December 1985, 400 hours per year before July 1981); state will partially reimburse employers for their portion of payments for 3–6 month period, with one extension possible	Indefinite, provided individual works certain minimum amount and government doesn't disapprove payment
Funding	Non-experience-rated payroll tax	General revenues	Non-experience-rated payroll tax

many, France, and Belgium and relevant aspects of each country's unemployment insurance system. These countries' policies are then contrasted with those in the United States.

3.1.1   Germany

The first law requiring German employers to give advance notice of dismissal to individual workers was passed during the 1920s. Today, required periods of notice to individual workers in Germany vary from two weeks to six months, depending upon whether the worker holds a blue-collar or a white-collar job and upon his or her seniority and age.[2]

In addition to stipulating advance notice for individual workers, German law gives the works council a legally mandated body of elected worker representatives, important powers in the event of a collective dismissal. Under current law, employers must keep both the works council and the local employment office advised of any developments that might lead to a collective dismissal over the next twelve months, and must consult the works council "as soon as possible" when contemplating such a layoff. The most important provision of the current law was introduced by the Works Constitution Act of 1972. That law requires, in cases of collective dismissal at an establishment normally employing more than twenty employees, that management and the works council must negotiate a social plan that stipulates compensation for workers who lose their jobs. In the event that the two parties cannot agree on a social plan, the law provides for binding arbitration.

Settlements in social plans vary considerably from case to case and depend upon the worker's tenure and wage as well as the company's financial condition. A study by Hemmer (1988) provides the best available data on the amounts of compensation paid out. In a sample of 145 social plans negotiated between 1980 and 1985, the median settlement was between DM 10,000 and DM 15,000 per recipient, or about fifteen to twenty-five weeks pay for a person with average blue-collar industrial earnings.

Between 1972 and 1985, the negotiation of a social plan was required if an employer laid off more than about 10 percent of the work force or more than thirty workers. The Employment Promotion Act of 1985 raised these thresholds to about 20 percent of the work force or more than sixty workers and gave new firms a four-year exemption from the social plan requirement. In addition, the new law made it easier for employers to hire workers on fixed-term contracts. German law regulates the use of fixed-term contracts so that employers cannot evade job-security regulations by hiring temporary workers who do not fall under the law's strictures. Prior to 1985, fixed-term contracts could last for no more than six months except under special circumstances. The 1985 law

---

2. A 1990 decision of the Federal Constitutional Court, the highest German court, declared the disparate treatment of blue-collar and white-collar workers under these statutes to be unconstitutional. This decision instructed the parliament to pass new legislation providing for equal notice periods for the two groups prior to June 30, 1993 (Brandes, Meyer, and Schudlich 1992, 22–23).

lengthened the allowable duration of fixed-term contracts to eighteen months and to twenty-four months for new small businesses.

German workers who are laid off are eligible to collect unemployment insurance benefits. The payroll tax that finances these benefits is not experience-rated, so that German employers incur no increase in unemployment insurance tax liability when they lay off workers. Because of the advance notice and other requirements associated with collective dismissals, temporary layoffs are virtually unknown in Germany, but the German unemployment insurance system does provide for short-time benefits. With the approval of the works council and the Employment Service, firms can reduce employees' hours of work, and those employees can collect prorated unemployment insurance benefits, which are financed in the same way as benefits to laid-off workers. Firms applying for short-time benefits must show that other measures for accommodating the fall in demand, such as reductions in overtime and rebuilding inventories, have already been taken. Since 1969, short-time benefits have been payable for six months under ordinary circumstances and for up to twelve months to employees of establishments in depressed regions or industries. In 1975 the allowable duration of benefit payment was extended to twenty-four months during periods of general recession.[3]

3.1.2 France

As in Germany, the requirement that workers be given advance notice of layoff has a long history in France. Under current law, the required period of notice is one month for workers with at least six months' service, two months for workers with at least two years' service, and three months for persons in middle management positions. French law also provides for severance payments to workers with at least two years' service who have not been fired for poor performance or other serious cause. The amount of severance pay guaranteed by law is one-tenth of one month's salary or twenty hours' pay for each year of service, though these amounts may be increased by the terms of applicable collective bargaining agreements.

French employers are required to meet additional legal requirements before carrying out collective dismissals involving as few as two workers over a thirty-day period. Before carrying out any such layoff, the employer is obliged to consult with the works council and advise the Labor Inspectorate of its plans. If ten or more workers are to be laid off, the law provides for minimum periods of consultation with the works council and notice to the Labor Inspectorate.

The most important changes to French labor law in recent years relate to these requirements. From 1975 through 1986, employers who wished to carry out any collective dismissal were required to obtain authorization from the Labor Inspectorate, which investigated both the reasons for the dismissal and the measures taken to avoid it. New rules effective as of 1987, however, have

---

3. For a more detailed discussion of German institutions, see Abraham and Houseman (1993).

eliminated this requirement. The same reform also eliminated all administrative oversight of layoffs involving fewer than ten employees and substantially reduced required periods of notice for larger layoffs.[4]

Like Germany, France also has a well-established structure for paying benefits to individuals whose hours of work have been temporarily reduced. The French system includes two types of payment, one from the state and the second from the employer under the terms of a 1968 national interindustry agreement. The former payment may be received except when workers are idled by an industrial dispute at their own establishment; the latter is not payable to workers idled by any industrial dispute. The public payment is a fixed hourly amount equal to 65 percent of the minimum wage for reductions in hours below thirty-nine per week. The complementary employer payment raises the short-time benefit to 50 percent of the worker's gross wage for reductions in hours below thirty-six per week, subject to a ceiling. Benefits currently may be paid for up to five hundred hours per year.

To encourage the use of short time, employers may be reimbursed for between 50 and 80 percent of their share of workers' short-time benefits. In practice, reimbursement rates of 70 to 80 percent are common. Agreements between an employer and the state concerning reimbursement of the employer's share of short-time benefit costs may last three months when the reimbursement rate is 70 percent or more, or six months when the reimbursement rate is 50 percent, with the possibility in both cases of one extension for a like term.[5]

3.1.3 Belgium

Like German and French employers, Belgian employers are required to give advance notice of dismissal to affected workers. For blue-collar workers past their probationary period, the notice period is twenty-eight days for workers with less than twenty years of service and fifty-six days for workers with more than twenty years of service. Since 1978, much longer notice periods have been required for white-collar workers, starting with a minimum of three months for those with less than five years of service and rising by three months for each successive five-year anniversary attained. In addition, highly paid white-collar workers were given the right to an amount of notice to be determined by the labor court. Subsequent court rulings effectively guaranteed these workers substantially longer notice periods.

Belgian law specifies no mandatory compensation to workers who are individually dismissed beyond the amount they are paid while serving out their period of notice. Belgian workers involved in a collective dismissal are entitled to special compensation from their employer in the amount of 50 percent of the difference between their previous net pay and their unemployment benefit

---

4. For discussions of French dismissal law and its evolution over time, see Rojot (1980, 1986) and EIRR (1985a, 1986).

5. For additional information on the French short-time system, see Grais (1983) and EIRR (1983). We have also benefited from conversations about the system with David Gray of the University of Ottawa.

or current net earnings. Workers who received less than three months' notice are entitled to receive this special payment for up to four months; the period of entitlement is reduced by one month for each extra month of notice received. Belgian law also contains special provisions for compensation to workers who lose their jobs because their plant closes.

In contrast to both German and French law, Belgian law does not require employers to justify dismissals. A law passed in 1972, however, requires that worker representatives be consulted before an employer carries out a collective dismissal. In addition, under the terms of a 1975 royal decree, which took effect in 1976, companies are required to provide detailed information to the state in the event of a planned layoff and to wait for at least thirty days after submitting this information before notifying affected workers of their dismissal. The introduction of this requirement was an important milestone in the development of Belgian labor law.[6]

Although the requirements imposed on employers who lay off blue-collar workers are less stringent in Belgium than in Germany and France, the growth of unemployment in the 1980s led to pressure for measures to increase employment flexibility. In addition to reducing periods of notice for white-collar workers, the reform package introduced in 1985 eased regulations concerning the use of fixed-term contracts and made a number of other smaller but collectively significant changes (EIRR 1984).

Among the three European countries we have studied, Belgium has the most liberal rules governing payment of short-time benefits to production workers. Production workers' short-time benefits are paid out of the regular unemployment insurance fund, which is financed by a payroll tax of a uniform percentage amount. Legislation that would have experience-rated the contributions that pay for short-time compensation was introduced in 1991 but did not pass (Vroman 1992, 22). Short-time compensation replaces 55 to 60 percent of a worker's net wages, depending upon his or her family situation. The rules governing payment of short time are complex but allow a blue-collar worker to collect short time indefinitely so long as he or she works a minimum of three days per week, or every other week if on a system of rotating layoffs, and the government does not disapprove the payment. Belgian white-collar workers are guaranteed full pay during slack periods and generally are not eligible for short-time benefits.[7]

3.1.4   United States

The requirements governing layoffs and the provision for short-time benefits described above offer a significant contrast to the general absence of similar arrangements in the United States. Prior to 1988, advance notice of layoffs and

---

6. Further details concerning Belgian dismissal law can be found in EIRR (1985b), Vranken (1986), and Blanpain (1989).

7. See Grais (1983), EIRR (1983), and Vroman (1992) for further discussion of the Belgian short-time system.

plant closings was required in only three states: Maine, Wisconsin, and Hawaii. In the absence of any national law requiring advance notice, workers often received little or no warning prior to being let go. In addition, workers who are permanently laid off often receive no severance pay.[8]

Although U.S. employers are not required to make severance payments to laid-off workers, the fact that the U.S. unemployment insurance system is experience-rated means that layoffs may lead to an increase in unemployment insurance tax liability. For a U.S. employer, the effective unemployment insurance cost of laying off a worker depends upon three things: his or her weekly benefit amount, the duration of benefit receipt, and the share of the benefit for which the employer ultimately pays through higher unemployment insurance taxes. Weekly benefit amounts average roughly 35 percent of weekly wages; the average duration of benefit receipt varies somewhat over the business cycle but has averaged about fourteen weeks; and, at the margin, a typical employer bears about 60 percent of the cost of benefits paid to laid-off workers (though many employers are already paying the maximum unemployment insurance tax rate and thus incur no increase in costs if they lay off additional workers).[9] Thus, a rough estimate of the unemployment insurance cost to a typical employer of laying off another worker is about three weeks' wages in the form of increased unemployment insurance tax liability.

Paying unemployment insurance benefits to workers whose hours have been reduced is a recent innovation in the United States. At present, only seventeen states have laws allowing prorated payment of unemployment insurance benefits to workers whose hours are reduced under approved work-sharing plans, and most of these laws were passed quite recently.

3.1.5   Implications for Labor Adjustment

Because of the institutional features of the German, French, and Belgian labor markets, we would expect that employers in these countries would respond quite differently to changes in production than would their U.S. counterparts. The advance notice and severance pay requirements that exist in all three countries can be expected to slow the adjustment of employment to changes in output. Given that mass layoffs are relatively costly in all of the European countries included in our study, we would expect greater reliance on attrition to achieve desired work force reductions there than in the United States.

While we would expect the adjustment of employment to be slower in these European countries than in the United States, we would not necessarily expect slower adjustment of total labor input. High employment adjustment costs should increase employers' reliance on hours adjustments. In addition, the

8. See General Accounting Office (1986) for survey results on the incidence of advance notice and severance pay.

9. *Unemployment Insurance Financial Data,* published by the U.S. Department of Labor, contains data on weekly benefit amounts, weekly wages in covered employment, and the duration of benefit receipt. Vroman (1989) discusses alternative estimates of the degree of experience rating.

availability of short-time compensation makes it less costly to adjust average hours per worker.[10] A priori, it is unclear whether German, French, and Belgian employers are, in fact, less able than U.S. employers to adjust labor input to changes in demand. Our empirical analysis looks at this question.

A final issue of interest is whether changes during the 1970s and 1980s to the job-security regulations in each of the three European countries studied affected the speed with which labor input adjusted to changes in output.

3.2 Model and Data

We have used a standard Koyck model of the dynamic demand for labor to study labor adjustment in West Germany, France, Belgium and the United States. The model assumes that employers seek to maximize the expected present value of current and future profits; that the costs of adjusting labor input are a quadratic function of the size of the adjustment made; and that changes in the determinants of the demand for labor other than output are sufficiently smooth that they can be captured by time trends. Under these conditions and given certain assumptions about how employers form their expectations of future demand, the adjustment of labor to changes in the level of output can be represented by the following equation:

$$(1) \qquad \ln L_t = \alpha + (1 - \lambda)\phi \ln P_t + \lambda \ln L_{t-1} + \delta_1 t + \delta_2 t^2 + \varepsilon_t,$$

where L represents employment, production employment, or production hours, P represents output, t is a time trend, and ε is the equation error. In this model, the parameter λ lies between zero and one and captures the speed of adjustment to changes in output. Larger values of λ are associated with slower adjustment speeds. A value of zero for λ implies that adjustment occurs instantaneously.

Note that, in interpreting cross-country differences in the estimated value of λ, a given difference in λ implies a larger difference in the speed of adjustment to a shock at high than at low values of λ. In the model specified, the proportion of the adjustment of labor input to a one-time change in output that occurs with a lag of t periods declines geometrically with t and equals $(1 - \lambda)\lambda^t$. The median lag in adjustment is the time required for 50 percent of the adjustment to be complete. In an equation using quarterly data, a drop in the estimated value of λ from 0.9 to 0.8 would imply a sizable drop in the median adjustment

---

10. Formal models of the effects of employment adjustment costs on both employment and hours are surveyed by Nickell (1986) and Hamermesh (1993). Burdett and Wright (1989) model the effect of access to short-time compensation through the unemployment insurance system. In their model, the short-time compensation subsidy associated with imperfect experience rating increases employers' reliance on hours adjustments and raises the volatility of average hours relative to the volatility of employment. Even in a perfectly experience-rated unemployment insurance system, giving liquidity-constrained employers access to short-time benefits for their workers may produce the same result.

lag, from 6 to 3 quarters. For values of λ of 0.5 or less, half or more of the adjustment to an output shock occurs concurrently, so that the median adjustment lag is zero quarters. Thus, a reduction in λ from, say, 0.4 to 0.3 would have no effect on the median adjustment lag. The mean lag in adjustment, which is the weighted average of the lag lengths $t = 0,1,2 \ldots \infty$ with the weight for each t equal to the share of adjustment occurring at that lag, is calculated as $\lambda/(1 - \lambda)$ (Maddala 1977, 360). A drop in the estimated value of λ from 0.9 to 0.8 would imply a drop in the mean adjustment lag from 9.0 to 4.0 quarters, whereas a decline in λ from 0.4 to 0.3 would imply a much smaller decline in the mean adjustment lag, from 0.7 to 0.4 quarters. When we report estimated values of λ for the purpose of making cross-country comparisons, we also report the values of the implied median lag and mean lag in adjustment.

Our specification treats output as exogenous. This assumption might be questioned, but as a practical matter there is no real alternative. Our model also assumes that the costs of adjusting labor input are a quadratic function of its change. Although the true structure of adjustment costs has been widely debated in the economics profession, we would expect larger adjustment costs (whatever their structure) to produce less-complete adjustment.[11] Moreover, although the model we have estimated was originally developed to explain the behavior of individual employers, larger adjustment costs should produce larger values of λ in models estimated using aggregate data, all else the same.

Finally, our specification assumes that information on current output is sufficient to generate employers' expectations concerning future output. In earlier work (Abraham and Houseman 1992), we found that making more complex assumptions about output expectations had little effect on the relative estimated speeds of adjustment across countries. We also have estimated finite distributed lag models of the labor adjustment process and reached qualitative conclusions generally similar to those based on the models reported here. In short, although there are certainly questions that could be raised concerning our model specification, we believe both that our choice is defensible and that our qualitative conclusions would not have been much different had we made a different choice.

We use equation (1) or a variant of it to assess the contribution of short-time work to observed labor adjustment and to assess the effect of changes in labor market regulation on the speed with which labor inputs are adjusted.[12] In all

---

11. For example, if adjustment costs are linear and there are periods during which firms choose not to hire or fire, then λ should approximately equal the fraction of periods during which no hiring or firing occurs, and that fraction should be larger when adjustment costs are higher (Anderson 1992). Similarly, the existence of fixed costs of adjustment should reduce the probability that a firm will adjust its labor input when output changes and should raise the estimated value of λ (Hamermesh 1989).

12. We also tested for differences in the speed of labor adjustment in response to negative versus positive output shocks. The differences, however, were always very small and generally statistically insignificant, and we do not report the results of this exercise.

models where Durbin-h tests indicated that there was first-order serial correlation in the error term, we made the appropriate correction.

Seasonally adjusted quarterly series for the West German, French, and Belgian manufacturing sectors and for selected manufacturing industries in those countries are used to estimate the models just described. Comparable estimates for the United States are also reported for purposes of comparison. Usable data on production employment and production hours are not available for France. Our principal measure of output for all four countries is an index of industrial production. We also make use of data on short-time hours for West Germany, France, and Belgium. Further details concerning data sources and construction are provided in the appendix.

3.3   Patterns of Labor Adjustment

The first part of our empirical analysis looks at the adjustment of employment and hours to changes in output over the 1973–90 period taken as a whole. In addition, we examine the contribution of the short-time system to labor adjustment in West Germany, France, and Belgium.

3.3.1   Employment and Hours Adjustment

Before turning to the estimation of formal adjustment models, we begin by examining plots of production, production worker employment, and production worker hours indices for West Germany, Belgium, and the United States.[13] Figure 3.1 displays these plots for the manufacturing sector as a whole and for the textiles; apparel; stone, clay, and glass; primary metals; automobiles; paper; printing; and chemicals industries. These industries were selected for inclusion both here and in the estimation reported below because there was a close correlation between the European and U.S. industry definition and because at least some usable time series data were available for at least two European countries. There are no plots of French data in figure 3.1 because suitable production employment and production hours series for France do not exist.

Consistent with our expectations, production employment in West Germany and Belgium moves smoothly and is unresponsive to short-run changes in output, whereas in the United States, movements in production employment closely follow those in output. In contrast, in both West Germany and Belgium, production hours—and by implication average hours per production worker—generally appear quite responsive to output changes, and German and Belgian hours adjustment appears to be much more similar to U.S. hours adjustment than German and Belgian employment adjustment is to U.S. employment adjustment.

Table 3.3 reports the estimated adjustment coefficients from Koyck models of employment, production employment, and production hours adjustment fit

---

13. Total employment behaves similarly to production employment but is omitted from the plots.

Fig. 3.1 Seasonally adjusted production, employment and hours: West Germany, Belgium, and the United States, 1973–1990

Fig. 3.1 (continued)

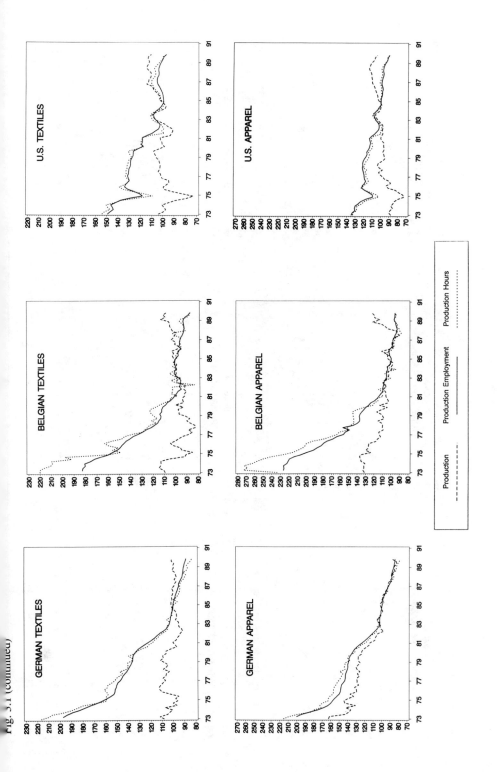

Fig. 3.1 (continued)

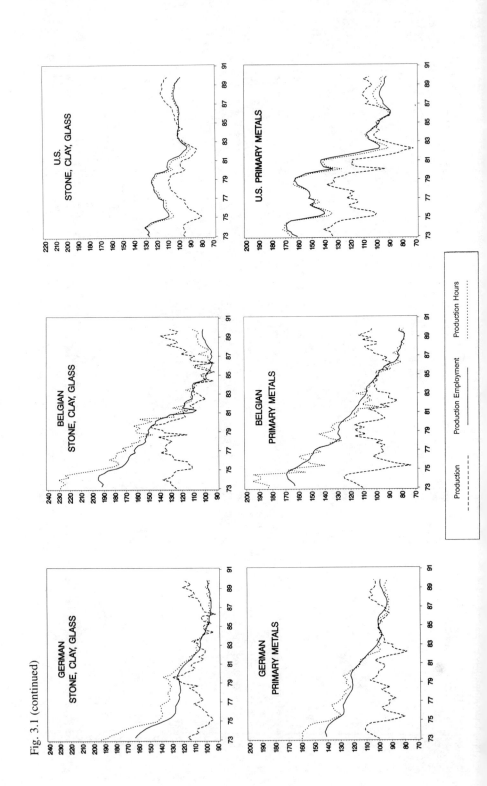

Fig. 3.1 (continued)

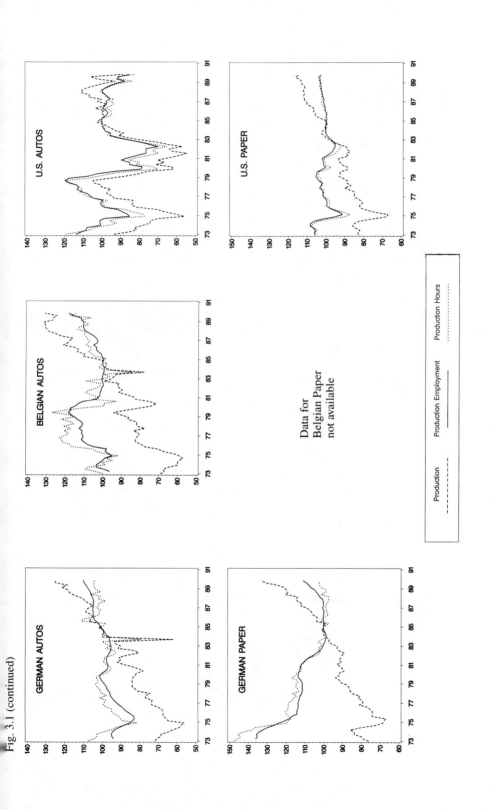

Fig. 3.1 (continued)

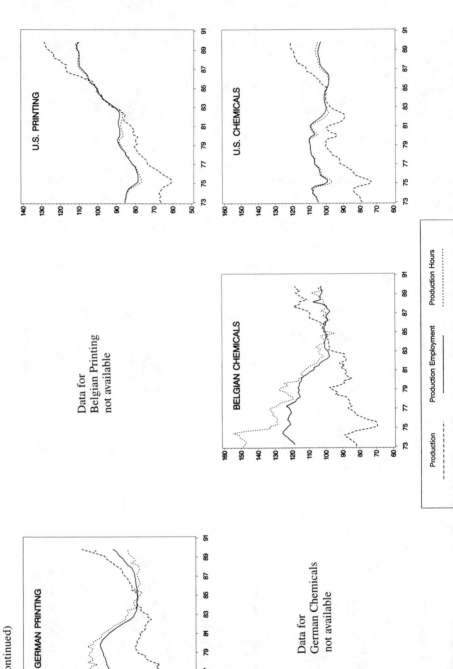

GERMAN PRINTING

U.S. PRINTING

Data for
Belgian Printing
not available

BELGIAN CHEMICALS

U.S. CHEMICALS

Data for
German Chemicals
not available

Production   Production Employment   Production Hours

Table 3.3   Estimated Speed of Adjustment in Manufacturing in the United States, West Germany, France, and Belgium, 1973–1990[a]

A. Employment Adjustment[b]

	West Germany	France	Belgium	United States
Manufacturing	.837	.935	.823	.383
	(.016)	(.026)	(.032)	(.039)
	[3, 5.1]	[10, 14.4]	[3, 4.6]	[0, 0.6]
Textiles	.918	.905	.950	.530
	(.024)	(.073)	(.044)	(.046)
	[7, 11.2]	[6, 9.5]	[13, 19.0]	[1, 1.1]
Apparel	.859	—	.710	.397
	(.066)		(.062)	(.091)
	[4, 6.1]		[1, 2.4]	[0, 0.7]
Stone, clay, and glass	.853	.924	.809	.568
	(.025)	(.026)	(.039)	(.032)
	[4, 5.8]	[8, 12.2]	[3, 4.2]	[1, 1.3]
Primary metals	.897	.937	.726	.504
	(.078)	(.048)	(.089)	(.039)
	[6, 8.7]	[10, 14.9]	[2, 2.6]	[1, 1.0]
Autos	.897	.934	.828	.331
	(.076)	(.037)	(.052)	(.049)
	[6, 8.7]	[10, 14.2]	[3, 4.8]	[0, 0.5]
Paper	.906	.910	—	.557
	(.046)	(.036)		(.048)
	[6, 9.6]	[7, 10.1]		[1, 1.3]
Printing	.864	.927	—	.858
	(.027)	(.031)		(.059)
	[4, 6.4]	[9, 12.7]		[4, 6.0]
Chemicals	—	.925	.877	.698
		(.036)	(.040)	(.055)
		[8, 12.3]	[5, 7.1]	[1, 2.3]

B. Production Employment Adjustment[b]

	West Germany	Belgium	United States
Manufacturing	.800	.792	.325
	(.017)	(.038)	(.041)
	[3, 4.0]	[2, 3.8]	[0, 0.5]
Textiles	.912	.924	.507
	(.027)	(.048)	(.044)
	[7, 10.4]	[8, 12.2]	[1, 1.0]
Apparel	.858	.607	.380
	(.090)	(.087)	(.094)
	[4, 6.0]	[1, 1.5]	[0, 0.6]
Stone, clay, and glass	.822	.547	.508
	(.024)	(.109)	(.027)
	[3, 4.6]	[1, 1.2]	[1, 1.0]
Primary metals	.885	.955	.458
	(.090)	(.056)	(.038)
	[5, 7.7]	[14, 21.2]	[0, 0.8]

(continued)

Table 3.3   (continued)

| | B. Production Employment Adjustment[b] | | | |
	West Germany	France	Belgium	United States
Autos	.883		.902	.276
	(.073)		(.038)	(.051)
	[5, 7.5]		[6, 9.2]	[0, 0.4]
Paper	.886		—	.540
	(.051)			(.044)
	[5, 7.8]			[1, 1.2]
Printing	.873		—	.873
	(.050)			(.053)
	[5, 6.9]			[5, 6.9]
Chemicals	—		.866	.551
			(.045)	(.064)
			[4, 6.5]	[1, 1.2]

| | C. Production Hours Adjustment[b] | | | |
	West Germany[c]	Belgium[c]	United States[c]	United States[d]
Manufacturing	.433	.441	.132	.362
	(.066)	(.066)	(.051)	(.051)
	[0, 0.8]	[0, 0.8]	[0, 0.2]	[0, 0.6]
Textiles	.714	.542	.295	.257
	(.058)	(.101)	(.059)	(.153)
	[2, 2.5]	[1, 1.2]	[0, 0.4]	[0, 0.3]
Apparel	.652	.063	.076	.547
	(.062)	(.105)	(.105)	(.189)
	[1, 1.9]	[0, 0.1]	[0, 0.1]	[1, 1.2]
Stone, clay, and glass	.512	.181	.340	.549
	(.052)	(.082)	(.036)	(.070)
	[1, 1.0]	[0, 0.2]	[0, 0.5]	[1, 1.2]
Primary metals	.621	.104	.314	.253
	(.064)	(.107)	(.038)	(.059)
	[1, 1.6]	[0, 0.1]	[0, 0.5]	[0, 0.3]
Autos	.363	.407	.119	.240
	(.072)	(.063)	(.041)	(.044)
	[0, 0.6]	[0, 0.7]	[0, 0.1]	[0, 0.3]
Paper	.381	—	.374	.475
	(.098)		(.057)	(.174)
	[0, 0.6]		[0, 0.6]	[0, 0.9]
Printing	.504	—	.830	.813
	(.071)		(.065)	(.052)
	[0, 1.0]		[3, 4.9]	[3, 4.3]
Chemicals	—	.621	.366	.596
		(.088)	(.065)	(.106)
		[1, 1.6]	[0, 0.6]	[1, 1.5]

[a]The speed of adjustment parameter is the coefficient on the lagged dependent variable from the following Koyck model: $\ln L_t = \alpha + (1 - \lambda)\phi \ln P_t + \lambda \ln L_{t-1} + \delta_1 t + \delta_2 t^2 + \varepsilon_t$, where L represents employment, production employment, or production hours and P is a measure of output.

Table 3.3	(continued)

[b]The standard error of the estimated adjustment parameter is reported in parentheses, and the implied median, mean adjustment lag in brackets.
[c]Estimates use production indices as the measure of output.
[d]Estimates use deflated shipments as the measure of output.

for West Germany, France, Belgium, and the United States, as permitted by available data. In the employment adjustment models reported in panel A of table 3.3, the differences between the estimated European adjustment coefficients and those for the United States are uniformly large and statistically significant. The larger European coefficients imply that employment adjustment there is substantially slower than in the United States. In manufacturing as a whole, for example, the implied median lag is 3 quarters in Germany, 10 quarters in France, and 3 quarters in Belgium, whereas over half (62 percent) of the adjustment in the United States occurs in the current quarter. Similarly, the mean adjustment lag is 5.1 quarters in Germany, 14.4 quarters in France, and 4.6 quarters in Belgium, but only 0.6 quarters in the United States. Consistent with the plots in figure 3.1, the production employment models reported in panel B of table 3.3 imply a similar contrast between the adjustment of production employment in West Germany and Belgium and that in the United States.

Our estimates of the speed of hours adjustment for West Germany, Belgium, and the United States are reported in panel C of table 3.3. Comparison of the German and U.S. coefficients shows that, for manufacturing as a whole and for five of seven disaggregate industries, German hours adjustment is significantly slower than U.S. hours adjustment. In all of these cases, however, the implied difference in the speed of German and U.S. hours adjustment is much smaller than the implied differences in the speeds of employment and production employment adjustment. For example, although they differ statistically, the German and U.S. hours adjustment coefficients for the manufacturing sector as a whole both imply a median adjustment lag of zero quarters and a mean adjustment lag of less than one quarter. The hours adjustment results for West Germany reported here are somewhat different than those we reported in an earlier paper (Abraham and Houseman 1992). In our earlier work, we estimated adjustment equations for the 1974–84 period for each of eleven manufacturing industries, using shipments deflated by a price index as our output measure. The estimated German coefficients in these models were more similar to those for the United States; for none of the eleven industries did we find evidence that German hours adjustment was significantly slower than U.S. hours adjustment.

Although no single factor accounts for all of the differences, the use of production rather than shipments as the measure of output for the United States seems to be the most important. For purposes of comparison, we also report the results of U.S. production hours adjustment models that use deflated shipments as the measure of output. For all of manufacturing and for several disaggregated industries—apparel; stone, clay, and glass; automobiles; and chemicals—the use of production rather than shipments as the measure of output for the United States substantially reduces the estimated speed of adjustment parameter, implying faster adjustment in the United States. Given that finished goods inventories may be used to buffer against demand changes, we might expect faster adjustment when production rather than shipments is used as the measure of output. For aggregate manufacturing and automobiles, the drop in the estimated coefficient for the United States also may be related to the way the production index was constructed; for these two industries, production hours account for 20 percent and 36 percent, respectively, of the production index. The use of production hours in the construction of the production index in these two cases would be expected to lower the estimated speed of adjustment coefficient. For aggregate manufacturing and the auto industry, estimates of hours adjustment in West Germany are quite similar to those in the United States when deflated shipments are used as the measure of output for the United States.

The results for Belgium in panel C of table 3.3 are even more similar to those for the United States. For three of the six disaggregated industries for which comparisons can be made, hours adjustment in Belgium is insignificantly different than that in the United States. In those industries where Belgian hours adjustment is slower than U.S. hours adjustment, the implied mean lag in Belgian adjustment is never more than one quarter longer than that in the United States.[14] Our findings for Belgium are generally consistent with those reported by Van Audenrode (1991), who, using a somewhat different model and a different output measure, concluded that hours adjustment in Belgian manufacturing was as rapid as that in U.S. manufacturing.

3.3.2   The Use of Short Time

It is of interest to ask how short-time work contributes to labor adjustment in the European countries we study. The available data allow us to address this question in somewhat different ways for West Germany, France, and Belgium.

For Germany, our general strategy is to ask how hours adjustment would have differed had no workers been placed on short time, assuming that employers' adjustment behavior otherwise remained unchanged. Using data on the number of manufacturing sector workers on short time and on the percentage reduction in hours experienced by those workers, we constructed estimates of the total number of production worker hours for which short-time compensa-

14. As in the United States, hours data are used in the construction of the Belgian production indices for aggregate manufacturing and the auto industry, comprising about 15 percent of the weight in each index.

Table 3.4   **Estimated Effects of Short Time on Adjustment in West German, French, and Belgian Manufacturing, 1973–1990**

	Speed of Adjustment	Standard Error	Median, Mean Adjustment Lag
West Germany: hours adjustment[a]			
Without short time	.655	.082	1, 1.9
With short time	.433	.066	0, 0.8
France: employment adjustment[b]			
With short time	.930	.030	9, 13.3
Assuming layoffs used in lieu			
of short time	.847	.044	4, 5.5
Belgium: hours adjustment[a]			
Without short time	.658	.070	1, 1.9
With short time	.441	.066	0, 0.8

[a]The German and Belgian with-short-time coefficients are the estimated λ's from the Koyck models with the logarithm of production hours as the dependent variable reported in table 3.3C. The without-short-time coefficients are the estimated λ's from similar models using the logarithm of production hours plus short-time hours as the dependent variable.

[b]The French without-short-time coefficient is slightly different from the estimated λ from the Koyck model with the logarithm of employment as the dependent variable reported in table 3.3A because the French short-time series begins in 1973:4. The with-short-time coefficient is the estimated λ from a similar model using the logarithm of employment minus short-time days during the quarter divided by 65 as the dependent variable.

tion was paid. The data on short time apply to all workers, not just production workers. The reported estimates assume that only production workers work short time, though the results are not much different if we assume that short-time hours are distributed between production and nonproduction workers in proportion to their share of total employment.[15]

Using this series, it is possible to show the contribution of fluctuations in short-time hours to the adjustment of production labor input. The results of this exercise are reported in table 3.4. The "with short time" adjustment parameter is the same number as was reported in panel C of table 3.3; the "without short time" number was derived by first constructing a total production hours series equal to hours actually worked plus short-time hours, then estimating our standard hours adjustment equation using this series. The results clearly indicate that the short-time system plays an important role in German employers' adjustment of labor input to changes in output.[16]

Because there is no usable French hours series, we carried out a somewhat different exercise for France, asking how much larger measured employment adjustment would have been had employers made layoffs to achieve the hours

15. Additional details concerning our procedures for constructing time series on West German production workers' short-time hours are reported in Abraham and Houseman (1993).

16. Results estimated using data for more disaggregated manufacturing industries confirm the importance of the role played by short time in West German hours adjustment.

reductions accomplished through short time. The French report quarterly data on the full-time equivalent number of days of authorized short time. We divided these numbers by sixty-five to yield a full-time employment equivalent usage measure and constructed a labor input series by subtracting this number of employees from the actual employment series. We then fit labor adjustment models, using both actual employment and this adjusted employment series to construct our dependent variable. Like the results for West Germany, the French results reported in table 3.4 indicate that the use of short time makes an important contribution to the adjustment of labor input. In particular, the results imply that the median and the mean adjustment lags for employment would fall by over half if layoffs were used in lieu of short-time work. By implication, in the short run, short-time work is a more important mechanism for adjusting labor input than is the adjustment of employment levels.

For Belgium, we were able to obtain monthly data on the number of full-time equivalent persons on short time for the aggregate economy. Although we did not have monthly short-time data disaggregated by sector, we did have data on the proportion of short-time work accounted for by manufacturing for two years. To construct a quarterly short-time hours series for Belgian manufacturing, we multiplied the short-time hours series for the aggregate economy by 0.475, the average of the proportion of short-time hours accounted for by manufacturing in 1985 and 1990, and aggregated the monthly data to yield quarterly figures. As was done for West Germany, we then added the short-time hours to production hours and estimated our standard hours adjustment equation with this series.

As table 3.4 shows, the results of this exercise are quite similar to those for West Germany and show that short-time hours make an important contribution to total hours adjustment in Belgium. Because the manufacturing sector is somewhat more cyclical than the aggregate economy, our estimates, if anything, understate the importance of short time in Belgian manufacturing hours adjustment.

3.4 Have Dismissal Laws Inhibited Labor Market Flexibility?

As already noted, we are particularly interested in whether the changes in job-security regulations in West Germany, France, and Belgium during the 1970s and 1980s affected the speed with which labor input adjusted to changes in output. By making it easier to reduce work force levels during periods of slack demand, argued proponents of weaker regulation, such changes also would make employers more willing to hire during periods of rising demand. There is, however, little empirical evidence on this issue.

To support their claims, proponents of weaker job-security regulation often appealed to employer surveys of the sort summarized in table 3.5. The em-

Table 3.5   **Selected Results from a 1985 European Community Survey of Manufacturing Employers[a]**

Response	West Germany	France	Belgium	United Kingdom
1. Insufficient flexibility in hiring and shedding labor as an obstacle to more employment				
Very important	23%	48%	38%	7%
Important	33	33	37	19
Not important	39	15	25	58
No answer	5	4	0	16
2. Expected effects on employment plans over next twelve months of shorter periods of notice and simpler legal procedures in case of layoffs or dismissals				
Significant positive	31%	18%	33%	6%
Little positive	32	30	41	22
No change	34	34	25	66
Negative	1	13	1	3
No answer	2	5	0	3
3. Expected effects on employment plans over next twelve months of relaxing restrictions on use of temporary contracts				
Significant positive	23%	13%	30%	4%
Little positive	51	41	33	23
No change	22	40	31	66
Negative	2	1	6	4
No answer	2	5	0	3
4. Expected effects on employment plans over next twelve months of reduction in redundancy payments that might have to be paid				
Significant positive	21%	7%	26%	6%
Little positive	25	15	37	17
No change	50	67	36	71
Negative	2	6	1	4
No answer	2	5	0	2

[a]Survey methodology and results summarized in Commission of the European Communities, *European Economy*, no. 27, March 1986.

ployer responses reported there are based on a survey conducted by the Commission of the European Communities in 1985. Over half of manufacturing employers in each of the three European countries we are studying cited "insufficient flexibility in hiring and shedding of labor" as a very important or important obstacle to increased employment. The percentage is particularly large (81 percent) in France, where at that point in time employers who wanted to dismiss workers were required to obtain the authorization of the Labor Inspectorate. Many manufacturing employers, particularly in West Germany and Belgium, believed that shorter notice periods, enhanced possibilities for using temporary workers, and lower severance payments would have a significant positive effect on their hiring plans. Comparable figures for the United Kingdom, where job-security regulations are much less stringent, are also reported to provide a point of reference. Not surprisingly, U.K. employers who responded to the survey were much less likely to cite hiring and firing rigidities as a barrier to employment.[17]

Our approach to assessing the effects of legal changes is to look for changes in the pace of labor adjustment that might have accompanied the introduction of more or less stringent regulations. For West Germany, we ask whether the speed of adjustment changed following passage of the Employment Promotion Act in 1985.[18] That law raised the number of employees who could be laid off without an employer being required to negotiate a social plan with the works council. It also liberalized the use of fixed-term contracts. The nature of these changes suggests that the responsiveness of employment to changes in output might have risen following the law's passage. To the extent that employers had not fully compensated for the slower adjustment of employment with the faster adjustment of average hours per worker, we also might expect that the weakening of employment protection laws would be accompanied by more rapid adjustment of total labor input.

Modified versions of equation (1) can be used to assess the effect of changes in labor market regulation on the speed with which labor inputs are adjusted. For example, to test whether the 1985 Employment Promotion Act raised the speed of labor adjustment in West Germany we estimate:

$$(2) \qquad \ln L_t = \alpha_0 + \alpha_1 D85{:}2 + (1 - \lambda_0 - \lambda_1 D85{:}2)\phi \ln P_t + \\ (\lambda_0 + \lambda_1 D85{:}2)\ln L_{t-1} + \delta_1 t + \delta_2 t^2 + \varepsilon_t,$$

where $D85{:}2$ is a dummy variable that takes a value of one in all quarters from 1985:2 onward and a value of zero prior to that date. The results of this test are reported in the three parts of table 3.6: total employment (panel A), production employment (panel B), and production hours (panel C). Had employment become more responsive, we would have expected negative values for λ_1; the estimated values vary in sign, though with one exception the coefficients are insignificant. Our finding that passage of the 1985 Employment Promotion Act did not raise the speed of employment adjustment is consistent with that of Kraft (1990), who reaches the same conclusion using a somewhat different specification.[19]

In France, the major change in dismissal regulation that we are able to study is the elimination in 1987 of the requirement that the Labor Inspectorate autho-

---

17. The responses to a similar survey of European employers in the retail trade sector show much the same pattern.

18. The West German data series that we use in the present paper begin in 1970 and thus in principle would permit us to test the effects of the social plan requirement introduced by the Works Constitution Act of 1972. However, the results of any test based on data containing only eight pre-1972 observations would be highly suspect.

19. The Works Constitution Act of 1972 changed West German job-security regulations more fundamentally than did the Employment Promotion Act of 1985. The 1972 act's requirement that employers who carry out a collective dismissal must negotiate a social plan with the works council might have been expected to slow employers' adjustment to changing economic conditions. In earlier research using a somewhat different approach, however, we found no evidence that this occurred (Abraham and Houseman 1993).

rize all dismissals of two or more workers.[20] Particularly given the large proportion of French employers who reported in 1985 that insufficient flexibility in the hiring and shedding of labor was a major obstacle to employment, it is plausible that this legal change would have had an important effect on the pace of employment adjustment. Again, however, our findings offer no strong support for this position.

If weaker job-security regulations encourage more rapid employment adjustment, we would expect negative values of λ_1 in the employment adjustment models reported for France in panel A of table 3.6. Although the estimated value of λ_1 is negative and significant for three of seven disaggregated industries, this result obtains neither for manufacturing as a whole nor for the remaining four disaggregated industries. We interpret these results as providing no more than weak support for the view that the weakening of French dismissal regulations has increased the speed of employment adjustment.

Although changes to dismissal law were less dramatic in Belgium than in the other two countries, significant reforms were introduced in 1976 and 1985. A royal decree in 1975, effective at the start of 1976, imposed the requirement that employers who make collective dismissals must notify the government thirty to sixty days in advance of carrying them out. In 1985 a package of reforms loosened employment regulations in a variety of ways. We would expect, therefore, that adjustment speeds would have fallen following the imposition of the 1975 royal decree (λ_1 positive in the models reported in table 3.6) and risen following the 1985 reforms (λ_2 negative in those same models). In certain of the Belgian equations, particularly those with the logarithm of total employment as the dependent variable, we obtain small estimates of λ_0 and large estimates of λ_1. This pattern probably is attributable to the fact that we have only twelve quarterly observations prior to the introduction of the 1976 reforms. Leaving these cases aside, our results offer no consistent support for the view that legislative changes have produced important changes in adjustment speeds. Our findings concerning the lack of any effect of the 1975 decree are consistent with those of Van Audenrode (1991), who fit separate adjustment equations using 1965–75 data and 1976–86 data and found no evidence of a change in the estimated model parameters between the two time periods.

Taken as a whole, then, our results provide no strong evidence that changes in the strength of job-security regulations since the early 1970s affected the speed of labor adjustment in West Germany, France, or Belgium. Various interpretations of this finding are possible. One could argue that the regulatory changes we have identified did not fundamentally change the relevant legal framework or that the constraints imposed by collective bargaining agreements are more important than those imposed by the laws we have considered, so that

---

20. Given that French data are available from the last quarter of 1972 onward, we could have reported tests of the effects of the 1975 introduction of the requirement that employers receive authorization for all dismissals. The results of this test, however, were implausible, presumably because of the small number of observations prior to the requirement's introduction.

Table 3.6   Estimated Effects of Changes in Employment Law on Speed of Adjustment

	Manufacturing	Textiles	Apparel	Stone, Clay, and Glass	Primary Metals	Autos	Paper	Printing	Chemicals
			A. Effects on Adjustment of Employment						
Germany[a]									
λ_0	.829	.920	.879	.850	.875	.874	.911	.864	—
(speed of adjustment)	(.017)	(.025)	(.058)	(.025)	(.075)	(.023)	(.048)	(.028)	
λ_1	.035	−.056	.407	.051	−.389	−.265	−.077	−.164	
(dummy 1985:2+)	(.025)	(.082)	(.239)	(.067)	(.350)	(.602)	(.468)	(.434)	
France[b]									
λ_0	.897	.757	—	.905	.853	.917	.871	.819	.875
(speed of adjustment)	(.032)	(.176)		(.029)	(.090)	(.059)	(.051)	(.052)	(.046)
λ_1	−.007	.090		−.194	−.008	−1.058	−.125	.037	−.305
(dummy 1987:1+)	(.034)	(.090)		(.083)	(.065)	(.276)	(.117)	(.081)	(.122)
Belgium[c]									
λ_0	.775	.049	.137	.042	.139	.817	—	—	.129
(speed of adjustment)	(.087)	(.040)	(.041)	(.032)	(.061)	(.112)			(.029)
λ_1	.056	.517	.215	.733	.442	.035			.877
(dummy 1976:1+)	(.089)	(.082)	(.068)	(.075)	(.153)	(.084)			(.120)
λ_2	.036	1.115	.377	−.055	.207	.139			−.293
(dummy 1985:1+)	(.037)	(.232)	(.125)	(.060)	(.129)	(.085)			(.201)
			B. Effects on Adjustment of Production Employment						
Germany[a]									
λ_0	.793	.906	.875	.820	.871	.892	.888	.869	—
(speed of adjustment)	(.018)	(.092)	(.079)	(.024)	(.076)	(.055)	(.054)	(.058)	
λ_1	.020	.092	.411	.048	−.458	−.281	−.158	−.296	
(dummy 1985:2+)	(.026)	(.035)	(.296)	(.061)	(.270)	(.422)	(.401)	(.528)	

Belgium[c]

λ_0	.658	.919	.620	.490	.949	.649	—	—	.976
(speed of adjustment)	(1.291)	(.068)	(.191)	(.562)	(.050)	(.157)			(.074)
λ_1	.351	-.043	-.041	-.030	-.002	.174			-.158
(dummy 1976:1+)	(1.291)	(.080)	(.125)	(.563)	(.036)	(.154)			(.115)
λ_2	-.044	.205	.110	.166	-.017	.101			-.148
(dummy 1985:1+)	(.025)	(.156)	(.203)	(.192)	(.041)	(.223)			(.109)

C. Effects on Adjustment of Production Hours

Germany[a]									
λ_0	.424	.716	.653	.515	.609	.372	.379	.486	—
(speed of adjustment)	(.066)	(.057)	(.063)	(.067)	(.061)	(.074)	(.100)	(.070)	
λ_1	.203	.591	.408	.078	-.045	-.156	.040	.271	
(dummy 1985:2+)	(.684)	(.586)	(.550)	(.114)	(.097)	(.118)	(.888)	(.546)	
Belgium[c]									
λ_0	.226	.394	.757	.200	-.393	.079	—	—	.178
(speed of adjustment)	(.119)	(.131)	(.157)	(.265)	(.183)	(.185)			(.209)
λ_1	.124	-.028	-.188	-.075	.457	.243			.517
(dummy 1976:1+)	(.103)	(.147)	(.097)	(.242)	(.214)	(.182)			(.228)
λ_2	.226	.521	.230	.061	.509	-.192			-.155
(dummy 1985:1+)	(.078)	(.257)	(.150)	(.150)	(.168)	(.220)			(.148)

[a]Reported coefficients (standard errors) are from the following model, using quarterly data over the 1972–90 period:
$\ln L_t = \alpha_0 + \alpha_1 D85{:}2 + (1 - \lambda_0 - \lambda_1 D85{:}2)\phi\ln P_t + (\lambda_0 + \lambda_1 D85{:}2)\ln L_{t-1} + \delta_1 t + \delta_2 t^2 + \varepsilon_t$, where L represents employment, production employment, or production hours and P is a measure of output.

[b]Reported coefficients (standard errors) are from the following model, using quarterly data over the 1975:2–1991:1 period:
$\ln L_t = \alpha_0 + \alpha_2 D87{:}1 + (1 - \lambda_0 - \lambda_1 D87{:}1)\phi\ln P_t + (\lambda_0 + \lambda_1 D87{:}1)\ln L_{t-1} + \delta_1 t + \delta_2 t^2 + \varepsilon_t$, where L represents employment, production employment, or production hours and P is a measure of output.

[c]Reported coefficients (standard errors) are from the following model, using quarterly data over the 1973–90 period:
$\ln L_t = \alpha_0 + \alpha_1 D76{:}1 + \alpha_2 D85{:}1 + (1 - \lambda_0 - \lambda_1 D76{:}1 - \lambda_2 D85{:}1)\phi\ln P_t + (\lambda_0 + \lambda_1 D76{:}1 + \lambda_2 D85{:}1)\ln L_{t-1} + \delta_1 t + \delta_2 t^2 + \varepsilon_t$, where L represents employment, production employment, or production hours and P is a measure of output.

legal changes had only limited effects. In the French context, these arguments do not seem plausible. There is widespread agreement that the elimination of the requirement for government approval of layoffs in France was an important change. Although the post-1972 changes in West German and Belgian dismissal regulation were less fundamental, observers in both countries have viewed the changes as significant.

In addition, although there is no clear theoretical reason for the Koyck adjustment coefficients we have estimated to be affected by differences in demand conditions, it is possible that our findings are contaminated by the different aggregate economic conditions of the 1970s and 1980s. Cleaner tests of the effects of different regulatory regimes may become possible if the European countries experience a deep downturn of the sort produced by the first oil price shock in the mid-1970s. In some cases, we also have relatively few observations either before or following a major change in legislation, thus raising the standard errors and lowering the significance of the coefficients capturing the effects of the change. In the future, with a longer time series it may be possible to construct a stronger test of the effects of the more recent legal changes.

Perhaps the most intriguing interpretation of our findings is that the changes to job-security regulations in West Germany, France, and Belgium during the 1970s and 1980s had little effect because employers had adapted to a strong job-security regime by using alternate adjustment mechanisms that have generally proved to be satisfactory and that they feel no compelling need to change. This interpretation is consistent with our earlier findings that the speed of hours adjustment, at least in Germany and Belgium, is more similar to that in the United States than is the speed of employment adjustment and that the availability of short-time compensation facilitates hours adjustment in these countries.

3.5   Conclusion

Our results suggest that, at least under certain circumstances, strong job security is compatible with labor market flexibility. Although the adjustment of employment to changes in output is much slower in the German, French, and Belgian manufacturing sectors than in the U.S. manufacturing sector, the adjustment of hours worked appears to be much more similar. Further support for the view that job-security regulations have not been burdensome for employers in the three countries we have studied comes from the fact that seemingly important changes in these regulations have not led to measurably different adjustment. A plausible interpretation of this finding is that, in spite of the important constraints imposed upon their behavior by existing job-security regulations, employers in these countries have developed alternate strategies that have given them adequate flexibility to adjust their labor input to changes in output.

Compared to the United States, then, labor market institutions in the European countries we have studied seem to have encouraged relatively greater reliance on hours adjustment and correspondingly reduced reliance on hiring and firing to alter the level of employment. This finding raises the question of how the competing systems we have examined should be evaluated.

Although the use of short time and temporary layoffs during a cyclical downturn may be reasonably close substitutes from the employer's point of view, they are quite different from the employee's perspective. Workers on temporary layoff are likely to face considerable uncertainty about whether they will ever be recalled. Those who are never recalled experience longer than average unemployment spells, in part because they tend not to look for new work while awaiting recall. These lengthy spells of unemployment represent a loss of income for the individual workers and a loss of resources to society. Extensive reliance on layoffs is also less equitable than work-sharing, for it concentrates the costs of adjustment on a relatively small number of workers who suffer large losses of income and other job-related benefits. Short-time work arrangements spread the costs of adjustment more evenly across members of the work force. These are important arguments in favor of short-time work to accommodate cyclical fluctuations in demand.

Short-time work may be used to accommodate structural as well as cyclical downturns. By extending the time over which these work force reductions occur, employers can make greater use of attrition and other alternatives to layoff. The use of short-time work in instances of structural adjustment is more controversial. Economists typically take the position that in the event of a permanent decline in demand, workers should be reallocated to other sectors as quickly as possible. To achieve this, large-scale layoffs, where necessary, have been advocated, on the assumption that dislocated workers will then be forced to find new employment. A number of recent studies of displaced workers in the United States show, however, that workers permanently laid off from their jobs often experience long periods of unemployment (see, for example, Podgursky and Swaim 1987, or Seitchik and Zornitsky 1989). By using short-time work as an interim adjustment measure and relying on attrition to reduce work force levels, firms can significantly reduce or even avoid layoffs. In this way, job reductions occur among those who have the most attractive outside opportunities or who are best able to relocate, and those who have poor outside opportunities or who are unable to relocate are not thrown out of work.

Currently, seventeen states in the United States have short-time compensation programs, but data show that in these states short-time compensation is used relatively little compared to regular unemployment insurance. The reasons for this low take-up rate are not entirely clear. One factor no doubt is that U.S. law makes it relatively easy for employers to lay off workers. Because there are no significant legal obstacles to continued reliance on layoffs, U.S. employers arguably have no compelling incentive to rethink their established adjustment strategies. Certain aspects of the way in which existing U.S. short-time programs have been administered also may have discouraged the use of short-time benefits.[21] For example, in contrast to Europe, where short-time payments are financed either through a non-experience-rated payroll tax or through general tax revenues, short-time benefits in the United States are financed through an experience-rated payroll tax, which may discourage their use. In addition, the maintenance of health care benefits for employed workers may be more of a disincentive to the use of short time in the United States than in Europe.[22] Whether and how U.S. employers should be encouraged to make greater use of short time remain important unanswered questions.

Appendix

Figure 3.1 and the estimates reported in tables 3.3, 3.4, and 3.6 make use of seasonally adjusted quarterly data on output, employment, production employment, and production hours, as available for each of the four countries included in the study.

For all four countries, the principal output measure is an index of industrial production (IPI). The German IPI is based on employer reports concerning the output of some 10,000 product groups. For France, 45 percent of the underlying series is based on production measured in physical units, 13 percent on input quantities, 18 percent on deflated turnover, 18 percent on hours worked, 5 percent on raw materials consumed, and 1 percent on orders converted into production. The Belgian IPI is based primarily on physical production data, but in metal working, which receives a weight of about 30 percent in the construction of the total manufacturing index, movements in deflated turnover and in hours worked serve as equal proxies for movements in output. Where available, information on physical output serves as the basis for the IPI for the United States. Information on energy usage is generally the preferred proxy for the level of production activity where output data are unavailable, but in some cases worker hours serve as a production activity proxy. The IPIs for the three European countries were obtained on tape from Eurostat, the Statistical Office of the European Community, and the U.S. IPI data are published by the Federal Reserve Board. We also make limited use of deflated shipments series for the United States. The U.S. shipments data were obtained from the Bureau of the Census's Manufacturer's Shipments, Inventories, and Orders data set and were deflated using, as appropriate, the manufacturing, durable goods, or nondurable goods producer price index.

21. See Abraham and Houseman (1993) for a more detailed discussion.
22. At least in Germany, however, special provisions concerning the maintenance of social insurance contributions as well as collective bargaining agreement provisions concerning vacation time and other special payments to workers imply that the fixed costs of keeping a worker on the payroll are substantial (Flechsenhar 1978, Abraham and Houseman 1993). These costs have not prevented German employers from making substantial use of the short-time system.

Monthly data on West German employment, production employment, and production hours were obtained directly from the Statistisches Bundesamt. Because employment is measured at the end of the month in Germany, rather than at midmonth as in the United States, we transformed the German employment numbers, defining:

(A1)
$$E_t' = \frac{E_t + E_{t-1}}{2}.$$

These transformed numbers were used in all analyses, though making this adjustment had little effect on any of our estimates. The West German hours numbers measure actual hours worked during the course of the month. For France, we used quarterly employment indices supplied by Eurostat. French production employment data are not available; although French hours data are published, they are not comparable over time. Eurostat supplied us with indices of employment, production employment, and production hours for Belgium. The Eurostat figures for Belgium are quarterly for the pre-1980 period and monthly from 1980 onward; to ensure comparability over time, the later figures were converted to quarterly numbers before seasonally adjusting. Belgian labor data for the manufacturing sector as a whole were reported by Eurostat only from 1980 onward; complete quarterly series on manufacturing employment, production employment, and production hours were obtained from Jean Lemaitre of Louvain University. The Belgian employment numbers refer to employment as of the pay period including the fifteenth of the month; the Belgian hours numbers measure hours worked during the month. The U.S. employment and hours data are monthly numbers published by the Bureau of Labor Statistics. The U.S. employment figures refer to payroll employment as of the payroll period including the twelfth of the month; the U.S. hours numbers measure hours paid during the same period.

None of the four countries' employment or hours series is adjusted for the effects of strikes. In cases where we knew that large strikes had occurred (e.g., in the West German automobile industry in 1984), we included dummy variables for the affected periods in our estimating equations.

In addition to the data just described, the estimates reported in table 3.4 required data on hours of short-time compensation. For West Germany, the underlying data are monthly figures on the number of workers in the manufacturing sector collecting short-time payments, and annual data on the distribution of workers collecting short-time payments according to the percentage reduction in their hours of work. These numbers were taken from *Amtliche Nachrichten der Bundesanstalt für Arbeit—Jahreszahlen* (various issues), published by the Bundesanstalt für Arbeit. For France, monthly data by industry on the number of full-time equivalent days of authorized short-time compensation are reported in *Statistiques du Travail: Bulletin Mensuel,* published by the Ministère des Affaires Sociales et de l'Emploi. We received unpublished data on short-time payments in Belgium, expressed in terms of the full-time equivalent number of workers supported, from Dirk de Bie of the Office Nationale de l'Emploi.

References

Abraham, K. G., and S. N. Houseman. 1992. Employment security and labor adjustment: A comparison of West Germany and the United States. Working Paper. College Park, Md.: University of Maryland.
———. 1993. *Job security in America: Lessons from Germany.* Washington, D.C.: Brookings Institution.
Anderson, P. 1992. Linear adjustment costs and seasonal labor demand: Evidence from retail trade firms. Working Paper. Princeton, N.J.: Princeton University.
Blanpain, R. 1989. The regulation of working conditions in the member states of the European Communities: Termination of the employment contract. Working Paper. Leuven, Belgium: Katholieke Universiteit Leuven.
Brandes, W., W. Meyer, and E. Schudlich. 1992. Pay classification systems: Monograph for Germany. ILO Research Project on Pay Classification in Industrialized Countries. Geneva: International Labor Organization.
Burdett, K., and R. Wright. 1989. Unemployment insurance and short-time compensation: The effects on layoffs, hours per worker, and wages. *Journal of Political Economy* 97:1479–96.
EIRR. 1983. Short-time and layoffs. *European Industrial Relations Review,* March, 15–19.
———. 1984. Important changes in Belgian labour law. *European Industrial Relations Review,* 30 (November): 12–14.
———. 1985a. Termination of contract: Belgium. *European Industrial Relations Review* 137 (October): 24–27.
———. 1985b. Termination of contract: France. *European Industrial Relations Review* 141 (June): 17–20.
———. 1986. Redundancy procedures revised. *European Industrial Relations Review,* March, 15–19.
Flechsenhar, H. R. 1978. Kurzarbeit: Kosten und finanzierung. *Mitteilungen aus der Arbeitsmarkt- und Berufsforschung* 9:443–56.
General Accounting Office. 1986. Dislocated workers: Extent of business closures, layoffs, and the public and private response. Briefing Report to the Honorable Lloyd Bentsen, United States Senate. Washington, D.C.
Grais, B. 1983. *Lay-offs and short-time working in selected OECD countries.* Paris: Organization for Economic Cooperation and Development.
Hamermesh, D. 1989. Labor demand and the structure of adjustment costs. *American Economic Review* 79:674–89.
———. 1993. *Labor demand.* Princeton, N.J.: Princeton University Press.
Hemmer, E. 1988. *Sozialplanpraxis in der Bundesrepublik: Eine empirische untersuchung.* Cologne: Deutscher Instituts-Verlag GmbH.
Kraft, K. 1990. Adjustment of employment. Working Paper. Kassel, Germany: University of Kassel.
Maddala, G. S. 1977. *Econometrics.* New York: McGraw-Hill.
Nickell, S. J. 1986. Dynamic models of labour demand. In *Handbook of labor economics,* ed. O. Ashenfelter and R. Layard, 473–522. Amsterdam: Elsevier Science Publishers.

Organization for Economic Cooperation and Development (OECD). 1986. *Flexibility in the labour market: The current debate.* Paris: OECD.

Podgursky, M. and P. Swaim. 1987. Duration of joblessness following job displacement. *Industrial Relations* 26:213–26.

Rojot, J. 1980. France. In *Bulletin of comparative labor relations,* no. 11, ed. R. Blanpain, 79–102. New York: Kluwer Law and Taxation Publishers.

———. 1986. France In *Bulletin of comparative labor relations,* no. 15, ed. R. Blanpain, 1–24. New York: Kluwer Law and Taxation Publishers.

Seitchik, A., and J. Zornitsky. 1989. *From one job to the next: Worker adjustment in a changing labor market.* Kalamazoo, Mich.: W. E. Upjohn Institute for Employment Research.

Soltwedel, Rüdiger. 1988. Employment problems in West Germany: The role of institutions, labor law, and government intervention. Carnegie-Rochester Conference Series on Public Policy 28:153–220.

Van Audenrode, M. 1991. Employment flexibility and labor hoarding. Working Paper. Berkeley: University of California.

Vranken, M. 1986. Deregulating the employment relationship: Current trends in Europe. *Comparative Labor Law* 7 (Winter): 143–65.

Vroman, W. 1989. Experience rating in unemployment insurance: Some current issues. Unemployment Insurance Occasional Paper no. 89–6. Washington, D.C.: U.S. Department of Labor, Employment and Training Administration.

———. 1992. Short-time compensation in the U.S., Germany, and Belgium. Working Paper. Washington, D.C.: Urban Institute.

4 Patterns in Regional Labor Market Adjustment: The United States versus Japan

Edward B. Montgomery

The past decade was a period in which the United States experienced a number of cyclical and secular shocks. While the early 1980s and 1990s were periods of recession, there was sustained growth in the mid-1980s. As seen in table 4.1, the overall performance of the U.S. economy between 1985 and 1990 was fairly strong in terms of job creation, gross domestic product (GDP) growth, low unemployment, and inflation. Although the United States lagged behind Japan in almost all measures of economic performance, it had greater employment growth and lower unemployment than most other Organization for Economic Cooperation and Development (OECD) countries. The ability to accommodate real-wage declines, rapid growth in employment, and falling unemployment have often been cited as signals of the greater flexibility of the labor market in the United States compared to other OECD countries.

Despite the fairly strong aggregate performance of the economy, the cyclical shifts in demand at the beginning and end of the decade interacted with relative-demand shocks within a number of industries to create a pronounced imbalance in the economic performance across regions of the economy. Unemployment rates varied substantially across states at both ends of the recent expansion. While some states had rates less than half the national average, others had double-digit unemployment rates for most of the decade.

These imbalances in regional growth raise questions about the flexibility of the labor market in the United States. *Flexibility,* in this paper, is taken to mean

Edward B. Montgomery is professor of economics at the University of Maryland and a research associate of the National Bureau of Economic Research.

The author thanks Timothy Bartik for providing his data. Katharine Abraham, Rebecca Blank, and Andrew Oswald provided helpful comments on an earlier draft of the paper. Anthony Blasingame and Yi-feng Chia provided research assistance, and Kari Foreback was most helpful in preparing the manuscript. The author acknowledges financial support from the Ford Foundation and the National Science Foundation (grant R11–9012706).

Table 4.1   Selected Comparative Economic Statistics: Average Annual
             Rates, 1985–1990

	United States	Japan	United Kingdom	Germany	Canada
Real GDP growth	2.7%	4.7%	3.2%	3.1%	3.0%
Inflation rate	4.3	1.4	6.7	2.2	4.9
Employment growth					
1985–90	2.0	1.6	2.0	1.9	2.4
1980–90	1.9	1.3	0.7	0.8	1.9
Unemployment rate	5.9	2.5	8.8	6.2	8.7
Nominal manufacturing compensation growth	2.7	3.9	7.1	4.0	5.3

Sources: International comparisons of hourly compensation costs for production workers in manufacturing, 1975–90 (1991) (Bureau of Labor Statistics); *Comparative labor force statistics* (1991) (Bureau of Labor Statistics); *Economic report of the president* (1992).

Note: The data use U.S. concepts for labor force statistics.

the sensitivity or speed of adjustment of labor markets to changes in market conditions. Because tests of this type of flexibility in the labor market at the aggregate level are likely to have little power, I investigate the labor market response to demand shocks at the regional level. I focus on two regional adjustment mechanisms: (1) relative wage changes and (2) worker movement, or migration, to other regions of the country. The flexibility of the labor market will be reflected in the extent to which these factors adjust. Clearly, flexibility along these dimensions will have implications for the persistence of differences in regional unemployment rates, so I also examine the sensitivity of regional unemployment rates to demand shifts.

I contrast the adjustment process in the United States with that of Japan, a country whose aggregate performance dominated the United States and whose labor market is often thought to be characterized by extreme flexibility. In particular, I examine the extent and persistence of regional imbalance in Japan and whether unemployment, wages, and migration there are more sensitive to demand shifts. Such a comparative analysis may yield insights into the roles of various government policies or institutions in affecting the speed and extent of market flexibility.

Cross-country differences in the dynamics of the regional labor market adjustment process may exist for a variety of reasons. Differences in preferences could alter labor supply elasticities, while variations in the extent of collective bargaining, regional concentrations of industries, and government social policies will influence the speed at which regional adjustments occurs. In the case of Japan, labor market flexibility is seen as the product of government employment policy, the Nenko payment system (described below), the widespread usage of bonus payments, and lifetime employment contracts. Thus, an examination of the nature of differences in how Japanese regional labor markets adjust could provide some insights into whether alternate policy and institutional environments generate added flexibility in regional labor markets.

Previous studies by Montgomery (1992), Hall (1970), and others have looked at the determinants of the equilibrium structure of wages, unemployment, or migration across regions in the United States. Further, Beeson and Montgomery (1993) and Bartik (1989) have looked at the role of taxes and other government policies aimed at affecting regional growth. These studies have generally focused on only one element of the labor market adjustment process and have not looked at the relative importance of these competing adjustment mechanisms. Further, they have not looked at how this process varies under different institutional settings. This paper will contribute to the literature along both of these dimensions.

Given the myriad of economic and institutional differences between the United States and Japan, the analysis in this paper is only meant to be suggestive. More definitive treatments need to endogenize these labor market variables and require richer data, preferably microdata.

4.1 Institutional Details

In doing a comparative analysis, it is obviously critical to have some feel for how labor market institutions differ in the countries being studied. One of the most commonly cited differences between Japanese and U.S. labor markets is that compensation in Japan is set by the Nenko pay system. Under this system, pay is almost exclusively based upon seniority, with the intention of encouraging worker loyalty and investments in specific human capital. Further, pay adjustments occur during the *Shunto*, or spring labor offensive, with the major firms setting patterns for smaller companies to follow. This coordinated wage setting on an aggregate level is thought to prevent the type of rigidities in U.S. wages that some authors attribute to the presence of long-term overlapping contracts.[1]

The payment of bonuses is found in almost all Japanese companies. These bonus payments, which can account for up to 20 percent of regular cash earnings, generate a profit sharing mechanism similar to Weitzman's (1984) share payments and are seen as providing a substantial degree of wage flexibility. This wage system facilitates or interacts with the often noted lifetime employment system to generate a high degree of employment stability and job tenure.

The stability of Japanese employment has been attributed to a three-pronged strategic response on the part of employers. First, short-term profits are sacrificed to avoid the loss of skilled workers with substantial amounts of firm-specific skills. Second, firms reduce the use of subcontractors or temporary

---

1. For a more detailed discussion and analysis of the Japanese labor market, see Hashimoto (1990). Montgomery and Shaw (1985) show that long-term contracting is of limited importance for aggregate wage flexibility.

workers so that employment adjustments are suffered by a periphery or buffer stock of workers (typically females) and not by the firm's core workers. Third, workers receive reduced bonus payments, thereby cutting labor costs and reducing the strain on short-term profits.

Abraham and Houseman (1989) have found that Japanese employers are slower than their U.S. counterparts to adjust employment to output shocks and that the magnitude of the adjustment is less. Hours adjustments in the short and longer term appear to be the same across the two countries, which leads to the conclusion that Japanese employers use hours adjustments *relatively* more than U.S. firms. Overall, total labor input adjusts less in Japan. There is also evidence of differences in wage and price flexibility between Japan and the United States. Yoshikawa and Takeuchi (1989) found that the slope of a standard Phillips curve is 3.112 for Japan but only .611 in the United States. This supports the notion of greater wage flexibility in Japan in response to excess demand, as measured by the unemployment rate.[2]

Thus, at the aggregate level, there appear to be differences in the nature and speed of labor market adjustments between Japan and the United States. If regional labor markets react in similar fashions to relative-demand shocks in the two countries, then one might expect greater wage flexibility and less unemployment in response to demand shifts in Japan than in the United States.

Although private sector institutions may explain much of these differences in labor market dynamics across the countries, part of this difference conceivably is due to differences in the nature of government labor market intervention. Although there are a number of national and local employment programs in both countries, those in the United States tend to be more remedial and limited in scope. The Humphrey-Hawkins bill in the United States and the Employment Measures Law in Japan both charge government with the task of maintaining full employment (4 percent in the United States and 2 percent in Japan). In the United States, the law gives equal weight to the goal of price stability, and there is no mechanism in the legislation for implementing the goal. In contrast, the Japanese Ministry of Labor is required to formulate long-term basic employment measures plans as well as to form and implement short-term annual employment plans. The actual administration of these programs is done at the national level by the Employment Security Bureau, at the prefectural level by Employment Security Sections, and locally by public employment service offices (PESOs). U.S. national, state, and local employ-

---

2. Although there is greater flexibility in response to unemployment changes, there is actually less responsiveness in Japan to output changes. The slopes of the implied Aggregate Supply (AS) curves are .084 in Japan versus .227 in the United States. This difference comes from the fact that unemployment does not vary much over the cycle because labor force participation in Japan is strongly procyclical. As noted in Yoshikawa and Takeuchi (1989) and Tachibanaki and Sakurai (1990), unemployment may not be as good an indicator of labor market conditions in Japan as in other OECD countries. Labor supply, particularly female labor supply, falls substantially during downturns, with the result that measured unemployment does not rise as much. Yoshikawa and Takeuchi suggest that this effect is over six times as big in Japan as in the United States.

ment policies are generally set independently, with little coordination. State and local areas engage in a host of independent initiatives in response to local conditions without federal (national) linkages.[3]

In both countries the public employment service office provides information on job openings. On the surface the job search assistance rendered in Japanese PESOs appears fairly extensive. The Ministry of Labor was to begin publication of a magazine listing job openings with detailed job descriptions and to prepare a computerized data base on job seekers and information on various employer subsidies and other support systems. However, as in the United States, the public employment service in Japan is not widely used. In a recent survey of firms, 30 percent claimed they never use the PESO. Over half of the firms responded that they could not get the appropriate types of workers, while workers consistently complained about the low quality of the jobs available.

In both countries, local public employment offices also serve to administer the unemployment insurance program. In the United States, eligibility and unemployment benefit levels are set at the state level, while Japan has a national structure. In both countries the unemployment insurance system is financed by a payroll tax on workers and employers. In Japan the system receives money to help *both* workers and firm; in the United States, money is provided only to workers. Japanese firms facing business fluctuations or located in targeted regions can get subsidies from the Employment Stabilization Fund if they agree to minimize layoffs and provide retraining. There is also money to help workers relocate or to get firms to locate new plants in depressed areas.

In both countries the government provides additional monies to ease the labor market impact of import competition or structural shifts. In the United States, the Trade Adjustment Assistance Act (TAA) provides training and supplemental unemployment benefits to *workers* who are unemployed because of imports.[4] The retraining component of this program, however, is rather limited, as less than 10 percent of the benefit recipients have received retraining or placement assistance.[5] Despite recent revisions in the law, it remains the case that displaced workers are only encouraged and not required to enter training programs.

In the United States, there are also state-level training and placement assistance programs for displaced workers, and several states have implemented advance-notice provisions to ensure that workers get prior notice of plant closures. Finally, states and local areas often give property and corporate tax abatements as incentives for firms to locate or remain in their area. These local initiatives have had limited success, and it remains true that the vast majority of states have no formal programs for retraining or assisting displaced workers or firms.

The structure of unemployment insurance benefits also differs across these

3. See Leigh (1989) for a discussion of these programs.
4. See Weir (1992) for a further discussion of employment policy in the United States.
5. See Leigh (1989) for a further description of displaced worker programs in the United States.

two countries. In Japan, experienced workers receive benefits of between 60 percent and 80 percent of their basic daily wage (which excludes bonus payments) when they become unemployed. This exceeds the typical U.S. replacement rate of 40–50 percent. In both countries, workers in high-unemployment areas can get extended benefits. One potentially important difference between unemployment insurance in Japan and in the United States is the fact that a worker in Japan who gets reemployed quickly or who is in a training program receives extra benefits.[6]

Overall, both countries have a plethora of government programs designed to help the unemployed. The focus on employment stabilization and the regional component of many of the Japanese programs would lead one to expect less regional dislocation in Japan. The relocation and retraining benefits should reduce mobility costs within and across local labor markets. Thus, the structure of private and public institutions in Japan would lead one to expect greater flexibility in terms of earnings, unemployment, and migration.

4.2 Model

Following Harris and Todaro (1970), Hall (1972), and Roback (1982), the long-run, or static, equilibrium structure of regional labor markets depends on the underlying distribution of nontraded goods (amenities). These amenities may enter the workers' utility function and/or the firm's production function. In equilibrium, workers must be indifferent to all locations, or, analogously, expected utility (V) is constant across areas j:[7]

(1) $$V(w_j^*, r_j; a_j) = k \quad V_{w^*} > 0, V_r < 0, V_s > 0,$$

where k is the nationally given level of utilty, w^* is the effective wage rate, r_j is the rental price of land in region j, and a_j is the value of local amenities. As in Hall (1972), the effective wage rate reflects expected wage or wages, adjusted for the likelihood of being employed:

(2) $$w_j^* = w_j(1 - u_j),$$

where the unemployment rate, u_j, is used to measure the probability of being employed and w_j is the real wage rate.

In the long run, firms must also be indifferent across locations, which for firms with constant return to scale production functions implies that, in equilibrium, unit costs equal price (assumed to be unity) in all areas:

(3) $$C(w_j^*, r_j; a_j) = 1 \quad C_{w^*} > 0, C_r > 0.$$

---

6. If a worker was eligible for ninety days of benefits and used less than forty-five, he would get thirty days of benefits as a bonus. If he were eligible for 300 days of benefits and used less than 100, he would get a bonus of 120 days.

7. Capital is assumed to be perfectly mobile and unaffected by amenities. Thus, the rate of return is equalized across areas and can be omitted from the expression.

If local amenities (e.g., absence of blizzards) enhance productivity, then $C_a < 0$. Hall (1972) argues that both real wages and local unemployment affect employer costs, as turnover costs are lower when the unemployment rate is high.

Equations (1) and (3) can be used to solve for w^* and r as functions of amenities, given k. The reduced-form hedonic wage equation is thus:

$$(4) \qquad w_j = f(u_j, r_j; a_j).$$

Equilibrium in this model need not imply equalization of wages or unemployment rates across areas. As long as amenities affect productivity or utilities, there is no reason to expect constant wage or unemployment rates. Long-run market equilibrium is thus consistent with persistent differences in wages, unemployment rates, or rental prices. The observed distribution of these factors across areas need only be conformable with utility and profit equalization across areas. The correlation between wages and unemployment in this long-run compensating differences model should be positive. Work by Blanchflower and Oswald (1992), however, suggests that in a world with efficiency wages this correlation could be negative. Efficiency wage payments may be lower in areas where the cost of job lost (unemployment) is high, and firms may also be hesitant to locate in high-unemployment areas due to inferior services, higher taxes, and so on. Whether these considerations will dominate is ultimately an empirical question.

Migration of workers or firms occurs to equalize utility or unit costs across areas in response to long-run shifts in tastes or technology. If migration is costly (due to transportation, opportunity, and psychic costs), the instantaneous flow of migrants will be less than the long-run response. We can thus express the migration rate between regions i and j in any period as a function of wages, unemployment, rents, and amenities in the two areas:

$$(5) \qquad mig_{ij} = g(u_i, u_j, w_i, w_j, r_i, r_j, d_{ij}; a_i, a_j),$$

where d_{ij} is the cost of moving between i and j, and mig_{ij} is the net migration rate between these areas.[8]

In this model, migration serves to maintain the long-run spatial equilibrium. In the short run, however, mobility costs may impede the instantaneous adjustment of labor markets to changing conditions. Topel (1986) considers such a dynamic model where, in the presence of mobility costs, permanent and transitory local-demand shocks affect migration rates, relative wages, and unemployment rates. Permanent (or anticipated) shifts in local demand get arbitraged away by migration, leaving the long-run spatial distribution of wages and unemployment described in the static models. Transitory (unanticipated)

---

8. Migration will depend on the relative values of unemployment, wages, and rents in the two areas, but the effects need not be symmetric. Previous research has rejected the restriction of symmetry or that it is only the difference in the values of these variables that determines migration (Hughes and McCormick 1989).

shifts in demand, in the presence of mobility costs, mean that current values of wages and unemployment adjust to local shocks and hence differ from their long-run values. A transitory negative shock to demand would reduce wages below long-run values and raise unemployment above its long-run values. Thus, a negative correlation between current wages and current unemployment can exist if mobility costs are important in the face of transitory demand shifts.[9] We now turn to an empirical analysis of these reduced-form spatial labor market models.

4.3 Stylized Facts and Empirical Results

The choice of the geographical unit for a study of regional labor markets is not clear-cut. Using cities or standard metropolitan statistical areas (SMSAs) might be preferred, as they correspond most closely to the area within which agents have good information and transportation costs are relatively minor. There are a number of problems, however, with using SMSAs as the geographical unit of analysis. First, in the United States the boundaries of SMSAs have changed over time in ways correlated with economic growth. This was particularly true in 1982, when many growing SMSAs had counties added to them to reflect the growing linkages across previously outlying areas. Second, some SMSAs extend over state lines (e.g., New York) so that residents in one part may face a different set of government policies than those in another part. To avoid this problem, I use states for my measure of regional labor markets in the United States. Clearly, mobility and information issues can be important within an area the size of a state, so the notion that a state represents a homogenous labor market is false. Where possible, I check the sensitivity of my results to the choice of geographic unit of analysis.

The forty-six prefectures in Japan are also used, as they are roughly analogous in concept to U.S. states. Like states, they have fixed geographic boundaries and their own governmental structure. Although Japan's prefectural and municipal governments are thought to have less autonomy than state and municipal governments in the United States, they do have some independent taxing and spending authority (Ito 1992, chap. 6). While grants to local governments from the national government are a more important source of local spending in Japan, individuals pay roughly similar proportions of their taxes to local jurisdictions in the two countries.[10]

Given the fact that the population of Japan is about 50 percent of the United States while it has only about 4 percent of the land size, there are substantial differences in the average population density and distance between the regional

---

9. Thanks to Andrew Oswald for bringing this point to the author's attention.

10. Grants account for 20 percent of the national budget in Japan versus 12 percent in the United States, and 43 percent of individual taxes went to state and local governments in the United States in 1987, while 36 percent went to prefectural and municipal governments in Japan. See Ito (1992) for a further discussion of fiscal policy in Japan.

units in the two countries. I attempt to standardize regional labor markets by adding controls for prefecture population and size to some of the Japanese analysis. Unfortunately, data limitations prevent checking the sensitivity of the Japanese results to the choice of regional labor market measure.

Since migration plays a crucial role in local labor market adjustments, it is useful to examine the magnitude and patterns of regional migration in the two countries. Table 4.2 presents migration rates for the United States and several other countries. The overall level of migration in the United States is higher than in Japan and the other OECD countries shown. Prefectural mobility in Japan is higher than regional mobility in the United Kingdom or country movement in Sweden and is comparable to state mobility in the United States and county movement in the Netherlands. However, when compared to migration rates of U.S. countries, which are more similar in size to Japanese prefectures, Japanese migration takes place at less than half the U.S. rate.

Migration may be less in Japan because shocks to the Japanese economy have been smaller than in the United States. Further, even if the level of shocks is similar across countries, the regional distribution of them may be more homogeneous in Japan than in the United States. As seen in table 4.3, the industrial distribution of employment at the aggregate industry level has changed much more dramatically in the United States than in Japan over the past thirty years. In Japan, manufacturing's share of employment has remained fairly constant, while it has declined markedly in the United States. Although these numbers hide within industry movements, they suggest that part of the difference in the level of regional labor market mobility may be due to differences in the size or regional distribution of shocks in the two countries.

For migration to help in labor market adjustment, it must also go in the right directions. Tables 4.4 and 4.5 show annual net migration rates for selected prefectures and states in Japan and the United States, respectively. The net migration rates for Japan are based on annual data and defined as in-migrants minus out-migrants, divided by the beginning-of-period population. Net migration rates for the United States are annualized values calculated using census data on the number of net migrants over various time intervals, divided

Table 4.2   **Selected Internal Migration Rates, by Country**

	United States	United Kingdom	The Netherlands	Japan	Sweden
Between regions	2.1%	1.01%			
Between states	3.09				
Between counties/prefectures	6.55		3.0%	2.9%	1.5%

Sources: For the United Kingdom and the United States, Hughes and McCormick 1989, and Gabriel, Shack-Marquez, and Wascher 1991; Japanese Bureau of Statistics; Björklund and Holmlund 1989; Dijk et al. 1989.

Note: There are nine census regions in the United States and ten regions in the United Kingdom.

Table 4.3   Percentage of Employment by Industry

	Japan			United States		
Industry	1960	1980	1989	1960	1980	1989
Agriculture	30%	10%	9%	9%	4%	3%
Mining	1	<1	<1	1	1	1
Construction	6	10	9	5	5	5
Manufacturing	22	25	24	28	22	17
Transportation	6	7	6	7	5	5
Trade	20	23	22	19	22	23
Finance	—	2	6	4	6	6
Services	13	18	21	12	19	24
Government	3	4	3	14	17	16

Source: Management and Coordination Agency, Labor Force Survey 1989; *Economic report of the president* (1992).

Note: Numbers may not add to 100 because of rounding.

Table 4.4   Japan's Selected Annual Prefectural Net Migration Rates

Prefecture	1970	1985
Hokkaido	−1.5%	−0.4%
Tokyo	−0.9	0.0
Niigata	−0.9	−0.3
Kyoto	0.1	−0.2
Osaka	0.7	−0.2
Nara	1.8	0.6
Saitama	3.5	0.7
Chiba	3.3	0.6
Aichi	0.9	0.1
Kagoshima	−2.3	−0.3

Note: Data on migration are described in the appendix.

Table 4.5   Annualized Net Migration Rates for Selected U.S. States

State	1970–80	1980–87
California	1.0%	2.6%
Florida	5.1	9.1
Illinois	−0.6	−0.6
Massachusetts	−0.5	−0.1
Minnesota	−0.2	−0.3
New York	−1.1	−0.3
Ohio	−0.8	−0.8
Pennsylvania	−0.5	−0.2
Texas	1.6	2.0
Virginia	0.6	1.0

Note: Data on migration rates are desribed in the appendix.

by the beginning-of-period population. Overall interprefectural migration rates range from 2.6 to 4.1 percent in Japan, and there is substantially more gross than net migration. Even the high-unemployment regions of Hokkaido and Kagoshima had substantial in- and out-migration. These data do show, however, that there have been consistent net migration flows toward Nara, Saitama, and Chiba prefectures and away from the Kagoshima and Hokkaido regions during the sample period. Similar patterns emerge in the United States, where states such as Illinois and Ohio have had negative net migration for almost twenty years.

To look further at this persistence in regional migration rates, I calculate rank correlation coefficients for area migration rates. These correlation coefficients indicate that regions in Japan appear to be consistently growing or declining for longer periods of time than in the United States.[11] Simple autoregressive estimates of regional net migration rates reinforce this conclusion of greater persistence in regional migration in Japan.[12]

These results may indicate either slower market adjustments (perhaps due to higher mobility costs) or that migration is being driven more by secular factors in Japan. If mobility costs are higher, then other regional labor market variables will need to adjust more. The autoregressive (AR) structure of relative earnings, employment growth, and unemployment in the two countries gives a simple way to characterize the behavior of these other labor market variables. Tables 4.6 and 4.7 show simple lagged dependent variable regressions for unemployment, employment growth, and earnings for Japan and the United States, respectively. It should be noted that because Japanese data at the prefecture level are at five-year intervals, the U.S. results are also presented using five-year lags for comparability. All variables represent deviations from means. The data used for these estimates are described in detail in the appendix.

The estimates presented in columns (1) of table 4.6 for each variable in Japan indicate there is substantial persistence in all the labor market variables even after five years. Unemployment growth and earnings have lagged coefficients of around .9. For the United States, the estimates in columns (1) of table 4.7 for each variable again show evidence of persistence at five-year intervals, especially in earnings and unemployment. There appears to be less serial persistence in the United Stats than in Japan for each of these labor market variables, especially for employment growth. Nonetheless, high earnings and unemployment areas appear to remain so for long periods of time in both countries.

The high degree of persistence in regional labor market variables also shows up in the rank correlations of prefecture or state labor market data. The rank

11. These results are available from the author upon request.
12. The coefficients on net migration lagged five years were .451 and .001 for Japan and .262 and −.543 for the United States in autoregressive regressions without and with area fixed effects.

Table 4.6   Univariate Models of Relative Earnings, Unemployment, and Employment for Japan (standard errors in parentheses)

	Log Monthly Contractual Earnings		Unemployment		Log Employment Change	
	(1)	(2)	(1)	(2)	(1)	(2)
Constant	.031	−.828	−.017	4.52	−.006	.855
	(.09)	(.05)	(.06)	(.31)	(.12)	(.44)
Dependent variable lagged five	.926	−.007	.971	.208	.701	.439
	(.03)	(.02)	(.03)	(.05)	(.03)	(.05)
Time	−.009	.0004	.002	−.023	3×10^{-5}	−.005
	(.03)	(.07)	(.01)	(.01)	(.03)	(.03)
$\bar{R}^2$	.89	.99	.80	.89	.67	.71
N	139	139	278	278	231	231

Note: Estimates of univariate equations use data described in the appendix. Periods of estimation are 1970–85 for earnings, 1960–85 for employment, and 1955–85 for unemployment. Column (2) estimates include prefecture fixed effects. All variables are deviations from national means.

Table 4.7   Univariate Models of Relative Wages, Unemployment and Employment for the United States (standard errors in parentheses)

	Log Wages		Unemployment		Log Employment Change	
	(1)	(2)	(1)	(2)	(1)	(2)
Constant	−.044	−.020	−.036	−.685	.0009	.001
	(.006)	(.01)	(.29)	(.39)	(.002)	(.005)
Dependent variable lagged five	.873	.189	.532	−.199	.059	−.174
	(.01)	(.04)	(.04)	(.04)	(.03)	(.03)
Time	.003	.0008	.004	.005	-7×10^{-5}	-8×10^{-5}
	(.0004)	(.0004)	(.03)	(.02)	(.0002)	(.0002)
$\bar{R}^2$	.88	.92	.26	.74	.01	.21
N	703	703	499	499	735	735

Note: Estimates of univariate equations use data described in the appendix. Periods of estimation are 1971–90 for average weekly manufacturing earnings, 1976–90 for unemployment, and 1970–90 for employment growth. Column (2) estimates include state fixed effects. All variables are deviations from national means.

correlations of area earnings are in excess of .70 in both countries, even over fifteen-year intervals.[13] The rank correlations of prefectural unemployment in Japan are also over .90 at fifteen-year intervals. Although the rank correlations of employment growth rates in Japan are lower than for earnings or unemployment, they still exceed .40 at fifteen-year intervals. In contrast, the rank correla-

13. These results are available upon request.

tions of unemployment and employment growth rates in the United States drop considerably over fifteen years, so that in some cases the rank correlations are even negative. High earnings, unemployment, and growth areas tend to remain so in Japan, while in the United States the picture is one of greater regional flux.

Simple AR models are suggestive but cannot discern whether this persistence represents the fact that the distribution of earnings and unemployment rates in Japan represent an unchanging equilibrium distribution generated by the presence of local amenities or whether migration and mobility are more stilted so that the reaction to shocks is substantially more protracted than in the United States.[14] Adding prefecture fixed effects to these regressions takes out the fixed-amenity effects and sheds some light on the degree of within-area persistence. Columns (2) of tables 4.6 and 4.7 show these results for Japan and the United States, respectively.

Within local markets in both countries, there is substantially less persistence over time for all of the labor market variables. There appears to be no persistence in earnings at five-year intervals in Japan, while there is still evidence of persistence in the United States. Conversely, there is no evidence of persistence in employment growth or unemployment at five-year intervals in the United States, while there is some in Japan. High cross-region but low within-region persistence in the two countries is consistent with the presence of a constant equilibrium structure of wages and unemployment across areas. The fact that within-area differences in persistence remain may suggest differences in regional labor market responsiveness in the two countries.

To explore more systematically the question of whether wages and unemployment react differently in the United States and Japan, I estimate several variants of equation (4). The parsimonious nature of the estimated regressions is largely due to data limitations for Japan. Previous studies (Hyclak and Johnes 1992; Neumann and Topel 1992; Eberts and Stone 1992; Montgomery 1992; Topel 1986; and others) have estimated regional wage and unemployment models for the United States, using a wider variety of controls. Since microdata, or individual data, are not available for Japan, I concentrated on estimating a simple Japanese labor market adjustment model and replicating it to as great a degree as possible using U.S. data. It should be emphasized that these reduced-form estimates suffer from endogeneity and hence must be interpreted with caution. Structural estimation is needed before definitive conclusions can be drawn, but this must wait future research.

Estimates for the Japanese and U.S. regional labor market model are presented in tables 4.8 and 4.9, respectively. All equations include fixed effects

---

14. These conclusions for the United States are not the result of using states as the measure of regional labor markets. The rank correlations across SMSAs for these series are remarkably similar to those for states. Further, the conclusions about constant relative wage structure are, if anything, strengthened if per capita personal income is used instead of wages as the measure of compensation.

Table 4.8   Relative Prefectural Unemployment and Earnings Equations for Japan (standard errors in parentheses)

	Log Monthly Contractual Earnings			Unemployment Rate	
	(1)	(2)	(3)	(1)	(2)
Constant	13.54	13.54	13.37	1.769	.822
	(.30)	(.81)	(.98)	(1.01)	(.12)
Log employment change	.025	.038	.038	−.141	−.297
	(.02)	(.02)	(.07)	(.06)	(.10)
Unemployment	−.063	−.062	−.133		
	(.02)	(.03)	(.11)		
Dependent variable lagged five	.001			.857	−1.13
	(.02)			(.14)	(.58)
Prefectural vacancy rate		−.118	.082	.069	−1.15
		(.08)	(.10)	(.08)	(.48)
Prefectural unionization rate		3.02	4.66	−5.04	−7.44
		(.77)	(2.89)	(2.26)	(4.61)
Consumer price index		6×10^{-6}			
		(.01)			
Housing rental prices			.0001		
			(.0001)		
$\bar{R}^2$	.99	.99	.94	.97	.22
N	139	139	139	139	92

Note: Data used are described in the appendix. All equations include prefecture fixed effects and time dummies controls. Column (2) for unemployment includes instrumental variable estimates for the lagged dependent variable.

and time dummies to take out period and constant area effects. Hsiao (1986) noted that fixed-effect models with lagged dependent variables yield biased estimates unless the number of time periods is large. Consequently, instrumental variable estimates are also presented for the earnings (columns 3) and unemployment (columns 2) equations in the United States and the unemployment equations (columns 2) in Japan. These regressions are estimated in difference form and use twice-lagged values of the dependent variable as instruments.

In both countries, for all specifications, regional earnings are inversely related to the level of unemployment. This is contrary to the findings of Hall but is consistent with international evidence by Blanchflower and Oswald (1992). Outsider pressures on wage premiums may thus be more important than the compensating differential notions suggested by Hall. The estimates also suggest that area earnings in Japan and the United States are significantly affected by area demand conditions as proxied by the rate of growth of employment. Prefectural earnings are consistently found to be positively related to demand (employment) growth, while state earnings are negatively related in the United States. The fact that increases in employment growth are associated with reductions in relative wages was found by Blanchard and Katz (1992) when they

Table 4.9   **Relative State Unemployment and Wage Equations for the United States (standard errors in parentheses)**

	Log Weekly Manufacturing Earnings			Unemployment Rate	
	(1)	(2)	(3)	(1)	(2)
Constant	3.42	4.91	−1.69	4.82	−.923
	(1.24)	(.33)	(.12)	(.56)	(.26)
Log employment change	−.475	−.177	−2.63	−33.01	−50.33
	(.10)	(.10)	(.17)	(2.67)	(5.53)
Unemployment	−.010	−.007	−.040		
	(.002)	(.002)	(.003)		
Dependent variable lagged five	.404	.187	4.88	−.018	.309
	(.05)	(.06)	(.29)	(.04)	(.14)
State unionization		.002	.012	.033	.234
		(.001)	(.001)	(.02)	(.05)
$\bar{R}^2$	.97	.97	.68	.87	.45
N	682	563	318	399	149

Note: Data are described in the appendix. All equations include state fixed effects and time dummies controls. Columns (2) for unemployment and column (3) for earnings include instrumental variable estimates for the lagged dependent variable.

used a sample period similar to the one used here. It is conceivable that the employment growth measure may represent supply shifts and not just area demand effects. As a check on this I instrumented for demand growth, using an estimate of area demand growth based on national one-digit industry growth rates for Japan and the United States. This instrument is similar to that used by Bartik (1991) for the United States and should be a valid measure as long as industry employment is not too concentrated in a particular state or prefecture, which at the one-digit level is unlikely to be the case. The qualitative nature of these results does not appear to be sensitive to the use of these alternative proxies.[15]

Finally, the extent of area unionism is positively associated with area relative wages in both countries. Unfortunately, state-level housing rental prices, cost of living, and vacancy data are not available for the United States, so we cannot replicate all of the results for Japanese labor markets. Overall, these results suggest that relative regional earnings in both countries are sensitive to local demand conditions and unemployment, as well as to the presence of noncompetitive forces such as unions.

It is important to know, in accessing flexibility, whether there are differences in the size or magnitude of the responses of earnings to these factors. Blanchflower and Oswald (1992) indicate that one important measure of flexibility is

15. These results are available from the author upon request.

the unemployment elasticity of earnings. The long-run values for this elasticity calculated from similar specifications (column 1 estimates in tables 4.8 and 4.9) are −.15 for Japan and −.11 for the United States.[16] The elasticity of earnings with respect to employment growth is .02 for Japan and −.02 for the United States. Thus, the higher persistence in regional earnings in Japan does not indicate that they are any less sensitive to unemployment or employment growth than in the United States.

In the regional unemployment equations for both the United States and Japan, there is evidence that employment growth (or instrumented employment growth) is negatively and significantly related to unemployment. Interestingly, we find no evidence that unions, despite their positive effects on relative wages, significantly increase unemployment rates in either Japan or the United States. The key finding again is that, despite the evidence of strong serial persistence in area unemployment rates in Japan, area unemployment rates are sensitive to demand shifts in both countries. Nonetheless, the long-run elasticity of unemployment with respect to employment growth from the estimates in columns (2) in the unemployment equations is .045 in Japan and .27 in the United States.[17] In contrast to the findings for earnings, unemployment appears to be less sensitive to demand (employment growth) in Japan than in the United States.

Given the evidence that demand shifts affect both wages and unemployment, our theoretical model would lead us to expect this to generate regional migration. To examine the sensitivity of net migration rates, we estimate variants of equation (5) for both Japan and the United States. The results from estimating these models without and with region fixed effects are reported in columns (1) and (2) of tables 4.10 and 4.11 for Japan and the United States, respectively.

Workers in both countries tend to migrate to those areas where employment is growing. Across areas there is no evidence that area unemployment significantly affects migration in Japan, but some evidence exists for the importance of unemployment in the United States. In the fixed-effect estimates (columns 2), high unemployment in an area increases out-migration in the United States but not in Japan. Regional earnings do not appear to have much impact on net migration in either country.

It is possible that the aggregate nature of the migration equation is obscuring the relationship between migration and income. Beeson and Montgomery (1993) and others have found such a relationship, using microdata in the United States. Matsukawa (1991) presents estimates of a place-to-place model of migration that allows migration rates from one area to another to be a func-

16. In specifications using lagged-once values of the dependent variable, the elasticities with respect to unemployment and employment growth for the United States are −.19 and −.003, respectively. Unfortunately, it is not possible to estimate this specification for Japan.
17. The elasticity using once-lagged values of the dependent variable for the United States is .28.

Table 4.10   **Prefectural Net Migration Rate and Commuting Equations for Japan (standard errors in parentheses)**

	Annual Net Migration Rate		Daytime/Nighttime Populations	
	(1)	(2)	(1)	(2)
Constant	−.028	−.366	.923	.776
	(.01)	(.08)	(.06)	(.14)
Log employment change	.006	.009	−.026	.006
	(.001)	(.001)	(.004)	(.002)
Unemployment rate	.0005	.003	.003	.001
	(.0006)	(.001)	(.004)	(.002)
Log monthly earnings	.001	.001	.006	−.005
	(.001)	(.001)	(.005)	(.002)
Vacancy rate	.003	.006	.022	−.001
	(.001)	(.001)	(.008)	(.002)
Housing rental prices	-2×10^{-6}	-3×10^{-6}	-7×10^{-6}	6×10^{-6}
	(1×10^{-6})	(1×10^{-6})	(-8×10^{-6})	(2×10^{-6})
Distance from Tokyo	-3×10^{-6}	.0004	1×10^{-5}	.0003
	(-2×10^{-6})	(.0001)	(2×10^{-4})	(.0002)
$\bar{R}^2$	.62	.87	.26	.98
N	139	139	139	139

Note: Columns (2) include prefecture fixed effects and time dummies. Data used are described in the appendix.

Table 4.11   **State Net Migration Equations for the United States (standard errors in parentheses)**

	Log Population Change		Annualized Net Migration Rate	
	(1)	(2)	(1)	(2)
Constant	.027	.018	−.026	−.036
	(.01)	(.05)	(.02)	(.01)
Log employment change	.213	.197	.307	.013
	(.02)	(.02)	(.03)	(.013)
Unemployment rate	.0004	−.002	.002	−.0008
	(.0002)	(.0003)	(.0005)	(.0002)
Log weekly wage	−.003	.006	.004	.007
	(.002)	(.008)	(.004)	(.002)
State unionization	−.0002	−.0001	−.0006	−.00002
	(.0001)	(.0001)	(.0001)	(.0001)
$\bar{R}^2$	.25	.74	.15	.94
N	585	585	536	536

Note: Data are described in the appendix. Columns (2) include state fixed effects and time dummies.

tion of relative wages and demand conditions in each area. His results suggest that income differentials matter in explaining migration behavior in Japan.

High housing prices also have a significant deterrent effect on regional net migration in Japan. The results hold even when area fixed effects are included. Unfortunately there is no equivalent state-level time series data on average house price series for the United States. Beeson and Montgomery, however, estimate a micro logit migration equation, using data from the 1980 census, and find some evidence that high housing prices have some, albeit insignificant, effect on migration in the United States.

The small size of Japan, and the availability of good rail transport, may mean that Japanese workers are more able to respond to changing economic conditions by commuting rather than by migrating to new areas. The potential importance of commuting behavior in Japan can be seen by looking at prefectural data on the ratio of daytime to total, or nighttime, population. This ratio, which will exceed one if there is net commuting to an area, is presented for selected prefectures in table 4.12. The Tokyo region experiences as much as a 28 percent population surge during the day, while Osaka and Aichi add between 2 and 5 percent to their population. On the other hand, Nara, Saitima, and Chiba have up to 13 percent of their residents commuting out to jobs. Thus, there appear to be substantial amounts of mobility in Japan that may not be reflected in net migration rates.

The correlation between prefecture commuting and net migration rates is positive (controlling for area fixed effects), suggesting that commuting and migrating may be substitutes. To see whether commuting behavior responds to local labor markets variables, the results from estimating of area commuting equations are presented in table 4.10, where the ratio of daytime to nighttime population is the dependent variable. In the fixed-effects specification (columns 2), the effects of local conditions on commuting are similar to their effects on net migration. While workers migrate and commute to high-growth areas, area unemployment does not appear to be a significant deterrent to either

Table 4.12   **Selected Prefectural Commuting Rates**

Prefecture	1970	1985
Hokkaido	1.00	1.001
Tokyo	1.111	1.181
Niigata	1.00	.988
Kyoto	1.008	1.004
Osaka	1.045	1.051
Nara	.903	.877
Saitama	.881	.869
Chiba	.906	.878
Aichi	1.013	1.018
Kagoshima	1.000	1.005

Note: Ratio of day population/total population.

commuting or migrating. Although wages do not appear to affect net migration, workers seem to commute to areas with high relative wages, holding distance and demand constant.

4.4 Summary and Discussion

In this study, I have examined regional labor market behavior in Japan and the United States. In contrast to the picture at the aggregate level, Japanese regional labor markets appear to exhibit substantially more persistence than their U.S. counterparts. Relative wages, unemployment rates, net migration, and employment growth rates all show substantial persistence in terms of both the level and ranking of areas. Within-prefecture persistence is less for all these labor market variables, suggesting a fairly constant spatial labor market structure but fluid within-area markets.

In the United States there is evidence of persistence in both the ranking and level of these labor market indicators, although it is less than in Japan. The most noticeable difference in the two countries is that there is very little correlation in area unemployment rates in the United States over ten-year intervals, while it remains high in Japan. The within-state persistence of the labor market variable for the United States is less than the across-area persistence but is higher than in Japan.

Estimates of reduced-form area earnings and unemployment equations suggest that, broadly speaking, regional labor markets in the two countries respond to similar factors. In contrast to the predictions of Harris and Todaro's (1970) compensating differential model, area earnings and unemployment rates are negatively correlated in both countries. This seems supportive of the efficiency wage considerations outlined in Blanchflower and Oswald (1992), in which worker wage premiums are reduced in areas where the costs of job loss are great. To further test between these models, it would be useful to distinguish between the effects of permanent versus transitory shifts in unemployment on earnings. Further, aggregation bias may have important effects here, as studies of the behavior of wages over the business cycle have found.

There was evidence of some important differences in labor market behavior in the two countries. First, employment growth seems to be positively correlated with area earnings in Japan but negatively correlated with earnings in the United States. This may suggest that regional employment growth differences were primarily supply driven in the United States but demand driven in Japan. Second, the long-run unemployment elasticity of earnings is slightly lower in the United States than in Japan. Conversely, regional unemployment in Japan is less sensitive to employment growth than in the United States.

Net migration rates are substantially higher in the United States than in Japan. Migration flows in Japan, however, are more persistent than in the United States and are not sensitive to area unemployment rates. Despite these differences, net migration flows in both countries respond to employment growth and wages in roughly similar fashions. There is some evidence that high housing prices have an important adverse effect on net migration in Japan, while they do not appear to have a significant effect in the United States. Perhaps because of high housing prices, commuting serves as a substitute for net migration in Japan.

This study finds only mixed evidence that regional labor markets in Japan are more fluid than in the United States. The lack of response in regional unemployment rates may reflect a greater regional homogeneity in demand shifts in Japan. Alternatively, if the valuation of location-specific amenities (such as being near Tokyo) are rising faster over time in Japan than in the United States, this could generate what appears to be a more limited regional response to short-run demand shifts. Conclusions about the importance of government regional aid and relocation policies based on this analysis must be tentative at best. Nonetheless, this study finds no evidence to support the conclusion that these policies succeeded in making regional unemployment rates in Japan more flexible than in the United States. Whether these same policies would have a pronounced effect in an economy with a different regional distribution of amenities remains an open question.

Appendix

U.S. Data

The U.S. data on wages, unemployment, and employment were provided by the INFORUM research group at the University of Maryland and are available via Internet.

Employment. The measure of employment is the establishment-based nonagricultural employment series from the Bureau of Labor Statistics (BLS). The data range is from 1970 to 1990. Employment growth rates are calculated as differences in the log of employment in periods t and $t - 1$.

Unemployment. The measure of state employment is from *Employment and Earnings* (BLS). The data range is from 1976 to 1990.

Wages. The measure of wages used is the BLS establishment-based average hourly earnings of manufacturing production workers from *Employment and*

Earnings. The data range is from 1971 to 1990.

Union. The unionization measure is taken from Current Population Survey (CPS) estimates of the percentage of employment in each state covered by a union contract. The data are from Curme, Hirsch, and Macpherson (1990) and Kokkelenberg and Sockell (1985). The data range from 1976 to 1988. Data for 1982 are derived from fitting a linear trend between the 1981 and 1983 series values.

Net Migration. There are two measures of net migration for the United States. One uses state-level population from the *Statistical Abstract* (Bureau of the Census, 1989). The data range from 1976 to 1990. Population growth rates are calculated as differences in the log of state population in periods t and $t - 1$. The second measure is census estimates of state-level numbers of net migration for the time intervals 1980–87, 1970–80, and 1960–70. The number of net migrants was divided by beginning-of-period population to get a net migration rate and then annualized.

Japanese Data

Wages. Wages are defined as average monthly contractual cash earnings per employee. The data are from establishments with more than thirty employees and are available for forty-six prefectures (forty-seven when data on Okinawa are available) every five years from 1970 to 1985, in *Annual Survey on the Wage Structure* (Ministry of Labor, Japan).

Employment and unemployment. These data are from the *Labor Force Survey* (Ministry of Labor, Japan). Unemployed persons are those over fifteen years old who were able to work, wanted to work, and sought work actively. Employment growth is calculated as the average annual change in the number of persons at work and those with a job but not at work. The data for forty-six prefectures (forty-seven when data on Okinawa are available) are available every five years from 1960 to 1985.

Distance. This is the number of kilometers from the capital of each prefecture to Tokyo.

The following Japanese data were all taken from the *Yearbook of Labor Statistics* (Labor Statistics and Research Department, Ministry of Labor, Japan).

Union. This is a measure of prefectural unionization based on a weighted average of one-digit industry unionization rates, where the weights are the share of prefectural employment in that industry. Data are available for 1970, 1975, 1979, and 1988.

Net migration. This is defined as the difference between the number of immigrants to a prefecture and the number of out-migrants from that prefecture, divided by initial population. Data are available by prefecture annually from 1960 to 1988.

Vacancies. These are defined as the ratio of monthly average active openings to active applications for persons registered at public employment security offices. The data by prefecture are available for 1970, 1980, 1985.

Nighttime and daytime population. These are taken from the population census. Nighttime population is the number of residents of each prefecture. Daytime population is calculated by subtracting from the nighttime population of each prefecture the difference between the number of persons (fifteen years of age and over) in each prefecture who are employed or attend school in another prefecture and those who reside in another prefecture but are employed or go to school there. Data are available by prefecture every five years for 1970 to 1985.

CPI. This is a measure of relative cost-of-living differences. It is based on the Regional Difference Indexes of Consumer Prices, which measure relative cost of living (Japan = 100) for prefectural capital cities. The data are available annually for 1971 to 1985.

Rent. Rent is defined as the average rental cost per month (in yen) of privately owned houses. The data, available annually from 1970 to 1989, are based on the *Retail Price Survey.*

References

Abraham, K., and S. Houseman. 1989. Job security and work force adjustment: How different are U.S. and Japanese practices? *Journal of the Japanese and International Economies* 3:500–521.

Bartik, T. 1989. The effects of demand shocks on local labor markets. Kalamazoo, Mich.: W. E. Upjohn Institute. Memorandum.

———. 1991. *Who benefits from state and local economic development policies?* Kalamazoo, Mich.: W. E. Upjohn Institute.

Beeson, P., and E. Montgomery. Forthcoming. The effects of colleges and universities on local labor markets. *Review of Economics and Statistics.*

Björklund, A., and B. Holmlund. 1989. Job mobility and subsequent wages in Sweden. In *Migration and labor market adjustment,* ed. J. Van Dijk, H. Folmer, H. Herzog, and A. Schlottman, 201–16. Dordrecht: Kluwer Academic Publishers.

Blanchard, O. J., and L. Katz. 1992. Regional evolutions. *Brookings Papers on Economic Activity* 1:1–75.

Blanchflower, D., and A. Oswald. 1992. International wage curves. Hanover, N.H.: Dartmouth University. Memorandum.

Curme, M., B. Hirsch, and D. Macpherson. 1990. Union membership and contract coverage in the United States, 1983–88. *Industrial and Labor Relations Review* 44:5–33.

Dijk, J. van, H. Folmer, and A. Schlottman, eds. 1989. *Migration and labor market adjustment.* Dordrecht: Kluwer Academic Publishers.

Eberts, R., and J. Stone. 1992. *Wage and employment adjustment in local labor markets.* Kalamazoo, Mich.: W. E. Upjohn Institute.

Gabriel, S., J. Shack-Marquez, and W. Wascher. 1991. Regional labor markets, cost-of-living differentials, and migration. Working Paper 91. Washington, D.C.: Board of Governors of the Federal Reserve.

Hall, R., 1970. "Why is the unemployment rate so high at full employment? *Brookings Papers on Economic Activity* 2:369–402.

———. 1972. Turnover in the labor force. *Brookings Papers on Economic Activity* 3:709–64.

Harris, J. R., and M. P. Todaro. 1970. Migration, unemployment, and development: A two-sector analysis. *American Economic Review* 60:126–42.

Hashimoto, M. 1990. *The Japanese labor market in a comparative perspective with the United States.* Kalamazoo, Mich.: W. E. Upjohn Institute.

Hsiao, C. 1986. *Analysis of panel data.* Cambridge: Cambridge University Press.

Hughes, G., and B. McCormick. 1989. Does migration reduce differentials in regional unemployment rates? In *Migration and labor market adjustment,* ed. J. Van Dijk, H. Folmer, H. Herzog, and A. Schlottman, 85–108. Dordrecht: Kluwer Academic Publishers.

Hyclak, T., and G. Johnes. 1992. *Wage flexibility and unemployemnt dynamics in regional labor markets.* Kalamazoo, Mich.: W. E. Upjohn Institute.

Kokkelenberg, E., and D. Sockell. 1985. Union membership in the United States, 1973–81. *Industrial and Labor Relations Review* 38:497–543.

Ito, T. 1992. *The Japanese economy.* Cambridge, Mass.: MIT Press.

Leigh, D. 1989. *Assisting displaced workers.* Kalamazoo, Mich.: W. E. Upjohn Institute.

Matsukawa, I. 1991. Interregional gross migration and structural changes in local industries. *Environment and planning A* 23:745–56.

Montgomery, E. 1992. Evidence on metropolitan wage differentials across industries and over time. *Journal of Urban Economics* 31:69–83.

Montgomery, E., and K. Shaw. 1985. Long-term contracts, expectations, and wage inertia. *Journal of Monetary Economics* 16:209–26.

Neumann, G., and R. Topel. 1991. Employment risk, diversification, and unemployment. *Quarterly Journal of Economics* 106:1341–66.

Roback, J. 1982. Wages, rents, and the quality of life. *Journal of Political Economy* 90:1257–78.

Tachibanaki, T., and K. Sakurai. 1990. Labour supply and unemployment in Japan. Kyoto: Kyoto Institute of Economic Research. Memorandum.

Topel, R. 1986. Local labor markets. *Journal of Political Economy* 94:S111–43.

Weir, M. 1992. *Politics of jobs: The boundaries of employment policy in the United States.* Princeton, N.J.: Princeton University Press.

Weitzman, M. 1984. *The Share Economy.* Cambridge: Harvard University Press.

Yoshikawa, H., and Y. Takeuchi. 1989. Real wages and the Japanese economy. *Bank of Japan Monetary and Economic Studies* 7:1–40.

5 Housing Market Regulations and Housing Market Performance in the United States, Germany, and Japan

Axel Börsch-Supan

Housing markets in most countries feature strong government involvement. This involvement typically takes the form of direct subsidies (e.g., housing allowances, public housing), tax incentives (e.g., mortgage interest deduction), and market regulations (e.g., tenure protection legislation), among other policy instruments. There are several objectives for this activist role of the government. First, it is claimed that housing markets are inefficient and need counterbalancing government actions to achieve pareto efficiency. A second motive is the belief that everybody merits reasonable housing and that society ought to provide this housing if an individual cannot afford it. Third, supporting housing consumption and investment serves as a convenient mechanism to redistribute income and wealth.

Many pages have been filled with discussions of these motives.[1] I do not want to repeat the merits and pitfalls of these arguments in this paper. Rather I want to concentrate on those programs that are intended to ensure social protection and analyze whether they achieve this goal and whether they have side effects on the performance of the housing market. In particular, I want to determine whether the social protection comes at the expense of economic flexibility hindering equilibrating market forces.

This task is complicated by the fact that housing markets are by no account good textbook examples of neoclassical spot markets. Market imperfections abound even in the absence of state intervention, particularly in the rental but

Axel Börsch-Supan is professor of economics at the University of Mannheim and a research associate of the National Bureau of Economic Research.

Parts of this paper are based on joint work with Yoshitsugo Kanemoto and Konrad Stahl. The author is indebted to Bernhard Boockmann, Stephanie Rau, Brian Sands, and Hanno Scholtz for able and committed research assistance. He appreciated the comments by Rebecca Blank, Yoshi Kanemoto, Barry McCormick, and Jürgen von Hagen. Support by the Ford Foundation is gratefully acknowledged.

1. See, for example, the textbook by Mills and Hamilton (1984).

also in the owner-occupied housing market segment. Housing is a durable good where prices are not necessarily defined by one-period spot market conditions alone. Therefore, expectations based on imperfect foresight play an important role in determining housing prices. High monetary and nonmonetary transaction costs are involved when consumption is changed by moving, creating thin or even missing markets. Property rights of the rental unit are given up only temporarily, giving the seller a strong incentive to care who the buyer is. And since the tenant's characteristics will be revealed only after some time, the problems of moral hazard and incomplete contracts hamper the functioning of the invisible hand. As is well known, if the two sources of potential inefficiency—intrinsic market imperfections and government intervention—are confused, inaccurate policy analysis and policy recommendations may occur when first-best solutions are proposed in a second-best environment. An important task of this paper is therefore to disentangle the effects of government intervention and the effects of intrinsic housing market imperfections.

Such an analysis is considerably eased by the possibility of comparing different countries. Empirical analysis of government intervention in one country alone frequently faces the impossibility of a with-and-without analysis, due to the fact that policy regime changes in a country are rare and that most housing market interventions are federal functions. Hence, time series data often have little temporal variation or are confounded by other historical changes, and cross-sectional data in a single country feature virtually no policy variation at all. In contrast, a cross-national comparison exploits the policy differences at a given point or during a short period of time. I draw empirical conclusions by comparing evidence in Germany and Japan with evidence from the United States. In all of these three countries, there is substantial government involvement in the housing markets. However, the programs that are in effect have very different intentions and designs. Moreover, they apparently create very different housing market outcomes. Examples are the different proportions of owner-occupancy and different mobility rates in the three countries.

Of course, international comparisons suffer from the confounding effects of cultural and attitudinal differences. The countries to be compared should not be so unequal as to make comparisons meaningless but should be sufficiently different to feature policy differences. This subtle balance restricts the choice of countries and requires a careful analysis that controls for other confounding factors. Germany and Japan have standards of living roughly comparable to that of the United States. They have become somewhat "Americanized" since World War II, particularly with respect to consumption patterns, but their histories and geographic features have led to very different policies.

I set the stage in section 5.1 with a summary of stylized facts about the German and the Japanese housing markets in comparison with the U.S. housing market. The policy discussion begins in section 5.2, with a brief description and evaluation of five types of government programs: tenants' protection legislation, housing allowance programs, the provision of public and social housing, indirect subsidies toward homeownership, and transaction regulations. Not all programs exist in all three countries, and some are designed quite differently; but the basic framework is shared in all three countries. However, it is not my intention to produce an exhaustive list of government programs in Germany, Japan, and the United States. Rather, these fives types of government intervention exemplify the main differences in how to approach housing policy in the three countries and therefore allow an assessment of efficacy and side effects of housing programs in general.

Sections 5.3 and 5.4 are devoted to more in-depth studies of the effects of the German tenants' protection legislation and of the U.S. and German home-ownership subsidies. I will relate the extent of these policies to measures of housing market performance, particularly flexibility. This is a difficult part of the paper, since measurement and even definition of economic performance and flexibility are vague. I will look at indicators such as cyclical stability and speed of adjustment to changing economic and demographic conditions on the macroeconomic level, as well as at housing affordability and mobility at the microeconomic level. The paper finishes with a synthesis in section 5.5.

5.1   Housing Market Facts in the United States, Germany, and Japan

This section summarizes the most important stylized facts about housing markets in Germany, Japan and the United States. Data sources are detailed in appendix A. For Germany, the data represent West Germany only. Due to its former political system and the inability of the current government to resolve the many land and house ownership disputes, the former East Germany still features a housing "market" totally dominated by state-administrated rental housing. However, the demographic structure of East Germany closely resembles that of West Germany, so that when the intended privatization of land and buildings finally takes place, East German housing consumption patterns should converge quickly to the West German ones.

5.1.1   Background: Demography, Income, Savings

I begin with a brief summary of those background facts that are most important to characterize housing markets.

The expected future *population size and structure* are very different among the three countries. While the population of the United States is projected to increase during the next forty years, albeit at a smaller rate than between 1950 and now, Japan's population is expected to stabilize at around half the current size of the U.S. population, and the German population is forecasted to decline substantially to about 80 percent of its current size (table 5.1).

However, there are two reasons to be cautious when drawing quick conclusions about future housing markets. First, immigration may completely upset

Table 5.1   **Population Size**

	Population (millions)			Immigration (thousands)		
	1950	1990	2030	1970	1980	1989
United States	152.3	248.5	302.2	373	531	1,091
West Germany	50.0	62.1	48.7	1,043	752	1,522
Japan	83.7	122.8	122.1	7.3	23.1	

Sources: OECD 1988, StAB, StJB, Kanemoto 1992.

Note: Immigration figures in Japan refer to changes in the stock of foreigners 1970–80 and 1980–90.

Table 5.2   **Population Structure**

	Average Household Size			% Aged 65 and More		
	1970	1980	1990	1950	1990	2030
United States	3.11	2.75	2.63	8.1%	12.2%	19.5%
West Germany	2.74	2.48	2.22	9.4	15.5	25.8
Japan	3.9	3.4	3.28	5.2	11.4	20.0

Sources: StJB, JHC, StAb, OECD 1988.

these projections. While the decline in the German population shown in table 5.1 (left panel) is about a third of a million per annum, actual net immigration in 1989 exceeded 1.5 million (right panel). Immigration into Germany is very high compared to the United States and Japan. It is expected to remain at about 1 million per year for the near future. Immigration into Japan is all but nonexisting. The United States, although much larger, has a lower *absolute* number of immigrants. Even if one doubles the U.S. figures to roughly account for unreported illegal immigration, per capita immigration into Germany still runs about 2.5 times higher than total per capita immigration into the United States.

The second reason to be cautious drawing conclusions about housing is that *population* counts do not translate one-to-one into *household* numbers. Table 5.2 (left panel) depicts the average household size in each of the three countries. Household size declines steadily in all countries and is substantially lower in Germany than in the United States or Japan. Part of this is due to the increasing percentage of elderly, who are most likely to live in single-person households. As the right panel of table 5.2 shows, this development is not likely to stop during the next forty years when the population aging process will reach its peak. Population aging is very pronounced in Germany; it is also very fast (although with a lower base) in Japan; and it is both slower and less dramatic in the United States.

The most important economic determinant of individual housing choices is *income*. Per capita gross domestic product (GDP) is substantially higher in the

Table 5.3   **Household Income (1990 U.S. $)**

	GDP per Capita, 1988	Net Household Income 1987	Income Distribution					
			Lower 20%	2d 20%	3rd 20%	4th 20%	9th 10%	Upper 10%
United States	$21,612	$41,085	4.7%	11.0%	17.4%	25.0%	16.9%	25.0%
West Germany	15,648	30,981	6.8	12.7	17.8	24.1	15.3	23.4
Japan	15,788	34,432	8.7	13.2	17.5	23.1	15.1	22.4

Sources: StAB 1991, 434, 843; StJB 1988, 554; Kanemoto 1992; World Bank, *World Development Record,* table 30.

Note: The income distribution figures represent the share of total income in the respective percentile. The data are from 1984 for West Germany, from 1979 for Japan, and from 1985 for the United States.

United States, compared to both Germany and Japan, as table 5.3 demonstrates. Amounts are in 1990 U.S. dollars converted by Organization for Economic Cooperation and Development (OECD) purchasing power parities.[2] Due to different household sizes and tax structures, this translates into a 16 percent lower net household income in Japan compared to the United States, and a 25 percent lower net household income in West Germany. Most of the difference between Germany and the United States is due to the 20 percent lower work hours in Germany and thus reflects different preferences for leisure rather than welfare differences.[3]

Moreover, income distributions differ dramatically (table 5.3, right panel). While the lowest 20 percent in the income distribution hold 6.8 to 8.7 percent of total income in Germany and Japan, they have only 4.7 percent in the United States. Conversely, the richest decile earns a quarter of total income in the United States but only 23.4 percent in Germany and only 22.4 percent in Japan. It is necessary to take these income differences into account when comparing housing consumption.

Finally, table 5.4 depicts the *macroeconomic parameters* most important for the housing market: Until 1990, Japan featured high gross national product (GNP) growth rates compared to the United States and Germany and a dramatically higher aggregate savings rate. Since 1990, Japanese GNP growth has somewhat slowed down, and the personal savings rate has fallen to the German level. As is well known, the United States features not only very low savings rates by international standards but also a unprecedented decline in savings during the past twenty years.

2. Precisely, DM and yen amounts have been inflated to 1990 by the domestic consumer price index (CPI) deflator (see *Economic report of the president, statistical tables* 1992, table B-105) and then converted into dollars using the purchasing power parities listed in OECD (1992).
3. In 1990, German workers averaged 1,506 hours, U.S. workers 1,847 hours.

Table 5.4   GNP Growth and Savings

	Annual GNP Growth			Aggregate Savings Rate		
	1971/75	1981/85	1990	1970	1980	1990
United States	2.3%	2.5%	1.0%	7.8%	5.8%	2.2%
West Germany	2.1	1.2	4.5	18.1	9.8	12.6
Japan	4.5	3.8	5.6	27.0	18.3	20.3

Sources: EcRep, statistical tables; Organization for Economic Cooperation and Development, National Accounts.

Table 5.5   Housing Consumption

	Rate of Owner-Occupancy	Floor Space of New Dwellings	
		Total	Per Person
United States	64.0%	149.0 m²	56.0 m²
West Germany	39.3	86.1	36.8
Japan	61.4	75.9	21.4

Sources: AHS 1987; GWZ 1987; JKDS 1988; and Kanemoto 1992.

Note: The Japanese numbers are multiplied by 1.15 to account for measurement differences in floor space (see Kanemoto 1992).

5.1.2   Housing Consumption

There are striking differences in housing consumption among the three countries. Most notable are the differences in tenure choice and dwelling size. Table 5.5 presents 1987/88 data.

Ownership rates are high in Japan and the United States but very low in Germany: 64 percent of all American households live in owner-occupied housing, 61.4 percent in Japan, but only 39.3 percent in Germany. Americans also have the largest dwellings. Newly constructed houses have on average 149 m² in the United States, while German houses have on average 86 m² and Japanese houses only 76 m². A correction for household size amplifies the relative smallness of Japanese dwellings: A Japanese person consumes on average 21.4 m², while a German person has about 1.7 times as much and an American 2.6 times as much space as a Japanese.

Table 5.6 gives a more detailed decomposition of housing demand. The differences in tenure choice are echoed in the differences between structure types. Whereas in Germany single-family structures (including duplexes) and multifamily structures have almost equal shares, single-family homes constitute the overwhelming share of structures in the United States. In all three countries, rental dwellings are much smaller than owner-occupied dwellings. This is most pronounced in Japan.

Table 5.6   **Housing Consumption by Tenure, Structure Type, and Dwelling Size**

	Structure Type		Dwelling Size		
Tenure	Single Family	Multi-family	1–4 Rooms	5+ Rooms	Total per Parameter
United States, 1987					
Rental	11.9%	24.1%	22.4%	13.6%	36.0%
Owner-occupied	55.7	8.3	8.7	55.3	64.0
Total	67.5	22.5	31.1	68.9	100.0
West Germany, 1987					
Rental	15.0	45.7	47.7	13.0	60.7
Owner-occupied	33.0	6.3	10.9	28.4	39.3
Total	48.0	52.0	58.6	41.4	100.0
Japan, 1988					
Rental	6.9	31.0	35.1	2.8	37.9
Owner-occupied	53.9	8.1	14.5	47.6	62.1
Total	60.8	39.1	49.6	50.4	100.0

Sources: United States: AHS 1987. West Germany: GWZ 1987. Japan: JHC 1988; Kanemoto 1992.

Table 5.7   **Mobility Rates**

	United States	West Germany	Japan
Total % of households having moved within 12 months	17.6%	6.6%	9.6%
Age of mover			
20–24 years	35.2	42.9	20.1
25–29	31.8	21.5	19.0
30–44	17.9	9.2	9.3
45–54	10.2	3.5	4.9
55–64	7.1	3.5	3.8
65–74	4.9	1.7	3.9
75 and above	4.7	2.0	4.5
Tenure			
Rental housing	37.5	9.0	19.8
Owner-occupied	8.5	3.4	3.6

Sources: AHS 1987; GWZ 1987; JHC 1988.

5.1.3 Mobility

The striking difference in internal mobility rates across countries is important to note for an analysis of market flexibility. Mobility rates in Germany are about three times lower than in the United States (table 5.7). Although German mobility is high at young ages, it virtually ceases after age 35. Of course, U.S. mobility rates also decline with age. However, Americans aged

75 and above move more frequently than heads of German households who are over age 35.[4] Japanese mobility rates are, on average, in between those of Germany and the United States. However, their age pattern is quite different. Mobility among the young is much lower, because first-home buying age is very late in Japan. In turn, mobility among the elderly is relatively high, mostly due to the Japanese tradition of taking in elderly parents.[5]

5.1.4   Housing Supply

I now turn to the supply side of the housing market. Table 5.8 presents the suppliers of the standing stock. In addition to differences in rental-owner shares, the rental housing segment itself features different suppliers. In Germany, almost a tenth of the housing stock is provided by public or nonprofit housing agencies. This percentage is a little lower in Japan, although, as a share of rental housing, public providers are more important in Japan. This contrasts with the United States, where the share of public housing is little more than 1 percent of total housing. Section 5.2.1 will explain that public housing in Germany and Japan is very different from public housing in the United States. Japan also has a substantial share of employer-provided housing, another segment cushioned from free-market mechanisms.

In all three countries, new construction is a small proportion of the total supply. Table 5.9 shows that this is particularly true for West Germany, while Japan had the most active new-construction segment. To account for the different business cycle phases in the three countries, I took averages from 1974 to 1988. During this time and on a per capita basis, U.S. construction activity was 60 percent of the Japanese, and the German about one-half. Neither Germany nor the United States ever reached new-construction activities as intense as the Japanese (almost 14 units per 1,000 inhabitants in 1988) nor did the U.S. and Japan ever drop as low as Germany in 1988 (only 3.4 units per 1,000 inhabitants).

5.1.5   Housing Market

Housing market features such as vacancy rates and the size of the second-hand market are very different in the three countries. The left panel of table 5.10 depicts vacancy rates for the three countries. The German vacancy rate is very low in comparison to both Japan and the United States. This vacancy rate fluctuates somewhat during the business cycle. However, the relative differences among the three countries are remarkably stable.

Germany and Japan have very thin second-hand markets in the single-family home market segment, in comparison to the United States. The right panel of table 5.10 displays the number of existing home sales, both absolute and rela-

---

4. The mobility rate for Germans aged thirty-five and above is 3.7 percent (SOEP 1987).

5. Regarding transactions costs, it is noteworthy that built-in kitchens are commonly part of rented dwellings in the United States, while they commonly belong to the household in Germany and Japan and are therefore being moved or sold in case of a move.

Table 5.8   **Housing Suppliers**

	United States 1988		West Germany 1989		Japan 1988	
Owner-occupied	64.0%		39.3%		62.1%	
Private rental	34.6	(96.1%)	51.4	(84.7%)	26.2	(69.0%)
Public/nonprofit	1.4	(3.9)	9.3	(15.3)	7.6	(20.0)
Employer-provided	—	—	—	—	4.2	(11.1)

Sources: StAb 1991; StBA (FS5.1) 1989; JHC 1988.
Note: Numbers in parentheses are percentages of rental housing.

Table 5.9   **New Construction (completed units), 1974–1988**

	Average			Minimum			Maximum		
	Units [000]	Per Capita	Year	Units [000]	Per Capita	Year	Units [000]	Per Capita
United States	1,549	6.8	1982	1,006	4.3	1978	1,868	8.4
West Germany	360	5.8	1988	209	3.4	1974	604	9.7
Japan	1,374	11.5	1983	1,137	9.6	1988	1,684	13.8

Sources: U.S. Department of Commerce, *Construction Review;* StBA(FS-5.1) 1989; JHC 1988; Kanemoto 1992.
Note: Per capita refers to number of newly constructed units per one thousand inhabitants.

Table 5.10   **Housing Market Features**

		Existing Home Sales	
	Vacancy Rate	Units [000]	Units per 1,000 Households
United States (1987)	8.9%	3,530	39.4
West Germany (1987)	2.7	69	2.7
Japan (1988)	9.4	152	4.1

Sources: AHS 1987 and StAb 1991; StJB 1988; JKDS 1990.
Note: The Japanese vacancy rate includes vacant second homes and unusable units.

tive to the number of households. In the United States, this market is almost fifteen times larger than in Germany and about ten times larger than in Japan. While it is very common in the United States to buy a used home, little more than 20 percent of homeowners do this in Germany. Most German first-home buyers move into new custom-built houses.

In summary, Germany has a relatively small market of newly built houses, a very thin second-hand market of single-family homes, and a thin rental segment since the vacancy rate is dominated by the rental sector. In this respect, it is very different from both Japan and the United States. Of course, this difference is mirrored in the low mobility rate.

5.1.6   Housing Prices

To conclude this *tour d'horizon* on U.S., German, and Japanese housing markets, table 5.11 presents housing prices in relation to income. At a first and superficial glance (columns 1 and 2), housing affordability does not seem to differ much across the three countries. However, this picture is deceiving. For one, the differences in metropolitan areas are much larger. Kanemoto (1992) reports that housing prices in Tokyo and Osaka are about twice as large as in New York and Los Angeles. Moreover, table 5.11 reports *expenditures* not corrected for differences in dwelling size and quality. They therefore say little about housing *prices*. In fact, as shown above, Japanese houses are much smaller than U.S. and German ones. I therefore calculate the price per square meter in relation to annual household income (column 3). Measured this way, housing is on average more than twice as expensive in Japan and Germany as in the United States.

A more careful computation for metropolitan areas in the United States and West Germany is presented by Börsch-Supan (1985) and is based on quality corrections by hedonic regressions for 1978.[6] Quality-corrected structure costs were about 80 percent higher in German cities than in U.S. Standard Metropolitan Statistical Areas (SMSAs). The main factor, however, is the 4.5-fold higher average price of land in German cities leading to a 40 percent share of land in total house values. The higher prices result in about 30 percent less consumption of housing (measured as a hedonic index composed of space and other housing quality attributes) and more than 40 percent less consumption of land.[7]

Table 5.12 provides a rough calculation of average land price and its changes over time in relation to income. Land values were computed from national accounting data and refer to arable land. Arable land is a small proportion of land in Japan, a much larger proportion in the United States, and virtually all land in Germany. It is also noteworthy that Japanese land values are dominated by the Tokyo area, while U.S. land values include substantial quantities of agricultural land.

Two observations stand out in table 5.12. First, Japan experienced a dramatic increase in land prices that was unparalleled in the United States and Germany. Second, arable land prices in 1988 are more than ten-fold in Germany and more than two hundred–fold in Japan in comparison to the United States. The stark contrast between the scarcity of land in Japan and central Europe and the abundance of land in North America is one of the basic facts that shape the housing markets in the three countries.

---

6. Based on the *American Housing Survey* (AHS) and the *Wohnungsstichprobe* (Housing Census) in 1978. Since then, Germany has not collected data on housing quality and household characteristics comparable to the AHS.

7. Average lot size in the United States is 1,578 m², in Germany only 922 m².

Table 5.11   **Housing Expenditures and Affordability of New Housing**

	Housing Expenditure Share	New-House Price Divided by Annual income	Price per m² Divided by Annual Income
United States (1987)	19.6%	3.4	0.023
West Germany (1986)	21.1	4.6	0.053
Japan (1989)	18.6	4.4	0.058

Sources: StAB 1991; StJB 1988; JKDS 1990; Kanemoto 1992; author's calculations.

Table 5.12   **Land Prices**

	Land Value per Arable km² / GNP per Capita				
	1970	1975	1980	1985	1988
United States	0.3	0.3	0.5	0.4	0.4
West Germany	5.7	6.3	5.6	5.1	5.5
Japan	49.5	56.2	65.2	69.7	110.1

Sources: Author's calculations based on Boone and Sachs 1989. For size of arable land: Kanemoto 1992, 667.

5.2   Housing Policies in the United States, Germany, and Japan

The discussion in the preceding section shows that the differences in housing consumption among the three countries are to some degree explainable by the relative scarcity of land in Japan and Germany, resulting in high land prices and substitution toward smaller dwelling sizes in comparison to the United States. One might be tempted to attribute the difference in the proportion of owner-occupied (and mostly single-family) homes between Germany and the United States to the same mechanism—if it were not for the large proportion of owner-occupied houses in Japan. Similarly, the striking differences in mobility and vacancy rates rates do not fit into such a simple explanation.

My main claim in this paper is that many differences are, to a large degree, generated by housing policies, particularly by homeownership subsidies and rental housing regulations. To this end, this section provides a brief description of the main housing policy programs in effect in the three countries since the midseventies.[8] Each subsection concludes with a short evaluation in terms of social protection and economic flexibility, and appendix B provides a summary of the programs.

8. Since housing choices are long-term decisions, it is important to look at the recent past as well as the current policy environment.

5.2.1   Public and Social Housing

The very first program to protect low-income households in terms of housing needs in the *United States* was the public housing program enacted in 1937. The public housing program was massive in the 1960s (the stock almost doubled from 593,000 units in 1960 to 1.1 million units ten years later) but has lost its importance since then. It never provided state-supplied housing for more than a small proportion of households. In 1960, 1.12 percent of all housing units were public housing, 1.82 percent ten years later at its peak, 1.64 percent in 1980, and only 1.41 percent in 1988.

As shown in table 5.8, Germany and Japan have considerably larger proportions of public and nonprofit housing. The associated programs, however, are very different from the U.S. public housing program.

German "social housing" is provided for by private nonprofit organizations that effectively operate under a rate-of-return constraint. Social housing is means-tested, but this test is applied only when households move into the unit. A large proportion of social housing is, in fact, used by households who have advanced into the middle class since their move. Moreover, unlike the concentrated multiunit public housing buildings in the United States, social housing in Germany is scattered throughout the community and is frequently located in small buildings.

In *Japan,* about a third of the public housing is not means-tested at all. Even in the most stringent means-tested "type 2 public housing," the annual income limit is $15,000.[9]

The problems of the U.S. public housing program are well-known. It is a textbook example (e.g., Mills and Hamilton 1984) of a policy failure because it failed to provided adequate housing and at the same time hindered economic flexibility. It turned out an economic failure because it was too expensive per housing unit provided—an advantage only to the construction industry. And it was a social failure because it accelerated the formation of ghettos and fostered discrimination. The German social housing program shares the problems of high supply costs (Barnbrook and Mayo 1985). It does, however, provide decent housing for low-income families—actually, sufficiently decent to attract many middle-class misusers of the program.

5.2.2   Rental Housing Subsidies

Private rental housing is indirectly subsidized in the three countries, primarily by subsidies to the construction of new multifamily homes and by accelerated depreciation schedules. In all three countries, expenses related to the provision of rental housing (including mortgage interest and depreciation) are deducted from rental income. Moreover, these expenses can often be used to

---

9. Precisely, 4,287,999 yen for type 1 and 3,359,999 yen for type 2 public rental housing (Kanemoto 1992).

offset income other than rental income. This mechanism is regarded as the most important subsidy toward rental housing and provides a scheme to arbitrage income taxes between renters with low marginal tax rates and landlords with high marginal tax rates.[10] Poterba (1984) provides a theoretical model of tenure selection along these lines.

Currently, the tax incentives for rental housing are not symmetric to those for owner-occupancy (see section 5.2.4). They are actually substantially lower. In the *United States,* the accelerated depreciation schedule for rental housing was abolished in the 1986 Tax Reform Act.[11] Moreover, capital gains on rented property are taxed in the United States, while owner-occupiers enjoy rollover provisions; and the transferability of tax losses to other income sources has been limited in the United States. Higher subsidies apply when housing is supplied to low-income families who were granted so-called Section 8 certificates.[12]

In *Germany,* owner-occupiers can use faster depreciation schedules than owners of rental property (although both are accelerated).[13] There is no capital gains tax unless real estate is sold within two years after purchase. Real estate losses can be used to offset other income without limitation. Similar to the U.S. Section 8 programs, higher subsidies apply if apartments are rented to low-income households.

Germany, unlike Japan and the United States, has adopted a direct subsidy of rental housing consumption in form of housing allowances (*Wohngeld*).[14] German housing allowances are fairly widespread entitlements. They cover about 11 percent of all renters (StJB 1990). About a third of all recipients are pensioners. The subsidy depends on the rent paid, income, and family size, similar to the housing gap formula applied in the U.S. Experimental Housing Allowances Program. The subsidy is rather deep: the average subsidy accounts for 33.2 percent of total rental expenditures.

It is important to note that although the amount of housing allowances granted is tied to the actual rent, housing allowances are paid as cash transfers to the household, not to the landlord. Therefore, two essential differences stand out in comparison with the rental subsidies in the United States. First, German housing allowances are entitlements, as opposed to the U.S. Section 8 certifi-

10. Rosen (1992, 436). Whether this is regarded as a subsidy depends on how comprehensive an income definition one applies.
11. Poterba (1992) provides an updated analysis of the effects of the 1986 Tax Reform Act on housing investment.
12. CBO (1988) provides a synopsis of the many programs that are and were in effect. The variants of the Section 8 program account for 71 percent of all rental housing subsidies.
13. However, Germany recently has introduced an emergency housing program with an accelerated depreciation schedule for newly built rental housing.
14. A large number of Japanese employers pay housing allowances. However, there is no tax incentive involved, as they constitute taxable income for the worker and are treated like wages for the firm. Employers pay nontaxable commuting allowances that are substantial. Their effect on housing consumption in terms of tenure and size is only indirect.

cates, which are rationed. Second, housing allowances are cash income, while most of the Section 8 certificates are in kind.[15]

In terms of social protection, the German housing allowances system has succeeded in preventing low-income families from living in lower than standard quality houses. Welfare recipients are able to cover their rent almost completely by housing allowances. This is unlike the United States, where the Congressional Budget Office classifies 36 percent of low-income households as having affordability problems and 14 percent as living in substandard housing (CBO 1988).

Because the German housing allowances are like cash income, distortions to consumption choices are small, at least in comparison to in-kind transfers. Moreover, discrimination is less of an issue, because housing allowances are granted to a large income segment and recipients do not have to reveal their status. In this respect, economic flexibility—interpreted here as noninterference in consumer and supplier choices—does not appear to be tangibly hampered by the German housing allowances program.

5.2.3   Rental Housing Market Regulations

There is no general tenants' legislation in the *United States*. Rent and eviction control legislation is at the discretion of the state or municipal level of jurisdiction. Some states and municipalities have enacted rather strict rent and eviction controls (most prominently New York), but most states and municipalities have none.

In addition to direct and indirect subsidies, Germany and Japan also regulate the rental housing market by tenants' protection legislations. In *Germany,* this legislation consists of two provisions. First, the law prohibits eviction of tenants aside from exceptional circumstances such as refusal to pay rent. Second, rent increases are limited by the average rent increase in the community. In addition, they are capped at 30 percent in three years. However, the initial rent level is unregulated. (More detail is provided in section 5.3.)

Japan has a more informal, but de facto even stricter rent and eviction control than Germany has.[16] Rental contracts are shielded by a special law from the general liberty of contract provisions in the Japanese civil law. This implies that a landlord must go to court and prove a "just cause" to change the contract (e.g., to increase the rent or to evict the tenant). In determining a just cause, the court compares the "need" of the tenant with that of the landlord. Obviously, few landlords are needier than their tenants. This clause therefore applies essentially only to tenants not paying rent. For land the law specifies a

15. The new Section 8 program allows renters to keep the difference between maximum eligible subsidy and actual rent. About 32 percent of Section 8 certificates are subject to this program variant.

16. The law was liberalized in 1991. Except for the possibility of legal temporary leases in the case of temporary job transfers (including sabbaticals), the "liberation" appears rather marginal. See Kanemoto (1991).

thirty-year contract period, none for housing. Specifying a short contract period, even if agreed to by both parties, is deemed ineffective. This leads to the absurd situation that there is no guarantee that a landlord can return to the unit after a temporary rental (e.g., during a sabbatical).

The rent control part of the Japanese tenants' protection legislation is similar to the German one. Initial rents are determined freely between owner and tenant, but rent increases thereafter must go through court, which is time consuming and costly. As in clauses specifying contract periods, the court may deem invalid all provisions in the contract that specify rent increases, even if both parties have originally agreed on such clauses.

Although there are many similarities between the Japanese and the German tenants' protection legislation, there is a crucial difference that renders the Japanese legislation much stricter. The burden of proof is on the tenant's side in Germany, while in Japan the landlord has to go to court.

It appears obvious that the stringent German and Japanese tenants' protection laws impede economic flexibility. Many Japanese authors claim that the Japanese tenants' protection legislation is the main cause for the scarcity of rental housing in Japan (Kanemoto 1992). In Germany, however, the balance between rental and owner-occupied housing is reversed. Thus, the claim of limited economic flexibility is less convincing. Whether tenants' protection laws achieve social protection is also not clear. Protection from arbitrary eviction may come at high rent levels and depressed supply, consequences of impeded economic flexibility. Section 5.3 will therefore provide an extended analysis of the effectiveness of tenants' protection legislation in Germany and the United States by comparing municipalities with and without rent control.[17]

5.2.4 Homeownership Subsidies

In spite of the many subsidies and regulations in the rental segment of the housing market, the major impact of housing policies from a U.S. perspective is actually in the owner-occupied market segment. In the *United States,* mortgage interest for home and land can be deducted from personal income taxes. The associated tax losses are ten times as large as all rental subsidies, including the public housing program. In *Germany,* accelerated accounting depreciation of the building can be deducted from personal income taxes, and a substantial tax credit is given to families with children who build new owner-occupied homes. In addition, savings toward down payments are subsidized. *Japan* subsidizes housing primarily by low-interest loans. The rationing rules favor people who buy a new house for themselves or build their own new house. In addition, Japan has a small tax credit for owner-occupancy. Imputed rental income escapes taxation in all three countries. Capital gains of owner-occupancy are not taxed in Germany and remain effectively tax free in the United States.

17. Unfortunately, there are no good microdata to extend this analysis to Japan.

More details of the applicable homeownership subsidies are provided in section 5.4. They were substantially higher in the United States than in Germany, although this difference has decreased due to recent changes in the tax laws. Due to the progressive tax structure, homeownership subsidies generally favor the middle class and the rich. Whether they also socially protect the poor depends on the highly controversial filtering effect. Because homeownership subsidies substantially exceed the subsidies toward rental housing, they are tilting the tenure choice toward owner-occupancy, which does not clearly hinder economic flexibility. By smoothing housing consumption over the business cycle, the subsidies may actually foster economic flexibility. Section 5.4 provides a more extended analysis.

5.2.5   Owner-Occupied Housing Market Regulations

Many regulations constrain consumption choices also in the owner-occupied housing market segment. Land use regulations, building codes, and zoning rules are interesting subjects for an investigation of the balance between social protection and economic flexibility but are beyond the scope of this paper (e.g., see Börsch-Supan, Kanemoto, and Stahl 1992).

Worth pointing out, however, are the very high transaction taxes accompanying a real estate sale in Japan. Three types of taxes are due: a real estate acquisition tax, a registration tax, and a stamp duty. For used houses, these taxes amount to between 8 and 10 percent of assessed values, which in turn are reconstruction costs minus a generous allowance for depreciation; the total is about 2 percent for newly constructed houses.[18] The effect of these transaction taxes on economic flexibility is clearly visible in table 5.10. Japan has only about 10 percent of the existing-home sales in the United States relative to the number of households.

Note that Germany has even less of a second-hand market than Japan. However, neither Germany nor the United States has substantial transaction taxes. As with the homeownership rates, one explanation alone does not explain all country-specific phenomena in these international comparisons.

5.3   Effects of Tenants' Protection Legislation

Tenants' protection legislation—the combination of rent controls and prohibition of eviction—is an intervention that quite prominently exemplifies the tension between social protection and economic flexibility.

Proponents of social protection claim that the legislation shields helpless tenants from exploitation and arbitrary eviction. They argue that it is necessary

---

18. The real estate acquisition tax is 3 percent for residential land and structures. The registration tax is 5 percent, and the stamp duty is 60,000 yen for the median-valued house (Kanemoto 1992).

to counterbalance the weak position of a tenant in a seller's market with a regulate pricing scheme. Specifically, proponents claim that without price regulation a landlord can exploit the exit barriers of high moving costs, thus gaining local monopoly power with the opportunity to raise rents. Proponents of the legislation also argue that the legislation would restrict or eliminate arbitrary and discriminatory eviction, which inflicts high moving costs on the tenants.

In terms of economic flexibility, on the other hand, opponents of tenants' protection legislation argue that crucial property rights—the right to evict an unpleasant tenant—are only given up against compensation for the money value of those rights. This would result in higher rents and depressed supply, which they claim will ultimately reduce tenants' utility. Opponents of the legislation also claim that it deters mobility and therefore creates housing market inflexibility in times of economic and demographic changes.

The aim of this section is an assessment of the positive and normative effects of tenants' protection legislation. I will first describe the German tenants' protection legislation and discuss its potential impacts on rent schedules, housing supply, and welfare. I will then exploit the diversity of U.S. rent and eviction regulations to evaluate the actual impact.

5.3.1 The German Tenants' Protection Legislation

In Germany, the *Wohnraumkündigungsschutzgesetz* (Law for the Protection of Tenants from Arbitrary Eviction) governs rental contracts. Versions of this law have been in effect since 1971. The law was strengthened in 1975, then weakened in 1983 and again in 1987, when short-term leases and prearranged rent changes were permitted. The law consists of two provisions. First, eviction is prohibited except under three conditions. Eviction is permitted (1) if the tenant severely breaches the contract (e.g., does not pay the rent); (2) if the landlord or a close relative wants to move into the unit and has a just cause for doing so; or (3) if the landlord is severely inhibited in the appropriate economic usage of his property (e.g., conversion into office space in areas assigned by zoning laws as a business district). The courts have been very restrictive on the two latter clauses and rarely permit such evictions.

The rent is not regulated when a new tenant moves in (usury is prohibited by general law). However, the second provision of the law indexes the rent for the sitting tenant. This rent regulation permits the landlord to pass on only cost increases, the annuitized value of upgrading and modernization expenses, and some part of general housing appreciation. Any rent increase is subject to the following procedure: The landlord has to quote the rent of three comparable units in the neighborhood. The landlord can then raise the rent up to the average rent of these units unless the rent increase exceeds 20 percent (nominally) within the last three years (30 percent before 1987). This procedure is time consuming, particularly if the tenant appeals (e.g., because the tenant has detected a cheaper comparable unit in the neighborhood). Therefore, the rent level for sitting tenants is effectively the lagged rent of comparable newly rented units (assuming a steady nominal rent increase).

5.3.2   Effects: Theory

There has been a long debate about the effects of rent and eviction control (e.g., the surveys of Olsen [1972, 1987]). Clearly, in a perfect neoclassical market any kind of restriction of property rights interferes with the pareto efficient market equilibrium. Hence, there is always a transfer scheme that could offset potential losses by renters and make both tenants and landlords better off if such controls were abandoned. This is the basic argument of the opponents of tenants' protection legislation.

In the case of the German (and the Japanese) legislation, which features free initial rents, this line of reasoning needs sophistication. Eekhoff (1981) shows that the primary effect of introducing this price regulation is a heavily frontloaded payment schedule, depicted in figure 5.1, which keeps profits at the prelegislation level. Losses (area B in fig. 5.1) in the second phase of the lease are compensated for by profits (area A) from the high initial rent in the first phase. The resulting actual rent profile is indicated by the bold horizontal line.

The argument made most frequently by opponents of tenants' protection legislation—namely, that the landlord's reduced profit expectations will reduce supply, raise initial rents, and thus make tenants and landlords worse off—is

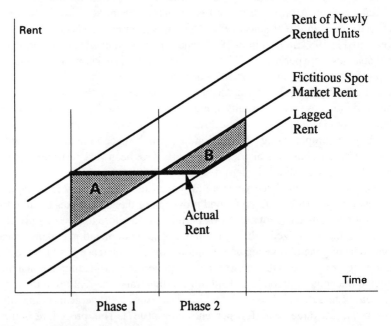

Fig. 5.1   Effect of price regulation
Source: Adapted from Eeckhoff 1981.

therefore incorrect in a perfect neoclassical environment. It is incorrect because initial rents can always be set sufficiently high to equilibrate the losses (are B in fig. 5.1) and the profits (area A). The legislation changes the timing of the rent streams but not their present discounted value. Hence, at least for perfectly anticipated length of tenure and perfect capital markets, there will be no effect on the landlords' profits or the tenant's utility.

The argument may, however, work in an imperfect rental housing market. Eekhoff (1981) points out that only the risk-neutral landlord is able to diversify the risk of having a tenant excessively enjoying his indexed rent in the second phase of his tenure. A risk-averse landlord, however, will charge a premium for this risk, resulting in even higher initial rents, which will reduce the tenant's utility.

Eckart (1983) presents another handle that makes the argument against tenants' protection work. The presence of liquidity constraints creates an intertemporal distortion because the tenant will be restricted in his or her housing consumption by the large initial rent. Eckart shows that under the assumption of either an expectation of increasing real rents or a perfectly elastic supply, the tenants' utility will indeed be reduced. However, Eckart also gives conditions under which this distortion actually increases the tenant's utility, contrary to the common belief and the assertions in Eekhoff (1981).

These arguments show that an assessment of the welfare effects of rent and eviction control is complicated and potentially ambiguous in a second-best world. In a highly stylized rental housing market model (Börsch-Supan 1986), I combine several second-best features with the main ingredients of the German tenants' protection legislation. These features include heterogeneity of landlords and tenants, and incomplete and asymmetric information. More precisely, tenants and landlords may belong to different types who do not like each other but cannot determine at the time of contract whether they match. Moreover, tenants and landlords cannot specify contracts that are contingent on a match or mismatch because this is subjective and cannot be verified in court. Nor can tenants and landlords form contracts that are binding for both sides because this is considered unethical in the court.[19]

The main result of this model is that tenants' protection legislation may or may not be pareto improving, depending on the balance between the mobility costs to the tenant who is evicted and the costs of a bad tenant to the landlord who is prohibited from evicting. If psychic and monetary moving costs inflicted on the evicted tenant are high, tenants' protection legislation is pareto improving. However, if the psychic and monetary costs inflicted on the landlord who is forced to keep a costly or unpleasant tenant are high, tenants' protection legislation reduces welfare.

---

19. In fact, tenants may always breach a rental contract as long as they provide a successor tenant. The lack of binding contracts is the crucial market failure in this model (see Schwager 1991).

In conclusion, theory alone cannot determine whether the German-type rent and eviction control is indeed a social protection of tenants against their landlords' greed or, in turn, whether rent and eviction control is an obstacle to the invisible hand that would otherwise achieve efficiency.

5.3.2   Effects: Evidence in West Germany

One implication of an effective German-type rent and eviction control is the growing gap between spot market rents and rents of sitting tenants, depicted in figure 5.1. In the absence of rent and eviction controls, landlords may increase the rent of sitting tenants because they can exploit their local monopoly power. I will therefore construct an empirical test of the efficacy of rent and eviction control, based on the relation between rent levels of sitting tenants and their length of tenure. The test consists in relating the rent differential between new and sitting tenants to the existence of rent and eviction control. If these controls were effective, the rent differential should be large in comparison to areas without rent and eviction control.

The gap between spot market rents and rents of sitting tenants—commonly termed tenure discount—can be estimated from long panel data or from cross-sectional data. In cross-sectional data this is measured as the difference in rent paid for comparable units by households that moved in at different times. Units are kept comparable by controlling for housing quality and neighborhood characteristics as well as tenants' and landlords' characteristics by applying hedonic regression techniques. A function of the form $R = f(t; X)$ is estimated in which the observed rent R depends on the length of tenure t, holding the vector X of housing quality, neighborhood, tenant, and landlord characteristics constant. Behring, Börsch-Supan, and Goldrian (1988) estimate a nonlinear rent profile for sitting tenants relative to the spot market rent level, based on 1 percent of West German households in 1978. The results, stratified by degree of urbanization, are displayed in table 5.13.

After one year of tenure, tenants pay 2 percent less rent than new tenants in comparable units. The discounts then increase quickly in the first five years of tenure, until they level off for very long lengths of tenure. They are essentially

Table 5.13   **Tenure Discounts in West Germany**

Length of Tenure (years)	High-Density Metropolitan Areas			Low-Density Urban Areas		Rural Areas
	Center	Suburbs	Environs	Center	Suburbs	
1	2%	2%	2%	2%	2%	2%
5	8	9	11	10	10	10
10	13	15	20	16	19	17
14 and more	19	25	27	19	25	26

Source: Behring, Börsch-Supan, and Goldrian 1988.

flat after a tenure of fourteen years and amount to more than a quarter of the rent a new tenant would pay.

The regression suffers from selectivity bias since high-rent contracts are more likely to be terminated than low-rent contracts. In order to perform a Heckman-type correction, data from at least two cross sections are required. Unfortunately no comparable German data set in a second year is available. Using U.S. data, Guasch and Marshall (1983) were able to perform such a selectivity correction. Their evidence, however, is inconclusive. Judging from their results, it appears most likely that positive, possibly smaller, tenure discounts would remain after a correction in the German data.[20]

The German tenants' protection legislation seems to be perfectly reflected in German rent profiles. However, this analysis suffers from the missing counterfactual. This counterfactual can only be provided by housing markets without tenants' protection legislation.

5.3.3   Rent Control in the United States

As opposed to Germany and Japan, there is no general tenants' legislation in the United States. Rent and eviction control legislation is at the discretion of the state or municipality. Some states and municipalities in the United States have enacted rather strict rent and eviction controls, but most have none and therefore do provide the counterfactual mentioned above.

Information about the presence of controls in the Standard Metropolitan Statistical Areas (SMSAs) of the United States during the years 1974–77 was collected by Baird (1980), Thibodeau (1981), and the National Multi-Housing Council (1982).

Since eviction and rent control laws vary a great deal across municipalities, I do not describe them in detail here. A rather comprehensive list can be found in the publications of the National Multi-Housing Council.

From this information, I construct two measures to assess whether the rental housing market in a specific SMSA was influenced by rent or eviction control. The stricter measure includes all SMSAs in which rent and eviction control was *in effect* in at least one jurisdiction; the weaker measure also includes SMSAs in which rent and eviction control was *pending*. Pending means that state legislation had been enacted so that municipalities could easily introduce rent and eviction control. Also included in this category are SMSAs in which rent control was a hot political issue or was rejected only by a small margin in the municipal government. The idea of this second category is to include all SMSAs in which landlords effectively faced or at least perceived an incentive to restrain themselves when pondering rent increases or eviction.

---

20. Ideally, one should analyze rent profiles over time for a given unit. This kind of panel data is not available. While the *American Housing Survey* provides geographic and structural information, units cannot be linked over time. In turn, panels such as the U.S. PSID and the German SOEP do not have sufficient structural information and do not disclose the municipality. Hence, I cannot test the interesting hypothesis that in areas with rent control larger tenure discounts will occur over time in the presence of (unexpected) housing price increases.

5.3.4   Effects: Evidence in the United States

Using the same methodology as in Germany, I employ estimated tenure discounts for fifty-nine Standard Metropolitan Statistical Areas based on hedonic regressions performed by Malpezzi, Ozanne, and Thibodeau (1980).[21] The rent profiles are based on the *Annual Housing Surveys* 1974–77 and were computed from the same cross-sectional hedonic specification as those by Behring, Börsch-Supan, and Goldrian for West Germany. The fifty-nine SMSAs are then categorized by their rent control legislation according to the two measures described in section 5.3.3.

Table 5.14 presents the results for a ten-year tenure length. The estimated shape is the same as in Germany: The percentage discounts increase quickly in the first five years of tenure, then level off and are essentially flat after twelve–fifteen years. As stated earlier, the percentages test the hypothesis that at long tenures rental prices will be lower in areas with rent and eviction control. The result, however, is astounding. Large and significant tenure discounts are also present in metropolitan areas in the United States in which rent and eviction control has never been in effect and which exemplify the spirit of free enterprise, such as Phoenix, Arizona. Average and median tenure discounts are highest where rent and eviction control is pending, but they are lowest where rent and eviction control is in effect. The difference between SMSAs completely with and without rent control is not statistically significant. Figure 5.2 plots the distribution of tenure discounts. The scatter plots for SMSAs with enacted and without any rent control are very similar. Moreover, a regression of the city-specific tenure discounts controlling for the number of housing units per capita, new construction per capita, net immigration rate, per capita income, and unemployment rate shows a significant effect of pending controls but cannot reject the hypothesis that tenure discounts are unaffected by rent and eviction control actually in place (see table 5.15).

These numbers do not provide convincing evidence that tenants' protection is a major explanation of tenure discounts. We have to accept them as a universal and independent phenomenon of rental housing markets. On average, landlords give discounts for a sitting tenant rather than exploit their monopoly power in order to extract the value of moving costs. To be precise, the result says that, whatever their causes, discounts cannot significantly be associated with rent and eviction control.

The theoretical analysis in Börsch-Supan (1986) provides a motivation for tenure discounts in an unregulated rental housing market: Landlords pay premiums to keep pleasant tenants from moving, because their move incurs a positive probability of drawing an unpleasant tenant.

---

21. Follain and Malpezzi (1980) and Goodman and Kawai (1982) estimate tenure discounts as a linear function of the length of tenure and arrive at much lower estimates. Due to the linearity, the estimates of Follain and Malpezzi tend to be biased downward, whereas the specification by Malpezzi, Ozanne, and Thibodeau (1980) suggests an upward bias due to the colinearity with their age-of-dwelling variable. Barnett (1979), Noland (1980), and Lowry (1981) reproduce estimates almost identical to the nonlinear specification of table 5.14.

Table 5.14   **Tenure Discounts and Rent Control in the United States, 1974–1977**

SMSAs without Enacted or Pending Rent and Eviction Control		SMSAs with Pending Rent and Eviction Control	
SMSA	Discount after 10 Years	SMSA	Discount after 10 Years
Minneapolis, MN	13.3%	Rochester, NY	22.6%
Dallas, TX	13.5	Anaheim, CA	25.0
Madison, WI	14.1	Springfield, MA	26.3
Las Vegas, NV	14.4	San Bernardino, CA	28.9
Cleveland, OH	16.7	San Diego, CA	29.5
Chicago, IL	17.9	Buffalo, NY	31.2
Omaha, NE	17.9	Honolulu, HI	33.7
Colorado Springs, CO	18.1	Providence, RI	34.3
St. Louis, MO	18.2	Albany, NY	36.4
Memphis, TN	18.4	Mean	29.8%
Indianapolis, IN	18.5	Median	29.5
Fort Worth, TX	18.6	Standard deviation	1.53
Hartford, CT	18.8		
Atlanta, GA	21.3		
Kansas City, KS/MO	22.0		
Portland, OR	22.0		
San Antonio, TX	22.3		
Phoenix, AZ	22.5		
Birmingham, AL	23.2		
Tacoma, WA	23.5		
Milwaukee, WI	23.7		
Newport News, VA	23.8		
New Orleans, LA	24.1		
Seattle, WA	24.2	SMSAs with Enacted	
Philadelphia, PA	24.4	Rent and Eviction Control	
Raleigh, NC	24.6		
Louisville, KY	25.1	SMSA	Discount after 10 Years
Columbus, OH	25.3		
Detroit, MI	25.5		
Orlando, FL	25.5		
Wichita, KS	26.3	Miami, FL	13.7%
Denver, CO	26.6	Washington, DC	18.6
Oklahoma City, OK	26.9	Newark, NJ	18.9
Cincinnati, OH	27.2	Los Angeles, CA	19.0
Grand Rapids, MI	28.6	Paterson, NJ	19.8
Houston, TX	30.8	Sacramento, CA	19.9
Salt Lake City, UT	31.0	Baltimore, MD	21.1
Allentown, PA	32.4	San Francisco, CA	22.2
Pittsburgh, PA	33.0	Boston, MA	30.2
Spokane, WA	34.2	New York, NY	31.0
Mean	23.0%	Mean	21.4%
Median	23.6	Median	19.9
Standard deviation	1.68	Standard deviation	0.85

Note: Standard deviation denotes standard deviation of the mean.

Source: Author's computations (see text).

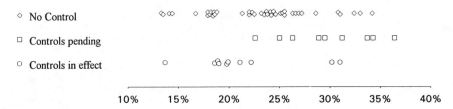

Fig. 5.2   **Tenure discounts after 10 years in 59 U.S. SMSAs**
Source: Author's computations.

Table 5.15   **Determinants of Tenure Discounts in the United States**

	Dependent Variable: Discount	
Independent Variable	Estimated Coefficient	*t-*Statistic
Constant	38.10	3.11
Controls in effect	1.07	0.50
Controls pending	6.08	2.86
Housing stock per capita	18.08	0.46
Permits per capita	−66.68	−0.52
Net migration per capita	0.0335	0.20
Average household income	−0.00443	−2.58
Unemployment rate	0.326	0.49
Number of observations		58
R-squared		0.254
Standard error of the regression		5.348
Durbin-Watson statistic		1.746

Source: Author's calculations.
Note: Ordinary least squares.

The lack of differences between SMSAs with and without controls does not exclude the existence of a minority of landlords who do not grant tenure discounts but rather exploit their local monopoly. In this sense, tenants' protection legislation provides social protection as an insurance for the tenant who does not know *a priori* which type of landlord is offering the lease.

Has rent and eviction control hindered economic flexibility? We have two yardsticks by which to measure economic flexibility in this respect. First, we look at whether mobility is suppressed by an effective rent and eviction control. Second, we investigate how the supply of rental housing reacts to differences in the stringency of the tenants' protection legislation.

The cross-national evidence and time series evidence on mobility rates contradict each other. As depicted in table 5.7, mobility rates are much lower in Germany and Japan than in the United States. This matches with the stringency

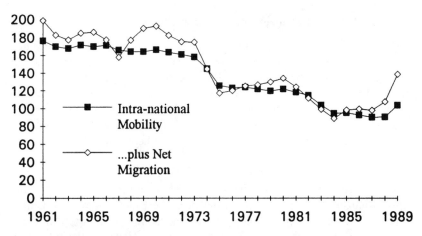

Fig. 5.3   German mobility rates (per thousand households)
Source: StJB, various years.

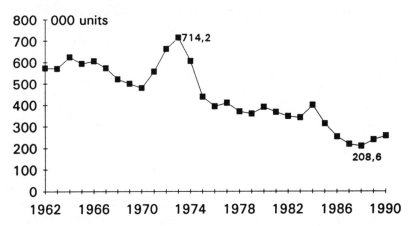

Fig. 5.4   New construction in Germany (thousands of units)
Source: StBA (FS-5.1).

of the tenants' protection legislation in these countries. However, German time series data display no reaction in mobility rates when the law was introduced in 1971 and no response to the liberalization of the tenants' protection legislation after the change of government in 1983 and after the change in the law in 1987 (fig. 5.3). Rather, mobility rates continued their secular decline. Similarly, the supply of newly constructed rental housing buildings was unaffected by changes in the law (fig. 5.4). Weighing the cross-national against the time series evidence, I conclude that the case against tenants' protection rests on weak empirical grounds.

5.4   The Effects of Homeownership Subsidies

One might wonder why a section on homeownership subsidies belongs in a paper on social protection and economic flexibility. As already mentioned in section 5.2.4, homeownership subsidies protect mainly the incomes of those households who have sufficiently high marginal tax rates to actually be able to apply the tax advantages. However, because the homeownership subsidies are quantitatively so important and because it is claimed that they, although indirectly, also help the poor, it is imperative to study them in more detail.

5.4.1   Homeownership Subsidies in the United States

The reduction in the personal income tax liability for owner-occupiers is the most prominent housing policy instrument in the United States. The United States subsidizes owner-occupancy by the deduction of mortgage interest. There is no upper limit on the deductible amount. However, the subsidy is effective only when deductions are itemized, wiping out this subsidy for low-income families. On the other end of the income distribution, the value of this subsidy is marginally reduced by the itemized-deduction phaseout.[22]

In addition, imputed rental income is not taxed, while property taxes can be deducted from personal income taxes. Property taxes can be substantial in the United States, even after deduction from the federal personal income tax. Nominal property tax rates range from 0.0 to 6.0 percent. They are at the discretion of the municipalities but, in some states, are capped by upper limits set by the state legislation. Because of generous rollover provisions, housing appreciation effectively escapes the U.S. capital gains taxation.

5.4.2   Homeownership Subsidies in Germany

In Germany the main mechanism for subsidizing homeownership is an accelerated depreciation allowance that can be deducted from federal income taxes.[23] The accelerated depreciation schedule provides, for eight years, a deduction of 5 percent of structure costs below $150,000.[24] It is applicable only to owner-occupied homes. Each individual can use this schedule only once in his or her life. Once the eight years are over, no further depreciation allowance is granted. It is important to note that this tax write-off depends on the value of the structure but not on the value of the land and that it is independent of the loan-to-value ratio. This changes the optimal capital-to-land ratio and tilts the symmetry between borrowing and lending.

Mortgage interest is deductible for rented buildings but generally not for owner-occupied homes. From time to time, however, when the government

---

22. This phaseout eliminates up to 20 percent of the deductions.

23. There are three basic depreciation schedules in Germany: an "accelerated schedule" with a cap on time and value, a "degressive schedule" applicable only to new structures, and the omnibus linear depreciation schedule. The first one is not applicable for rented property.

24. The temporary emergency housing act increased this percentage to 6 for the first four years.

feels that housing construction needs more encouragement, the government introduces temporary mortgage interest deduction programs. At the end of 1991, for example, the German government announced that for a limited time (until repeal) it will be possible to deduct up to $5,500 annually of mortgage interest payments during the first three years of a newly constructed building. A similar program was in effect from 1983 through 1987.

Families with children enjoy another important tax advantage if they build a house: an accelerated depreciation deduction. For each child, the deduction is raised for eight years.

The imputed rent of owner-occupancy is not taxed in Germany. German property tax is a minor tax, due to both low assessed values and low rates. Finally, capital income through capital gains is tax free unless the house is sold within two years of purchase.

Another loophole in German tax law that was closed in 1983 is worth mentioning because it shows how owner-occupiers react to the special features of the tax law. Until 1983, mortgage interest could be deducted in addition to the accelerated depreciation allowances plus all maintenance expenses in houses with two dwelling units. This included also those two-unit houses that had one unit owner-occupied and the other unit "rented" to a family member without actual money ever flowing. Not too surprisingly, this "fake two-family house" was very popular until the loophole was closed (in 1977 it constituted 17.3 percent of all buildings, about 40 percent of all one- and two-unit owner-occupied houses).

Finally, savings for the down payment were subsidized by a special incentive program when they were funneled into building societies.[25] Until recently, this subsidy was both deep and widespread. About 50 percent of all households had a building society savings account, and the subsidy reached 33 percent of annual savings.[26] In 1990 this program was severely reduced. The maximum subsidy rate is now 10 percent.

5.4.3 Homeownership Subsidies in Japan

Japan subsidizes housing primarily by low-interest loans. The rationing rules favor people who buy a new house for themselves or build their own new house. There are upper limits for these loans, and it is usually necessary to complement them with commercial loans. Eligibility is also dependent on income, house price, and floor space. For incomes below $53,000, the subsidy amounts to an interest reduction of about 2 percent; for higher income households the reduction is about 1.5 percent. About 53 percent of all newly constructed houses received some form of public interest subsidy.

Neither mortgage interest nor depreciation is deductible from the Japanese federal income tax. There is, however, a small, newly introduced tax credit for

---

25. See Börsch-Supan and Stahl (1991) for a detailed description and analysis.
26. For a median-income family with three children saving DM 936 annually.

owner-occupancy, currently 1 percent of the remaining balance of the mortgage, up to about $1,000 annually for the first six years after purchasing a house.

Imputed rental income of owner-occupancy is not taxed in Japan. In most Japanese municipalities, the nominal property tax rate is 1.4 percent, and only 3.5 percent of the Japanese municipalities have property tax rates between 1.4 and 2.1 percent of assessed values. However, assessed values are low, and both residential land and newly constructed buildings (up to three years old) are subject to substantially reduced rates. On average, Japanese homeowners pay twice as much in property taxes as Germans but less than half as much as Americans. Capital gains are taxable when the house is sold. Moreover, the substantial transaction taxes summarized in section 5.2.5 apply in this case.

5.4.4   Effects: Theory

The homeownership subsidies reduce the user cost of housing. Because the magnitude of these subsidies depends on different facets of housing choices in the three countries, they have different impacts on housing consumption. In the *United States,* mortgage and property tax payments are reduced by the homeownership subsidies in proportion to the marginal personal income tax rate if deductions are itemized. The subsidy is then

$$HS_{USA} = (i_m m + p_e) \cdot t \cdot V,$$

where i_m denotes the mortgage interest rate, m the loan-to-value ratio, p_e the effective property tax rate, t the marginal personal income tax, and V the value of the home.

Hence, the subsidy tilts housing decisions toward larger and more expensive homes financed by higher loan-to-value ratios.

In *Germany,* homeownership subsidies[27] in the first years after construction currently consist of the depreciation deduction, the (temporary) mortgage interest deduction, and the child supplement:

$$HS_{GER} = CS + t \cdot (L^{max} + d \cdot s \cdot V^{max}),$$

where d denotes the applicable accelerated depreciation rate and s the share of construction costs in total value. The subsidies are independent of the house value, unless the caps V^{max} on total value and L^{max} on the loan are lower than actual total value and actual loan. However, these caps are low, so this is rarely the case. Because the subsidies depend on the structure-to-land ratio as the only housing choice–related variable, housing decisions are less tilted to more expensive projects and do not favor high loan-to-equity ratios as in the United States. However, there is an incentive to substitute housing capital for land.

In *Japan,* user costs are reduced by the interest subsidy and the small tax credit *TC.*

27. I abstract from the effect of the savings subsidies.

Hence, the subsidy

$$HS_{JAP} = TC + r \cdot L^{max}$$

depends on the interest gap between market and subsidized interest rate r and the cap L^{max} for subsidized loans. However, subsidies do not depend on the marginal tax rates, as they do in Germany and in the United States. When we compare the three countries, Japan has the least and the United States the most distortive homeownership subsidies, with Germany in between.

The homeownership subsidies have been much more substantial in the United States than in Germany. Table 5.16 compares the homeownership subsidies in the United States and in Germany for typical income levels and house values in the first few years of a new home. The subsidies changed considerably from 1978 to 1992. In 1992, the subsidies in Germany remain smaller for expensive houses but not for small houses. Moreover, the child supplement is large, so for families with two or more children the homeownership subsidies in Germany are now larger than in the United States. Japan has even higher subsidies for median-income families. However, these subsidies decrease dramatically for larger incomes.

By decreasing the user costs of housing, the homeownership subsidies foster new construction. Because the U.S. and German subsidies mainly affect households with high marginal tax rates, this new construction takes place at the top end of the quality scale. However, it is claimed that this mechanism unfreezes housing at lower quality levels in a chain reaction and therefore pro-

Table 5.16	Homeownership Subsidies, 1978 and 1992 (1990 U.S. dollars)		
Value	United States		West Germany
Lower Middle Class Household in 1978			
$100,000	$1,865		$ 662
240,000	3,870		1,383
400,000	3,870		1,383
Upper Middle Class Household in 1978			
$100,000	$2,546		$1,163
240,000	5,594		2,366
400,000	8,220		2,366
Median Income Household in 1992			
Value	United States	West Germany [+ Child supplement]	Japan
$100,000	$1,604	$2,503 [+1,675]	$ 4,018
200,000	3,207	3,498 [+1,675]	7,115
300,000	4,811	3,996 [+1,675]	10,211

Sources: Börsch-Supan 1985; author's calculations based on 1990 tax codes.

Note: Married couple, 20 percent equity-to-loan ratio in the United States and Japan, 40 percent land-to-value ratio in Germany. Lower-middle-class income in 1978 = $32,000; upper middle class = $50,000. Child supplement is for each child.

vides more, thus also cheaper, housing for lower-income groups. In this sense, subsidies for the rich help protect the poor. This "filtering" mechanism is described in Sweeney (1974). Its working depends on the speed of this chain reaction, thus on the possibility and costs of moving. Mobility is also the key issue in terms of economic flexibility. Owner-occupied housing is said to tie people to particular pieces of property, thus decreasing the willingness to move when labor market changes may require relocation of labor.

5.4.5   Evidence

In order to gauge the evidence, we will ask three questions. First, do home-ownership subsidies induce substitution from rental to owner-occupied housing? Second, do we observe filtering? Third, is mobility reduced when ownership is high?

We have noted already in section 5.1 that the difference in ownership rates between Germany and the United States corresponds to the historical differences in homeownership subsidies. Table 5.17 gives a more careful look at this matter by conditioning on income. The exercise exemplifies the problems of an international comparison. Columns 2 and 3 depict ownership rates by income for the United States in 1987, while columns 4–9 present corresponding rates for Germany. But what is corresponding? Columns 4 and 5 hold relative social status constant and compute ownership rates for the corresponding income percentiles. German ownership rates are much lower, reflecting what we have seen in table 5.5. Columns 6 and 7 convert the income categories in column 1 by the ratio of the two countries' average income. Since income is distributed more equally in Germany, this results in much fewer households in the top and bottom income categories. Measured this way, ownership rates are still much lower in Germany than in the United States but not as drastically as in columns 4 and 5. Finally, columns 8 and 9 use purchasing power parities for conversion. Since German income levels are lower than U.S. ones, this shifts many well-to-do Germans into relatively low U.S. income categories. Even here, however, German ownership rates are lower than American ones.

These tables are suggestive but do not separate the effects of homeownership subsidies from other cross-country differences. For a more causal link between ownership rates and homeownership subsidies, I refer to the Börsch-Supan (1985) study based on 1978 data. In that paper, I estimated discrete choice housing demand equations for a sample of married couples in urban areas, conditional on the differences in tax advantages and other explanatory variables such as income and age.[28] In order to separate the effect of preference differences from differences in the tax treatment, I simulated each country's choice between renting and owning at the other country's tax laws and preferences. Table 5.18 summarizes the results.

---

28. The choices include renting versus owning, single-family versus multifamily house, and small versus large unit.

Table 5.17   Homeownership by Income, 1987

Annual Net Income [1986 $thousands] (1)	United States		West Germany					
			Equivalent Income Distribution		Equivalent Average HH-Income		Purchasing Power Parity	
	Ownership rate (2)	Percent Households (3)	Ownership rate (4)	Percent Households (5)	Ownership rate (6)	Percent households (7)	Ownership rate (8)	Percent Households (9)
< 6.0	36.2%	8.8%	21.8%	8.8%	—	1.0%	21.7%	5.1%
6.0–12.0	45.9	12.3	24.2	12.3	22.5%	7.8	24.3	22.7
12.0–21.0	51.9	17.1	31.4	17.1	26.5	24.7	37.5	40.7
21.0–30.0	60.0	14.6	36.5	14.6	35.2	22.6	50.7	20.9
30.0–42.0	68.3	16.3	41.6	16.3	45.4	26.8	62.1	8.5
42.0–60.0	79.3	15.9	48.6	15.9	58.6	12.5	72.3	1.3
≥ 60.0	89.1	15.8	61.8	15.8	70.4	4.6	—	0.3

Sources: AHS 1987; SOEP 1987; JCHS 1988.

Notes: Column 1: Income converted using U.S. CPI and Deutsche Marks-to-dollar conversion rates as explained in notes 3, 4, and 5. Columns 2 and 3: Ownership rates based on JCHS and CPS (see sources above). Columns 4 and 5: Ownership rates by income groups corresponding to percentiles of U.S. income distribution. Columns 6 and 7: ownership rates by income groups; currency conversion by ratio of average household incomes in the United States and West Germany. Columns 8 and 9: Owner-ship rates by income groups; currency conversion by 1987 purchasing power parity.

Table 5.18   Simulated Homeownership Rates, 1978

Simulation	(1)	(2)	(3)	(4)	(5)	(6)
Basic data	U.S.	U.S.	U.S.	German	German	German
Preferences	U.S.	German	U.S.	German	U.S.	German
Tax Laws	U.S.	U.S.	German	German	German	U.S.
Homeownership	76.9%	79.4%	70.5%	42.2%	39.8%	80.3%

Source: Börsch-Supan 1985.

The table presents six simulations. The first three are run on the U.S. sample, the second three on the German sample. Simulations 1 and 4 represent the baseline ownership rates.[29] Simulations 2 and 5 isolate the effects of preference differences, while simulations 3 and 6 isolate the effects of the different tax laws.[30]

Predicting either country with the other country's preferences does not change the tenure choice very much. However, predicting each country's housing consumption at the other country's tax code effective at that time produces drastic shifts into ownership in Germany and a substantial but much small corresponding shift toward rental housing in the United States. The asymmetry is due to tax law peculiarities and the discrepancy in land prices. Because Germany has very high land prices (in addition to higher structure costs), Germans could deduct a much higher proportion of their income under the 1978 U.S. tax code than Americans actually did at that time. Hence, simulated ownership rates jump from 42 percent to 80 percent. In turn, the German tax code was unfavorable to high house values but provided tax advantages comparable to the United States for typical U.S.-priced houses. Thus, the simulated change is much smaller than the corresponding one based on German data.

As a third piece of evidence on the effectiveness of homeownership subsidies, I look at changes over time. Since 1978 the tax laws have changed dramatically (see table 5.16). These changes are also reflected in the homeownership rates, as table 5.19 demonstrates. Ownership rates decreased in the United States, while they increased in Germany. Moreover, the increase in Germany is largest at middle-class and high incomes, that is, for those who have marginal tax rates above 25 percent (the top rate is 52 percent).

In summary, we have rather conclusive evidence that homeownership subsidies do induce substitution toward ownership. What does this mean in terms of social protection? The evidence for induced new construction is less overwhelming because price elasticities of housing are rather low. More important, there appears to be little direct evidence for the filtering process. Mills and Hamilton (1984), for example, state that the process had an adverse effect for

29. Due to the estimation procedure, the predicted market shares at the baseline specification are exactly the observed market shares.
30. Of course, because these simulations are drastic interferences with the steady states, they are qualitative guidelines rather than accurate quantitative predictions.

Table 5.19   **Changes in Homeownership by Income Categories, 1974/78–1987**

United States				Germany			
Annual Net Income	Ownership Ratio			Annual Net Income	Ownership Ratio		
(1990 U.S. $ thousands)	1974	1978	Change	(1990 U.S. $ thousands)	1978	1987	Change
$ < 6.0	42.8%	36.2%	−6.6%	$ < 8.0	23.9%	23.6%	−0.3%
6.0–12.0	48.7	45.9	−2.8	8.0–12.0	25.2	24.0	−1.2
12.0–21.0	53.8	51.9	−1.9	12.0–16.0	29.5	30.6	+1.1
21.0–30.0	58.7	60.0	+1.3	16.0–25.0	36.2	42.5	+6.3
30.0–42.0	69.3	68.3	−1.0	25.0–30.0	42.3	49.1	+6.8
42.0–60.0	78.6	79.3	+0.7	30.0–40.0	50.6	58.3	+7.7
≥ 60.0	86.2	89.1	+2.9	≥ 40.0	61.6	68.0	+6.4
Total	64.7	64.0	−0.7	Total	37.6	39.3	+1.7

Sources: AHS 1974 and CPS 1987 as quoted from JCHS 1988; WS 1978 and SOEP 1987.

the United States because it created abandoned houses in the city centers. For Germany, a large and carefully designed study by Weissbarth and Thomae (1978) shows that the filtering process works well in supplying medium-quality housing but that the moving chains are rather short. Thus, the filter process is unlikely to reach those households who really need social protection.

The evidence on mobility is unambiguous (see table 5.7). Mobility rates are dramatically lower for those households who live in owner-occupied housing. Moves occur 4.4 times more frequently for renters in the U.S. and 2.6 times more often in Germany. Thus, indirectly by encouraging homeownership, the subsidies hinder economic flexibility by reducing mobility in general and interregional mobility in particular.

A final issue is worth mentioning. It is claimed that the homeownership subsidies help flatten the business cycle. Tax deductions that rest on marginal tax rates do not accomplish this aim, because they are smaller in times of low income. However, the German system of subsidized dedicated savings contracts has this effect because it detaches mortgage interest rates in building societies from the business cycle. This effect is indeed visible in figure 5.5. This figure plots construction put in place as percentage deviation from a linear trend. Except for the boom in the early 1970s, the German time series is smoother than the U.S. one. As mentioned above, subsidies to the building society system were severely reduced in the 1980s. It would be premature, however, to ascribe the increasing amplitude of the building cycle in the 1980s solely to this policy change.

5.5   Conclusions

This international comparison provides us with a rich but by no means simple collection of results. Housing markets in the United States, Germany, and

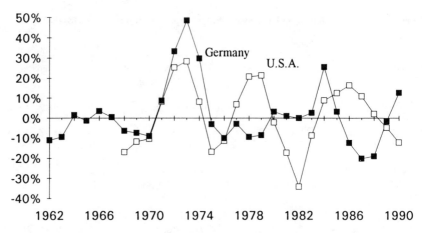

Fig. 5.5   Newly constructed units in West Germany and the United States (percentage deviation from linear trend)
Sources: U.S. Department of Commerce, *Construction Review;* StBA (FS-5.1).

Japan respond to the incentives provided by the various government programs. For some programs, the reactions are strong and unambiguous, such as the response of homeownership rates to homeownership subsidies. In all three countries, housing subsidies favor homeownership, but they do so much more strongly in the United States and Japan. This also solves the puzzle of why the United States and Japan have high and Germany a low ownership share although the United States has low but Germany and Japan very high land and housing prices.

However, the response to rent and eviction control is much less clear. It is claimed that the Japanese tenants' protection legislation is the cause for drying out the rental housing market in Japan. Unfortunately, we have no data to test this claim. In Germany, rent profiles are in line with those predicted under rent and eviction control. However, they are also similar in those areas of the United States where no controls exist. In fact, there is no statistically detectable influence of rent and eviction control on the evolution of rental prices for sitting tenants.

What does all of this mean in terms of social protection and economic flexibility? There is no evidence at all that homeownership subsidies help the poor by filtering abundant housing on higher quality levels down to the poor. In turn, the evidence clearly links high homeownership rates with low mobility, and the causes are obvious as homeownership ties people to their property. Insofar as mobility helps economic flexibility, homeownership subsidies are thus hindering economic flexibility. The German housing financing system— in which the government used to subsidize savings in building societies that are detached from the capital market—had the positive effect of smoothing the business cycle; thus, it reduced construction industry unemployment in recession periods and cooled down labor market stress in boom periods.

Rent and eviction control of the German design (i.e., with unregulated initial rents) appears to be a successful insurance mechanism protecting tenants from being exploited. The evidence on economic flexibility—again, measured in terms of the willingness to move—is less than perfect. Clearly, Germany and Japan, with their omnipresent controls, have lower mobility than the United States. However, time series do not react to changes in the stringency of the laws, and mobility is lower in Germany than in Japan although the controls are tighter in Japan.

This chapter could not analyze all housing-related issues affecting economic flexibility and social protection without crowding out the space this volume can provide. Important topics not dealt with here are land use regulations, zoning, and building codes. The jury is still out in a fascinating case.

Appendix A
Data Sources

The following data sources have been used in constructing the tables:

Germany

   StJB: *Statistical Yearbook of the Federal Republic of Germany*
   StBA (FS-5.1): Statistisches Bundesamt, Fachserie 5.1
   VZ: Volkszählung (Census of Population)
   GWZ: Gebäude- und Wohnungszählung (Census of Housing)
   SOEP: Sozio-Ökonomisches Panel (Socioeconomic Panel)

Japan

   JHC: Japanese Housing Census (Housing Survey of Japan)
   JMC: Japanese Ministry of Construction, *Construction Dynamics Series*
   JKDS: Juutaku Keizai Data Shu (Collection of Economic Housing Data)

United States

   StAb: *Statistical abstract of the United States*
   EcRep: *Economic report of the president, statistical tables*
   AHS: *American housing survey*
   CPS: *Current population survey*
   USCCR: U.S. Bureau of the Census, *Construction reports*
   JCHS: Joint Center of Housing Studies, *The state of the nation's housing*
   PSID: *Panel studies of income dynamics*

Data Availability

Except for the microdata sets (SOEP, PSID) and the JCHS reports, all data are available in printed volumes edited by the German, Japanese, and U.S.

government printing offices, respectively. The JCHS *Reports on the state of the nation's housing* are available from the Joint Center for Housing Studies of Harvard University, Cambridge, Massachusetts 02138. The German Socioeconomic Panel (SOEP) is available in public use form with English documentation from the International Aging Project at the Maxwell School, Syracuse University, Syracuse, New York 13244.

Appendix B
A Summary of Housing Policies

	United States	Germany	Japan
Public and social housing	Government provided, means-tested, scarce	Provided by nonprofit organizations, means-tested only at move	Government provided, only partially means-tested (if so, generous)
Rental housing subsidies to landlord	No accelerated depreciation, capital gains taxed, limited transferability of tax losses	Accelerated depreciation, capital gains essentially tax free, full transferability of tax losses	None
Housing allowances (to renter)	Limited number of Section 8 certificates, partially in kind and partially like cash	Entitlement to *Wohngeld,* deep subsidy, like cash	None
Rent and eviction control	Varies by local jurisdiction, most have none	Federal law restricts eviction and limits rent increases for sitting tenants	All changes in rental contracts subject to a "just cause" claim in court
Homeownership subsidies	Mortgage interest and property tax deductible from income tax, imputed rent not taxed	Depreciation and small part of mortgage interest deductible from income tax, imputed rent not taxed, additional tax credits for families with children	Mortgage interest subsidies, small tax credit

References

Baird, C. W. 1980. *Rent control: The perennial folly.* San Francisco: Cato Institute.
Barnbrook, I., and S. Mayo. 1985. Rental housing subsidy programs in West Germany and the United States. In *U.S. and German housing markets: Comparative economic analysis,* ed. K. Stahl and R. Struyk. Washington, D.C.: Urban Institute Press.

Barnett, C. L. 1979. Using hedonic indexes to measure housing quality. Santa Monica: Rand Corporation, R-2450-HUD.

Behring, K., A. Börsch-Supan, and G. Goldrian. 1988. *Analyse und Prognose der Nachfrage nach Miet und Eigentümerwohnungen.* Berlin: Duncker und Humblot.

Boone, P., and J. Sachs. 1989. Is Tokyo worth four trillion dollars? An explanation for high Japanese land prices. Mimeograph.

Börsch-Supan, A. 1985. Tenure choice and housing demand. In *U.S. and German housing Markets: Comparative economic analysis,* ed. K. Stahl and R. Struyk. Washington, D.C.: Urban Institute Press.

————. 1986. On the West German tenants' protection legislation. *Journal of Institutional and Theoretical Economics (Zeitschrift für die gesamte Staatswissenschaft)* 142:380–404.

————. 1991. Implications of an aging population: Problems and policy options in the U.S. and Germany. *Economic Policy* 12:104–39.

Börsch-Supan, A., Y. Kanemoto, and K. Stahl. 1992. *House price booms, financial liberalization, and policy traps: Housing markets in Germany, Japan, and the United States.* University of Mannheim and University of Tokyo. Manuscript.

Börsch-Supan, A., and K. Stahl. 1991. Do dedicated savings increase personal savings and housing consumption? An analysis of the German Bausparkassen system. *Journal of Public Economics* 4:233–55.

Congressional Budget Office (CBO). 1988. *Current housing problems and possible federal responses.* Washington, D.C.: U.S. Government Printing Office.

Eckart, W. 1983. A welfare analysis of the German tenants' protection legislation. Working Paper in Economic Theory and Urban Economics no. 8308. University of Dortmund.

Eekhof, J. 1981. Zur Kontroverse um die ökonomischen Auswirkungen des Zweiten Wohnraumkündigungsschutzgesetzes. *Zeitschrift für die gesamte Staatswissenschaft* 137:62–77.

Follain, J. R., and S. Malpezzi. 1980. *Dissecting housing value and rent: Estimate of hedonic indices for thirty-nine large SMSAs.* Washington, D.C.: Urban Institute.

Goodman, A. C., and M. Kawai. 1982. Length of Residency discounts and rental housing demand: Theory and evidence. Working Paper no. 108. Baltimore: Johns Hopkins University.

Guasch, J. L., and R. C. Marshall. 1983. A theoretical and empirical analysis of the length of residency discount in the rental housing market. Working Paper no. 834. San Diego: University of California.

Kanemoto, Y. 1991. The housing market in Japan. Tokyo: University of Tokyo. Mimeograph.

————. 1992. Housing problems in Japan. Paper prepared for the European meetings of the Regional Science Association, August, in Brussels.

Lowry, I. S. 1981. Rental housing in the 1980s: Searching for the crisis. In *Rental housing: Is there a crisis?* ed. J. C. Weicher. Washington, D.C.: Urban Institute.

Malpezzi, S., L. Ozanne, and T. Thibodeau. 1980, *Characteristic prices of housing in fifty-nine metropolitan areas.* Washington, D.C.: Urban Institute.

Mills, E. S., and B. W. Hamilton. 1984. *Urban economics.* Glenview, Ill.: Scott, Foresman.

National Multi-Housing Council. 1982. *The spread of rent control.* Washington, D.C.: NMHC.

Noland, C. W. 1980. Assessing hedonic indexes for Housing. Santa Monica: Rand Corporation, N-1505-HUD.

Organization for Economic Cooperation and Development (OECD). 1988. *Aging populations: Social policy implications.* Paris: OECD.

————. 1992. *Purchasing power parities and real expenditures.* Paris: OECD.

Olsen, E. 1972. An econometric analysis of rent control. *Journal of Political Economy* 80(4): 1081–100.

———. 1987. What do economists know about rent control? Discussion Paper no. 1750. Charlottesville: Department of Economics, University of Virginia.

Poterba, J. 1984. Tax subsidies to owner-occupied housing. *Quarterly Journal of Economics* 94:363–72.

———. 1992. Taxation and housing: Old questions, new answers. NBER Working Paper no. 3963. Cambridge, Mass.: National Bureau of Economic Research. August.

Rosen, H. S. 1992. *Public finance. 3rd ed.* Homewood, Ill.: Irwin.

Schlicht, E. 1983. The tenant's decreasing willingness to pay and the rent abatement phenomenon. *Zeitschrift für die gesamte Staatswissenschaft* 139:155–59.

Schwager, R. 1991. Efficiency of housing markets with uncertain types of agents and uncertain future incomes. *Journal of Institutional and Theoretical Economics (Zeitschrift für die gesamte Staatswissenschaft)*. Forthcoming (Spring 1994).

Sweeney, J. 1974. A commodity hierarchy model of the rental housing market. *Journal of Urban Economics* 1:288–323.

Thibodeau, T. 1981. *Rent regulation and the market for rental housing services.* Washington, D.C.: Urban Institute.

Weissbarth, R., and M. Thomae. 1978. Sickereffekte verschiedener Formen der Wohnbau und Bausparförderung. *Wohnungsmarkt und Wohnungspolitik,* Nr. 07.003. Bonn: Bundesministerium für Raumordnung, Städtebau und Wohnungswesen.

6 Health Insurance Provision and Labor Market Efficiency in the United States and Germany

Douglas Holtz-Eakin

> Worker mobility is one of the most important values in an entrepreneurial society, where most jobs are created by small businesses. The present health care system is a big brake on that.
>
> President Bill Clinton

Health insurance and health care provision have claimed a prominent place on the policy agenda in the United States. Critics argue that the *status quo* has led to spiraling health care costs, an inequitable distribution of quality medical care, and a failure to provide care to many individuals. Further, there is a perception that the dominant form of providing health insurance in the United States—private provision as part of employee compensation—interferes with smooth functioning of the labor market. The statement (above) by President Bill Clinton[1] is characteristic of claims that individuals are locked into jobs because of their fear of large changes in their health insurance status if they change jobs. Clearly, to the extent that this is true, a U.S.-style system of providing this fundamental part of the social safety net interferes with the efficient matching of employers and employees. Other things equal, one would prefer to avoid such a labor market inefficiency when providing health insurance.

Do individuals forgo changing jobs on the basis of health insurance? In a recent *CBS/New York Times* survey, roughly 30 percent of respondents indicated that they had stayed in a job to retain their current health insurance cover-

Douglas Holtz-Eakin is associate professor of economics at Syracuse University and a research associate of the National Bureau of Economic Research.

Access to the Socioeconomic Panel of Germany and the Panel Study of Income Dynamics was made possible by the generosity of the Cross-National Studies in Aging Program at Syracuse University. David Gross and Jonathan Ratner of the General Accounting Office provided a valuable briefing on the intricacies of the German health insurance system. The author also thanks the Metropolitan Studies Program at Syracuse University for its aid; Mary Daly, Michelle Harter, and, especially Steve Rhody for research assistance; and Karin D'Agnostino and Esther Gray for their help in preparing the manuscript. This paper has benefited from the insightful comments of Rebecca Blank, Jonathan Gruber, Stephen Machin, Brigitte Madrian, Harvey S. Rosen, two anonymous referees, seminar participants at Syracuse University, and attendees of the conference.

1. Quotation from Greider, W., P. J. O'Rourke, H. S. Thompson, and J. S. Wenner (1992), The Rolling Stone interview: Bill Clinton, *Rolling Stone,* 17 September, 44.

age.[2] In other suggestive evidence, a KPMG Peat Marwick survey cited in the *Wall Street Journal* indicated that job switching may be impeded by the absence of coverage for preexisting conditions, a situation affecting over two-thirds of employees.[3] In addition, researchers have begun to analyze the job lock issue. The results in Madrian (1992), the first careful econometric analysis of the issue, suggest the presence of job lock from health insurance in the United States.

In contrast to the U.S. system, virtually all German citizens are guaranteed health insurance as part of a privately operated but compulsory health insurance system. As a result, the insurance is apparently portable, and one would expect that it would have no impact on job arrangements. However, one feature of the German system is that individuals may pay different—perhaps very different—premiums for essentially the same coverage. Moreover, the cost of coverage will depend upon the insurance company, or sickness fund, chosen by each employer. Accordingly, health insurance may be portable, but the *price* is not. In some circumstances, however, individuals—not their employers—choose the sickness fund that provides for their health insurance, thereby providing portability of both coverage and price. *Ceteris paribus,* one would anticipate a greater propensity to move among those individuals whose insurance does not change in price across jobs. To the extent that this is an important issue, changes in the price of health insurance when switching jobs offer a potential impediment to the smooth functioning of the German labor market.

The basic goal of this paper is to assess the empirical magnitude of health insurance–related impediments to job mobility in the United States and Germany. It is important to stress at the outset that the impact on labor market efficiency is not the sole, or even the best, means by which to gauge the performance of a health insurance system. One might, for example, wish to assess the efficiency of the insurance market itself.[4] Still, a comparison of the U.S. and German experiences may provide input in assessing the relative strengths of the alternative systems.

To anticipate the basic results, I find little evidence that health insurance provision interferes with job mobility in either the United States or Germany. The outline for the remainder of the paper is as follows. Section 6.1 looks at health insurance and labor market mobility in the United States, focusing on the job lock hypothesis. In section 6.2, I examine the role of health insurance financing in labor market mobility in Germany. The final section contains a summary and assesses the implications of the results.

2. *New York Times* (1991), 26 September, 1. The question asked was: "Have you or anyone else in your household ever decided to stay in a job you wanted to leave mainly because you didn't want to lose health coverage?"
3. *Wall Street Journal* (1991), 31 December, A1.
4. Fuchs (1991) provides an overview of the issues.

6.1   Health Insurance and the Labor Market in the United States

As noted at the outset, policy toward health insurance is currently much debated in the United States. In part, this reflects the increasing share of national resources devoted to health care expenditures; the share of such spending in net national product rose from 4.8 percent to 13.7 percent between 1950 and 1990 (Aaron 1991, table 3-1). In addition, there is widespread concern that the large number of uninsured families leaves a critical part of the population, especially children, needlessly vulnerable to health problems. Finally, there is the notion that the tradition of packaging health insurance along with other job-related benefits may have detrimental effects on labor market efficiency.

Some suggestive evidence on the latter issue—the job lock conjecture—in the United States is displayed in table 6.1. As detailed below, the 1984 wave of the Panel Study of Income Dynamics (PSID) identifies individuals receiving employer-provided health insurance. The table shows the frequency with which those who do and do not receive such health insurance change employers in subsequent years. The job transition rates are for the one-year period from 1984 to 1985 and the three-year span between 1984 and 1987.[5] To the extent that job lock is a significant feature of labor market dynamics, transitions between employers should be relatively higher among the uninsured and relatively lower among those who receive health insurance. That is, in terms of the table, the proportion of the entries in the first row of each category, under "Job Change," should be greater than the proportion of the entries in the second row. Looking first at the transitions for married individuals, one finds exactly the predicted pattern for both one-year and three-year transitions.[6] Also reported below each transition category is a Chi-square test statistic. In each case, the transition rates of the insured are significantly different from those of uninsured. Turning to single individuals, one finds the same pattern: transition rates are lower for the insured. Once again, the differences are statistically different.

To be sure, transition tables focus on a single variable—insurance here—and thus ignore many aspects of the decision to change jobs. For this reason, they are not a powerful test of the job lock hypothesis. This section is devoted to developing a more complete assessment of the role of job lock. Before doing so, however, I begin with a brief review of private and public health insurance institutions in the United States. In the subsequent subsection, I discuss information available regarding health insurance in the PSID, the source of individual-level data for the United States in this study. Section 6.1.3 discusses

---

5. The sample consists of full-time employed individuals aged twenty-five to fifty-five. I follow the recommendations of Brown and Light (1992) in identifying job changes.

6. At each step in the analysis that follows, results for two-year transitions are quite similar to those for the three-year horizon. To conserve space, these are not reported.

Table 6.1   Job Transition in the United States

	One-Year Transition		Three-Year Transition	
	No Change	Job Change	No Change	Job Change
Married individuals				
No insurance	1,707	399	1,283	757
	(0.834)	(0.166)	(0.629)	(0.371)
Insurance	1,789	234	1,499	524
	(0.884)	(0.116)	(0.741)	(0.259)
χ^2	21.4**		59.1**	
Single individuals				
No insurance	500	152	367	258
	(0.767)	(0.233)	(0.563)	(0.437)
Insurance	429	96	341	184
	(0.817)	(0.183)	(0.650)	(0.350)
χ^2	4.41*		9.11**	

Notes: Numbers in parentheses = column entry ÷ (no job change + job change). χ^2 = Chi-square test statistic for the null hypothesis that those with and without insurance have the same transition rates.

*Significant at the 5 percent level.
**Significant at the 1 percent level.

the empirical facts regarding the uninsured as revealed by these data.[7] In the final section, I undertake some simple multivariate analyses designed to quantify the importance of health insurance in reducing labor market mobility.

6.1.1   The Provision of Health Insurance

For working-age individuals and their dependents, employer-provided private coverage is the dominant source of health insurance in the United States. Two out of every three Americans under the age of 65, constituting roughly 75 percent of employees, are covered by employer-provided private insurance (Aaron 1991, 54). The precise terms of this coverage, however, vary widely. In part due to the existence of alternative health care providers such as health maintenance organizations (HMOs) and in part because many employers support more than a single plan, the variance in actual coverage and its cost is enormous.

There is widespread government involvement in the provision of health insurance as well. Perhaps the most important policy is the exclusion of premiums for employer-provided insurance from taxable income under the U.S. individual income tax. The value of this exclusion is nearly $80 billion[8] and

7. As discussed below, the PSID does not ask directly about insurance coverage. Instead, individuals are classified as uninsured if they do not receive employer-provided health insurance.

8. Calculated from Congressional Budget Office (1992, 258). The taxation of employer-paid insurance would generate $230 billion in income tax revenues and $160 billion in payroll tax revenues over the period 1993–97. Converting the total ($390 billion) into an annual average yields the number in the text.

provides a clear incentive to add health insurance as a fringe benefit.[9] In addition, Medicare and Medicaid are large-scale programs that provide health insurance. Retired individuals who worked in employment covered by Social Security or railroad retirement are eligible for Medicare, which began in 1966. The program is divided into two parts: Part A covers the costs of hospitalization and some nursing home care; Part B covers physicians' charges. Part B is limited to covering 80 percent of allowable charges above a $100 deductible, so there is an incentive to purchase private, "medigap" insurance.[10]

Medicaid is a health insurance program for low-income individuals that covers roughly 9 percent of the population (Wolfe 1992). In practice, it consists of individual programs in each of the states, operating under general guidelines from the federal government. The federal government finances part of the cost by offering matching grants to those states that offer specified services to target populations. In particular, states are required to offer benefits to recipients of Aid to Families with Dependent Children (AFDC) and Supplemental Security Income (SSI).

6.1.2 Analyzing Health Insurance, Using the PSID

The empirical analysis presented below uses the Panel Study of Income Dynamics. The PSID offers many advantages, in particular a wealth of longitudinal data on labor market performance and a structure comparable to that of the Socioeconomic Panel of Germany (GSOEP) data used in the empirical analysis of Germany.[11] Unfortunately, there are drawbacks as well, the most important of which is the relative paucity of information on the health insurance status of individuals. Ideally, one would like to have annual information on the type, cost, and coverage from all sources of health insurance. Instead, even the relatively circumscribed information on health insurance coverage is limited to a single year.

In the 1984 wave of the PSID, individuals were asked the question: "Does your employer pay for any medical, surgical, or hospital insurance that covers any illness or injury that might happen to you when you are not at work?" For married couples, there is an identical question regarding the payment of health insurance by the spouse's employer. In what follows, those individuals who answered "yes" are classified as having employer-provided health insurance, and those who answered "no" will be referred to as "uninsured."[12] Clearly, this is a great departure from the ideal. In particular, some of those categorized as

---

9. See, for example, Sloan and Adamache (1986) or Hamermesh and Woodbury (1990) for a discussion of the relationship between tax policy and the provision of fringe benefits.

10. In 1990, Congress placed limits on the medigap insurers, especially limiting their ability to exclude those with preexisting conditions, mandating experience rating, and requiring a minimum ratio of benefit payments to premium income. See Rovner (1990).

11. For a description of each data source, see the appendix.

12. Those that answered either "don't know" or "not applicable" were eliminated from the sample.

uninsured may have purchased private insurance or obtained access in some other way. Further, there is no information regarding the extent or *cost* of coverage, especially the degree to which spouses are covered by any plan. In what follows, I will interpret the results, using the assumption that individuals are eligible for coverage under their spouse's plan, if present, but a degree of caution is clearly warranted. Lastly, the focus below is on private health insurance. To the extent that the absence of private insurance is offset by Medicare or Medicaid, the labor market behavior of individuals will be altered.[13]

6.1.3   Who Are the Uninsured?

Estimates indicate that there are thirty to forty million uninsured individuals in the United States, including a substantial fraction that are uninsured throughout each year (Wolfe 1992). In addition, there is concern that the fraction of the population that is uninsured has risen over the past decade.[14] As noted above, the PSID does not contain information regarding health insurance provision for multiple years. Thus, it is not possible to address many interesting questions regarding the dynamics of insurance, such as the extent to which uninsured status is transitory, the extent to which the rise in the number of uninsured reflects changes in family structure, and so forth. It is possible, however, to take a "snapshot" view of the uninsured population.

In doing so, I focus on employed individuals ages twenty-five to fifty-five, the same group for which I test the job lock hypothesis. Thus, this section is best viewed as providing a glimpse at the characteristics of the working uninsured. The basic facts are laid out in table 6.2. Part A focuses on married individuals. In the top table the upper-left entry indicates for 49 percent of the married individuals who did not have insurance, neither did their spouses. In contrast, the upper-right entry indicates that the remaining 51 percent of the uninsured were married to individuals whose employers provided health insurance. The second row of the matrix gives corresponding information for those with insurance. Notice that the probability of having a spouse with insurance is higher for the uninsured than for the insured. Put differently, the probability of having insurance is negatively correlated among spouses. The Chi-square statistic (16.4) indicates that this correlation is statistically significant at the 1 percent level. Thus, spousal insurance tends weakly to offset the lack of insurance for a married individual.

From here, I proceed in two routes. The data on the left investigate the relationship between the individual reporting employer-provided insurance (Indi-

---

13. In practice, two pieces of evidence suggest that the existence of government-provided insurance does not have a significant impact on the results. First, there is no significant difference in behavior between those belonging to the low-income subsample and those in the remainder of the PSID. Second, eliminating all individuals who report assistance from any income assistance program (Aid to Families with Dependent Children, Supplemental Security Income, unemployment insurance, or Medicaid) does not affect the basic nature of the results.

14. Most counts of the uninsured are based on the Current Population Survey, and the wording of the questions in this survey has changed over time. As a result, there is some ambiguity in interpreting changes in the number of uninsured (see Swartz 1989).

Table 6.2   **Insurance Relationships: Characteristics of Insured and Uninsured Individuals, Married and Single**

	A. Married Individuals					
	Spouse Uninsured			Spouse Insured		χ^2
Uninsured	0.494			0.506		
						16.4**
Insured	0.557			0.443		
	Individual			Individual or Spouse		
Characteristic	No Insurance	In-surance	χ^2	No Insurance	In-surance	χ^2
Gender						
Male	0.352	0.646	350**	0.496	0.500	0.0520
Female	0.648	0.354		0.504	0.500	
Race						
Nonwhite	0.257	0.251	0.209	0.297	0.240	13.2*
White	0.743	0.749		0.703	0.760	
Health						
Good	0.971	0.995	34.0**	0.957	0.991	49.6**
Poor	0.029	0.005		0.043	0.009	
Union member						
Nonunion	0.967	0.727	454**	0.961	0.810	134**
Union	0.033	0.273		0.039	0.190	

	B. Single Individuals			
Characteristic	No Insurance	Insurance	χ^2	
Gender				
Male	0.333	0.404	6.33*	
Female	0.667	0.596		
Race				
Nonwhite	0.661	0.410	74.3**	
White	0.339	0.590		
Health				
Good	0.929	0.983	18.6**	
Poor	0.071	0.017		
Union membership				
Nonunion	0.952	0.762	91.8**	
Union	0.048	0.238		

Notes: Each entry is the number of individuals, expressed as a decimal fraction of the total (e.g., male plus female) in that category (e.g., no insurance). χ^2 denotes the Chi-square test statistic for independence of the rows and columns.

*Significant at the 5 percent level.
**Significant at the 1 percent level.

vidual") and the characteristics of such individuals. In contrast, in the data on the right, we undertake the same comparisons, using instead as the measure of insurance whether either the individual or the spouse (or both) has employer-provided insurance ("Individual or Spouse").

Consider first the results for those that report receiving employer-provided coverage. A glance down the column reveals (statistically) significant differences along three major dimensions. First, the uninsured are more likely to be female than are the insured. Second, the uninsured are more likely to report that they are in poor health (in 1984, 2.9 percent in poor health, compared with 0.5 percent of the insured). Third, and not very surprising, the insured are much more likely to be union workers than are the uninsured population. The latter suggests that large changes in the status of unions may be related to changes in the uninsured population in the United States. Interestingly, the uninsured have roughly the same racial composition as the insured.

When one looks at the data on the right, a slightly different picture emerges. Recall that an individual is classified as insured here if either the individual or the individual's spouse (or both) report receiving employer-provided medical insurance. Using this definition, the gender composition of the uninsured and the insured populations is essentially the same. In contrast, we now find differences along racial lines. The uninsured population has a greater fraction of nonwhite individuals, and the difference is statistically significant at the 1 percent level. The remaining two relationships are unchanged: the uninsured are more likely to be in poor health and to be nonunion workers.

Part B of table 6.2 undertakes a comparable analysis for single individuals. The same patterns emerge from the data. Just as with married individuals, the uninsured tend to be female, nonwhite, in poor health, and nonunion workers.

Of course, it is desirable to examine these relationships simultaneously rather than in a sequence of bivariate comparisons. The probit analysis in table 6.3 is designed for this purpose. The table shows the results of estimating a probit model in which the dependent variable is equal to one if the individual has employer-provided insurance, and zero otherwise.[15] It is important to note that these probit estimates are designed to be descriptive; there is no putative causal relationship. Instead, they serve to summarize the empirical relationship between uninsured status and a myriad of other (endogenously determined) variables.

There are several interesting results. First, the coefficients on age, education, and number of children are insignificant.[16] The last in particular indicates no differential propensity for those with children to be at risk of not having health insurance. Similarly, the lack of correlation with race persists in this analysis; neither of the coefficients for white and black individuals is individually significant. (Also, one cannot reject the null that they are equal.)

There are a wide variety of variables that do enter significantly. The dummy variables to control for occupation and industry capture statistical differences

15. A more expansive definition of coverage would include those whose spouses have employer-provided insurance. Estimating a probit using this definition yields results broadly similar to those in table 6.3. To the extent that they differ, the probability of coverage rises with age, declines for nonwhites, and is unrelated to sex and tenure.

16. One cannot reject the joint hypothesis that both age and age squared have coefficients equal to zero.

Table 6.3   Probit Analysis: Probability of Employer-Provided Insurance*

Variable	Coefficient (standard error)	Variable	Coefficient (standard error)
Age	−0.0387	Children	−0.00842
	(0.0275)		(0.0207)
Age squared × 10⁻³	0.312	Wages × 10³	0.00134
	(0.350)		(0.00132)
Education	0.0193	Assets × 10⁻⁶	−0.764
	(0.0117)		(0.156)
White	0.157	Tenure	0.0204
	(0.162)		(0.00513)
Black	0.0645	Union member	0.565
	(0.165)		(0.145)
Female	−0.134	Union job	0.273
	(0.0565)		(0.133)
Poor health	−0.255	Spouse insured	0.0124
	(0.215)		(0.0556)
Married	−0.0988	Spouse wages × 10⁻³	0.00259
	(0.0651)		(0.00198)
Average unemployment	−0.0160	Public sector	1.95
	(0.00578)		(0.147)
Professional	0.474	Retail sales	1.55
	(0.0807)		(0.129)
Sales	0.492	Real estate	1.90
	(0.0811)		(0.151)
Blue-collar	0.426	Business services	1.33
	(0.0846)		(0.158)
Agriculture, fisheries, forestry	0.942	Personal services	1.34
	(0.202)		(0.156)
Mining	2.51	Entertainment	1.34
	(0.325)		(0.285)
Construction	1.17	Professional services	1.78
	(0.156)		(0.123)
Manufacturing	2.20	Public administration	2.14
	(0.133)		(0.144)

*Based on 5,037 observations. The dependent variable is equal to one if the individual has employer-provided insurance, and zero otherwise.

in coverage across different sectors of the economy and job levels within firms. Similarly, the more detailed characteristics of the job also help to predict insurance coverage. The probability of medical insurance rises with wage earnings by the individual, tenure on the job, union membership, and whether the individual's job is covered by a collective bargaining agreement ("union job"). Thus, the presence of medical insurance reflects good jobs—that is, jobs with good wages, stability, and other benefits.

Individual characteristics matter as well. Females are less likely to be insured, although separate probits for married and single individuals (not reported) reveal that this finding stems from married females. (This also explains the negative but statistically insignificant effect on the variable for married individuals.) The probability of insurance falls with net assets, likely reflecting the ability of wealthy individuals to purchase insurance directly or forgo it altogether. An individual's work history also enters the likelihood of having insurance in a significant fashion; the probability of being insured falls when the average number of weeks of unemployment between 1981 and 1983 ("average unemployment") rises.

Finally, in contrast to the raw correlation in table 6.2, the probit analysis indicates no significant correlation between the presence of a spouse who has employer-provided insurance and the probability of having health insurance. A difficulty in interpreting such a reduced form, however, stems from the fact that some spouses may elect to decline insurance coverage. In such circumstances, it is not obvious how the individual will answer the survey question on insurance coverage.

6.1.4   Health Insurance and Job Mobility

Should employment-based health insurance reduce job mobility? At a first pass, the likely answer seems to be no. Health insurance is only part of the overall compensation package for a worker. Thus, one might anticipate that wages or other noninsurance aspects of the total compensation package would vary so as to offset differences in the cost of providing health insurance. Indeed, Gruber (1992) finds that changes in the costs of insuring workers for maternity benefits are reflected by almost identical offsets in wages. Thus, if workers differ in terms of the cost of health insurance, the result could still be a compensation package that matches the productivity of each worker.

Changes in health status, however, complicate this simple story. Consider an individual who experiences a significant decline in health. As part of his or her current group plan, say, he or she may be relatively inexpensive to insure. As a result of experience rating, however, this cost would rise if the individual moved to another firm, and the individual would be a less attractive candidate for other jobs unless he or she was willing to accept lower wages in the new job. Thus, in the current firm, the individual could receive health insurance of the same value and a larger wage income than in another firm. In this way, employment-based insurance may act as a "tax" on labor mobility by driving a wedge between the cost of insurance in a new firm versus the current employer. Notice, however, that even this effect may be short lived. To the extent that insurance companies raise premiums, even the current employer may move to a mix of greater health insurance and less wage income.

A similar scenario may follow from clauses precluding coverage for preexisting conditions. A 1987 survey indicated that 57 percent of employers had clauses limiting or excluding coverage for expenses stemming from preexisting conditions in their insurance arrangements. For smaller firms these are even more prevalent, with 64 percent of small employers (less than five hundred employees) having such clauses.[17] These features of the insurance market have led to many calls for reforms that move away from employer-based insurance (see, e.g., Mitchell 1990) on the grounds that the features trap workers in their current jobs. Still, firms have the option of paying more to cover preexisting conditions, so the presence of job lock behavior and its efficiency consequences is ultimately an empirical issue.

While there is a relatively large literature on the relationship between fringe benefits and job mobility (especially pensions), there is a paucity of studies examining the role of health insurance alone.[18] The major exception is Madrian (1992), who finds some evidence of job lock, using the 1987 National Medical Expenditure Survey. Madrian focuses on three comparisons to find evidence of job lock: (1) the job mobility of insured men whose spouses have health insurance coverage versus those whose spouses do not, (2) the behavior of men with large versus small families, and (3) the behavior of men with pregnant spouses versus those who are not expecting a child. In each case, mobility is lower in those situations where the current insurance coverage is more valuable. Indeed the empirical magnitudes are quite striking. Madrian estimates that voluntary mobility differentials due to job lock range from 25 percent (estimated using the first parameter) to 50 percent (using the third). The existence of mobility differentials of this magnitude suggests that an insurance system divorced from employment status (see, e.g., Mitchell 1990) would enhance efficiency.

To see the nature of the test for job lock, consider the following simplified model. Let the probability of changing employers be given by

(1) $$p(\text{change}) = \phi(z) + \alpha_1 d_1 + \alpha_2 d_2 + \alpha_3 d_3 + \alpha_4 d_4,$$

where $\phi(\cdot)$ captures non-insurance-related aspects of the job change decision. The variable d_1 is a dichotomous variable equal to one if the individual is the only person in the household to have insurance and equal to zero otherwise; d_2 is defined similarly and indicates that only the individual's spouse has insurance; d_3 equals one if both the individual and the spouse are insured, and d_4 indicates that neither has insurance. (It is assumed that if the spouse has insurance, the individual can be covered by it.) If the lack of portable insurance impedes job transitions, it should be apparent only when employment and in-

---

17. The survey of two thousand employers offering health insurance was conducted by Foster Higgens, an employee benefits consulting firm (see Cotton 1991).

18. Mitchell (1982, 1983) explores the link between fringe benefits and job mobility. There is also a substantial literature examining the degree to which pension plans (and their vesting rules) produce additional job attachment (see, e.g., Allen, Clark, and McDermed 1991). Gustman and Steinmeier (1990), however, find that jobs with pensions also contain a wage premium that dominates the financial effects of pension provision; they conclude that the wage premium is the source of lower propensities to leave these jobs. As was noted above, the probability that a job provides health insurance is also positively correlated with the wages received by the individual.

surance are tied. In terms of equation (1), this corresponds to having $d_1 = 1$. For all others, the access to insurance is independent of employment. For example, if $d_2 = 1$, then the individual is covered by the spouse's policy, which is unaffected by a change to a new employer. Or if $d_4 = 1$, the individual has no insurance to lose, and it is therefore not a factor when changing jobs.

It turns out to be useful to express this in a slightly different form:

(2) $p(\text{change}) = \phi(z) + \beta_0 + \beta_1 Self + \beta_2 Spouse + \beta_3 Both$,

where *Self* indicates that the individual has insurance, *Spouse* indicates that the spouse has insurance, and *Both* is the interaction (product) of these two variables. A bit of algebra reveals the correspondence between equations (1) and (2):

(3) $p(\text{change}) = \phi(z) + (\beta_0 + \beta_1)d_1 + (\beta_0 + \beta_2)d_2 +$
$(\beta_0 + \beta_1 + \beta_2 + \beta_3)d_3 + \beta_0 d_4$.

Consider now equation (1). As argued above, if individuals are locked into their current jobs by health insurance, it should be apparent only when $d_1 = 1$. Note that the other states are equivalent from the perspective of health insurance—the individual loses no insurance if he or she leaves a job. Hence, one would expect $\alpha_2 = \alpha_3 = \alpha_4$. Thus, the notion that employer-based insurance affects job transitions amounts to testing the null hypothesis that $\alpha_1 = \alpha_2 (= \alpha_3 = \alpha_4)$. This has several implications for the parameters in equation (3): (1) $\alpha_2 = \alpha_3$ implies that $\beta_1 + \beta_3 = 0$; (2) $\alpha_3 = \alpha_4$ implies that $\beta_1 + \beta_2 + \beta_3 = 0$, so that these together require that $\beta_2 = 0$; and (3) $\alpha_1 = \alpha_2$ implies that $\beta_1 = \beta_2$, so that β_1 must also be zero. Collecting results, this requires that β_3, the coefficient on the interaction variables (*Both*), be zero. Thus, this line of reasoning suggests the (not surprising) result that one should test whether all of the coefficients on the insurance variables in equation (2) are equal to zero. If they are, this is consistent with the notion that health insurance has no effect on transitions among jobs. Rejecting this null hypothesis, however, suggests the presence of job lock due to health insurance.

However, one could argue that the presence of an employer-provided insurance plan is really serving as an indicator of whether the individual has a "good job"; the probit analysis in table 6.3 leads directly to this notion. If so, all that such an exercise establishes is that people are less likely to leave good jobs than bad jobs. In terms of equation (1), the "good jobs" argument essentially says that $\phi(\cdot)$ does not control completely for attributes of the job that are correlated with the presence of insurance. It is likely, then, that the coefficients on d_1 and d_3 are contaminated by these job-related attributes. A similar argument may be put forward with regard to spouses; that is, the coefficients on d_2 and d_3 reflect unobserved attributes of the spouse. Thus, one may rewrite equation (1) as:

(1′) $$p(\text{change}) = \phi(z) + (\alpha_1 + j)d_1 + (\alpha_2 + s)d_2 + (\alpha_3 + j + s)d_3 + \alpha_4 d_4 ,$$

or

(4) $$p(\text{change}) = \phi(z) + \gamma_1 d_1 + \gamma_2 d_2 + \gamma_3 d_3 + \gamma_4 d_4 ,$$

where j is the contamination due to job effects and s is the corresponding contamination due to spouse effects. Because of the presence of s and j, it is not possible to test the relevant hypothesis regarding the coefficients in equation (1). Indeed, one cannot even learn about health insurance effects by looking at $(\gamma_2 - \gamma_1)$, $(\gamma_3 - \gamma_1)$, or $(\gamma_4 - \gamma_1)$, because each contains either s or j. However, bringing equation (3) into play allows one to compare the differences of the differences, thereby eliminating the unobserved attributes and isolating the effect on job changes. Algebraically, $(\gamma_3 - \gamma_2) - (\gamma_1 - \gamma_4) = (\alpha_3 - \alpha_2) - (\alpha_1 - \alpha_4)$, which does not depend on s or j. Under the null hypothesis, this should equal zero. Returning to equation (3), it is straightforward to verify that $(\alpha_3 - \alpha_2) - (\alpha_1 - \alpha_4) = \beta_3$. Thus, testing the null hypothesis in the presence of job effects and spouse effects involves testing whether the coefficient on the interaction variable differs from zero. Intuitively, in the absence of health insurance effects on transitions, the impact of having an employer-provided plan should not depend on whether the worker can be covered by a spouse's plan.

Table 6.4 looks at the propensity to change employers for married individuals who have employer-provided medical insurance. Within each gender the

Table 6.4   **Job Transitions in the United States for Married Individuals with Employer-Provided Health Insurance**

	One-Year Transitions		Three-Year Transitions	
	No Change	Job Change	No Change	Job Change
Men				
Uninsured spouse	789	87	655	221
	(0.901)	(0.099)	(0.748)	(0.252)
Insured spouse	376	55	322	109
	(0.872)	(0.128)	(0.747)	(0.253)
χ^2		2.39		0.001
Women				
Uninsured spouse	212	39	176	75
	(0.845)	(0.155)	(0.701)	(0.299)
Insured spouse	412	53	346	119
	(0.886)	(0.114)	(0.744)	(0.256)
χ^2		2.49		0.218

Notes: Numbers in parentheses = column entry ÷ (no job change + job change). χ^2 = Chi-square test statistic for the null hypothesis that those with and without insurance have the same transition rates.

rows display the mobility rates for those whose spouses do not have insurance versus those whose spouses have employer-provided insurance. Consider the results for married males. For one-year transitions, one finds that 12.8 percent of males with an insured spouse undertook a job transition, and this exceeds the 9.9 percent rate for those whose spouses do not receive insurance. The greater propensity to change jobs is suggestive of the job lock phenomenon. As indicated by the Chi-square test statistic, however, the difference in behavior is not statistically significant.[19] The lack of an effect from spousal insurance is even clearer in the three-year transition matrix. Here the transition rates are virtually identical in each row.

Table 6.4 displays analogous transition data for married women. In both time spans, the propensity to change employers is greater, not smaller, for those whose spouses do not have insurance. Again, however, the differences are not statistically significant. Thus, the raw data reveal little linkage between insurance status and job mobility.

Intuitively, one would also expect job lock (if any) to become more important as insurance became more valuable to the individual. Using the information from the PSID, one may focus on several indicators of the value of insurance. First, the PSID contains measures of health status for 1984 and 1986 and of the change in health status between 1982 and 1984. Thus, for example, one might expect that health insurance would be more valuable to those with poor health in 1984.[20] In a probit equation for job mobility, then, this would lead one to anticipate that the interaction between poor health and the provision of health insurance would tend to decrease mobility; that is, the sign of the coefficient on such an interaction variable should be negative. In contrast, poor health should raise the value of access to medical insurance via one's spouse. I investigate these interactions in the analysis of the PSID.

The use of 1984 health status places the emphasis on contemporaneous relationships. Alternatively, it may be that individuals anticipate the need to address developing health conditions, and they value their current insurance more highly as a result. To gain a feel for this aspect of the data, I perform an analogous examination of the effects of interacting future health status (that reported for 1986) with the provision of health insurance in 1984. As before, one would anticipate that the coefficient on such an interaction variable should be (if anything) negative.

Of course, the discussion of preexisting conditions indicates that job lock may hinge on the *change* in health status as much as or more than on the state of the individual's health. The 1984 wave of the PSID also contains survey

19. The difference between the mobility rate of *uninsured* males whose spouses do and do not have insurance is 0.037. Thus, the differences-in-differences point estimate of the effect of insurance is negative: $-0.008 = 0.029 - 0.037$.

20. I focus on the "poor health" response in what follows. Attempts at first distinctions in health status provided no additional insights.

information on health status in 1984 versus 1982. I focus on those who report that their health is *worse* in 1984 than in 1982.[21] The logic of preexisting conditions indicates that the worsening of health condition should make health insurance more valuable and thus lower mobility. As before, I check the degree to which the data are consistent with this hypothesis by examining the coefficients on an interaction between the variable indicating provision of health insurance and that indicating a worsening of health status over the two years prior to 1984.

As a last check on the interaction between the value of insurance to the individual and job mobility, I focus on interactions with the age of the individual. Here, the basic notion is simple: as one ages, the expected cost of medical care rises, *ceteris paribus*. Thus, as before, the interaction between age and employer-provided health insurance should serve to reduce mobility.

Thus far, the discussion has focused on the health status of the individual. However, the health status of others living with (and covered by the policy for) the individual may have just as important an effect on the perceived value of the benefit. I use the number of children living in the family to proxy for the expected value of the insurance policy. If correct, one would expect the coefficient on such an interaction variable (number of children and employer-provided insurance) to be negative.

No empirical strategy is entirely without pitfalls, and the approach used herein is no exception. Thus far, for example, the discussion has treated health insurance status as exogenous. To the extent that this is not the case, two related problems arise. First, it is difficult to understand the notion of job lock when the health insurance package is (in part) self-inflicted. Second, the right-side variables in the probit equations below will be endogenous, and more-refined statistical techniques will be required to identify residual evidence of job lock. A conceptually similar issue arises in the literature on pensions. Allen, Clark, and McDermed (1991), for example, model the endogenous determination of pension status. In addition, when health insurance status is endogenous, there may be some gain to explicitly modeling the distribution of insurance among spouses. These extensions are beyond the scope of this paper.

Another caveat is that the absence of information on the benefits package for health insurance makes the interpretation of the dummy variables more tenuous. While the interaction effects discussed above are designed to reveal the differential value of insurance across individuals, they are unlikely to capture fully such variations in the net benefits of insurance coverage.

Last, two minor footnotes on legal institutions are in order. First, the Consolidated Omnibus Reconciliation Act of 1986 (COBRA) contains provisions (effective 1 July 1986) guaranteeing access to health insurance for up to eighteen months after separating from a job. (For a full discussion of COBRA, see

21. Again, attempts to make finer distinctions yielded little additional insight.

Flynn 1992.) Thus, while I examine job changes as late as 1987 below, those that occur after 1985 are subject to the caveat that COBRA may make job transitions easier. Similarly, even prior to COBRA many states had state-specific laws regarding access to employer medical insurance after leaving a job.[22]

6.1.5   Probit Analysis

The results of testing for health insurance–related job lock in the PSID are summarized in table 6.5 and table 6.6. Begin by looking at table 6.5, which reports the coefficient estimates for three variables indicating health insurance status. The first is a dichotomous variable equal to one for those that have employer-provided health insurance. The second is an analogously defined variable indicating that the spouse has health insurance. The final variable is the interaction between the first two variables and indicates that both the individual and the spouse have insurance. For single individuals, the last two clearly are not appropriate.

Part A of the table reports the coefficient estimates for one-year transitions, while Part B is devoted to three-year transitions. Within each part, two sets of estimates are reported for each sample. The "No Controls" estimates are obtained by estimating a probit equation for job transitions in which only the insurance variables (and a constant) appear on the right-hand side. The "Controls" estimates contain a rich set of noninsurance control variables and are discussed below. Examination of the "No Controls" estimates suggests two broad conclusions. First, for the probits analyzing married men and women, the coefficient on the interaction variable "Both insurance" is always on the wrong sign and statistically insignificant. Recall from the earlier discussion that this variable is the natural point of focus when one suspects that the specification does not fully capture attributes of jobs or spouses that are correlated with the provision of employer health insurance. The "No Controls" estimates in table 6.5 are an extreme case because no other controls are included in the equation. Second, from a job lock perspective, even the econometric performance of the "Own insurance" variable is somewhat uneven; only for married men is it uniformly negative and statistically significant.

The columns labeled "Controls" in table 6.5 contain the results for the insurance variables of fully specified mobility equations for one-year and three-year transitions, respectively.[23] Before discussing the variables related to the job lock hypothesis, consider the variables included in the probit to control for other aspects of job mobility. Each probit equation contains dummy variables for occupation and industry, reflecting differential conditions in these markets. In an attempt to control, albeit incompletely, for non–health insurance attributes of individuals' jobs, I include reported tenure on the job, dummy vari-

---

22. A statistical test of the importance of dummy variables for each state did not reject the null hypothesis of no significant differences across states.

23. Complete results are available from the author.

Table 6.5   **Probit Analysis of Job Transitions (standard errors in parentheses)**

	A. One-Year Transitions							
	Married Men		Married Women		Single Men		Single Women	
	No Controls (1)	Controls (2)	No Controls (3)	Controls (4)	No Controls (5)	Controls (6)	No Controls (7)	Controls (8)
Own insurance	−0.251**	−0.143	0.00519	−0.0341	−0.223	0.291	−0.175	−0.050
	(0.0901)	(0.134)	(0.117)	(0.141)	(0.133)	(0.236)	(0.111)	(0.217)
Spouse insurance	0.160	0.247	0.0618	−0.0568				
	(0.120)	(0.140)	(0.0854)	(0.129)				
Both insurance	−0.00209	0.0860	−0.270	−0.233				
	(0.155)	(0.164)	(0.150)	(0.163)				
	B. Three-Year Transitions							
	Married Men		Married Women		Single Men		Single Women	
	No Controls (1)	Controls (2)	No Controls (3)	Controls (4)	No Controls (5)	Controls (6)	No Controls (7)	Controls (8)
Own insurance	−0.175**	−0.0912	−0.0671	−0.156	−0.291*	0.304	−0.204	−0.0451
	(0.0748)	(0.110)	(0.0366)	(0.120)	(0.123)	(0.224)	(0.0960)	(0.180)
Spouse insurance	0.174	0.164	0.0344	−0.0692				
	(0.105)	(0.120)	(0.0268)	(0.108)				
Both insurance	−0.181	−0.0518	−0.0833	−0.104				
	(0.132)	(0.140)	(0.0458)	(0.136)				
Observations	2007	2007	2024	2024	420	420	738	738

*Significant at the 5 percent level.
**Significant at the 1 percent level.

ables for each of the following: whether the job is covered by a collective bargaining agreement, whether the job provides dental insurance, whether it provides life insurance, and whether there is a pension plan. To further refine the pension measures, two additional variables are included. The first identifies those who have been vested in the pension plan, while the remaining variable indicates those who participate in a defined contribution pension plan.

Also present in the equation are individual attributes such as age, education, race, an indicator variable for health-related work limitations, an indicator variable for poor health (in 1984), the number of children in the household, and union membership status.

Finally, the equations control for resources and prices associated with the mobility decision by including wage earnings in the current job and net assets of the individual. For married individuals, the wages of the spouse are included as well. (Descriptive statistics for key variables are shown in appendix table 6A.1.)

Consider now the variables related to medical insurance. For married individuals, as discussed earlier, the interaction variable is the focus of attention. For single individuals, such an interaction is not available. However, one may be able to discern evidence of job lock by looking at the interaction between insurance and health status or other variables. I return to these tests below.

Column 2 of part A in table 6.5 shows the estimates for married men when focusing on job changes over the one-year period 1984–85. The coefficient for having insurance is −0.14 but not statistically significant. As argued above, however, neither this coefficient nor the coefficient on spouse insurance (0.25) is the proper center of attention. Instead, the coefficient on the interaction variable is likely to be the most reliable indicator of job lock. The estimated coefficient is positive (0.09), which is suggestive of job lock but not statistically significant at conventional levels. Thus, in contrast to Madrian (1992), these data do not provide evidence of health insurance–related job lock.

The results for married women present a slightly different picture, as the coefficient on "Own insurance" is positive and imprecisely estimated. However, the interaction variable is of the "wrong" sign from the job lock perspective and, as in the case of married men, statistically insignificant.

The basic thrust of these results is reinforced by those reported in part B, which shows the estimates for three-year transitions. For both married men and married women, the point estimate of the interaction variable is negative and has a large standard error. In sum, using the presence of spouse insurance to test for job lock gives little support to the proposition. Thus, these estimates do not favor identifying health insurance as a major culprit in job market inefficiencies.

Recall from the discussion surrounding equation (4) that the coefficient on the own insurance variable may be contaminated by correlation with unobserved attributes of the job. If one could be confident that such unobserved heterogeneity was quantitatively small, then it would be possible to test for job lock by direct examination of the own insurance variable, a testing procedure that would permit examination of the results for single individuals (columns 6 and 8 of parts A and B as well. In this context, a comparison of the No Controls and Controls columns is relevant. The estimated coefficients for the insurance variables appear somewhat sensitive to the inclusion of controls for differences among individuals and jobs. This argues against focusing on the own insurance variable. Moreover, as noted earlier, the pattern of estimated coefficients for the own insurance variable in the No Controls columns does not support the job lock notion. This conclusion is amplified by the results in the Controls columns.

A simple indicator variable may not adequately capture differences across individuals in the value of insurance. Hence, as noted earlier, using interactions between the insurance variable (both insurance) and indicators of the value of insurance such as poor health, or worsened health, may provide better insight into the significance of job lock. Moreover, to the extent that these variables are significant in the mobility equations for single individuals, they permit one to detect job lock where the use of the spouse insurance interaction was not feasible.

Table 6.6 is devoted to summarizing the results of such an exercise. The table contains t-statistics to test the null hypothesis that the coefficient on the interaction between the insurance variable and the variable shown in each row is zero. Thus, for example, consider the entry in the first row of column 1 of the table. To generate the test statistic, I estimate a variant of the basic mobility probit, which also includes the interaction between the both insurance variable and the dummy variable for poor health in 1984. The test statistic, 1.52, indicates that one cannot reject the null hypothesis that the coefficient for the interaction is zero. This procedure is repeated for each of the variables shown in the table. (For single individuals, the own insurance variable is used for these interactions.)

Table 6.6   *t*-test Statistics for Interactions with Insurance Variables

	One-Year Transitions	Three-Year Transitions
Married men		
Poor health, 1984	1.52	1.18
Poor health, 1986	0.239	3.02**
Worse health, 1982–84	1.66	0.400
Children	0.007	−1.36
Age	0.585	0.709
Married women		
Poor health, 1984	−0.039	1.22
Poor health, 1986	1.17	1.43
Worse health, 1982–84	0.672	0.773
Children	−0.584	−0.406
Age	−1.36	−0.973
Single men		
Poor health, 1984	1.07	1.02
Poor health, 1986	1.83	1.34
Worse health, 1982–84	3.04**	3.17**
Children	−0.248	−0.552
Age	1.79	1.77
Single women		
Poor health, 1984	1.71	1.15
Poor health, 1986	−0.161	0.644
Worse health, 1982–84	2.12*	1.28
Children	−0.854	1.07
Age	−0.176	−0.704

Note: Test statistics for the null hypothesis that the interaction between the "Both Insurance" variable (for single individuals, "Own Insurance") and the row variable is zero.

*Significant at the 5 percent level.

**Significant at the 1 percent level.

What results emerge? There is little in the table to suggest an important or pervasive effect of job lock. Few of the interactions are statistically significant, and one that is—the interaction of worsening health status with insurance among single men—is of the wrong (positive) sign. In sum, using a variety of indicators of the value of health insurance to the individual does not provide evidence of job lock in the United States.

6.2   Health Insurance and the Labor Market in Germany

The German systems of health care provision and finance have attracted rising attention in the United States. As in the United States, the majority of care in Germany is provided by private sector doctors operating in private hospitals and financed by health insurance provided by private companies ("sickness funds," see below). Also in the United States, these private markets are subject to large-scale government intervention to ensure satisfactory health and budgetary outcomes. In 1987, however, health expenditures were only 8.1 percent of gross domestic product in West Germany, compared with 11.2 percent in the United States (Aaron 1991, 80, table 4-1). Moreover, mandatory insurance coverage for virtually all Germans precludes the possibility of large numbers of uninsured people. For these reasons, some analysts have pointed to the German system as a model for U.S. reforms.[24]

6.2.1   Health Insurance Provision in Germany

The German system of social health insurance[25] was introduced by Bismarck in 1883 and has gradually expanded to cover roughly 90 percent of the population.[26] The core of the financing system is provided by the roughly 1,150 private sickness funds, or insurance companies. Regional associations of sickness funds, in turn, bargain with regional associations of physicians to determine the rates charged for specific services.[27] Similarly, there are negotiations with each hospital for specific in-patient rates. All these negotiations are undertaken within the guidelines for rate increases established by the national committee (Concerted Action) set up in the 1977 health care reform to control the growth rate of health costs.

In some broad sense, then, the fund system is decentralized and self-governed by autonomous administrations. That is, it resembles a private system in that there are no explicit government agencies. German law requires, how-

24. In this context, it is somewhat ironic that the West German health care and finance system underwent major reforms in 1977, 1982, 1983, and 1989, in part to address dissatisfaction over the inability to contain costs.

25. This brief overview draws upon excellent surveys by Glaser (1991), GAO (1991), Henke (1990), and Reinhardt (1990).

26. The system dates from the Social Insurance Code of 15 June 1883 (Commission of the European Communities 1990, 50).

27. German physicians do not directly bill the sickness fund for services rendered. Instead, the regional association of physicians pays its members out of premium income collected from the sickness funds.

ever, that all persons with incomes below a cutoff (in 1989, DM 54,900, or roughly $27,300 in 1990 U.S. dollars) receive mandatory health insurance coverage. Those people with incomes above the cutoff may voluntarily join the mandatory system, purchase private health insurance, or remain uninsured.[28]

In large part, individuals receive insurance from the sickness fund chosen by their employer. (I will return to the exceptions below.) The retired are covered by the sickness fund of their former employer, and the unemployed receive insurance from the sickness fund of their previous employer. Self-employed individuals must enroll in one of the sickness funds. The health insurance premiums are financed from a variety of sources. The bulk of contributions take the form of a payroll tax rate, which is statutorily split equally between the employer and the employee. Government subsidies contribute toward the cost of covering the retired, the unemployed, and full-time students.

The payroll tax base consists mainly of wage and salary income.[29] Health insurance premiums, and thus payroll tax rates, are based on the average cost of insurance within each sickness fund. To calculate the rate, an insurance fund effectively divides the expected insurance costs by the total payroll tax base of its members. The result is a single payroll tax rate that is applied to the earnings of each individual (and his or her employer) in the fund. In this way, the German system embodies a form of "community rating" in which insurance rates are independent of the medical risks of individuals and their dependents.[30] Rates do depend, however, upon the sickness fund of the insured, with the result that West German rates ranged from 8 percent to 16 percent in 1990 (Schneider 1991).

Such a system provides clear incentives to migrate from high-cost insurance funds. Freedom of choice, however, is carefully circumscribed in the German insurance system. As noted above, employers choose the sickness fund that covers most of their employees. The most common sickness funds are the General Local Sickness Funds, or local funds organized on a regional basis. In addition, companies may organize their own establishment sickness funds, or company funds, to provide insurance to their employees. White-collar workers, however, also have the option of joining alternative private funds known as substitute funds, which are organized on a national basis.[31] In addition, there are several sickness funds for specific occupations (guild funds) and for miners, farmers, and mariners.[32] In the end, approximately 50 percent of individu-

28. Prior to the 1989 reforms, individuals whose incomes fluctuated first above, then below the income cutoff simply rejoined the mandatory system, an option that is no longer available.

29. Recently, some pension income has been included in the payroll tax base.

30. It is illegal to charge rates that discriminate by age, but in practice the system moves beyond even this restriction.

31. As a result of the 1989 reforms, the options of blue-collar workers are now comparable to those of white-collar workers.

32. The breakdown is as follows: 266 local sickness funds, 691 company sickness funds, 152 guild sickness funds, 19 agricultural sickness funds, 1 seamen's fund, 1 miners' fund, and 15 substitute sickness funds.

als may choose their own health insurance fund. Note that most of the variation across funds occurs in the cost of coverage, not benefits received (HCFR 1989, 94).

6.2.2   Health Insurance Information in the GSOEP

With the PSID as the standard for comparison, the German Socioeconomic Panel (GSOEP) provides relatively good information regarding the insurance status of each individual. Each year, information is collected regarding whether the individual has insurance and, if so, from which type of sickness fund. In addition, there is information about whether the individual is a voluntary or compulsory member of the sickness fund. Like the PSID, however, the GSOEP does not contain information on the health insurance premium paid by each individual.[33]

6.2.3   Health Insurance and Job Turnover

Although the German system is designed to provide universal coverage, its features potentially generate a job lock phenomenon. In this regard, the key aspect is the degree to which the price of insurance is portable across jobs. Several cases are straightforward. Individuals with private health insurance, for example, have insurance that is portable in both access and price. Similarly, members of guild or substitute sickness funds (each of whom is, by definition, a voluntary member) will be equally unencumbered by their insurance status.

For the remainder, the possibility of a nonportable price arises. Members of company funds—voluntary or compulsory—face a change in the cost of health insurance if they change employers, and the empirical averages indicate that it will be a higher cost. Schulenburg (1989) reports that the company funds have the lowest average payroll tax rate among types of sickness funds.[34] Similarly, both voluntary and compulsory members of local sickness funds may have to change funds if the employment switch takes them outside of the current area or if their new employer chooses not to use the local sickness fund.

To deal with the ambiguity, I create two variables identifying candidates for job lock on the basis of health insurance. The first, "Insurance Lock 1," consists of company fund members, local fund members, and compulsory members of the "other" category.[35] If all employment changes involve interregional moves, this variable appropriately identifies candidates for job lock. The second variable, "Insurance Lock 2," excludes members of local funds and is appropriate

---

33. There have been attempts to impute premiums to individuals, but the imputation scheme does not reflect differences in types of sickness funds. Experimentation with these imputed payroll tax rates did not prove fruitful, and the analysis presented below does not rely on these measures.

34. See table 6.6. Schulenburg reports that in 1988 the average payroll tax rate required for health insurance was highest (13.5 percent) in local sickness funds and lowest (11.5 percent) in company funds.

35. The latter assignment was done on the basis of testing whether the coefficient on such a variable was different from that on the health lock variable. I could not reject this hypothesis.

only for intraregional moves. While only a conjecture, it would seem likely that the large number of local funds and relatively small land area would combine to make the first measure more appropriate on the whole.[36]

As with the analysis of the PSID, I begin with a simple look at the data in the GSOEP. Tables 6.7 and 6.8 contain transition data computed for those with and those without "Insurance Lock" status. Consider table 6.7, which shows the transition rates of for individuals with and without the Insurance Lock 1 status. The table first shows a comparison of job mobility rates for married individuals. For comparability with the analysis of the U.S. data, I restrict the sample to individuals ages twenty-five to fifty-five who are full-time employees. The combination of excluding those in the very early stages of their labor market experience and the general nature of the German labor market contributes to the low overall rate of job transition that characterizes both tables.

Looking at the transition rates in table 6.7, one finds that they are in accord with the simple hypothesis for both one-year transitions (between 1984 and 1985) and three-year transitions (between 1984 and 1987). Only the former differences, however, are statistically significant. For single individuals, job transition rates for the insurance locked are lower over both the one-year and the three-year horizon; indeed, they are less than one-half the rates for the control group. Moreover, as shown by the Chi-square statistics, these differences are significant.

Table 6.8 repeats the analysis using Insurance Lock 2, the more circumscribed definition, as the indicator of insurance lock-in. Here the results are qualitatively similar—transition rates are uniformly lower for married and single individuals in the insurance lock category—but the details of statistical significance differ. As with the transition data from the PSID, such a simple test is hardly conclusive, so I turn now to a multivariate analysis intended to shed additional light on the issue.

6.2.4   Probit Analysis

The results of the probit analysis for job lock in the GSOEP, presented in table 6.9, are organized in a fashion parallel to those for the United States.[37] As before, I begin by analyzing transition equations that include only the insurance lock variables. Because of the low overall rate of job transitions, the use of such a parsimonious specification avoids the pitfall of overfitting the equations. Further, in a fashion analogous to the discussion earlier, comparison of these estimates with those from a richer specification sheds light on the degree to which the insurance variables are correlated with unobserved heterogeneity in

36. The public use sample of the GSOEP does not contain geographic identifiers, thus precluding direct examination of this issue.

37. The sample size for married women who are full-time employed was too small to obtain satisfactory estimates, so I restrict my attention to married men, single men, and single women. Full results are available upon request.

Table 6.7   Job Transitions for Germany: Insurance Lock 1

	One-Year Transitions		Three-Year Transitions	
	No Change	Job Change	No Change	Job Change
Married individuals				
Insurance Lock 1	703	9	670	42
	(0.987)	(0.013)	(0.941)	(0.059)
No lock	717	20	692	45
	(0.973)	(0.027)	(0.939)	(0.061)
χ^2	3.88*		0.027	
Single individuals				
Insurance Lock 1	971	24	945	50
	(0.976)	(0.024)	(0.950)	(0.050)
No lock	331	21	309	43
	(0.940)	(0.060)	(0.878)	(0.122)
χ^2	10.2**		20.9**	

Notes: Numbers in parentheses = column entry ÷ (no job change + job change). χ^2 = Chi-square test statistic for the null hypothesis that those with and without insurance have the same transition rates.

*Significant at the 5 percent level.

**Significant at the 1 percent level.

Table 6.8   Job Transitions for Germany: Insurance Lock 2

	One-Year Transitions		Three-Year Transitions	
	No Change	Job Change	No Change	Job Change
Married individuals				
Insurance Lock 2	212	2	209	5
	(0.991)	(0.009)	(0.977)	(0.023)
No lock	1,208	27	1,153	82
	(0.978)	(0.022)	(0.934)	(0.066)
χ^2	1.46*		5.98*	
Single individuals				
Insurance Lock 2	230	4	227	7
	(0.983)	(0.017)	(0.870)	(0.030)
No lock	1,072	41	1,027	86
	(0.963)	(0.037)	(0.923)	(0.077)
χ^2	2.33		6.75**	

Notes: Numbers in parentheses = column entry ÷ (no job change + job change). χ^2 = Chi-square test statistic for the null hypothesis that those with and without insurance have the same transition rates.

*Significant at the 5 percent level.

**Significant at the 1 percent level.

Table 6.9   **Probit Analysis of Job Transitions (standard errors in parentheses)**

| | A. One-Year Transitions | | | | | |
| | Married Men | | Single Men | | Single Women | |
	No Controls	Controls	No Controls	Controls	No Controls	Controls
Insurance Lock 1	−0.261	−0.501*	−0.446**	−0.381	−0.459	−0.583
	(0.168)	(0.227)	(0.140)	(0.262)	(0.244)	(0.530)
Insurance Lock 2	−0.342	−0.348	−0.373	−0.107	−0.242	0.317
	(0.279)	(0.315)	(0.246)	(0.285)	(0.419)	(0.538)
	B. Three-Year Transitions					
	Married Men		Single Men		Single Women	
	No Controls	Controls	No Controls	Controls	No Controls	Controls
Insurance Lock 1	0.179	−0.153	−0.447**	−0.409*	−0.691**	−0.952*
	(0.114)	(0.153)	(0.138)	(0.207)	(0.199)	(0.396)
Insurance Lock 2	−0.477*	−0.509*	−0.542**	−0.384	−0.273	0.102
	(0.199)	(0.213)	(0.204)	(0.226)	(0.329)	(0.377)
Observations	1,173	1,173	879	879	453	453

*Significant at the 5 percent level.
**Significant at the 1 percent level.

job attributes for the individuals. The results for separate probits using each insurance lock measure are shown in the No Controls columns of table 6.9.

With a single exception—three-year transitions for married men—each of the estimated coefficients is negative, which is consistent with the job lock notion. In terms of statistical significance, the effect appears to be centered among the single individuals, with the more expansive definition of insurance lock performing the best.

As in the case of the PSID, it is useful to see whether this pattern survives in the context of a multivariate analysis. I begin by noting the noninsurance variables entered in the probit equation to control for other aspects of job changes. Each probit in the Controls columns includes controls for the type of employment (blue-collar, civil servant).[38] The equations also include individual attributes such as age, indicator variables for alternative educational backgrounds, an indicator of health-related work limitations, an indicator of poor health (in 1984), and the number of children in the household.

Finally, the equations control for resources and prices associated with the mobility decision by including wage earnings in the current job, household income (for married men) and the capital income (dividends and interest) of the individual.[39] Descriptive statistics for key variables are shown in the appendix table 6A.2.

38. Experiments with including industry dummy variables yielded very large standard errors but had only a small effect on the point estimates for the insurance lock variables.
39. In contrast to the PSID, these equations do not have a control for job tenure (which is not available) or pension characteristics.

Returning to table 6.9, part A looks at one-year job transitions between 1984 and 1985. For married men, the coefficient on the Insurance Lock 1 variable is negative and exceeds its standard error by roughly 1.9. Thus, especially if one employs a one-tailed test for a negative value, there is suggestive statistical evidence that job mobility is lower among those individuals who belong to insurance funds for which the price of insurance is not portable. The result for Insurance Lock 2 is qualitatively similar but even less precisely estimated. The pattern is reversed for three-year transitions among married men; both coefficients are negative, but that for Insurance Lock 2 is weakly significant.

Recall as well from table 6.7 that the results for one-year transitions were somewhat stronger for single individuals than for married men. In the probit analysis, however, this is not the case. Looking at the estimated coefficients for single men and women in part A, one finds that they are typically of the anticipated sign but are not statistically significant at conventional levels in either one- or two-tailed tests.

Are these results special to one-year transitions? Consider the estimates for three-year transitions between 1984 and 1987. Again, there is no strong pattern of reduced mobility for those having insurance lock status. For both single men and single women, the coefficient on Insurance Lock 1 is negative but is significant only at the 5 percent level. Moreover, the results from using the Insurance Lock 2 variable instead are even weaker.

Taken as a whole, the parameter estimates in table 6.9 raise the possibility that the low rate of job mobility is reduced further by the institutions of the German health insurance system. At the same time, the statistical link is not sufficiently firm to warrant a strong position on the basis on this evidence alone.[40] Rather, the picture that emerges is one that does not support any conjecture of widespread labor market interference as a result of the health insurance system in Germany.

6.3 Summary

The potential for employer-provided insurance to interfere with the smooth working of the labor market has attracted considerable attention in the United States, and some analysts have pointed to Germany as a model for a system that avoids impediments to labor market mobility. As in the United States, however, the provision and cost of health insurance in Germany are in part determined by individuals' employers. Although it has not attracted comparable attention, the German system also generates the potential for insurance-related job lock.

---

40. I experimented with interactions of the health insurance lock variable and age, number of children, and health status. The anecdotal evidence suggests that the benefits package does not differ widely across sickness funds. If so, one would not expect these variables—which proxy for differences in the value of benefits across individuals—to be significant. They were not.

To date, much of discussion of job lock has been restricted to the use of anecdotal evidence. As a step toward filling the research void, this paper has been devoted to gauging the empirical magnitude of the job lock phenomenon. On the whole, these initial results suggest no evidence of job lock in either country. For the United States, analysis of the PSID suggests little in the way of correlation between insurance variables and the probability of changing employers. Some suggestive correlations are present when the health insurance variables are analyzed in isolation. However, in the presence of a rich set of noninsurance variables to control for other aspects of the incentives to change employers, their apparent importance disappears. This suggests that access to richer data for each individual and employer may explain the apparent difference between these findings and those in, for example, Madrian (1992).

The results of analyzing the GSOEP data for West Germany have the same flavor. When viewed in isolation, membership in a sickness fund for which the price of insurance is not portable across jobs is correlated with lower mobility. When analyzed simultaneously with a larger set of socioeconomic variables, however, the link becomes more tenuous. A difficulty unique to this analysis is the low overall rate of mobility among employers reported in the GSOEP.

From a slightly different perspective, the results of the empirical analysis in each country suggest a very important result. The health insurance systems in these countries should not be judged by their secondary effects on labor mobility, as these effects are small at best. Instead, they should be judged by their primary effects: access to health care and the efficiency of the provision of health insurance.

Appendix
Data Sources

The empirical analyses use data from two longitudinal data sets: for the United States, the Panel Study of Income Dynamics (PSID); for Germany, the Public Use Version of the Socioeconomic Panel of Germany (GSOEP). Since 1968, the PSID has interviewed annually a representative sample of some five thousand families. At least one member of each family was either part of the original families interviewed in 1968 or born to a member of one of these families. (See Survey Research Center 1984 for a complete discussion.)

The GSOEP is a more recent longitudinal data set developed at the Universities of Frankfurt and Mannheim in cooperation with the Deutsches Institut für Wirtschaftsforschung, Berlin (DIW) and initially financed by the German National Science Foundation. In 1990 the DIW assumed control of the panel with funding through 1995 from the Bund-Länder-Kommission für Forschungsförderung. The panel started in the spring of 1984. It comprises about six thousand families. Nine yearly waves have been conducted (1984–92), and six waves (1984–89) are available, providing information on calendar year 1983 through 1988. (In 1990 the GSOEP was expanded to include a representative sample of East Germans.) The data are representative of the German population, including "guest workers." Wagner, Burkhauser, and Behringer (1993) contains a detailed discussion of these data.

Table 6.A.1   Descriptive Statistics for Key Variables: PSID

	Married Men	Married Women	Single Men	Single Women
Job change 1984–85	0.1266	0.1512	0.2548	0.1789
	(0.3326)	(0.3583)	(0.4363)	(0.3835)
Job change 1984–87	0.2795	0.3463	0.4381	0.3726
	(0.4489)	(0.4759)	(0.4967)	(0.4838)
Own insurance	0.6457	0.3498	0.5000	0.4173
	(0.4784)	(0.4770)	(0.5006)	(0.4935)
Spouse insurance	0.3189	0.6275		
	(0.4662)	(0.4836)		
Both insurance	0.2113	0.2263		
	(0.4083)	(0.4185)		
Age	37.64	37.18	34.76	38.00
	(8.301)	(8.565)	(7.566)	(9.155)
Education (years)	12.66	12.60	12.51	12.04
	(2.626)	(2.210)	(2.702)	(2.350)
White	0.7514	0.7451	0.5429	0.4052
	(0.4323)	(0.4359)	(0.4988)	(0.4913)
Black	0.2327	0.2288	0.4333	0.5867
	(0.4227)	(0.4201)	(0.4961)	(0.4928)
Children	1.593	1.501	0.3643	1.098
	(1.214)	(1.205)	(0.8892)	(1.285)
Own wages, 1984	21,707	7,920	15,870	9,437
	(17,632)	(8,391)	(14,115)	(8,790)
Spouse wages, 1984	7,390	21,647		
	(8,207)	(20,986)		
Tenure	10.70	7.563	7.833	8.696
	(7.995)	(5.843)	(7.027)	(7.283)
Union member	0.2148	0.08646	0.1429	0.1179
	(0.4108)	(0.2811)	(0.3503)	(0.3227)
Poor health, 1984	0.01545	0.01976	0.02619	0.05556
	(0.1234)	(0.1392)	(0.1599)	(0.2292)
Poor health, 1986	0.02691	0.02223	0.02857	0.05149
	(0.1619)	(0.1475)	(0.1668)	(0.2212)
Worse health, 1982–84	0.09866	0.9289	0.1214	0.1626
	(0.2983)	(0.2903)	(0.3270)	(0.3693)

Table 6A.2   Descriptive Statistics for Key Variables: GSOEP

	Married Men	Married Women	Single Men	Single Women
Job change, 1984–85	0.02090	0.01103	0.03600	0.02838
	(0.1470)	(0.1046)	(0.1864)	(0.1663)
Job change, 1984–87	0.06372	0.04412	0.07537	0.05677
	(0.2444)	(0.2057)	(0.2641)	(0.2317)
Local fund, 1984	0.3339	0.3897	0.5928	0.5109
	(0.4718)	(0.4886)	(0.4916)	(0.5004)
Company fund, 1984	0.1453	0.06985	0.1766	0.1245
	(0.3525)	(0.2554)	(0.3816)	(0.3305)
Guild fund, 1984	0.06627	0.02574	0.04387	0.01965
	(0.2489)	(0.1586)	(0.2049)	(0.1390)
Substitute fund, 1984	0.2702	0.4044	0.08661	0.2795
	(0.4442)	(0.4917)	(0.2814)	(0.4492)
Other fund, 1984	0.04344	0.02214	0.02931	0.006550
	(0.2039)	(0.1474)	(0.1688)	(0.08076)
Private insurance, 1984	0.1325	0.09927	0.06637	0.06550
	(0.3392)	(0.2996)	(0.2491)	(0.2479)
No insurance, 1984	0.01956	0.003690	0.01237	0.002183
	(0.1385)	(0.06075)	(0.1106)	(0.04673)
Age	40.97	38.77	38.93	38.16
	(8.351)	(9.145)	(8.429)	(8.781)
Blue-collar	0.4435	0.2500	0.7840	0.5480
	(0.4970)	(0.4338)	(0.4117)	(0.4982)
Civil servant	0.1487	0.06985	0.05287	0.03712
	(0.3559)	(0.2554)	(0.2239)	(0.1893)
Chronic illness	0.2574	0.2427	0.1856	0.2576
	(0.4374)	(0.4295)	(0.3890)	(0.4378)
Health limitation	0.05438	0.09191	0.06412	0.09170
	(0.2269)	(0.2894)	(0.2451)	(0.2889)
Wages	44,998	32,098	36,140	28,231
	(19,814)	(28,577)	(22,317)	(11,355)
Capital income	306.8	301.9	190.2	131.5
	(2052)	(1301)	(2099)	(1581)
Children	1.037	0.5441	1.051	0.7249
	(0.9518)	(0.8138)	(1.239)	(1.022)

References

Aaron, H. 1991. *Serious and unstable condition.* Washington, D.C.: Brookings Institution.

Allen, S., R. Clark, and A. McDermed. 1991. Pensions, bonding, and lifetime jobs. Raleigh: North Carolina State University. Mimeograph.

Brown, J., and A. Light. 1992. Interpreting panel data on job tenure. *Journal of Labor Economics* 10:219–57.

Commission of the European Community. Directorate of General Employment, Industrial Relations, and Social Affairs. 1992. Health care. In *Social protection in the member states of the community: Situation on July 1st 1990 and evolution*, 50–72. Paris: Commission of the European Community.

Congressional Budget Office. 1992. *Reducing the deficit: Spending and revenue options*. Washington, D.C.: U.S. Government Printing Office.

Cotton, P. 1991. Preexisting conditions 'hold Americans hostage' to employers and insurance. *Journal of the American Medical Association* 265, 15 May, 2451–53.

Flynn, P. 1992. Employment-based health insurance: Coverage under COBRA continuation rules. Washington, D.C.: Urban Institute. Mimeograph.

Fuchs, V. 1991. National health insurance revisited. NBER Working Paper no. 3884. Cambridge, Mass.: National Bureau of Economic Research.

General Accounting Office (GAO). 1991. Health care spending control: The experience of France, Germany, and Japan.

Glaser, W. 1991. *Health insurance in practice: International variations in financing, benefits, and problems*. San Francisco: Jossey-Bass.

Gruber, J. 1992. The efficiency of a group-specific mandated benefit: Evidence from health insurance benefits for maternity. NBER Working Paper no. 4157. Cambridge, Mass.: National Bureau of Economic Research.

Gustman, A., and T. Steinmeier. 1990. Pension portability and labor mobility: Evidence from the Survey of Income and Program Participation. NBER Working Paper no. 3252. Cambridge, Mass.: National Bureau of Economic Research.

Hamermesh, D., and S. Woodbury. 1990. Taxes, fringe benefits, and faculty. NBER Working Paper no. 3455. Cambridge, Mass.: National Bureau of Economic Research.

Health Care Financing Review (HCFR). 1989. Annual supplement.

Henke, K. 1990. The Federal Republic of Germany. In *Advances in health economics and health services research*. Supplement 1: Comparative health systems, 145–68. Greenwich, Conn.: JAI Press.

Hurst, J. 1991. Reform of health care in Germany. *Health Care Financing Review* 12:73–86.

Madrian, B. 1992. Employment-based health insurance and job mobility: Is there evidence of job-lock? Cambridge: Massachusetts Institute of Technology. Mimeograph.

Mitchell, O. 1982. Fringe benefits and mobility. *Journal of Human Resources* 17:286–98.

———. 1983. Fringe benefits and the cost of changing jobs. *Industrial and Labor Relations Review* 17:70–80.

———. 1990. Employee benefits and the new economy: A proposal for reform. *California Management Review* 32:113–30.

Reinhardt, U. 1990. West Germany's health-care and health-insurance system: combining universal access with cost control. In *A call for action*, 3–16. U.S. Bipartisan Commission on Comprehensive Health Care. Supplement to the Final Report.

Rovner, J. 1990. Congress tightens regulation of medigap insurance plans. *Congressional Quarterly Weekly Report*, 3 November, 3720.

Schneider, M. 1991. Health care cost containment in the Federal Republic of Germany. *Health Care Financing Review* 12:87–101.

Schulenburg, J. 1989. The West German health care financing and delivery system: Its experiences and lessons for other nations. Paper presented at the International Symposium on Health Care Systems. Mimeograph.

Sloan, F., and K. Adamache. 1986. Taxation and the growth of non-wage compensation. *Public Finance Quarterly* 57:115–38.

Survey Research Center. 1984. *User guide to the Panel Study of Income Dynamics*. Inter-University Consortium for Political and Social Research. Ann Arbor, Mich.

Swartz, K. 1989. Counting uninsured Americans. *Health Affairs* 8:193.

Wagner, G., R. Burkhauser, and F. Behringer. 1993. The English language public use file of the German Socio-Economic Panel. *Journal of Human Resources* 28:413–15.

Wienand, M. 1988. Health insurance. In *The social system and social work in the Federal Republic of Germany,* 43–45. Bonn: German Association for Public and Private Welfare.

Wolfe, B. 1992. Reform of health care for the poor. IRP conference paper. University of Wisconsin, Madison.

7 Social Security and Older Workers' Labor Market Responsiveness: The United States, Japan, and Sweden

Marcus E. Rebick

Social security and other public transfer programs aimed at improving the welfare of the elderly have been well established in all Organization for Economic Cooperation and Development (OECD) countries. A secondary goal of public support programs for older individuals has been to open job opportunities for younger individuals by encouraging earlier retirement of older workers. This kind of program has been explicitly tried in several European countries, including the United Kingdom. In part as a result of the adoption of better social support for older people, the age of full retirement from the labor force has fallen substantially in the OECD, and there is some debate as to whether the programs have encouraged the retirement of too many individuals who would prefer to continue working.[1] There is also an argument that these programs have exacerbated unemployment problems for older workers through the creation of work disincentives.[2]

This paper examines some of the outcomes of public assistance programs for the middle-aged and older individual that have been adopted in three countries in the OECD: the United States, Japan, and Sweden. I address the ques-

Marcus E. Rebick is assistant professor of labor economics and international and comparative labor at Cornell University.

The author thanks the Japan Development Bank, the National Bureau of Economic Research, and the Ford Foundation for support for this research. Debra Dwyer provided excellent research assistance. The author benefited from helpful comments from Morio Kuninori, Maria Hanratty, George Jakubson, Olivia Mitchell, Ronald Dore, Annika Sunden, participants at the preconference and conference, seminars at the Japan Development Bank and Cornell University, and two anonymous discussants. He is especially indebted to Rebecca Blank for her comments and suggestions. He is also grateful to the Japanese Ministry of Welfare, to the Japan Institute of Labor, and to Annika Sunden and Margarita Henkel for help in obtaining data. All errors are the author's own.

1. An excellent survey of early retirement programs in the OECD that addresses this question may be found in OECD (1992a), chap. 5.

2. An example of this argument applied specifically to older workers in Japan may be found in Shimada et al. (1982).

tion of whether the growth of these programs has discouraged economic flexibility by encouraging older individuals to either retire early or to remain in the state of unemployment during downturns in the business cycle. In particular, I examine fluctuations in employment and participation rates for different demographic groups over the business cycle and look for evidence that these fluctuations have become more severe since the expansion of benefits during the 1960s and early 1970s. I also look directly at how participation in benefits of such programs varies with economic conditions.

I have chosen these three countries because of their widely differing institutions in the labor market, because of their different ideological orientations toward social protection programs, and also because they face the common challenge of a rapidly aging labor force. In addition, all three countries share the feature that they have responded relatively well, by European standards, to the economic circumstances of the 1970s and 1980s, so that failing economic performance is less likely to be a concern for this study.

The countries differ substantially in the kinds of social programs that have been developed to support earlier retirement. The United States saw the introduction of an early retirement program as early as 1961 (1956 in the case of women). Since that time, most of the initiative in encouraging earlier retirement has come through changes in the provisions of private employee pension plans. Sweden is notable for its introduction in 1976 of a partial pension program designed to encourage partial retirement, a program that has been a model for other European countries. Sweden had also relaxed the qualifications necessary for receipt of disability benefits in the early 1970s. In the Japanese case, the age of normal retirement is 60, rather than 65, as it is in the other two countries.

In this study, I propose to examine the extent to which various government labor market programs, including early retirement programs, are used by older individuals in response to economic fluctuations. I begin section 7.1 of the paper with a brief survey of the different government labor market programs used in each of three countries. Section 7.2 provides an overview of the conditions for mature and older workers by examining secular trends in labor force participation rates, unemployment rates, and indicators of well-being in the three countries. Section 7.3 looks at cyclical movements in participation and employment over the business cycle. Time series analysis of participation and employment is used to show the relative responsiveness of different demographic groups in the labor force. Section 7.4 then looks at the response during subperiods within each country to see how the cyclical response of employment of older demographic groups has changed over time as the social programs have grown and matured. In section 7.5, I present direct evidence on changes in the participation rates in public benefits over the business cycle, and in section 7.6, I offer conclusions.

7.1 Social Security Programs for the Mature and Older: Institutional Description

All countries in the OECD have developed public pension systems (known in the United States as Social Security) for the purpose of ensuring economic security for the elderly.[3] Although there were existing pension systems for parts of the labor force, Sweden introduced a national pension system in 1913, the United States introduced Social Security in 1935, and Japan developed its National Pension System in 1946. The existence of social security systems on paper, however, may have very little potential impact on labor supply. Instead, it is the size of the benefits, the extent of coverage of the population, and the conditions for benefit eligibility that influence aggregate behavior for specific demographic groups. Benefits may reduce labor supply through (1) the income effect of increased lifetime unearned wealth and (2) the substitution effect if benefits are reduced by working. This is particularly true of unemployment insurance and public pension systems that include an earnings test.

In general, the level of benefits, the extent of coverage, and the eligibility for benefits at earlier ages all increased over time in all three countries. It is this consistent trend that will allow me to test for changes in labor supply behavior caused by growth in the social insurance system. I begin this section with a brief summary of the different benefits and eligibility conditions in the three countries. I then describe the changes in the level of benefits and the extent of coverage over time. Finally, I look briefly at the effects of private pension plans and at the public pension financing arrangements on the labor market.

7.1.1 Public Economic Security Programs

Table 7.1 provides a summary description of the principal forms of public benefits, including unemployment insurance offered to older individuals, in each of the three countries. (A more comprehensive description of the different programs is provided in appendix A.) Here I list the main points that are particularly important in distinguishing the programs offered.

1. The *United States* offers the least variety in the way of programs targeted for its older workers. Unemployment insurance (UI) benefits are only available if one is dismissed from one's job. The normal age of retirement under the Social Security system is 65, but since 1956 and 1962 an early retirement option has been available for women and men, respectively, at age 62. Early retirement involves a reduction in the lifetime annuity and also includes an earnings test that reduces the benefit if the individual continues to work.

---

3. Throughout this paper, all income figures are evaluated at 1990 levels and converted to U.S. dollars, using the purchasing power parity index for consumption goods developed by the OECD for the year 1990. These levels may be found in OECD (1992b), table 2.5, row 1. Gross domestic product (GDP) deflators used were: United States—*Economic Report of the President, 1992,* table B-3; Japan and Sweden—World Bank, *World Tables 1992,* pp. 348–49 and 576–77, respectively.

Table 7.1   **Public Early Retirement and Disability Schemes in the United States, Japan, and Sweden, 1961–1990 (1990 U.S. dollars)**

Country	Retirement Age Normal	Early	Program	Conditions for Eligibility	Amount of Pension
United States	65[1]	62	Early retirement option (began 1956 for women, 1961 for men)		Benefits reduced 5/9 of 1% for each month prior to normal age[2]
			Disability insurance program	Person is unable to work due to physical or medi-cal impairment expected to last at least 1 year or result in death	
			Unemployment insurance	Involuntary separation	50% replacement rate
Japan	60 (males) 56 (females)		Employee pension	Full retirement, partial retirement (less than 3/5 of full-time work), or below earn-ings test point	Approximately 40% of income includ-ing bonuses
			Disability pension	Must qualify as having disability	
			Unemployment insurance		60–80% replacement rate for up to 300 days, up to $35/day
Sweden	65	60	Actuarially reduced pension (began 1963)		Pension reduced by 0.6% per month for each month prior to age 65
		60	Early retirement (began 1972)	Unemployment benefit has been paid for maxi-mum period, or labor market as-sistance been paid for 450 days and opportunity to earn a salary is permanently reduced by one-half	Full pension
		60	Flexible retirement with part-time employment (began 1976)	Employed 5 out of the last 12 months; worker must transfer	65% of salary lost due to part-time employment[3]

Table 7.1   (continued)

Country	Retirement Age		Program	Conditions for Eligibility	Amount of Pension
	Normal	Early			
Sweden (cont.)				from full- to part-time work and work at least 17 hours a week	
			Disability (began 1960)	Working capacity reduced by one-half due to physical or mental impairment or on grounds of redundancy (special medical examination not required, 1972–1991); partial disability available on grounds of premature aging or mental incapacity	Full pension
			Unemployment insurance	Must have worked 5 months out of last year	90% of earnings up to $50 per day; up to 450 days
			Labor market assistance	No longer eligible for unemployment insurance	$21 per day; up to 300 days before age 60; after age 60, available until age 65

Sources: United States and Sweden: Excerpted from Mirkin (1987), exhibit 1, and augmented from appendix 1. Japan: appendix A (this paper).

[1]In 1983, eligibility age for full retirement benefits was raised from 65 to 67.

[2]In 1983, the early retirement reduction in benefits claimed at age 62 was raised from 20 percent to 30 percent, to be phased in gradually between 2002 and 2027.

[3]65%, except for 1981–1987, where it was 50 percent.

2. *Sweden* offers the largest spectrum of different kinds of assistance programs, including an old-age pension with a normal retirement age of 65 (67 before 1976) and an early retirement option with actuarially reduced benefits and, unlike the United States, no earnings test. Other programs include partial pensions (up to 65 percent replacement of lost earnings for reduced working hours since 1976); liberal unemployment benefits (up to 90 percent replacement rate for 450 days); labor market assistance (smaller unemployment insurance benefits that are available after regular benefits run out) up through age 65, since 1971. Among the most important early retirement benefits are those

offered by disability pensions. Between 1972 and 1991, mature and older workers have been able to take the disability pension if they experienced difficulty finding jobs. As a result, roughly 13 percent of Swedes ages 55–59 and more than 30 percent of ages 60–64 were receiving disability pensions in the late 1980s. This was by far the most popular early retirement program.[4] Disability pensions given for difficulty in finding jobs will resemble unemployment insurance in their impact on labor supply. The impact will be even greater, however, since these pension benefits are typically much larger than those offered by unemployment insurance.

3. *Japan* allows individuals to collect both unemployment insurance and public pensions at the same time. Japan currently has the earliest normal retirement age for employees: age 60 for men and age 56 for women. The retirement age for women is being increased from 56 to 60 over the period from 1986 to 2000. The self-employed, part-time workers, and nonworking spouses have a normal retirement age of 65. Japan has an earnings test on wage income that is substantially relaxed after age 65.[5]

Japan's pension system provides unequal levels of protection for its entire population, since the average employee receives benefits starting at age 60 that are about four times larger than those received by the self-employed starting at age 65. Families in which the self-employed members are the top earners still make up almost a quarter of individuals covered directly or indirectly under the Japanese pension system. For these individuals the pension system offers very low benefits (table 7.4), well below the minimum poverty line.

7.1.2   Trends in the Levels of Benefits and Extent of Coverage

At present, the replacement rates on Swedish public pensions (57 percent) are higher on average than in the United States (43 percent) or Japan (42 percent) (Japan 1991, 202–3). As indicated in Table 7.1 through 7.4, however, there have been some significant changes to the programs offered over time, changes that could have important implications for labor supply and the timing of retirement.

Tables 7.2–7.4 present evidence on the average level of benefits paid out for different pension systems over the period from 1960 to the present. Prior to 1970, all three countries increased the coverage of their pension systems.[6] Since the public pension plans pay benefits based on the number of years of coverage, there is a time lag before the increase in coverage translates into increases in the number of older workers who have sizable public pension ben-

---

4. For comparison, the rate of disability recipiency in the United States is only 7 percent of those eligible for benefits in the age group 55–59. In Sweden, the second most popular program, the partial pension, was used by some 13 percent of men and 7 percent of women ages 60–64.

5. Appendix A indicates that there are loopholes in the system that allow one to avoid the earnings test.

6. For a description of these trends, see Quinn, Burkhauser, and Myers (1990) for the United States, Japanese Ministry of Welfare, *Jigyō Nenpo,* for Japan, and Lagerström (1976) for Sweden.

Table 7.2   **OASDI[a] Retiree and Disability: Average Monthly Benefits in the United States, by Age and Sex (1990 U.S. dollars)**

Year	Retiree 62–64	Retiree 65–69	Disability 55–59	Disability 60–64
Men				
1960	—	$393	$403	$408
1970	365	444	465	469
1980	568	630	635	649
1990	612	648	681	685
Women				
1960	234	274	335	332
1970	282	347	372	376
1980	378	465	447	456
1990	388	459	445	438

Source: Social Security Administration 1960–1991.
[a]OASDI = Old-Age, Survivors, and Disability Insurance.

Table 7.3   **Sweden's Basic Old-Age, Supplementary, Disability, and Partial Pensions: Average Monthly Benefit, 1978–1988[a] (1990 U.S. dollars)**

Year	Basic and Supplementary Old-Age 65–69	Basic and Supplementary Disability 60–64	Partial Pension 60–64
1978	$649	$653	$416[b]
1983	899	760	317
1988	950	764	362

Sources: National Insurance Board (1978, 1983, 1988), *Allmän Försäkring* (National Insurance) (Stockholm).
[a]All benefit averages were deflated to 1990 kronur and then converted to 1990 dollars.
[b]1979.

Table 7.4   **Japan's Employee Pension and National Pension: Average Monthly Benefit, 1970–1990[a] (1990 U.S. dollars)**

Year	Employee Pension (New Recipients) Men	Employee Pension (New Recipients) Women	National Pension
1970	$190		$ 53
1975	417		104
1980	552		128
1985	$773	$437	143
1988	818	435	153

Source: Japanese Ministry of Welfare, *Jigyō Nenpo* (Annual Report) (Social Insurance Bureau).
[a]All benefit averages were deflated to 1990 yen and then converted to 1990 dollars.

efits to consider in their retirement decisions. All three countries also increased the real levels of benefits through the 1970s and, in the case of Sweden and Japan, in the 1980s as well. The increases in Japan are the most dramatic, with the employee pension increasing threefold on average. In the United States and Sweden, the level of old-age benefits doubled over the 1970s. In an exception to the general trend, Sweden saw a decrease in the average level of benefits paid out for the partial pension during the period 1980–86 as the government cut the replacement rate for forgone earnings from 65 percent to 50 percent over this period.

7.1.3   Financing Arrangements and Their Effect on the Labor Market

Both social security systems and unemployment insurance are supported through payroll taxes in the three countries. The United States is closest to being fully funded today, although that was not always the case. Japan is closest to having a pay-as-you-go system (Clark 1991). In general, payroll tax rates for public pensions have increased over time in all three countries because of (1) aging of the population in the presence of less than full funding of social security, (2) the move toward full funding in the United States, and (3) the increase in defined benefits relative to real wages. In the first two cases, increases in payroll tax rates may reduce labor supply if the substitution effect of lower after-tax wage rates dominates the income effect of lower take-home pay. For the third case, however, the accompanying increase in defined benefits makes the computation more complex. The aforementioned substitution and income effects may largely disappear, since there is also an increase in the rate of deferred compensation in the form of the pension. At the same time, however, there is an increase in lifetime wealth (from previous years of participation in the system) that may reduce labor supply. A detailed analysis of the effects of public pension payroll tax increases is beyond the scope of the paper, but in general the trends toward increased tax rates should reinforce the effects on labor supply caused by the increase in benefit levels and coverage.

The United States is the only country with partial experience rating for unemployment insurance, with the degree of experience rating varying by state. Experience rating may have some effect on the willingness of firms to lay off older workers in the case of the United States, and this may be one reason why movement of older workers out of the U.S. labor force is less likely to be seen in the form of unemployment.

7.1.4   Private Pension Coverage

Private pensions are important components of compensation in all three countries, but there are some important differences in terms of their effect on retirement and of their share of total retirement income. The important differences from the perspective of his paper are (1) the relative share of private pensions in postretirement income and (2) the manner in which retirement wealth accrues to those still working (Kotlikoff and Wise 1989).

In the *United States,* private pensions exist as both defined benefit plans and defined contribution plans; the former is still the most prevalent, with 80 percent of all pension plan participants in 1985 (Clark and McDermed 1990, 2). Defined benefit plans set a retirement date based on either age alone or some combination of age and service that usually results in a retirement age between 60 and 65. The provisions of private pension plans vary, but the typical U.S. defined benefit pension plan offers substantial incentives for retirement on or before the normal retirement date of the Social Security program (Quinn, Burkhauser, and Myers 1990; Hurd 1990). In 1990, private pensions made up roughly one-fifth of nonearnings income for individuals over age 65 in the United States. Social security made up roughly two-fifths of nonearnings income for the same group (Social Security Administration 1960–1991).

In *Sweden,* private pensions are offered by all employers in the Swedish Employers' Confederation. Their level of benefits is roughly one-sixth of the levels offered by the basic and supplementary public pensions. There is no earnings test on the pensions, and (unlike in the United States) delaying retirement does not delay payment of these pensions. Therefore, their impact on retirement is likely to be similar to that of the public pensions.

In *Japan,* employers have the options of making lump-sum payments, offering fixed-period annuities, or augmenting the level of benefits paid through the public pension system. These benefits are usually calculated at the age of mandatory retirement (ages 55 to 60). As a result, working past the age of 60 has no effect on pension wealth, and the private pension system does not offer direct incentives to retire in the sense of U.S. pensions.[7] Japanese private pensions are also unlikely to provide major incentives to retire by providing greater economic security. The average lump-sum severance payment represents three years of base salary, or a lifetime annuity of approximately 22 percent of base salary.[8] This is approximately one-third the size of the employee pension annuity and not likely to be a major component of income after retirement.

This concludes the overview of economic security systems in the three countries. The next section begins an examination of the characteristics of the labor markets of the three countries, looking at secular trends in employment and labor force participation over the past 20 years.

7.2 Secular Trends in Employment and Participation and Well-being

Table 7.5 gives the labor force participation rates for older men and women between 1971 and 1990.[9] For the men, the most notable trends are the substan-

---

7. The augmented portion of the employee pension is not subject to the earnings test.

8. The figures for the size of the lump-sum pension (37.7 months of base salary) come from Japanese Ministry of Labor (1987), *Taishokkin no Shikyū Jittai* (Survey of Severance Payments). The annuity is calculated assuming the individual lives twenty years after mandatory retirement and the real rate of interest is 4 percent.

9. Five-year averages are used to avoid confusing secular changes with short-term economic fluctuations.

Table 7.5   Labor Force Participation Rates in the United States, Japan, and
                 Sweden, by Sex and Age Groups

Group	1971–75	1986–90	Change
Men			
55–59			
United States	85.5%	78.8%	−6.7%
Japan	92.2	91.3	−0.9
Sweden	89.9	86.6	−3.3
60–64			
United States	68.0	54.3	−13.7
Japan	80.5	71.9	−8.6
Sweden	75.8	63.9	−11.9
65+			
United States	22.3	15.8	−6.5
Japan	46.3	36.0	−10.3
Sweden	23.9	13.4	−10.5
Women			
55–59			
United States	47.9	53.1	+5.2
Japan	49.5	51.5	+2.0
Sweden	57.7	78.5	+20.8
60–64			
United States	34.0	34.0	0.0
Japan	38.1	38.9	+0.8
Sweden	35.6	50.5	+14.9
65+			
United States	8.3	7.4	−0.9
Japan	16.0	15.7	−0.3
Sweden	7.2	4.4	−2.8

Source: Organization for Economic Cooperation and Development (OECD), Labor Force Statistics.

tial 5- to 15-point declines in the participation rates for the 60–64, and 65-and-
over age groups in all three countries. U.S. men age 55–59 also show a substantial decline of 7 points in their labor force participation rate. In all three
countries, the trends for women exhibit a sharp contrast to the male trend, with
increasing participation rates for 55- to 64-year-olds in Sweden and for 55- to
59-year-olds in the United States and Japan. The trends for Swedish women
are the most dramatic, with age groups 55–59 and 60–64 showing 21- and 15-
point increases, respectively, over the past two decades. Finally, Japan is notable for having higher labor force participation rates than the other countries.
Japan's labor force participation rates in the 65-and-older age group were the
highest among the seven largest economies in the OECD.[10]

10. A problem with the Japanese figures stems from the extent of self-employment in Japan.
The extent to which the self-employed are actually working is open to question (Rebick 1993).

Turning to trends in unemployment, table 7.6 gives a matching set of age-specific unemployment rates. Unemployment rates have been fairly steady in the United States and Sweden over the 1970–90 period, although the early 1980s were a period of higher unemployment. The unemployment rates of both Japanese men and women show a rising secular trend over this period, especially for men in the 60–64-year-old age group. In Sweden, there is a drop in the unemployment rate for older men after the mid-1970s that corresponds to the lowering of the normal retirement age from 67 to 65 in 1976. At the same time, unemployment insurance benefits were restricted to those under the age of 65.

The secular trends in labor force participation for older men can be imputed to rising private and public pension levels and to increased pension coverage. The trends for women seem to be related to the increased labor force participation rates of women in more recent birth cohorts (Laczko and Phillipson 1991) and to the fact that women typically have poorer pension benefits because pen-

Table 7.6   **Unemployment Rates in the United States, Japan, and Sweden, by Sex and Age Groups**

Group	1971–75	1986–90	Change
Men			
55–59			
United States	3.0%	3.9%	+0.9%
Japan	2.2	3.2	+1.0
Sweden	1.5	1.3	−0.2
60–64			
United States	3.4	3.6	+0.2
Japan	2.2	6.5	+4.3
Sweden	2.8	2.5	−0.3
65+			
United States	3.7	2.8	−0.9
Japan	1.4	1.5	+0.1
Sweden	3.6	0.3	−3.3
Women			
55–59			
United States	3.7	3.1	−0.6
Japan	1.0	2.0	+1.0
Sweden	1.7	1.3	−0.4
60–64			
United States	3.4	2.9	−0.5
Japan	0.7	1.7	+1.0
Sweden	2.7	3.2	+0.5
65+			
United States	3.8	2.8	−1.0
Japan	0.0	0.5	+0.5
Sweden	2.4	0.3	−2.1

Source: Organization for Economic Cooperation and Development (OECD), Labor Force Statistics

sion levels are tied to length of employment and wage levels. On the other hand, the trends in the unemployment rates in Sweden and Japan seem to come in part from changes in public support programs. In Japan the 60–64 age group receives better benefits today than in 1970, while in Sweden unemployment benefits for those over the age of 65 have been eliminated.

The effects the increased benefits from the social programs have on well-being are not in doubt. All three countries have seen substantial declines in the poverty rates of older groups. Table 7.7 shows the trends in poverty rates for older groups in each of the three countries over time. Although the poverty measures are not necessarily comparable between the three countries, the table does indicate that the trend toward lower poverty among the older groups of the population have been similar in all three countries.

A question of importance in the discussion of well-being is the issue of *who* retires early. Studies in the United States (Quinn, Burkhauser, and Myers 1990) and Japan (Seike 1989) indicate that the less healthy and the more poorly educated tend to retire earliest, other things equal. Although these studies suggest that the social protection programs are effective in reaching the least advan-

Table 7.7   **Trends in Poverty for Older-Age Groups in the United States, Sweden, and Japan**

	Year				
	1967	1970	1975	1980	1985
United States[a]					
Age 60–64					
Men	13%	11%	10%	8%	10%
Women	19	16	13	13	12
Age 65 and over					
Men	24	19	11	11	9
Women	34	28	18	19	16
Sweden[b]					
Married, over 45					
Employed	2			2	
Not employed	11			0	
Single, over 45					
Employed	7			3	
Not employed	17			5	
Japan[c]					
Age 60–64			34.4	16.6	11.7
Age 65–74			41.4	20.1	14.4

Sources: Bureau of the Census, *Current Population Reports,* Series P-60: No. 95, table 1; No. 106, table 11; No. 133, table 11; No. 158, table 7. Japan: Preston and Kono 1988, table 11.6. Sweden: Erikson and Fritzell 1988, table 12.3.

[a]Percentage below official absolute poverty line (post–1969 definition).

[b]Percentage below relative poverty line (one-half medial disposable income of whole population).

[c]Percentage of Japanese living in households with monthly expenditures less than $509 (1990 U.S. dollars).

taged, other evidence in the United States also shows that the lowest-paid workers are least likely to retire early, probably because their total wealth including pensions is insufficient (Quinn, Burkhauser, and Myers). This suggests that the social protection programs may be inadequate in providing protection for some of the neediest.

A more difficult question is the extent to which the programs ameliorate the income losses experienced with job loss. In order to examine this question carefully, analysis of longitudinal data is required. One study of the 1969–79 decade in the United States found that 11 percent of couples without pensions fell into poverty during the one- to two-year period immediately following retirement (Burkhauser and Duncan 1988). At the same transition, only 2 percent of those with pensions fell into poverty, illustrating the importance of private pensions as a supplement to social security. The evidence from Sweden given in table 7.7 also suggests that improvements in the level of social security and unemployment benefits lowered the poverty rates for the mature and older unemployed between 1967 and 1980. The poverty rate for not-employed single individuals over age 45 fell from 17 percent to 5 percent.

In conclusion, it appears that the increase in coverage and levels of benefits in all three countries was successful in achieving the goal of greater social protection. At the same time, the labor force participation rates for men fell, possibly as a result of these changes in social benefits.

7.3   Cyclical Movements in Employment Levels of Older Workers

This section looks at the extent to which employment and participation movements over the business cycle are more severe for the older age groups. As mentioned earlier, Japan and Sweden offer better job protection for younger and prime-age workers. One way to see how strongly unemployment hits different demographic groups is to look at cross-sectional profiles of the age structure of unemployment. Figure 7.1 shows the unemployment profiles for men and women in the G7 countries and Sweden during 1987. It is apparent that there is considerable variation across countries in the extent to which unemployment is concentrated in the older age groups. The United States, Italy, and Japanese women show relatively low unemployment rates for older participants, while Japanese men, Sweden, France, West Germany, and the United Kingdom show relatively high unemployment rates for older participants in comparison with prime-age participants.

The variation in the age structure of unemployment across countries may be due to differences in the methods of providing benefits to nonworking individuals. For example, the relatively high unemployment rates for older people in Sweden and Japan may actually reflect retirement from the labor force, when unemployment benefits are used in addition to or in place of pensions as an income support for those who stop working. In order to avoid the reporting problems that result from differences in protection programs in the three countries, it is useful to look at movements in both unemployment rates and partici-

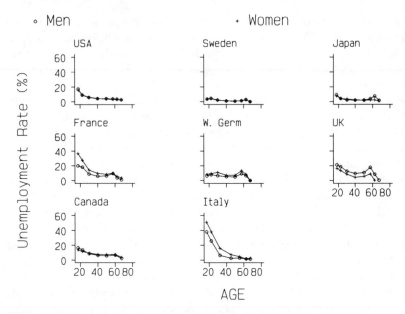

Figure 7.1   Unemployment rates for G7 countries and Sweden in 1987, by age
Source: OECD, Labor Force Statistics.

pation rates over the business cycle. In this way, fluctuations in the numbers of discouraged workers may also be considered.

Adopting a method used by Clark and Summers (1981), I use a simple time series analysis to analyze employment fluctuations by different demographic groups over the business cycle. Clark and Summers developed this method explicitly to compare the differential response of different demographic groups to business conditions in the United States, assuming that some groups will exhibit stronger discouraged-worker effects than other. Using their approach, I focus on the employment/population ratio rather than the unemployment rate as an indicator of labor movements over the business cycle. Decomposition of the employment/population ratio into the employment rate and the labor force participation rate yields:

$$(1) \qquad \log E_{it}/N_{it} = \log E_{it}/P_{it} + \log P_{it}/N_{it},$$

where E_{it} is employment, N_{it} is the population, and P_{it} represents participants for the ith demographic group at time t. I then examine the cyclical movements in all of the terms, using current and lagged values of the unemployment rate of prime-age males (who show the strongest attachment to the labor force) as a measure of the business cycle:

$$(2) \qquad \log E_{it}/N_{it} = \alpha_0 + \Sigma \, \alpha_j \, UR_{t-j+1} + \alpha_{25} t + \varepsilon_t$$

$$(3) \qquad \log E_{it}/P_{it} = \beta_0 + \Sigma \, \beta_j \, UR_{t-j+1} + \beta_{25} t + \varepsilon_t$$

(4) $$\log P_{it}/N_{it} = \gamma_0 + \Sigma \, \gamma_j \, UR_{t-j+1} + \gamma_{25} \, t + \varepsilon_t,$$

where UR refers to the unemployment rate of prime-age males, defined as 35- to 44-year-old men in the case of the United States and Sweden and 30- to 39-year-old men for Japan. The sums $\Sigma \, \alpha_j$ and $\Sigma \, \beta_j$ and $\Sigma \, \gamma_j$ of the coefficients on the current and lagged values of UR will then show the respective percentage responses of the employment/population ratio, the employment rate, and the labor force participation rate to a one-point change in the unemployment rate of prime-age males over the long run. The use of lagged terms allows for longer-term adjustments to shocks in the business cycle, including adjustment costs and the role of future expectations.

An advantage of using the unemployment rate of prime-age males as an explanatory variable, rather than a more conventional measure such as de-trended output, is that there is less reason to expect a simultaneous equation bias.[11] In addition, I am able to examine the relative response of the older groups to a labor market measure of the business cycle. The labor force partici-pation rate of prime-age males is unlikely to show a major response to cyclical fluctuations, and so the unemployment rate of prime-age males provides a use-ful metric by which the responsiveness of other groups can be measured. If other groups show a response similar in magnitude to that of prime-age work-ers, then the sums of the coefficients on the contemporaneous and lagged un-employment rates of prime-age men should come to approximately minus-one for the employment/population ratio and the employment rate, and zero for the labor force participation rate. These sums represent the long-run response of different demographic groups to the business cycle.

I use a monthly deseasonalized time series[12] and twelve monthly lags in my estimations.[13] As in Clark and Summers (1981), I include a time trend to allow for secular shifts in the average participation and employment rates. I model the error structure as an AR1 process, and use a maximum-likelihood proce-dure (TSP) to estimate the generalized least-squares model.[14] The lagged vari-ables are estimated using an Almon distributed lag model of order 6 for ease in estimation.[15] I report more details on the results of the regressions them-selves in appendix B. For ease of exposition, I show only the estimates of the long-run responses $\Sigma \, \alpha_j$ and $\Sigma \, \beta_j$ and $\Sigma \, \gamma_j$ in table 7.8. In each case I have

11. I have also repeated the procedure using the detrended growth in gross domestic product as a measure of the business cycle. Although the results for specific demographic groups are slightly different, the overall conclusions of the paper are not affected. These results are available from the author on request.

12. The time series span the period 1949–92 for the United States, 1976–92 for Sweden, and 1962–92 for Japan.

13. Increasing the number of lags slightly increases the size of the long-run response but does not affect the overall conclusions of the paper.

14. A simultaneous equations model was also estimated with the cross-equation restriction that the long-run responses obey the identity in equation (1). The basic results of the paper remain the same.

15. Results are virtually unchanged if an unconstrained lag model is used.

Table 7.8   Cyclical Response of Participation and Employment: United States–Sweden–Japan Comparisons, by Age Group (standard errors in parentheses)

Demographic Groups	Dependent Variable	United States 1949–1992	Sweden 1976–1992[a]	Japan 1962–1992
Men Age 55–64	Employment Population	−1.20* (0.37)	−2.36* (0.18)	−1.39* (0.13)
	Employment Labor force	−1.14* (0.05)	−1.54* (0.12)	−0.93* (0.05)
	LFPR[b]	−0.16 (0.33)	−0.77* (0.16)	−0.46* (0.12)
Age 65+	Employment Population	−1.35 (0.90)	−10.67* (4.03)	−3.33* (0.34)
	Employment Labor force	−0.60* (0.10)	0.31 (0.23)	−0.43* (0.06)
	LFPR[b]	−0.61 (0.86)	−10.99* (3.92)	−2.91* (0.33)
Women Age 55–64	Employment Population	0.004 (0.93)	−1.39* (0.41)	−1.36* (0.31)
	Employment Labor force	−0.74* (0.06)	−1.59* (0.18)	−0.25* (0.03)
	LFPR[b]	0.48 (0.89)	0.28 (0.38)	−1.13* (0.30)
Age 65+	Employment Population	−1.58 (1.25)	7.98 (6.05)	−3.30* (1.21)
	Employment Labor force	−0.29* (0.08)	1.41* (0.64)	−0.15* (0.04)
	LFPR[b]	−1.12 (1.23)	6.81 (6.09)	−3.14* (1.17)

Sources: United States: *Employment and Earnings.* Japan: Labor Force Survey. Sweden: Labor Force Survey.

Note: Figures reported in the table are sums of coefficients of prime-age male contemporary and eleven lagged unemployment rates in regressions where the dependent variables are the log(employment/population rate), log(employment rate), and log(participation rate) for different age groups. Results are multiplied by 100 × the detrended standard deviation of the explanatory variable for comparability across countries. Prime-age males are 35–44 in the United States and Sweden and 30–39 in Japan. All data are deseasonalized, monthly observations covering the period from 1949 to 1991 for the United States, 1962 to 1991 for Japan, and 1976 to 1991 for Sweden. A time trend and constant term are included in all regressions. The Japanese regressions include an additional dummy variable set to one for the period after October 1967, when the methods of the Labor Force Survey changed. Regressions correct for AR1 autocorrelation using a maximum likelihood procedure. Details of estimates are shown in appendix B.

[a]The estimates are for the period 1976–1985 in the case of men and women over age 65.

[b]LFPR = Labor Force Participation Rate.

*Significantly different from zero at the 5 percent level.

multiplied these estimates by one standard deviation in the detrended unemployment rate of prime-age males, the explanatory variable used to represent the business cycle. The two age groups that I analyze are *mature,* defined as ages 55 to 64, and *older,* defined as over 65.

The results given in table 7.8 indicate some differences in the behavior of mature and older workers across the three countries. For the employment/population variable, the overall Japanese response is significantly larger than that of the United States, for all women and older men. The differences are much more striking for the older groups. This is interesting, given that the standard deviation in prime-age male unemployment (measured in percentage terms) is much smaller in Japan at 0.3 than in the United States at 1.23. Similarly, Sweden shows larger responses than the United States for men and mature women and no significant difference for older men. Again, this is interesting in light of the fact that in Sweden, one standard deviation in the prime-age male unemployment rate is only 0.7. Japan and Sweden, countries known for stable employment and low unemployment, rely on their mature and older workers for a substantial proportion of flexibility in aggregate employment levels.[16] Despite this tendency, however, the absolute size of the response to the business cycle of the mature groups in these two low-unemployment countries is only slightly larger than that seen in the United States.[17]

Looking at the breakdown of the response in the employment/population ratio into the employment/labor force ratio and the labor force participation rate (LFPR), it is clear that the unemployment age profiles of figure 7.1 by themselves do not accurately portray the relative response of mature and older groups. This is especially true for women and older men in Japan and older men in Sweden, where the fluctuations in the labor force participation rates dominate the response in the overall employment/population ratio. The LFPR response is not statistically significant for any of the older groups in the United States, but the results shown here indicate that this is not a universal phenomenon.

Although the behavior over the business cycle of Japanese, Swedish and U.S. labor markets for mature and older workers are substantially different, it is unlikely that all of these differences are related to supply-side effects gener-

16. Abraham and Houseman (1989) and Hashimoto (1993) note that the relative importance of hours reductions for labor input flexibility is greater in Japan than in the United States, especially over the short run. The data that I am using do not allow me to investigate this factor for separate demographic groups. Hashimoto also reports on the importance of *kyūgyōsha,* workers who are sent home on reduced pay during slack business periods. These workers are not unemployed from the perspective of economic security since they remain employed by their firms, but the prevalence of the practice indicates that the flexibility of labor input is greater than simple hours and unemployment rate fluctuations would indicate. The same paper estimates that the *kyūgyōsha* may represent up to 2 percent of the labor force during economic downturns.

17. For similar results from a comparison of Germany and the United States, see Abraham and Houseman (1993), pages 110–14.

ated by the social security benefits offered by the different countries. The availability of benefits will not affect behavior over the business cycle unless wages are lowered during downturns to induce workers to leave their jobs. Rather, total business cycle response of the employment/population ratio will be related to demand-side factors such as whether or not firms preferentially fire older workers during business downturns.[18] The effect of social programs will primarily be to determine the breakdown of the employment/population response into employment and labor force participation responses. For example, the relative importance of the labor force participation response for mature men in Sweden and Japan (in comparison with the United States) may be due to the fact that it is easier to take public pensions in these countries and then return to work without penalty. In the U.S. case, the early retirement pension lowers Social Security benefits for the rest of the retiree's life and will be subject to an earnings test if the individual returns to work.

To account for the difference in overall response on the demand side, it is necessary to look beyond the social security programs to other institutions in the labor markets of these countries. In the United States, age discrimination–discouraging legislation and the seniority preference system of unions make older U.S. workers less vulnerable in comparison with their Japanese counterparts. The steepness of seniority-earnings profiles in Japan also provides a stronger financial incentive for Japanese firms to dismiss their older workers if the compensation for the oldest workers is greater than their value to the firm. If firms have specific investments in all workers, then dismissal of older workers during downturns would be rational since their asset value to the firm is lower, given the shortness of the remainder of their working life. Finally, older workers are less likely to be a deliberate target of company dismissal policy when, as in the United States, they have lower participation rates, even in the best economic conditions.

In Sweden, older workers are explicitly protected by legislation drafted during the 1970s, a period of many plant closings. Workers over the age of 45 must be given six months notice of dismissal, and employers must try to find other jobs for those who have lost the ability to perform their usual jobs (Ginsberg 1985). In addition, Swedish unions use a seniority rule for layoffs, also protecting their older workers.

Some evidence on the extent to which labor market responses may have been affected on the supply side by economic security programs may be inferred by looking at participation and employment responses during periods when the benefits available were different from those offered today. This is the subject of the next section.

---

18. It is possible that personnel management practices may be affected by the availability of benefits—it is easier both psychologically and politically to fire workers if they will be provided for. This point is emphasized in OECD (1992a).

7.4 Changes in the Pattern of Response over Time within Countries

To examine changes in the response pattern of demographic groups, I modify models (2), (3), and (4) used in the previous section to allow for different subperiods to be examined. This is done by interacting a dummy variable set equal to zero in the first subperiod and one in the second subperiod, with the lagged prime-age male unemployment rates and the time trend to generate an additional set of thirteen terms. If the sum of the twelve coefficients on the interactive unemployment rate terms is not significantly different from zero, then we can conclude that the null hypothesis, that there is no difference in business cycle response between the two periods, is supported by the data.[19]

In table 7.9, I report the results of this procedure for the United States and Japan.[20] The two subperiods chosen for the United States are 1949–75 and 1977–92. The size of pension benefits increased in real terms until 1975 and then remained constant. Therefore, the 1977–92 period represents a period of higher benefits, where we should expect to see an increase in the response of the employment/population ratio if social protection programs are responsible for the kinds of response shown in table 7.8. For Japan, the two periods covered are 1962–75, and 1977–92, the latter period having much higher public pension benefits and extension of unemployment benefits for mature and older workers.[21]

For each country in table 7.9, the column on the left shows the response of the dependent variable to the contemporaneous and lagged levels of prime-age male unemployment for the first subperiod, just as table 7.8 showed the response over the entire sample period. The right-hand column then shows the *change* in the response that occurs in the second period, and its significance. The actual second-period response point estimate would be given by the sum of the point estimates in the two columns. For example, mature men in the United States show a statistically significant employment/population response of −1.18 from 1949 to 1975. From 1977 to 1992 the response was −1.37 (−1.18 − 0.19), but the change between the two periods was not significant, as the standard error of .60 for the −.19 change indicates.

The U.S. results indicate that mature and older women have seen some increase in the responsiveness of their employment/population ratio response to fluctuations in the prime-age male unemployment rate, but the results have low significance. This effect comes from an increased response in their labor force participation rate. At the same time, the response of the employment/labor

19. The model actually used for estimation is slightly more complex, in that I include a third set of interactions to cover the one-year period after the beginning of the second period in order to remove a one-year transition from consideration and to sharpen the statistical test.

20. Sweden does not have age-specific employment and participation data available prior to 1970, and the brevity of the period 1970–76 makes analysis using time series difficult. Consequently, this section presents results for only Japan and the United States.

21. The detailed results of the regressions are provided in supplementary tables available from the author.

Table 7.9   Cyclical Response of Participation and Employment, United States and Japan: Comparisons between Subperiods (standard error in parentheses)

		United States		Japan	
		1949–1975	1977–1992 Additive Change in Sum	1962–1975	1977–1992 Additive Change in Sum
Demographic Groups	Dependent Variable	Sum of Lagged Unemployment	of Lagged Unemployment	Sum of Lagged Unemployment	of Lagged Unemployment
Men	Employment	−1.18*	−0.19	−0.98*	−0.54*
Age 55–64	Population	(0.43)	(0.60)	(0.25)	(0.20)
	Employment	−1.30*	0.16*	−0.69*	−0.12
	Labor force	(0.06)	(0.06)	(0.11)	(0.09)
	LFPR	−0.13	−0.11	−0.33	−0.39*
		(0.38)	(0.55)	(0.23)	(0.18)
Age 65+	Employment	−3.08*	3.14*	−4.37*	1.49*
	Population	(0.94)	(1.02)	(0.68)	(0.56)
	Employment	−1.14*	0.81*	−0.32*	0.17*
	Labor force	(0.08)	(0.08)	(0.10)	(0.08)
	LFPR	−1.91*	2.36*	−4.06*	1.33*
		(0.95)	(1.04)	(0.68)	(0.55)
Women	Employment	0.63	−2.52	−3.25*	1.63*
Age 55–64	Population	(1.06)	(1.56)	(0.59)	(0.48)
	Employment	−0.88*	0.24*	−0.24*	−0.06
	Labor force	(0.07)	(0.07)	(0.08)	(0.07)
	LFPR	1.03	−2.24	−3.16*	1.83*
		(1.01)	(1.51)	(0.57)	(0.47)
Age 65+	Employment	−0.47	−1.46	−9.02*	7.73*
	Population	(1.47)	(1.52)	(1.22)	(0.98)
	Employment	−0.68*	0.60*	−0.16	0.04
	Labor force	(0.09)	(0.09)	(0.09)	(0.08)
	LFPR	0.37	−2.22	−8.99*	7.90*
		(1.45)	(1.49)	(1.21)	(0.97)

Sources: United States: *Employment and Earnings.* Japan: Labor Force Survey. Sweden: Labor Force Survey.

Note: Figures reported in columns 1 and 3 of the table are sums of coefficients of prime-age male contemporary and eleven lagged monthly unemployment rates in regressions where the dependent variables are log(participation rate), log(employment rate), and log(employment ratio) for different age groups. Columns 2 and 4 contain the sums of the coefficients on the lagged prime-age male unemployment rates interacted with a dummy variable set equal to one during the second period. In addition, there is a time trend and set of lagged variables interacted with a dummy variable for a transition period of one year between the two main periods. For other details, see table 7.8. Detailed results available from the author.

*Significantly different from zero at the 5 percent level.

force ratio has significantly declined, partly offsetting the increase in the participation response. The size of this significant decline in the response of the employment/labor force ratio, however, is smaller than the (less significant) increase in the response of the labor force participation rate. Mature U.S. men show a similar decline in the employment/labor force response, but overall there is no significant change in their employment/population ratio responsiveness. Older U.S. men show a significant decline in *both* participation and employment responses during the second period.

Turning to the estimates for Japan, mature Japanese men show an increase in their employment/population response after 1975, mainly from an increased response in the participation rate. Mature and older Japanese women as well as older Japanese men show a significant *decrease* in their employment/population response, also coming from a decline in the participation response. The data used here indicate that changes in the unemployment insurance legislation in 1975 did not give rise to a major increase in the unemployment response of older groups. Increases in the level of benefits in the employee pension system may have doubled the participation response of mature Japanese men, but the absolute size of this effect remains small—an increase in prime-age male unemployment of one standard deviation now yields a 0.7-point drop in the labor force participation rate of mature men as opposed to the 0.3-point drop it would have yielded in the years 1962–75.

In conclusion, evidence from employment series taken by different subperiods provides little evidence that introduction and/or extension of social benefit programs for older workers has greatly increased the responsiveness of their employment rates over the business cycle. The exceptions to this may be mature Japanese men, a group that showed significantly higher responses in the employment/population ratio after 1975, and U.S. women, who show some evidence of a greater discouraged-worker effect after 1975. In the next section, I look directly at fluctuations in the rate of participation in pension and unemployment benefits over the business cycle.

7.5 Participation in Public Support Benefits over the Cycle

This section of the paper examines the use of public support programs over the past twenty to thirty years in the three countries. In particular, I distinguish secular and cyclical trends and attempt to look at the impact of changes in legislation during the period. In general, my procedure is to regress the percentage of individuals in a given age group that are receiving benefits on the unemployment rate of prime-age men and a time trend.[22] Since most of the data on benefits are only available as annual data, I use only current unemployment rates of prime-age men as an explanatory variable.

22. For the United States, I use the fraction of those eligible for benefits that receive them (the take-up rate).

7.5.1   United States

Table 7.10 displays the results for the United States. Women show a positive correlation between participation in the old-age pension for both the 62–64 age group and the 65–69 age group, but the significance level is not high. Men only show a low-significance positive response for the over-65 age group. More important than the significance levels, the estimated elasticity of the response is very low. There is little change in participation in Social Security benefits over the business cycle. Recipients of disability pensions also show no variation over the business cycle. As expected, unemployment insurance recipients in the 55–64 age group are positively correlated with the prime-age male unemployment rate, but the elasticities are less than one for both men and women (which is consistent with the results on the employment rate from column 2 in table 7.8). I conclude that with the exception of unemployment insurance, U.S. old-age, survivors, and disability insurance (OASDI) is unlikely to have had much effect on the fluctuations in employment of mature workers in the United States over the business cycle.

Table 7.10   **Cyclical and Secular Changes in Benefit Participation Rates: United States, 1960–1987 (dependent variable is the log of the fraction of those eligible receiving the benefit)**

Explanatory Variable	Full Pension		Actuarially Reduced Pension		Disability Pension[a]		Unemployment Insurance	
	Men 65–69	Women 65–69	Men 62–64	Women 62–64	Men 55–59	Women 55–59	Men 55–64	Women 55–64
Log unemployment rate, prime-age men	.031 (.020)	.026 (.017)	−.01 (.06)	.039 (.024)	−.024 (.11)	−.06 (.13)	.84* (.13)	.54* (.13)
Time trend	.007* (.001)	.003* (.0008)	.035* (.003)	.021* (.001)	.21* (.005)	.027* (.007)	−.039* (.007)	−.014 (.007)
Constant	−.60* (.13)	−.34* (.11)	−3.85* (.39)	−2.55* (.16)	−4.92* (.69)	−5.1* (.86)	2.22* (.84)	−1.3 (.82)
R^2	.80	.62	.90	.96	.67	.51	.65	.40
Exponential of mean of dependent variable	.83	.82	.32	.33	.072	.057	.030	.016

Sources: Social Security Administration, *Annual Statistical Supplements; Employment and Earnings; Labor Force Statistics Derived from the Current Population Survey, 1948–87,* U.S. Department of Labor Bulletin 2307.

Note: Standard errors in parentheses.

[a]1981 is not included for disability pensions.

*Significantly different from zero at the 5 percent level.

7.5.2   Sweden

The evidence for Sweden is shown in table 7.11, using data for the period 1975–88. Evidence is shown only for the various pension programs. The uptake of the basic and supplementary old-age pension increases during periods of high unemployment; the elasticity of response is statistically indistinguishable from one. Although the participation in disability benefits among 60 to 64-year-olds shows no statistically significant correlation with prime-age male unemployment, new participation of individuals claiming disability pensions on the basis of labor market difficulties does show a significant positive response for women and, to a lesser degree of significance, for men as well. The elasticities are statistically indistinguishable from one. In all cases, the secular trends for participation in these benefits are positive.

The estimates for the partial pension system show no significant correlation between the business cycle and participation in benefits. The declining secular

Table 7.11   **Cyclical and Secular Changes in Benefit Participation Rates: Sweden, 1976–1988 (dependent variable is the log of the fraction of the demographic group receiving the benefit)**

Explanatory Variable	Basic pension		Disability Pension[a]		Disability Pension For Labor Market Difficulties (new take-ups only)		Partial Pension[b]	
	Men 60–64	Women 60–64	Men 60–64	Women 60–64	Men 60–64	Women 60–64	Men 60–64	Women 60–64
Log unemployment rate, prime-age men	.62* (.20)	.97* (.33)	−.015 (.06)	−.02 (.04)	.62 (.48)	.71* (.31)	−.09 (.31)	.13 (.25)
Time trend	.05* (.02)	.05 (.025)	.04* (.004)	.05* (.002)	.14* (.03)	.09* (.02)	−.06* (.02)	−.01 (.02)
Constant	−5.2* (1.9)	−3.7 (3.1)	−5.5* (.47)	−6.19* (.33)	−13.5* (3.9)	−9.3* (2.5)	2.61 (2.5)	−.99 (2.1)
R^2	.82	.73	.90	.96	.72	.78	.51	.73
Exponential, mean of the dependent variable	.03	.02	.12	.12	.01	.01	.13	.07

Sources: Sweden Labor Force Survey; National Social Insurance Board, *Allmän Försäkring,* (National Insurance), (Stockholm).

Note: Standard errors in parentheses.

[a]1970–1988.

[b]1977–1988.

*Significantly different from zero at the 5 percent level.

trend in the participation rate for men reflects the fact that benefit levels were cut back from 65 percent replacement of the reduction in earnings to 50 percent of the reduction in earnings between 1980 and 1986. Given the limited number of observations, changes in the replacement rates may overwhelm any observable effect from the business cycle for this pension plan.

7.5.3 Japan

The results for Japan are shown in table 7.12. The number of pension recipients and the number of unemployment insurance recipients both show a positive elasticity with respect to the unemployment rate of prime-age men, but the unemployment insurance (UI) recipients show a substantially higher elasticity. The earnings test–reduced pension shows negative elasticities of the recipient rate with respect to the unemployment rate (as would be expected).

As the time trend coefficient estimates indicate, the rates of employee pen-

Table 7.12   **Cyclical and Secular Changes in Benefit Participation Rates: Japan, 1981–1990 (dependent variable is the log of the fraction of the demographic group receiving the benefit)**

Explanatory Variable	Employee Pension		Full Employee Pension		Earnings Test–Reduced Pension		Unemployment Insurance[a]
	Men 60–64	Women 60–64	Men 60–64	Women 60–64	Men 60–64	Women 60–64	Men 55–64
Log unemployment rate, 30–39-year-old men	0.17* (.03)	0.13* (.01)	0.38* (.04)	0.24* (.02)	−.74* (.18)	−.30* (.10)	.73* (.10)
Time trend	0.02* (.001)	0.05* (.0006)	0.03* (.002)	0.07* (.001)	0.013 (.007)	−.03* (.004)	−.03* (.005)
Post–1984 dummy							−.38* (.05)
Constant	−2.7* (.14)	−5.3* (.07)	−2.4* (0.20)	−6.4* (0.1)	−6.8* (.87)	−1.9* (.47)	2.0* (.68)
R^2	.99	.99	.98	.99	.78	.90	.98
Exponential, mean of the dependent variable	0.39	0.24	0.32	0.20	0.07	0.04	0.03

Sources: Unemployment rates and population figures: Labor Force Survey. Numbers of benefits recipients: Social Insurance Bureau, *Jigyō Nenpo*; Japanese Ministry of Labor *Employment Insurance Annual Report.*

Note: A dummy variable set to one for the period 1985–90 is used in the regression for the unemployment recipient rate, since recipients over age 65 are included in the period 1975 to 1984. Standard errors in parentheses.

[a]1976–1990.

*Significantly different from zero at the 5 percent level.

sion participation for both men and women increased over the 1980s, reflecting the decline in labor force participation over this period, the increased availability of pensions for women, and the decline in self-employment by cohort. The UI recipient rate also shows a declining trend over time, with a sharp drop in 1985 when UI benefits were cut back.

From these observations we can conclude that both pensions and unemployment benefits are used for income support during downturns in the business cycle. Since both the employee pension and unemployment insurance may be collected at the same time, this is not surprising.

In conclusion, the participation rates in most of the social benefits increase with downturns in the business cycle, in accordance with the labor market responses estimated in section 7.3. Notable exceptions are the actuarially reduced early retirement schemes in the United States and Sweden. In these cases, there are no financial advantages to receiving the benefits, so workers may prefer to wait and find work, in the U.S. case, or take benefits from another program, as in the Swedish case. Finally, there is no evidence that the benefits have affected the decision whether or not to work during economic downturns.

7.6 Conclusions

In this study, I examined the extent to which government labor market programs, including early retirement programs, are used by older individuals in the United States, Japan, and Sweden in response to economic fluctuations. I found that these programs are more heavily used by workers in Sweden and Japan, where the responsiveness of older demographic groups to economic conditions is greater than that shown by older groups in the United States. There has been a significant decrease in poverty rates of older demographic groups over the time period in which these programs were expanded. This suggests that these programs have had a major impact in improving the well-being of older individuals.

Previous research indicated that the introduction of social programs for the elderly affected overall trends in participation of older workers. This paper shows that there is no conclusive evidence that introduction of these programs had major effects on the labor market responsiveness of the older demographic groups, in terms of fluctuations in employment over the business cycle. Labor market responsiveness varies among the three countries for a variety of reasons, likely related to differences in institutions that constrain a firm's ability to adjust its demand for labor of different demographic groups. Consequently, evaluation of programs for older individuals should concentrate on their long-run impact on labor force participation rates and on the efficiency with which they improve economic security, rather than on their impact on labor market flexibility.

Appendix A
Description of Unemployment and Pension Programs

Foster (1990) provides a good survey of general information on employee benefits in the United States and Sweden. For Japan, see Japanese Ministry of Welfare, *Outline of Social Insurance in Japan* (Social Insurance Agency).

United States

The United States offers both unemployment insurance and old-age pension benefits to older retirees. Normal retirement benefits begin at age 65 in the United States, with early retirement benefits available from age 62. Formerly it was possible for a retiree to collect both a pension and unemployment insurance at the same time, although this depended on individual state practice. Since 1980, this has not been possible in any state (Hamermesh 1980).

Unemployment Insurance. Unemployment insurance benefits are available only to employees who have lost their jobs involuntarily. Unemployment insurance benefits replace 50 percent of earnings (up to a maximum of $419 per week in 1990 dollars).

Public Pensions. Pensions are calculated on a formula based on "average indexed monthly earnings," which provides a replacement ratio that varies inversely with the level of earnings. There is a ceiling on covered earnings ($51,300 in 1990). Early retirement benefits are available as early as age 62, with an actuarial reduction of 0.9 percent in the benefit level for each month they are taken before age 65. The pension computation also includes an earnings test that reduces benefits by one-half of the income earned over a minimum threshold ($6,840 in 1990), for those aged 62 to 64. The earnings test reduction rate is lowered to one-third after age 65, while the minimum threshold is raised.

Sweden

In comparison with the United States and Japan, Sweden offers the widest range of different support programs for retirees, including early receipt of public pensions at reduced benefit levels, partial pensions (for part-time workers), unemployment insurance, and disability pensions.

National Pension. Public pensions of a *national basic pension (AFP)* of fixed value calculated from a base amount paid to every Swedish resident at retirement along with the *national supplementary pension (ATP)* with benefits related to earnings during preretirement years. There is a ceiling (7.5 times the base amount) on pensionable earnings. The full pension for thirty years of insured earnings is set at 60 percent of the average of the pensionable income for the fifteen best years. The normal retirement age in Sweden is 65 (67 prior to 1976), and there is an option for early retirement at age 60 (62 before 1976). There is no earnings test for pensions in Sweden.

Partial Pensions. This program has been available since 1976. Between ages 60 and 64, workers whose hours are reduced by at least five hours per week are eligible for the partial pension if they have ten years of pensionable income since age 45. The pension replaces 65 percent of the earnings lost by reducing hours (50 percent between 1980 and 1987), not counting any reduction in the wage rate that may accompany the reduction in working hours. For those who enroll in this program, there is no reduction in regular pension benefits after age 65.

Disability Pensions. This pension provides for the loss of at least 50 percent of earnings capacity or permanent unemployment after age 60. The latter provision was abolished in 1991. The pension pays between 50 percent and 100 percent of the retirement pension, according to the degree of disability.

Unemployment Insurance. Two kinds of benefits are available: *unemployment insurance,* and *labor market assistance.* Unemployment insurance benefits range from $16 to $50 per day and are available for 450 days for those over the age of 55. Labor market assistance is available after unemployment insurance benefits run out; it pays $19 per day. Between age 55 and 59, these are available for 300 days. After age 60, they are available until age 65. Unlike the case of Japan, any pensions received from the social security system or a private plan are subtracted from the benefit.

Japan

Japan offers two major kinds of public assistance programs that could be used for early retirement: unemployment insurance and public pensions.

Unemployment Insurance. Unemployment insurance benefits replace between 60 percent and 80 percent of wage earnings up to a maximum benefit ($37 per day in 1989). In order for a person to qualify for benefits, they must have been covered by the system for at least six months prior to leaving their job. They must also report to a public employment center for help with job placement. Unemployed individuals are not required to take a job that pays less than 60 percent of the most recent wage, that pays less than the unemployment benefit, that is unsuitable for the person's skills, or that involves an unreasonable commute or change of residence. In practice, most public employment offices are not strict about forcing beneficiaries to engage in job search.

Benefits are paid for up to 300 days in the case of 45- to 65-year-olds, although the period of benefits is tied to tenure at the last job (with the exception of the period between 1975 and 1984). There are also possible extensions to the 300-day maximum in the case of individuals whose circumstances make it especially difficult for them to find new work.

Public Pensions. The main public pension for private sector employees is the *employee pension,* part of the national pension program. The employee pension is available to women at age 56 and to men at age 60. The pension is computed on a formula that includes a fixed part and a part that is proportional to the average wages earned during the time that the individual has been enrolled in the system:

$$\text{Pension} = (a_1 + [a_2 \cdot \text{Average wage}]) \cdot \text{Months of coverage} \cdot \text{COLA},$$

where COLA refers to a cost-of-living adjustment. There is a cap on months of coverage (480 in 1990) and a cap on monthly wages that are used for the computation of the average wage ($2,807 in 1989). The major reforms of the early 1970s doubled the size of the fixed coefficient a_1 in real terms. More important, past wages were substantially revalued to take account of both inflation and economic growth. This led to a substantial increase in the real value of the pensions. A second factor increasing real values of the pension after 1973 has been the increase in the coverage period for the average individual as the pension system matured.

There is an earnings test (substantially relaxed after age 65). Up to age 64, at selected earnings cutoff points, the pension is reduced by fixed percentages with 100 percent of the pension lost when monthly earnings exceed $1,159 in 1990 dollars. The Japanese earnings test produces a fairly flat budget constraint (with notches) up to the point where benefits are reduced to zero. The earnings test is not applied, however, to those employees who are employed for less than three-fifths of normal working hours in the firm. Also, bonuses are not considered earnings from the perspective of the public pension system. By increasing the bonus portion of pay, employers can keep covered earnings below the earnings test points, even in the case where employees are working full time (Rebick 1993). There is no reliable statistical evidence on how widespread this practice is.

Appendix B
Regression Results for Table 7.8

Table 7B.1   **Cyclical Response of Participation, Employment, and Employment/ Population Ratio: United States, 1949–1992**

Demographic Group	Dependent Variable	Constant	Trend	Sum Lagged	ρ	R^2
Men						
	Employment	−0.39	−5.7e–04	−0.97	0.97	1
Age 55–64	Population	(0.024)	(6.5e–05)	(0.3)	(0.0097)	
	Employment	0.0033	3.6e–05	−0.93	0.66	0.92
	Labor force	(0.002)	(3.3e–06)	(0.039)	(0.033)	
	LFPR[a]	−0.39	−5.9e–04	−0.13	0.98	1
		(0.026)	(7.2e–05)	(0.27)	(0.0081)	
	Employment	−1.9	−2.2e–03	−1.1	0.93	1
Age 65+	Population	(0.042)	(8.9e–05)	(0.73)	(0.016)	
	Employment	−0.0093	4.3e–05	−0.48	0.73	0.7
	Labor force	(0.0043)	(7.3e–06)	(0.083)	(0.03)	
	LFPR[a]	−1.9	−2.2e–03	−0.5	0.93	1
		(0.04)	(8.3e–05)	(0.7)	(0.017)	
Women						
	Employment	−0.76	1.0e–03	0.0031	0.99	0.98
Age 55–64	Population	(0.088)	(2.5e–04)	(0.76)	(0.0071)	
	Employment	−0.0086	2.5e–05	−0.6	0.62	0.73
	Labor force	(0.0026)	(4.4e–06)	(0.051)	(0.035)	
	LFPR[a]	−0.74	1.0e–03	0.39	0.99	0.99
		(0.09)	(2.6e–04)	(0.72)	(0.0067)	
	Employment	−2.5	−5.3e–04	−1.3	0.89	0.91
Age 65+	Population	(0.054)	(1.0e–04)	(1)	(0.02)	
	Employment	−0.025	−1.8e–06	−0.23	0.52	0.34
	Labor force	(0.0035)	(5.8e–06)	(0.068)	(0.038)	
	LFPR[a]	−2.5	−5.3e–04	−0.91	0.89	0.91
		(0.054)	(1.0e–04)	(1)	(0.019)	

Sources: U.S. Population Bureau, *Employment and Earnings,* (monthly series), 1949 to March 1992.

Notes: The dependent variable is the log of the participation rate, employment rate, or employment/population ratio for the demographic group. "Sum Lagged" refers to the sum of the coefficients on the current and lagged unemployment rates of prime-age males (age 35–44) over the last year. "Trend" is a simple time trend. Regressions were estimated using TSP's AR1 procedure, maximum likelihood method. Standard errors lie below the regression coefficients estimates.

[a] LFPR = Labor Force Participation Rate.

Table 7B.2 **Cyclical Response of Participation, Employment, Employment/Population Ratio: Sweden, 1976–1992[a]**

Demographic Group	Dependent Variable	Constant	Sum Lagged	Trend	ρ	R^2
Men						
	Employment	−0.28	−3.6	−3.7e−04	−0.1	0.75
Age 55–64	Population	(0.0045)	(0.28)	(2.0e−05)	(0.073)	
	Employment	0.0086	−2.4	3.6e−05	0.4	0.73
	Labor force	(0.0029)	(0.18)	(1.4e−05)	(0.068)	
	LFPR[b]	−0.29	−1.2	−4.1e−04	−0.18	0.73
		(0.0039)	(0.25)	(1.8e−05)	(0.072)	
	Employment	−1.9	−16	−4.9e−04	0.05	0.37
Age 65+	Population	(0.17)	(6.2)	(7.0e−04)	(0.097)	
	Employment	−0.013	0.48	−4.0e−05	0.064	0.077
	Labor force	(0.0097)	(0.35)	(4.0e−05)	(0.097)	
	LFPR[b]	−1.9	−17	−4.5e−04	0.044	0.39
		(0.16)	(6)	(6.9e−04)	(0.097)	
Women						
	Employment	−0.36	−2.1	1.5e−03	0.37	0.94
Age 55–64	Population	(0.01)	(0.62)	(4.6e−05)	(0.069)	
	Employment	0.0072	−2.4	3.9e−05	0.55	0.73
	Labor force	(0.0046)	(0.28)	(2.1e−05)	(0.062)	
	LFPR[b]	−0.37	0.43	1.5e−03	0.37	0.95
		(0.0093)	(0.57)	(4.3e−05)	(0.069)	
	Employment	−4	12	−4.3e−03	−0.12	0.37
Age 65+	Population	(0.25)	(9.2)	(1.1e−03)	(0.097)	
	Employment	−0.081	2.2	−3.7e−04	0.17	0.17
	Labor force	(0.027)	(0.97)	(1.1e−04)	(0.11)	
	LFPR[b]	−3.9	10	−4.0e−03	−0.13	0.35
		(0.26)	(9.3)	(1.1e−03)	(0.097)	

Source: Labor Force Survey (monthly series), January 1975 to March 1992.

Note: See note to table 7B.1 for details of estimation.

[a] The estimates are for 1976–85 in the case of the older (65+) men and women.

[b] LFPR = Labor Force Participation Rate.

Table 7B.3   **Cyclical Response of Participation, Employment, Employment/Population Ratio: Japan, 1962–1992**

Demographic Group	Dependent Variable	Constant	Constant1	Trend	Sum Lagged	ρ	R^2
Men							
	Employment	−0.16	0.014	−1.1e−04	−5	0.62	0.95
Age 55–64	Population	(0.01)	(0.0036)	(2.3e−05)	(0.47)	(0.043)	
	Employment	0.018	−0.0026	2.1e−05	−3.3	0.54	0.95
	Labor force	(0.0041)	(0.0014)	(9.3e−06)	(0.19)	(0.046)	
	LFPR[a]	−0.17	0.016	−1.2e−04	−1.7	0.63	0.88
		(0.0097)	(0.0033)	(2.2e−05)	(0.44)	(0.042)	
	Employment	−0.84	−0.037	−9.6e−04	−12	0.59	0.98
Age 65+	Population	(0.027)	(0.0092)	(6.0e−05)	(1.2)	(0.044)	
	Employment	0.013	−0.0033	2.8e−05	−1.5	0.5	0.71
	Labor force	(0.0046)	(0.0016)	(1.0e−05)	(0.21)	(0.047)	
	LFPR[a]	−0.85	−0.034	−9.8e−04	−10	0.59	0.98
		(0.026)	(0.0090)	(5.8e−05)	(1.2)	(0.044)	
Women							
	Employment	−0.67	−0.019	2.8e−04	−4.9	0.64	0.63
Age 55–64	Population	(0.025)	(0.0084)	(5.5e−05)	(1.1)	(0.042)	
	Employment	−0.0089	0.0046	−2.4e−05	−0.89	0.26	0.73
	Labor force	(0.0027)	(9.5e−04)	(6.0e−06)	(0.12)	(0.052)	
	LFPR[a]	−0.66	−0.023	3.0e−04	−4	0.63	0.63
		(0.024)	(0.0082)	(5.4e−05)	(1.1)	(0.042)	
	Employment	−1.6	−0.1	−2.2e−04	−12	0.83	0.93
Age 65+	Population	(0.095)	(0.0028)	(2.2e−04)	(4.3)	(0.03)	
	Employment	0.0023	0.0033	9.9e−06	−0.52	0.07	0.11
	Labor force	(0.0029)	(0.0010)	(6.5e−06)	(0.13)	(0.054)	
	LFPR[a]	−1.6	−0.11	−2.2e−04	−11	0.82	0.93
		(0.092)	(0.028)	(2.1e−04)	(4.2)	(0.031)	

Source: Monthly Labor Survey (monthly series), September 1960 to March 1992.

Note: Prime-age males are age 30–39. Constant 1 is a dummy variable set to one from October 1967. For other details, see note to table 7B.1.

[a] LFPR = Labor Force Participation Rate.

Appendix C
Statistical Sources

All data used in this paper are available to the public, mainly through published documents.

United States

Labor force data from the Current Population Survey are published monthly in *Employment and Earnings* by the U.S. Population Bureau. All data used on the benefit levels and participation in benefits come from the *Annual Statistical Supplement* of the Social Security Administration.

Sweden

Monthly labor force data are from the Swedish Labor Force Survey. These are not published but are available from Statistiska centralbyrän, AM-avdelningen, 115 81 Stockholm. Data on benefits and participation in benefits come from an annual publication *Allmän Försäkring* (*National Insurance*), published by the National Insurance Board, Stockholm.

Japan

Monthly labor force data after 1968 are available from the Japanese *Labor Force Survey*. This is published as annual volumes by the Japanese Ministry of Labor. For monthly data before 1968, it is necessary to use the monthly reports put out by the same ministry. Data on the level of benefits and participation in benefits may be found in the *Jigyō Nenpo* (Annual Report), an annual volume published by the Social Insurance Bureau of the Japanese Ministry of Welfare.

References

Abraham, K., and S. Houseman. 1989. Job security and work force adjustment: How different are U.S. and Japanese practices? *Journal of the Japanese and International Economies* 3:500–521.

———. 1993. *Job security in America: Lessons from Germany*. Washington, D.C.: Brookings Institution.

Burkhauser, R., and G. Duncan. 1988. Life events, public policy, and the economic vulnerability of children and the elderly since 1939. In *The vulnerable*, ed. Palmer, J. L., T. Smeeding, and B. B. Torrey. Washington, D.C.: Urban Institute.

Clark, K., and L. Summers. 1981. Demographic differences in cyclical employment variation. *Journal of Human Resources* 16:61–77.

Clark, R. 1991. *Retirement systems in Japan*. Homewood, Ill.: Dow Jones–Irwin.

Clark, R., and A. McDermed. 1990. *The Choice of pension plans in a changing regulatory environment*. Washington, D.C.: American Enterprise Institute Press.

Erikson, R., and J. Fritzell. 1988. The effects of the social welfare system in Sweden on the well-being of children and the elderly. In *The vulnerable,* ed. Palmer, J. L., T. Smeeding, and B. B. Torrey. Washington, D.C.: Urban Institute.

Erikson, T. 1988. Evaluation of the flexible retirement age system in Sweden. In *The role of research in social security.* Geneva: International Social Security Association.

Esping-Andersen, G., L. Rainwater, and M. Rein. 1988. Institutional and political factors affecting the well-being of the elderly. In *The vulnerable,* ed. Palmer, J. L., T. Smeeding, and B. B. Torrey. Washington, D.C.: Urban Institute.

Fields, G., and O. Mitchell. 1984. *Retirement, pensions and social security.* Cambridge: MIT Press.

Foster, H. 1990. *Employee benefits in Europe and USA.* London: Longman.

Ginsberg, H. 1985. Flexible and partial retirement programs for Norwegian and Swedish workers. *Monthly Labor Review* 108(10): 33–43.

Hamermesh, D. S. 1980. *Unemployment insurance and the older American.* Kalamazoo, Mich.: W. E. Upjohn Institute.

Hashimoto, M. 1993. Aspects of labor market adjustments in Japan. Part 1. *Journal of Labor Economics* 11 (January): 136–61.

Hurd, M. 1990. Research on the elderly: Economic status, retirement, and consumption and saving. *Journal of Economic Literature* 28:565–637.

Japan. 1991. *Aging society handbook* (Kōreishakai Tokeiyōran). Kōnenreishai Koyō Kaihatsu Kyōkai.

Kotlikoff, L., and D. Wise. 1989. *The wage carrot and the pension stick: Retirement benefits and labor force participation.* Kalamazoo, Mich.: W. E. Upjohn Institute.

Laczko, F., and C. Phillipson. 1991. *Changing work and retirement.* Milton Keynes: Open University.

Lagerström, L. 1976. *Pension systems in Sweden.* Stockholm: Kugel Tryckeri AB.

Mirkin, B. A. 1987. Early retirement as a labor force policy: An international overview. *Monthly Labor Review* 110(3): 19–33.

Organization for Economic Cooperation and Development (OECD). 1991. Unemployment benefits. Chap. 7 of *Employment outlook.* Paris: OECD.

———. 1992a. Labour market participation and retirement of older workers. Chap. 5 of *Employment Outlook.* Paris: OECD.

———. 1992b. *Purchasing Power Parities and Real Expenditures.* Paris: OECD.

Preston, S., and S. Kono. 1988. Trends in well-being of children and the elderly in Japan. In *The vulnerable,* ed. Palmer, J. L., T. Smeeding, and B. B. Torrey. Washington, D.C.: Urban Institute.

Quinn, J., R. Burkhauser, and D. Myers. 1990. *Passing the torch: The influence of economic incentives on work and retirement.* Kalamazoo, Mich.: W. E. Upjohn Institute.

Rebick, M. E. 1993. The Japanese approach to finding jobs for older workers. In *As the workforce ages: Costs, benefits, and policy challenges,* ed. Olivia Mitchell, 103–124. Ithaca, N.Y.: ILR Press.

Schulz, J. E., et al. 1991. *Economics of population aging: The "graying" of Australia, Japan, and the United States.* New York: Auburn House.

Seike, A. 1989. The effect of the employment pension on the labor supply of the Japanese elderly. *A Rand Note* N-2862. June.

Shimada, H., et al. 1982. *Rōdō Shijō Kikō no Kenkyū* (Studies in the Structure of Labor Markets). Economic Research Center Studies Series no. 37. Tokyo: Economic Planning Agency.

Smolensky, E., S. Danziger, and P. Gottschalk. 1988. The declining significance of age in the United States: Trends in the well-being of children and the elderly since 1939. In *The vulnerable,* ed. Palmer, J. L., T. Smeeding, and B. B. Torrey. Washington, D.C.: Urban Institute.

Social Security Administration. 1960–1991. *Social Security Bulletin,* Annual Statistical Supplement Series. Washington, D.C.: U.S. Department of Health and Human Services, Social Security Administration.

8 Public Sector Growth and Labor Market Flexibility: The United States versus the United Kingdom

Rebecca M. Blank

Expansions in transfer and income security programs have direct effects on the behavior and well-being of those who are eligible for them. But such expansions also have indirect economic effects that may be equally important to understand in evaluating the impact of these programs. In most cases, these programs are run through the public sector and produce an increase in government expenditure and in public sector employment. If public sector labor markets operate differently than private sector labor markets, then expansions of the public sector can change the nature of labor market equilibrium. This could happen, for instance, if public sector jobs require a different set of worker skills, if the public sector wage-setting process is different, or if the elasticity of public employment and wages to demand changes is lower.

Major expansions of government-run programs throughout the post–World War II industrialized world resulted in increases in the size of the public sector. Table 8.1 shows the share of government outlays in gross domestic product (GDP) and the share of public employment in total employment for six advanced industrial countries over the last three decades.[1] Most European countries experienced a large increase in the relative size of the public sector and in public employment between 1960 and 1980, while the United States experienced more moderate growth in the public sector over these two decades. In

Rebecca M. Blank is professor of economics at Northwestern University, faculty affiliate at Northwestern's Center for Urban Affairs and Policy Research, and a research associate of the National Bureau of Economic Research.

The author thanks the Ford Foundation, the National Bureau of Economic Research, and the Center for Urban Affairs and Policy Research, Northwestern University, for their support for this project. Excellent research assistance was provided by Yasuyo Abe, Jennifer Bivens, and Rebecca London. Particularly useful comments were provided by Tom Downes, Douglas Holtz-Eakin, and Stephen Jenckins.

1. For more extensive data on public sector comparisons across a variety of countries, see Rose (1985), OECD (1982), or Heller and Tait (1983).

Table 8.1   **Trends in Government Expenditure and Employment among Industrialized Nations**

A. Government Outlays as a Share of GDP

	1960	1980	1990
United States	27.0%	33.7%	36.1%*
United Kingdom	32.2	44.8	42.1
West Germany	32.4	48.5	46.0
France	34.6	46.1	49.9
Sweden	31.0	61.6	61.4
Total European Economic Community	31.8	45.2	48.7
Japan	17.5	32.6	32.3

*1989 statistic

B. Government Employment as a Share of Total Employment

	1960	1980	1990
United States	14.7%	15.4%	15.0%
United Kingdom	14.8	21.1	19.2
West Germany	8.0	14.6	15.1
France	—	20.0	22.6
Sweden	12.8	30.3	31.7
Total European Economic Community	11.1	16.9	17.6
Japan	—	6.7	6.0

Source: Organization for Economic Cooperation and Development (1992), *Economic outlook, historical statistics, 1960–90* (Paris: OECD), table 6.5 (for part A above), table 2.13 (for part B above).

contrast, the expansion of the public sector stops or slows substantially in all countries in the 1980s.

This paper investigates the implications of changes in the relative size of public and private sector labor markets in the United States and the United Kingdom. These two countries provide a particularly interesting comparison for at least three reasons. First, they both have relatively unregulated private sector labor markets;[2] thus, public/private differences between these countries will primarily reflect differences in the public sector. Second, the composition of the public sector in each country is quite different. The United States has a larger military sector, while the United Kingdom has more publicly owned industries, including a nationalized health sector. This potentially allows me to investigate the extent to which public/private differences can be ascribed to the different mix of goods produced in the public sector. Third, the pattern and timing of public and private sector growth has been quite different in the two countries. Both countries had similarly sized public sectors in 1960, but the

2. The unionization rate in the private sector in the United Kingdom is higher than in the United States. Coleman (1991) cites a United Kingdom unionization rate of about 38 percent in the mid-1980s in the United Kingdom. Freeman and Ichniowski (1988) cite a United States figure of 14 percent in 1986 in the United States.

United Kingdom saw greater relative public sector growth than the United States over the 1960s and 1970s and a greater decline in the public sector over the 1980s. The question is whether these differences have had differential effects on employment patterns and employment flexibility.

In the 1980s, the political winds in the two countries blew in similar directions, as both countries witnessed the election of conservative political leadership at the end of the 1970s. Both Ronald Reagan and Margaret Thatcher promised to shrink the size of government, to create greater competitive pressures in the public sector, and to better align public and private wages. In the United Kingdom, Thatcher embarked on major privatization efforts. Over the 1980s, more than twenty companies moved out of public ownership, while those companies that remained publicly owned were restructured to encourage more competitively based operations.[3] In addition, Thatcher implemented major changes in the wage-setting process in the public sector. Local governments were given more control over wage setting for local government workers. The structure for public wage setting was altered, as existing definitions of public/private comparability were changed. One of the more visible symbols of these changes was Thatcher's very public deunionization of a group of civil servants in the General Communication Headquarters (GCHQ) in 1984.

The Reagan administration made fewer nationally mandated changes in public sector labor markets over the 1980s. Because the United States never had the nationalized industries that existed in the United Kingdom, no major federal privatization occurred, although a number of state and local governments experimented with privatizing certain services, such as publicly owned jails and hospitals. Similar to Thatcher's GCHQ incident, the event that became the symbol of Reagan's concern about high wage levels in the public sector occurred in 1981, when he fired all striking air traffic controllers and decertified their union. The largest changes of the 1980s occurred at the state and local levels, where large numbers of jurisdictions conducted major comparability studies and realigned public and private sector wages, typically as an outgrowth of the discussion over comparable worth.[4]

This paper investigates the effect of the public sector on labor market flexibility in three ways. First, the paper compares the differences in employment and wages in the two sectors and investigates whether these differences simply reflect a different mix of product demands in the two sectors. Second, the paper investigates the nature of public/private wage differentials in the two countries and tests whether these differentials decreased over the 1980s when both countries made an effort at greater "wage alignment." Third, the paper looks at the

---

3. Companies that moved out of public ownership include British Telecom, Rolls-Royce, British Airways, and British Petroleum. For a thorough discussion of British privatization efforts and their effect, see Kay, Mayer, and Thompson (1986) or Vickers and Yarrow (1978).

4. While few jurisdictions actually implemented explicit comparable-worth plans, many updated their comparability wage-setting techniques in order to prevent or quiet criticism by local unions.

long-term adjustment process of employment and wages in both countries and investigates whether there is evidence of substantially different responses to aggregate demand changes in the two sectors.

8.1   Should the Public Sector Differ?

If there were no difference in the operation of the public versus the private sector, it would matter little whether services were provided by one or the other. In fact, however, there are at least three reasons why the labor markets in these two sectors could differ. First, many researchers have suggested that there is less market competition within the public sector. The public sector disproportionately provides public goods or creates and maintains monopolies in the production of goods, limiting the amount of market competition for public sector workers and their services.[5] The result might be public/private differences in the level and distribution of pay, in the quantity of workers hired and retained, and in the adjustment in pay and employment as demand changes. For instance, this lack of competition may increase the tendency toward strong internal labor markets in the public sector (e.g., the civil service or the military), which typically increases pay rigidities. Similarly, the monopolistic provision of socially necessary goods such as police or fire protection may lead to different levels of unionization and worker bargaining power. In recognition of this problem, many public sector wages in both countries are set through comparability surveys, designed to determine pay levels for equivalently skilled private sector workers whose wages are assumed to be market based.

Second, the public sector might have more diverse employment goals than the private sector. While the private sector's primary concern is profit maximization, the government may be pursuing social welfare goals or political goals as well as production-related goals in its employment decisions. For instance, the public sector might seek to reverse historical patterns of discrimination in the employment and promotion of women or minority workers. Alternatively, nonmarket political pressures may affect pay determination and expenditure decisions by public officials whose primary concern is the next election. These political and social concerns could result in different relative employment and wage levels among workers in the public sector.

Third, because the goods provided by the public sector differ from those provided by the private sector, there may be differences in the skill demands generated by public sector versus private sector expansions. In essence, the government buys a different bundle of goods and services than do consumers. To the extent that there is a trade-off between public demand and private demand, increases in public sector demand will disproportionately benefit those workers whose skills are more useful in the production of public than

5. Among local public sector employers, of course, there may be substantial cross-jurisdictional competition for workers.

of private goods. Some observers have further suggested that public sector goods, because they are heavily service oriented, are less likely to experience productivity-enhancing technological change. In this case, a growing public sector will have long-term productivity and cost implications for the economy.

Modeling the behavior of the public versus the private sector is a complex problem. To fully capture the complete set of possible differences, one would have to account for differences in the competitive environment, in the type of goods produced, and in the decision-making process of government versus private sector employers. While models have been developed that investigate each of these issues separately, there is no integrated model of public sector behavior currently available.

This paper is primarily an empirical exploration, investigating differences in the employment and wage outcomes in the public sector versus the private sector. To the extent that these findings shed some light on theoretical predictions of different causal theories, that will be noted. But these theories are impossible to disentangle empirically in any satisfactory manner with the data available for this paper.

8.2   U.S. and U.K. Public Sector Employment and Wages

Aggregate employment patterns in the United States and the United Kingdom have been very different over the past several decades, as have patterns of public sector employment. Table 8.2 shows trends in employment in the public and private sectors in both countries. All of the employment data discussed in this section come from the National Income and Product Accounts (NIPA) data of the two countries. Data are available from 1961 to 1990 for the United Kingdom, and from 1948 to 1990 for the United States.[6]

Within the United Kingdom, private employment was virtually flat throughout the 1960s and 1970s, showing an increase only in the 1980s. In contrast, public sector employment grew steadily to a peak in 1979 and then declined while private employment grew in the 1980s. Local government employment grew faster in the 1960s, while central government employment grew faster in the 1970s. Employment in nationalized industries was largely constant until 1980, although its share fell as other public employment expanded. After 1980 it fell steeply as many of these industries were privatized. Panels A through D of fig. 8.1 depict employment patterns in these sectors in the United Kingdom.

Within the United States, private employment grew strongly over the past three decades, almost doubling between 1960 and 1990. Public sector employment showed equally strong growth from 1960 through 1980; thus, the share

---

6. See appendix A for more information on data sources. Employment figures for the United States are reported as full-time equivalents over the entire period. Within the United Kingdom, full-time equivalent numbers are only available for the last decade, so I use actual employment numbers. Because of an expansion in part-time work in the United Kingdom, the full-time equivalent numbers show less employment growth over the 1980s than is reported here.

Table 8.2   **Employment Trends in the United States and the United Kingdom**

A. *United Kingdom*

	1961	1970	1980	1990
Total employment (thousands)	24,458	24,752	25,328	26,914
Share of total (%)				
Private employment	76.0	73.7	70.8	77.6
Public employment	24.0	26.3	29.2	22.4
Total public employment (thousands)	5,860	6,515	7,387	6,040
Share of total (%)				
Central employment	30.5	29.6	32.4	38.0
Local employment	31.9	39.3	40.0	49.1
Public enterprise	37.5	31.1	27.6	12.9

B. *United States*[a]

	1960	1970	1980	1990
Total employment (thousands)	56,312	70,671	86,346	104,918
Share of total (%)				
Private employment	81.9	80.0	81.9	83.1
Public employment	18.1	20.0	18.1	16.9
Total public employment (thousands)	10,209	14,117	15,620	17,734
Share of total (%)				
Federal employment	43.0	37.0	27.3	25.4
State/local employment	46.8	53.2	62.6	64.5
Public enterprise	10.1	9.7	10.1	10.1

Source: National Income and Product Accounts, United States and United Kingdom.

[a]For the United States, employment is reported as full-time equivalents.

of public sector employment remained almost constant. Over the 1980s, public employment grew, but less steeply than private employment, leading to a fall in the public share. Within the public sector, federal employment peaked in 1968, due to the large military buildup during the Vietnam War. State and local employment grew strongly over this entire time period, more than doubling in size. Employment in public enterprises in the United States is extremely small compared with the United Kingdom and grew at about the same rate as overall employment.[7] Panels A through D of fig. 8.2 depict the employment patterns in these sectors in the United States.

Table 8.3 analyzes the changing composition of employment within different parts of the public sector.[8] In the United Kingdom, the military's employ-

7. The U.S. NIPA include state/local and federal public enterprise employees in their counts of total state/local and federal employment. In the United Kingdom, public enterprise is considered a separate category from local and central employment. For comparability, whenever subsectoral data are presented in this paper, public enterprise employees are treated as a separate group of public employees in the United States.

8. The United Kingdom has only two levels of government, central and local. The United States, with a federalist system of government, has three levels, federal, state, and local. The data used in this section do not allow me to distinguish between state and local workers in the United States. In addition, the U.S. NIPA data do not provide as detailed a subsectoral breakdown of public employment as do the U.K. NIPA data.

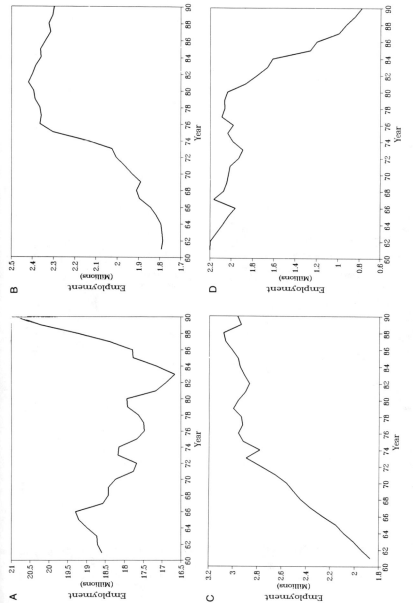

Figure 8.1 Employment patterns in the United Kingdom: (A) private employment; (B) central government employment; (C) local government employment; (D) public enterprise employment

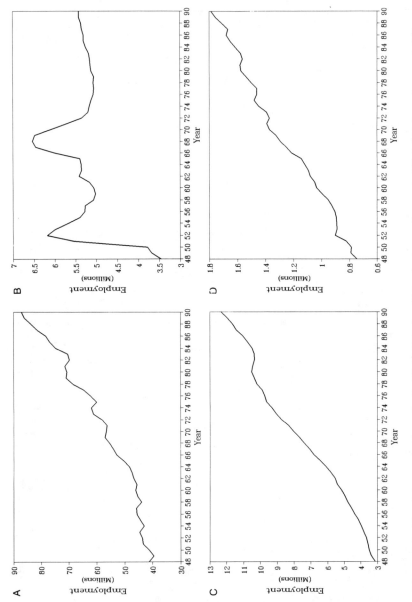

Figure 8.2 Employment patterns in the United States: (A) private employment; (B) federal employment; (C) state/local employment; (D) public enterprise employment

Table 8.3   **Public Sector Employment Components in the United States and the United Kingdom**

A. United Kingdom

	1961	1970	1980	1990
Central government employment, share of				
Military	26.5%	19.3	13.5%	13.2%
National Health Service	32.1	38.4	49.1	53.4
Civilian (except NHS)	41.4	42.4	37.4	33.4
Local government employment, share of				
Education	42.0	48.5	50.8	48.2
Social services	9.1	10.4	11.7	14.0
Police	5.8	5.7	6.1	6.7
Other	43.2	35.5	31.4	31.1

B. United States

	1960	1970	1980	1990
Federal government employment, share of				
Military	61.3%	62.6%	51.8%	50.6%
Civilian	38.7	37.4	48.2	49.4
State/local government employment, share of				
Education	52.1	56.2	55.6	57.5
Other	47.9	43.8	44.4	42.5

Sources: National Income and Product Accounts, United States and United Kingdom.

ment share steadily declined, while the National Health Service (NHS) expanded to over 50 percent of central government employment by 1990. At the local level, education has accounted for approximately half of all local employees in the United Kingdom since 1970. The share of employees in social services has expanded steadily over time, as has the share in police services.

In the United States, the military accounts for a much larger share of federal employment, although this share has fallen as the size of the armed forces has shrunk. At the state and local level, education accounts for a little over half of all employees. As in the United Kingdom, this share has been relatively flat since 1970.

In short, the United States experienced far more overall employment growth, both public and private, over the last three decades, while U.K. private sector labor markets were virtually stagnant for much of this period. Within the United Kingdom, the central government had twice the share of total employment in 1990 as the U.S. government did. This occurred despite much larger armed forces employment in the United States and partially reflects the presence of National Health Service workers as central government employees in the United Kingdom. As a share of total employment, local employment in the United Kingdom is about equivalent to state and local employment in the United States and seems to be composed of similar types of spending. U.K. government enterprise accounts for a much larger share of total employment than in the United States, even after extensive privatization over the last decade.

It is worth noting that the most rapid public sector employment growth in both countries occurred at the state and/or local level. Much of this was due to the expansion of public employment in education, which increased particularly rapidly in the 1960s as both countries experienced strong population growth among the young.[9] This makes it difficult to attribute the overall sluggish labor market growth within the U.K. private sector to the larger public sector employment share in that country. In fact, the public sector component (local employment) that was growing most rapidly in the United Kingdom grew just as rapidly in the United States, accounted for just as much total employment, and clearly did not prevent private sector employment growth in that country.

The U.S. NIPA data include average annual earnings as well as employment by sector, but the U.K. NIPA data do not. From 1978 on, the New Earnings Survey (NES), a random national sample of workers in the United Kingdom, provides information on average gross weekly earnings among private and public sector workers.[10] Public and private sector wage trends from these two data sources are presented in table 8.4.[11]

Within the United Kingdom, there is little evidence of public/private earnings differences in the NES data, except in public enterprise in 1980. Between 1980 and 1990, relative public/private sector earnings declined among all public sector workers. Panel A of fig. 8.3 graphs public and private earnings trends from 1978 to 1990. Panel B of fig. 8.3 graphs earnings trends among central government, local government, and public enterprise workers. Real earnings generally increased among all workers over this time period.

Within the United States, there are positive public/private earnings differentials among federal workers and public enterprise workers. Unlike in the United Kingdom, there is no evidence of a decline in these differentials over the 1980s, and in fact they appear to grow somewhat. Panel A of fig. 8.4 graphs public and private earnings trends in the United States from 1948 to 1990. Panel B of figure 8.4 graphs trends in federal, state/local, and public enterprise earnings over this time period. Real earnings rose substantially among all groups of workers during the 1950s and 1960s and the 1980s.

---

9. The U.K. population under age 15 grew 10 percent in the 1960s, compared to U.S. growth of 5 percent in the same decade.

10. The NES data are not exactly comparable to the NIPA data. They do not include part-time or very low wage workers. This will lead to something of an overstatement of wage levels.

11. For comparability, weekly earnings in the United Kingdom are put into 1990 U.K. pounds, using the U.K. GDP deflator (at market prices), and then translated into U.S. dollars, using the 1990 purchasing power parity calculation by the OECD that sets £0.597 equal to $1. U.S. earnings are reported in 1990 U.S. dollars, using the U.S. GDP deflator.

Table 8.4   **Earnings Trends in the United States and the United Kingdom (1990 U.S. dollars)**

A. United Kingdom

		1980		1990	
	1960	Wages[a]	Public/ Private Ratio	Wages[a]	Public/ Private Ratio
Private wages	—	$333		$445	
Public wages	—	350	1.05%	429	0.96%
Central employment	—	331	0.99	404	0.91
Local employment	—	345	1.04	442	0.99
Public enterprise	—	380	1.14	446	1.00

B. United States

		1980		1990	
	1960	Wages[b]	Public/ Private Ratio	Wages[b]	Public/ Private Ratio
Private employment	$21,082	$24,755		$25,889	
Public employment	20,156	25,057	1.01%	27,585	1.07%
Federal employment	20,516	27,109	1.10	28,711	1.11
State/local employment	19,576	23,650	0.96	26,711	1.03
Public enterprise	21,310	28,223	1.14	30,343	1.17

Sources: New Earnings Survey (U.K. data); National Income and Product Accounts (U.S. data).
[a]Real average gross weekly earnings of full-time workers age 21 and over.
[b]Real average annual earnings of full-time equivalent workers.

The public/private earnings comparisons in table 8.4 are somewhat difficult to interpret, since they do not control for hours of work over the year or for differences in worker skills and characteristics between sectors. We will investigate public/private wage differentials more closely in section 8.4 of this paper, using microdata samples of workers in each country.

8.3   Public/Private Differences in Skill Demands and Worker Characteristics

As noted above, the type of workers employed in the public sector may differ from those hired in the private sector. This could be due to differences in the mix of public versus consumer goods, differences in the goals of public sector employers, and preferences for public sector jobs among certain groups of workers. To the extent that public sector expansions disproportionately increase employment options among certain workers, this can affect the long-run composition and productivity of the labor force.

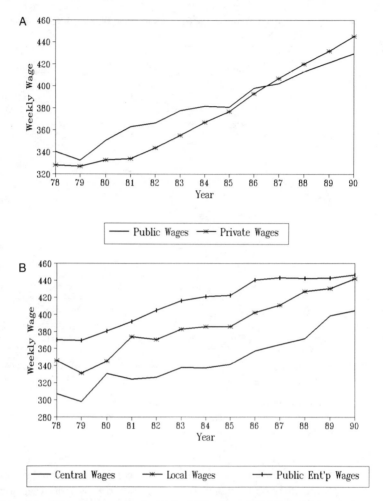

Figure 8.3   Wage patterns in the United Kingdom (1990 U.S. dollars): (A) public and private wages; (B) public sector wages

Previous research has documented differences in the characteristics of public and private sector workers.[12] In the United States, many studies have indicated that the public sector employs a substantially higher proportion of women and minorities. Its employees are also, on average, more skilled. Within the United Kingdom, there is less empirical evidence on this topic, but similar patterns seem to occur. The public sector hires more women and white-collar workers (Gregory 1990) and has more actively worked to hire racial minority and disabled individuals (Beaumont 1981). The effort to privatize large nation-

12. For a review of this research, see Ehrenberg and Schwarz (1986).

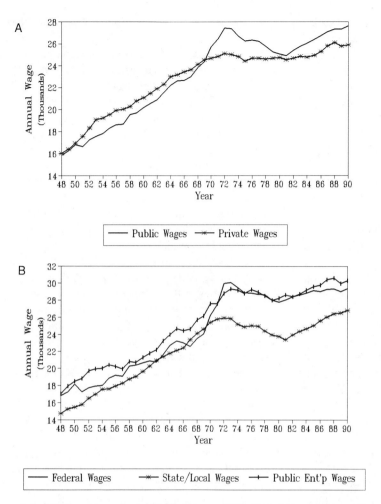

Figure 8.4   Wage patterns in the United States (1990 U.S. dollars): (A) public and private wages; (B) public sector wages

alized industries over the past decade has changed the mix of public employees (Kay and Thompson 1986).

This section investigates differences in skill demands and worker characteristics, updating previous research with evidence from the late 1980s. This section and the following two sections utilize two microdata random samples of workers in the United States and the United Kingdom. Within the United States, I use the Current Population Survey (CPS), which every March asks a barrage of questions about workers' employment and income during the previous year, including whether they were employed in the public sector or in a federal, state, or local government job. Because I am interested in changes over the past decade, I extract a sample of workers age 18 to 64 from the 1990 and 1980 March CPS.

Within the United Kingdom, microdata with information on public sector employment are less available. The General Household Survey (GHS), an annual random survey of households, asked workers whether they were employed in the public or the private sector in the survey years 1983, 1985, and 1987. Unfortunately, this question did not ask whether public employees were in central, local, or public enterprise jobs. In the results reported here, I use samples of workers age 16 to 64 from the 1983 and the 1987 GHS.[13]

Table 8.5 reports the characteristics of public and private sector workers in the United Kingdom (in 1987) and the United States (in 1989). Both countries show very similar sectoral patterns. As others have noted, public sector workers in both countries have more education, are older, are more likely to be nonwhite,[14] and are more likely to be female. In the United Kingdom, public sector workers are also more likely to work part-time.

The bottom part of table 8.5 shows the occupational distribution of jobs in the public and private sectors in the two countries, using roughly comparable occupational categories. Similarities in the public/private occupational distribution of the two countries are apparent. Over one quarter of public sector employees are health, education, and welfare professionals, while less than 5 percent of private employees are in this area. The public sector has a higher proportion in service occupations and a much lower proportion in sales and blue-collar occupations. In the United Kingdom the public sector also has a smaller share of workers in general management positions, although in the United States the two sectors are about equivalent. Conversely, in the United States the public sector appears to employ a greater share of clerical workers, while the shares are equivalent in the United Kingdom.

Even within specific occupational groups, public sector workers are typically more highly educated and older. The greater use of nonwhite workers in the U.S. public sector is apparent among all U.S. occupations, while the greater use of part-time workers in the U.K. public sector is particularly concentrated among manual workers. Within the U.S. data, where I have enough observations to look at quite detailed occupational categories (e.g., "elementary school teacher"), these sectoral differences remain. This implies that there are probably differences in the entire labor market process by which employees are hired and retained in the public sector.

I have also looked at the changes in relative worker characteristics over time. As discussed above, there were major efforts to retrench the public sector in both the United Kingdom and the United States over the 1980s. As it turns out,

---

13. In the U.S. data, there are 69,974 workers in the 1990 March CPS sample and 74,059 workers in the 1980 March CPS. In the U.K. data, there are 7,519 workers in the 1983 GHS sample and 8,838 workers in the 1987 GHS sample.

14. In the United States, these are workers who report themselves as black and/or Hispanic. In the United Kingdom, these are respondents who are assessed by the interviewer to be "colored."

Table 8.5   **Characteristics of Public and Private Sector Workers**

	United Kingdom[a]		United States[b]	
	Public	Private	Public	Private
All workers				
Years of education	12.2	11.4	14.2	12.8
Age	39.2	35.7	39.1	35.6
Percentage nonwhite	3.7	3.4	17.9	13.7
Percentage part-time	26.4	22.1	15.9	16.8
Percentage female	53.0	44.8	53.7	46.0
Occupational shares (%)				
Health, education, and welfare				
professionals	27.1	3.2	27.0	4.8
Science and Engineering				
professionals	4.7	5.3	3.0	3.0
Managers, administrators, and				
other professionals	8.4	15.5	13.2	12.6
Clerical	18.8	18.6	23.3	15.9
Sales	0.3	10.4	1.0	13.5
Services	24.3	11.4	16.8	12.3
Farm, fishing, construction,				
and mining	4.7	3.5	2.7	6.7
Production, craft, and				
assembly	7.2	23.0	3.9	16.8
Transportation and materials				
moving	3.4	6.2	3.1	4.5
Labor and miscellaneous[c]	1.2	1.9	5.9	10.0

[a]1987 data.

[b]1989 data.

[c]Due to definitional differences in occupational categories between the two countries, many of the workers counted here for the United States are subsumed in other categories in the U.K. data.

there are few changes in the relative age or education levels in these two sectors over these years in either country. In the United States, there is also little evidence of changes in the relative use of part-time or minority workers in the two sectors. In the United Kingdom, there is an increase in the relative use of both part-time and female workers in the public sector.

It is clear from table 8.5 that expansions in the public sector will lead to growth in the share of white-collar, clerical, and service-sector jobs.[15] If there is any trade-off between public and private sector growth, blue-collar male workers will be most negatively affected by public sector expansion. Such expansion would increase the employment of women and (particularly in the United States) minority workers. These sectoral differences, however, reflect both demand and supply effects. There is evidence from the United States that

15. Of course, this assumes that any expansion in public sector demand results in expanded demand for the same mix of services currently provided by the public sector.

women and minorities are much more likely to select public sector jobs (Blank 1985). To the extent that the public sector provides more attractive job opportunities to workers (women and minorities) who are often considered disadvantaged in the labor market, this may increase long-term labor market productivity. Public sector expansions in the United Kingdom will also increase the share of part-time jobs, which may provide jobs to workers who would otherwise be unemployed. This could be viewed as increasing labor market flexibility, but the disadvantage of such flexibility is a larger share of the work force in lower-paid employment.

8.4   Public/Private Wage Differentials and Their Changes over Time

If public/private differences are solely due to differences in demand mix, then there is little reason to worry about the size of the public sector; if the private sector produced these goods, it would also demand the same mix of workers. If, however, these employment differences reflect an entirely different wage/employment equilibration process within the public sector, then this will be reflected in public/private wage differentials, even among workers in relatively similar jobs.

Most research in the United States indicates that substantial public/private wage differentials exist (Ehrenberg and Schwarz 1986), although this work has largely not tried to test underlying theories about these differences.[16] Initial work in the United States by Smith (1977) suggested that federal workers had higher wages than comparable private workers; state and local workers showed less consistent differences. Women and minorities were almost uniformly better paid in the public sector. More recent work has suggested that the wage advantage has eroded for federal workers, due primarily to the erosion of federal wages among more skilled employees (Freeman 1987; Krueger 1988b; Katz and Krueger 1991). Public/private wage differentials remain substantial even after controlling for selectivity into the public or private sector (Venti 1987; Gyourko and Tracy 1988).

Within the United Kingdom, there is much less empirical research on public/private wage differentials. Looking at raw public/private wage differences, Gregory (1990) finds higher pay for white-collar workers and lower pay for manual workers in the public sector, with no clear trends over time between 1970 and 1982. Recent attempts by the British government to substantially alter the determination of comparable pay levels has led to much discussion of how to determine effective public pay (Cappelli 1983; Kessler 1983; Kessler 1990), but there is little empirical work testing the effects of these changes.[17]

16. An exception is Katz and Krueger (1991), who find support for the theory that greater government bureaucracy and the nonprofit nature of the government affect public/private wages but unionization differences and changes in discretionary job categories do not.

17. Analysis of public/private pay differentials from other industrialized countries provides no evidence of consistent public/private patterns. Auld et al. (1980) find little difference in public/

This section investigates both aggregate and occupation-specific differences in public and private sector wages in the United States and the United Kingdom. To provide more detailed information on the nature of public/private wage differentials, four selected occupational groups are used: senior managers and professionals, professionals in health, education, or welfare–related occupations (hereafter HEW professionals), clerical workers, and manual workers. All of these occupational groups have substantial employment in both the public and private sectors. Appendix B defines these four groups in more detail.

I am particularly interested in changes in public/private wage differentials over the 1980s. As noted above, there was an effort in both countries to better align public and private sector wages during this decade. If the public sector was indeed out of line in its wage payments and if reforms over the 1980s were well directed, then the result should be a decline in public/private wage differences over the 1980s.

It is worth noting that wage changes might differ in the two sectors if productivity changes are occurring at a different rate among public and private sector jobs. Baumol (1967) first suggested that public sector jobs might experience little productivity change because of their labor-intensive nature. Empirical investigation of this issue, however, has indicated that public sector jobs experienced substantial productivity growth in recent decades,[18] and there is little reason to believe that productivity in the public sector has grown more slowly.

Table 8.6 presents the simple differences in log wages between the public and private sector in the early and late 1980s in columns 1 (U.K.) and 3 (U.S.).[19] In these data, there is a substantial difference in the level of public and private pay in the United Kingdom in 1983, larger than that reported in the New Earnings Survey, which shows essentially no public wage advantage. These two surveys are reporting on somewhat different samples; most notably, the New Earnings Survey includes only full-time workers, includes elderly workers, and excludes very low-wage workers. But the magnitude of the difference is problematic. In the 1983 GHS data, public sector workers receive 23.5 percent higher wages than public sector workers. Senior managers in the public sector are paid 11.2 percent more, while clerical workers are paid 34.1 percent more. Between 1983 and 1987, all of these differences decline substantially.

---

private wage changes in Canada between 1967 and 1975. Keller (1981) finds that skilled public sector employees in the Netherlands have higher relative wages. Zetterberg (1990) finds a similar pattern in Swedish data and also indicates that the overall public/private wage differential shrank in Sweden over the 1970s. Pederson et al. (1990) use Danish data from 1976 to 1985 to show that as public sector programs have expanded in that country, public sector wages have been reduced.

18. For a U.S.-based discussion of this issue, see Gramlich (1982). For a U.K.-based discussion, see Levitt and Joyce (1987).

19. In the United States, the wage data are the result of dividing annual earnings by annual hours of work. In the United Kingdom, the wage data are usual gross weekly earnings. Thus, the control for part-time work is presumably more important in the U.K. data than in the U.S. data.

Table 8.6   **Public/Private Differentials in Log Wages Over Time (standard errors in parentheses)**

Worker sample	(1) Simple Log Wage Difference	(2) Public Sector D.V. Regression Coefficient	(3) Simple Log Wage Difference	(4) Aggr. Public	(5) Federal	(6) State/Local
				Public Sector D.V. Regression Coefficients		
					Separated into:	
	United Kingdom (1983)			United States (1979)		
All	.235**	.140**	.090**	.001	.189**	−.048**
	(.018)	(.011)	(.006)	(.006)	(.012)	(.006)
Selected occupations						
Senior managers and professionals	.112*	.020	.117**	.029	.197**	−.029
	(.056)	(.049)	(.022)	(.025)	(.046)	(.029)
HEW professionals	.355**	.242**	−.022	−.009	.077*	−.015
	(.089)	(.049)	(.028)	(.015)	(.042)	(.015)
Clerical workers	.341**	.147**	−.034*	−.047**	.108**	−.090**
	(.031)	(.025)	(.016)	(.017)	(.031)	(.018)
Manual workers	.168**	.083**	.113**	.040	.090	.035
	(.024)	(.021)	(.033)	(.033)	(.091)	(.034)
	United Kingdom (1987)			United States (1989)		
All	.154**	.105**	.181**	.031**	.180**	−.010*
	(.019)	(.012)	(.007)	(.007)	(.013)	(.007)
Selected occupations						
Senior managers and professionals	−.073*	−.090*	−.004	−.099**	.032	−.147**
	(.057)	(.048)	(.021)	(.022)	(.040)	(.025)
HEW professionals	.318**	.159**	−.018	−.017	.153**	−.024*
	(.068)	(.039)	(.027)	(.017)	(.057)	(.017)
Clerical workers	.258**	.123**	.021	−.011	.111**	−.040*
	(.035)	(.028)	(.022)	(.023)	(.047)	(.025)
Manual workers	.085**	.094**	.265**	.152**	.235*	.145**
	(.036)	(.031)	(.033)	(.037)	(.113)	(.038)
	Difference: 1987−1983			Difference: 1989−1979		
All	−.081**	−.035*	.091**	.030**	−.009	.038**
	(.026)	(.017)	(.009)	(.009)	(.018)	(.010)
Selected occupations						
Senior managers and professionals	−.185**	−.110*	−.121**	−.128**	−.165**	−.118**
	(.079)	(.069)	(.031)	(.034)	(.063)	(.036)
HEW professionals	−.037	−.083*	.004	−.026	.076	−.009
	(.112)	(.063)	(.039)	(.022)	(.071)	(.022)

Table 8.6   (continued)

	(1)	(2)	(3)	(4)	(5)	(6)
		Public Sector D.V. Regression Coefficient		Public Sector D.V. Regression Coefficients		
	Simple Log Wage Difference		Simple Log Wage Difference	Aggr. Public	Separated into:	
Worker sample					Federal	State/Local
	Difference: 1987–1983			Difference: 1989–1979		
Clerical workers	−.083*	−.024	.055*	.036*	.003	.050*
	(.046)	(.037)	(.027)	(.028)	(.056)	(.031)
Manual workers	−.083*	.011	.152**	.112*	.145	.110*
	(.043)	(.037)	(.046)	(.050)	(.145)	(.051)

Note: In addition to public sector dummy variable, U.K. regressions include controls for education, experience, sex, region, marital status, color, country of birth, and part-time job. U.S. regressions include education, age, sex, region, marital status, race, and part-time job.
*Significant at 10 percent level.
**Significant at 1 percent level.

The log difference in public/private sector wages in the United States in 1979 (column 3) is substantially smaller. These CPS data are consistent with the public/private earnings differences in the NIPA data and indicate a public wage advantage of 9.0 percent. Among HEW professionals and clerical workers, U.S. public sector workers appear to be paid less. Quite in contrast to the United Kingdom, overall public/private pay differences between 1979 and 1989 rise on average in the United States, from 9.0 percent to 18.1 percent. These unadjusted differences in pay, however, may reflect differences in the skills needed on public and private sector jobs and therefore may reflect productivity-related differences in the group of workers hired into public versus private jobs. Column 2 presents the log wage regression coefficient on a dummy variable equal to 1 if a worker is employed in the public sector in the United Kingdom, controlling for education, experience, sex, region, race, marital status, and part-time employment. Thus, the regression coefficient measures any public/private difference in wages that remains after holding constant other standard determinants of wages. Column 4 presents a similar log wage regression coefficient on a public sector dummy variable in the United States. Columns 5 and 6 estimate separate public sector coefficients for federal and state/local workers in the United States.

The results in column 2 for the United Kingdom indicate that controlling for worker and job characteristics reduces public/private wage differences, although it does not eliminate them. The regression-adjusted public/private wage difference declined 3.5 percent between 1983 and 1987; thus, in the United Kingdom, relative public/private wages did move closer together over the 1980s. This trend did not occur uniformly over all occupations, however. Clerical and manual workers saw little change in their public sector wage advantage. HEW professionals saw a clear decline, from a 24 percent wage advantage to a 16 percent wage advantage. But senior managers went from relatively comparable wages to public sector wages that were significantly lower than those in the private sector by the late 1980s.

Within the United States, the public sector coefficients (column 4) are also smaller than unadjusted differences.[20] Once worker characteristics are controlled for, there is no public sector advantage in 1979 and a small (3.1 percent) public sector advantage in 1989. There is little evidence in column 4 that the 1980s brought the wages of public sector workers more in line with their private sector counterparts. Senior public managers saw their wages go out of alignment, HEW professionals remained in alignment, and low-skilled manual workers saw substantial increases in their public sector advantage.

With the U.S. CPS data, I can estimate adjusted public wage differentials within the federal and the state/local sectors. The last two columns in table 8.6 do this. The results provide strikingly different conclusions that one would reach looking only at the aggregate public/private regression coefficients in column 4. There appears to be no net public sector wage differential, not because there is no difference in public/private wages but because there is a significant positive public wage advantage at the federal level offset by a significant negative public wage disadvantage at the state/local level. While the federal wage differential does not change over the 1980s, the negative state/local differential appears to come into better alignment with regard to public/private wages. Thus, the overall public sector wage differential appears to worsen, but this is entirely due to aggregation between federal and state/local effects.

Several conclusions should be drawn from table 8.6. First, both countries appeared somewhat successful at bringing wage levels more in line between the public and the private sector over the 1980s, although in the United States this consisted more of bringing state/local workers up to private sector wage levels, while in the United Kingdom this was the result of bringing down higher relative public wages. To the extent that both countries pursued a goal of bringing public and private wages into better alignment, this appears to have been achieved. Second, in both countries, senior public managers saw extensive relative wage declines. HEW professionals in the United Kingdom also experienced wage declines, but this did not happen in the United States. Third, the United States saw substantial relative wage gains among less-skilled manual workers, although this trend was not apparent in the United Kingdom. The

---

20. The results in this section are quite similar to those previously reported in Freeman (1987), Krueger (1988a), and Katz and Krueger (1991).

result of these changes among more- and less-skilled public sector workers in both countries should be to narrow the relative wage distribution in the public sector versus the private sector, a point I will pursue further below. Fourth, the substantial differences in the behavior of the U.S. federal and state/local sectors should create hesitation about drawing strong conclusions from the aggregate U.K. public/private wage changes. Disaggregating the U.K. public sector coefficient into the effects within the central, local, and public enterprise subsectors of the economy could result in a very different picture of public/private pay movements. In particular, privatization efforts within the United Kingdom could have changed the nature of jobs and workers within the public sector over these years, thus changing the selectivity of workers into the public sector. It would be extremely useful to be able to separate changes in public enterprises from changes in other public sector jobs, but unfortunately the data do not allow this.

Table 8.7 presents results similar to those in table 8.6 but focuses on differences between male and female workers. We noted above that women appear to be disproportionately more likely to be hired by the public sector. In table 8.7 we can investigate whether women in the public sector also receive a greater wage advantage. Columns 1 and 4 of the table repeat the aggregate "public sector wage effect" estimated from a regression controlling for worker and job characteristics in the United Kingdom and the United States, respectively. Columns 2 and 5 present similar results for male workers in the two countries, and columns 3 and 6 present results for female workers.

The primary conclusion from table 8.7 stands out sharply for both countries and for all occupations: women have larger public sector wage advantages than men, or they have smaller public sector wage disadvantages in virtually all occupations and years. Male public sector workers in the United Kingdom in 1983 have an 8.0 percent wage advantage, while female workers have a 21.4 percent advantage. In the United States in 1979, men have a 7.3 percent wage disadvantage in the public sector, while women have a 7.6 percent advantage. This wage advantage could be one reason for the greater presence of women in the public sector. In results not shown here, I have estimated probit models of public sector employment, including expected public/private wage differences in the regression. While the wage differences are important, women are more likely to be in the public sector, even after controlling for their larger public/private wage differential. This could imply that women prefer public sector work beyond its wage advantages, or it could indicate that public sector employers both give hiring preferences to women and pay them better than their public sector alternatives. (In other words, it is difficult to judge whether the additional propensity of women to select into the public sector is coming from the supply or the demand side of the labor market.)

At least three important omitted variables in the regressions reported in tables 8.6 and 8.7 might be affecting these results. First, as many have speculated, there may be substantial differences in the nonwage characteristics of

Table 8.7   **Public/Private Differentials in Log Wages by Gender over Time: Public Sector Dummy Variable Regression Coefficients (standard errors in parentheses)**

Worker Sample	All (1)	Male (2)	Female (3)	All (4)	Male (5)	Female (6)
	United Kingdom (1983)			United States (1979)		
All	.140**	.080**	.214**	.001	−.073**	.076**
	(.011)	(.014)	(.019)	(.006)	(.008)	(.009)
Selected occupations						
Senior managers and	.020	.027	−.042	.029	−.050*	.193**
professionals	(.049)	(.051)	(.137)	(.026)	(.028)	(.055)
HEW professionals	.242**	.041	.316**	−.009	−.061**	.030*
	(.049)	(.077)	(.062)	(.015)	(.023)	(.019)
Clerical workers	.147**	.083*	.153**	−.047**	−.084	−.047**
	(.025)	(.058)	(.025)	(.017)	(.140)	(.017)
Manual workers	.083**	.076**	.229*	.040	.017	.089*
	(.021)	(.021)	(.139)	(.033)	(.045)	(.046)
	United Kingdom (1987)			United States (1989)		
All	.105**	.029*	.164**	.031**	−.024**	.088*
	(.012)	(.015)	(.020)	(.007)	(.009)	(.009)
Selected occupations						
Senior managers and	−.090*	−.131**	−.104	−.099**	−.186**	.024
professionals	(.048)	(.052)	(.113)	(.022)	(.029)	(.035)
HEW professionals	.159**	.056	.219**	−.017	−.041*	.012
	(.039)	(.052)	(.054)	(.017)	(.030)	(.020)
Clerical workers	.123**	.037	.133**	−.011	.224	−.008
	(.028)	(.055)	(.030)	(.023)	(.216)	(.023)
Manual workers	.094**	.054*	.484**	.152**	.081*	.285**
	(.031)	(.031)	(.156)	(.037)	(.048)	(.059)
	Difference: 1987−1983			Difference: 1989−1979		
All	−.035*	−.051**	−.050*	.030**	.049**	.012
	(.017)	(.020)	(.027)	(.009)	(.012)	(.013)
Selected occupations						
Senior managers and	−.110*	−.158*	−.062	−.128**	−.136**	−.169**
professionals	(.069)	(.073)	(.177)	(.034)	(.040)	(.065)
HEW professionals	−.083*	.015	−.097	−.026	.020	−.018
	(.063)	(.093)	(.082)	(.022)	(.038)	(.028)
Clerical workers	−.024	−.046	−.020	.036*	.308	.039*
	(.037)	(.080)	(.040)	(.028)	(.258)	(.029)
Manual workers	.011	−.022	.255	.112*	.064	.196**
	(.037)	(.037)	(.209)	(.050)	(.066)	(.074)

*Significant at 10 percent level.
**Significant at 1 percent level.

public and private sector jobs, such as job security, fringe benefits, or work environment. If these differences are substantial, wage alignment between the two sectors might actually be an indication that total compensation is not in alignment. Unfortunately, I have no information on the nonwage characteristics of jobs in my data sets.

One way to infer information about total compensation is to look at the demand for public sector jobs. Katz and Krueger (1991) use U.S. federal applications data to indicate that there appear to be far more applications per job for blue-collar federal jobs than for white-collar federal jobs. Krueger (1988a, 1988b) also shows evidence of queues among federal workers in jobs with wage advantages. This implies that the pay differences we observe translate into total compensation differences, increasing the demand among workers for these jobs.

A second possible omitted variable is union status in the public and private sectors. Some have argued that public sector unions might be able to achieve higher wages because they can threaten to disrupt vital citizen services. Again, I do not have information on this variable in my data sets. Within the United States, there is little consistent evidence of greater public/private wage differences among unionized workers (Ehrenberg and Schwarz 1986; Trejo 1991), although some differences in wages and employment appear to occur under different bargaining arrangements (Zax 1989; Ichniowski, Freeman, and Lauer 1989). In the United Kingdom, there is little empirical work on this issue. Dickerson and Stewart (1992) have found few differences in the propensity of public sector unions to strike, once other factors are controlled for. Major changes in legislation and regulations governing trade unions in the United Kingdom over the past decade are generally believed to have weakened public sector union power (Saran and Sheldrake 1988; Towers 1989).

A third omitted variable problem is more amenable to investigation. It has been suggested that some of the public/private sector differences are due to differences in the average size of public versus private sector establishments. Existing research in labor economics indicates that larger establishments tend to offer different labor market contracts than smaller establishments do.[21] Larger corporations are likely to be more bureaucratic in their behavior, to have more strongly developed internal labor markets, and may be better able to smooth cyclical fluctuations. Some of the difference between public and private sector workers may be due to the fact that public sector jobs are more comparable to jobs in large corporations than those in small firms. In this case, an establishment size variable would act as a proxy for the different types of jobs and job contracts available in larger firms.

In the U.S. CPS data, I have no way to control for establishment size, but

21. Katz and Krueger (1991) look at this question for the United States, and Green, Machin, and Manning (1992) look at it for the United Kingdom. Neither paper looks at the wage effect of establishment size by public and private sector.

the U.K. GHS data includes this information. The GHS data for 1987 show that public sector workers are indeed more likely to be in larger establishments (see table 8.8 for frequency distribution). If there are differences in the labor market contracting arrangements of smaller and larger establishments, it is clear that the public/private wage differential will reflect these differences.

Table 8.9 presents the regression coefficients for public sector jobs, interacted with establishment size. Rows 1 through 4 report the results from a single regression, which interacts the public sector dummy with four dummy variables for each of the four establishment sizes coded into the GHS data. The results in the first four rows of table 8.9 appear to indicate that there is a differential wage level in public sector jobs that grows as establishment size increases, among both men and women. Workers in public sector establishments with over 1,000 workers received 15.6 percent higher wages in 1987, while workers in public sector establishments of less than 25 workers received only 4.9 percent higher wages.

If the wages of all workers differ by establishment size, however, this first regression might be misleading. The last four regressions presented in table 8.9 estimate separate wage regressions for workers in each size of establishment. These regressions tell quite a different story, indicating that both public and private workers in large establishments get higher wages. Within establishment size groups, the largest wage advantage for public sector workers appears to occur in the smallest establishments. In fact, in establishments of 25 workers or more, there are relatively small and frequently insignificant coefficients on the public sector dummy variable.

The results in table 8.9 confirm that establishment size is an important omitted variable in regressions that attempt to measure the impact of public sector employment on relative wages. As the bottom row of table 8.9 indicates, if I take the estimated public sector effects by establishment size, based on the four regressions at the bottom of table 8.9, and weight them by the share of public sector employment in each establishment size, I get an aggregate public/private wage differential of 4.3 percent in 1987. This compares to an estimated aggregate wage differential among all workers in 1987 of 10.5 percent when establishment size differences are not controlled for (table 8.6). In 1983, the estimated aggregate public wage differential is 6.8 percent, compared to an estimate of 14.0 percent when establishment size is not controlled for. Thus,

Table 8.8   Frequency Distribution of U.S. Workers, by Establishment Size

Establishment Size	Public Sector Workers	Private Sector Workers
1–24 workers	21.0%	39.0%
25–99	26.2	23.6
100–999	35.4	27.8
1000+	17.4	9.6

Table 8.9   **Interactive Effect of Establishment Size and Public Sector Placement on Wages of U.K. Workers (standard errors in parentheses)**

	All Workers (1)	Male (2)	Female (3)	All Workers (4)	Male (5)	Female (6)
		1983			1987	

Regression 1: Public sector and establishment size interacted
Coefficient on:
Public sector,*

	All Workers (1)	Male (2)	Female (3)	All Workers (4)	Male (5)	Female (6)
Size < 25	.007	−.001	.037	.049*	−.030	.106**
	(.023)	(.032)	(.032)	(.023)	(.033)	(.032)
Public sector,*						
25 ≤ size < 100	.127**	.047*	.211**	.082**	.013	.135**
	(.020)	(.025)	(.030)	(.021)	(.027)	(.031)
Public sector,*						
100 ≤ size < 1,000	.174**	.073**	.306**	.129**	.036*	.223**
	(.016)	(.019)	(.027)	(.018)	(.021)	(.030)
Public sector,*						
size ≥ 1,000	.205**	.146**	.299**	.156**	.081**	.200**
	(.021)	(.023)	(.039)	(.025)	(.029)	(.041)

Regression 2: Sample of establishment size < 25 only
Coefficient on

	All Workers (1)	Male (2)	Female (3)	All Workers (4)	Male (5)	Female (6)
public sector	.155**	.107**	.208**	.206**	.104**	.259**
	(.029)	(.039)	(.041)	(.029)	(.041)	(.041)

Regression 3: Sample of 25 ≤ establishment size < 100 only
Coefficient on

	All Workers (1)	Male (2)	Female (3)	All Workers (4)	Male (5)	Female (6)
public sector	.076**	.042*	.111**	.019	−.026	.049*
	(.022)	(.029)	(.033)	(.023)	(.029)	(.036)

Regression 4: Sample of 100 ≤ establishment size < 1,000 only
Coefficient on

	All Workers (1)	Male (2)	Female (3)	All Workers (4)	Male (5)	Female (6)
public sector	.049**	.003	.122**	.016	−.009	.032
	(.016)	(.019)	(.026)	(.017)	(.021)	(.029)

Regression 5: Sample of establishment size ≥ 1,000 only
Coefficient on

	All Workers (1)	Male (2)	Female (3)	All Workers (4)	Male (5)	Female (6)
public sector	.016	.027	−.019	−.064**	−.069**	−.122**
	(.021)	(.024)	(.039)	(.024)	(.029)	(.046)
Estimated aggregate public sector wage effect, using results from regressions 2 through 5	.068**	.030*	.120**	.043**	−.007	.071**
	(.010)	(.013)	(.017)	(.011)	(.014)	(.019)

Note: See table 8.6 for a list of control variables included in regression. Each cell represents a separate regression. Columns 1 and 4 estimated with all workers; columns 2 and 5 estimated with male workers only; columns 3 and 6 estimated wtih female workers only.
*Significant at 10 percent level.
**Significant at 1 percent level.

differences in labor market payments by establishment size seem to explain a little more than half of the public/private wage difference in the United Kingdom. On the other hand, significant public/private wage differences still remain, albeit at a smaller level, even after establishment size is controlled for. In addition, the same over-time trends are visible in the size-adjusted public sector effects, as the U.K. public/private differential shrinks by about one-third between 1983 and 1987.

The evidence in table 8.9 indicates that, in the United Kingdom, a little over half of the public/private wage differential is due to differences in wage contracts between establishments of different size, where public sector workers are disproportionately likely to be in larger establishments. The evidence that public sector workers in large establishments are paid similarly to private sector workers in large private firms provides little evidence of a less market-oriented public sector. On the other hand, there do appear to be wage advantages for public sector workers in smaller firms, which could indicate a greater degree of bargaining power or market protection than such workers have in the private sector. At least in part, this must be due to the fact that many U.K. public sector workers have their wages set through national agreements, and thus there are smaller wage differences between public sector workers in large and small establishments than among private workers employed in different establishment sizes.

8.5 Distribution of Public and Private Sector Wages

Both the United States and the United Kingdom experienced changes in the wage distribution over the 1980s. In the United States there were real increases in the wages of more-skilled workers and real decreases in the wages of less-skilled workers (Danziger and Gottschalk 1993). Within the United Kingdom there is also evidence of widening in the earnings distribution (Schmitt 1992), but the trends appear to be somewhat less pronounced than in the United States. One test of "sectoral differences" is to see whether the public sector mirrored the private sector in these distributional changes. The results in table 8.6 indicate that more-skilled public workers saw declining relative wages and less-skilled public workers saw increasing relative wages over the 1980s. This indicates that the public wage distribution did not widen as rapidly as the private wage distribution. Katz and Krueger (1991) have already confirmed this phenomenon for the United States.

Table 8.10 presents direct evidence on the relative wage distribution in the two sectors. It shows public and private wages at the 10th and the 90th percentile and the ratio of these wages to mean wages for both countries over the 1980s. Thus, the first row of the table indicates that the ratio of wages at the 10th percentile in the United Kingdom to mean public sector wages was 0.30 in 1983, while the equivalent ratio at the 90th percentile was 1.71. In the private sector, in contrast, these ratios were 0.23 and 1.78, respectively. This im-

Table 8.10   **Wage Distribution in the Public and Private Sectors (1990 U.S. dollars)**

	Gross Weekly Wages				Hourly Wage Rates			
	10th Percentile		90th Percentile		10th Percentile		90th Percentile	
	Wage Level	Ratio to Mean	Wage Level	Ratio to Mean	Wage Level	Ratio to Mean	Wage Level	Ratio to Mean
	United Kingdom (1983)				United States (1979)			
All workers								
Public	110	0.30	632	1.71	4.36	0.42	17.70	1.69
Private	73	0.23	563	1.78	3.79	0.38	17.70	1.77
Public/private	1.50	1.30	1.12	0.96	1.15	1.10	1.00	0.96
Senior managers and professionals								
Public	355	0.57	889	1.44	6.67	0.45	23.61	1.59
Private	237	0.40	984	1.65	5.45	0.38	25.44	1.77
Public/private	1.49	1.42	0.90	0.87	1.22	1.19	0.93	0.90
HEW professionals								
Public	159	0.38	680	1.62	5.63	0.48	17.94	1.53
Private	59	0.17	744	2.11	4.60	0.39	19.85	1.66
Public/private	2.71	2.24	0.91	0.77	1.22	1.25	0.90	0.92
Clerical workers								
Public	154	0.50	453	1.47	4.04	0.56	10.55	1.45
Private	88	0.36	406	1.67	4.18	0.54	11.07	1.43
Public/private	1.75	1.39	1.11	0.88	0.97	1.03	0.95	1.02
Manual workers								
Public	269	0.67	548	1.36	3.60	0.48	11.07	1.47
Private	191	0.54	521	1.46	2.79	0.37	11.30	1.51
Public/private	1.41	1.24	1.05	0.94	1.29	1.28	0.98	0.97
	United Kingdom (1987)				United States (1989)			
All workers								
Public	82	0.25	583	1.77	4.09	0.35	19.71	1.68
Private	61	0.20	571	1.85	3.16	0.30	19.23	1.82
Public/private	1.33	1.25	1.02	0.96	1.29	1.16	1.02	0.92
Senior managers and professionals								
Public	267	0.52	755	1.47	5.77	0.38	24.04	1.60
Private	255	0.43	10.4	1.68	5.38	0.34	30.77	1.72
Public/private	1.05	1.21	0.75	0.88	1.07	1.14	0.78	0.93
HEW professionals								
Public	149	0.38	614	1.57	5.45	0.39	21.63	1.54
Private	65	0.20	659	1.98	3.95	0.29	24.04	1.78
Public/private	2.26	1.90	0.93	0.79	1.38	1.32	0.90	0.86
Clerical workers								
Public	108	0.42	406	1.56	3.85	0.47	11.78	1.43
Private	61	0.27	392	1.75	3.69	0.44	13.19	1.57
Public/private	1.77	1.56	1.04	0.89	1.04	1.06	0.89	0.91
Manual workers								
Public	122	0.37	481	1.46	3.61	0.48	12.02	1.59
Private	124	0.39	490	1.53	2.38	0.38	11.06	1.79
Public/private	0.98	0.95	0.98	0.95	0.66	1.24	1.09	0.89

plies that U.K. public sector wages were less dispersed both below and above the mean than were private sector wages.

It is clear that at both points in time, public sector workers in both countries faced more compressed wage distributions than did private sector workers. For almost every occupation in every year in both countries, both the 10th percentile and the 90th percentile of wages in the public sector are closer to mean public sector wages than are 10th percentile and 90th percentile of wages in the private sector.

Over time, the data in table 8.10 indicate that the wage distribution in the public and private sectors of both countries widens over the 1980s, as both real wages and wages relative to the mean fall at the bottom and rise at the top of the distribution. The widening in the U.S. public sector occurs more slowly, however, so that there is a growing divergence in distribution between the public and private sectors. In contrast, the U.K. public sector appears to experience more widening than the private sector, and the distributions move closer together.

The results in table 8.10 indicate that the public sector was not immune to the distributional changes over the 1980s. Particularly in the United Kingdom, there is little evidence that the public sector did not react to the market forces that led to a widening wage distribution in that country. In the United States, the fact that the distribution of public sector wages did not widen as rapidly as the distribution of private sector wages could be an indication that the public sector is somewhat more protected from market forces and can be seen as evidence of at least somewhat different timing in the adjustment of the public sector to market changes.

8.6   Change and Cyclicality in Employment and Wage Adjustments

The evidence presented above indicates that there were substantial changes in the relative wage position of public sector workers in the United States and United Kingdom over the 1980s. Given the emphasis throughout that decade on the need for greater responsiveness and flexibility in the public sector in both countries, these wage changes can be read as a sign that efforts to increase public sector responsiveness were successful. But observations on two points in time provide limited information on the issue of market responsiveness. This section uses aggregate time series data on employment and wages in the United States and the United Kingdom to investigate the relative flexibility of public versus private sector labor markets in the two countries. There is only a limited amount of research on this topic in the United States[22] and no British research on it to date.

---

22. Freeman (1987) indicates that state/local employment is countercyclical, while federal employment has little cyclical responsiveness. Katz and Krueger (1991) find that state and local wages appear to move with private sector wages, while federal pay is less responsive to the cycle.

In this section, I return to the NIPA data on employment by sector and sub-sector within the United States and the United Kingdom. This provides information on U.S. employment and wages since 1948 and on U.K. employment since 1961. Unfortunately, as noted above, the U.K. NIPA do not report wages by sector. The NES data on public/private earnings reported in table 8.4 are only available since 1978, too short a time period for time series analysis. As a result, for the United Kingdom I use alternative wage series from the New Earnings Surveys that are available since 1970.[23] Compared to the U.S. wage data, these data provide much more inaccurate and approximate information on U.K. wages by sector and subsector.

Table 8.11 reports statistics on the general variability in sectoral employment and wages for these two countries. A simple story of "public sector rigidity" would imply that public sector employment and wages both have less variance over time. Column 1 of table 8.11 reports the standard deviation in first differences of log employment over time; column 3 reports the standard deviation in the difference in log wages.[24]

The results for employment and wages in the United Kingdom and the United States are somewhat unexpected. In both countries, the evidence indicates that public sector employment and wages are as variable as or more variable than private sector employment and wages. Within the United Kingdom, employment in public enterprise is particularly variable, largely due to declines in public enterprise employment over the 1980s with privatization. Within the United States, federal military employment is highly variable, while overall federal civilian employment shows much less variability. The U.K. wage data show somewhat higher variability in the public sector, although the more questionable nature of this data makes firm conclusions about U.K. wages difficult. There is little evidence of substantial variance in U.S. wages in either the public or private sectors.

The results in columns 1 and 3 of table 8.11 indicate that there is at least as much change occurring in employment and wages within the public sector as within the private sector, although the amount of variability differs by subsector. But it is not entirely clear how to interpret these results. There are at least two more causal questions that a simple standard deviation coefficient cannot

23. For private sector workers, I use average weekly wages among all workers. I use weekly wages among workers in the industry designated as "public administration" as a proxy for overall public sector wages. Among all central government workers, I use average weekly wages among executive-grade workers covered by national wage agreements; for local government workers, I use wages among administrative-, professional-, and technical-grade local government workers covered by national agreements. For National Health Service workers, I use wages among nurses and midwives covered by national agreements. For education workers, I use an occupational wage series for elementary and secondary teachers; for the police, I use an occupational wage series on police. See appendix A for more detailed descriptions.

24. I have also duplicated this analysis using standard deviations in the level value of log employment and log wages, as well as standard deviations in the residuals of a regression of log employment against a time trend. The results are similar to those reported here for log first differences.

Table 8.11   Variability in Public and Private Sectors for Log Employment and Log Wages (standard errors in parentheses)

	Employment		Real Wages	
	Standard Deviation in Log First Difference (1)	Regression Coefficient on Change in Log per Capita Disp. Income[a] (2)	Standard Deviation in Log First Difference (3)	Regression Coefficient on Change in Log per Capita Disp. Income[b] (4)
United Kingdom				
Private sector	.023	.059 (.077)	.023	.377* (.174)
Public sector	.022	−.003 (.073)	.040	.058 (.346)
Central—all	.019	.023 (.063)	.078	.437 (.668)
Central—NHS	.029	−.018 (.094)	.079	−.788 (.656)
Central—civilian (except NHS)	.025	.047 (.081)	—	—
Local—all	.025	.019 (.084)	.040	−.140 (.341)
Local—education	.030	.018 (.100)	.072	.133 (.622)
Public enterprise	.065	−.085 (.216)	—	—
United States				
Private sector	.026	1.127** (.164)	.013	.232* (.118)
Public sector	.038	.396 (.348)	.018	.136 (.166)
Federal—all	.070	.597 (.642)	.028	.208 (.260)
Federal—civilian	.040	.443 (.365)	.026	.139 (.245)
State/local—all	.017	.062 (.156)	.017	.022 (.161)
State/local—education	.019	.161 (.178)	.021	−.084 (.192)
Public enterprise	.021	−.039 (.196)	.020	.187 (.187)

Sources: U.K. employment: 1961–90 NIPA data; U.K. wages: 1970–90 New Earnings Survey data (see Appendix A for definitions). U.S. employment: 1948–90 NIPA data; U.S. wages: 1948–90 NIPA data.
[a]Regression is Δlog(employment) = α + β*Δlog(real disposable income/population)
[b]Regression is Δlog(real wage) = α + β*Δlog(real disposable income/population)
*Significant at 10 percent level.
**Significant at 1 percent level.

address. First, it would be interesting to know how public versus private sector employment and wages respond to cyclical change. Second, it would be interesting to know how public and private sector employment responds to demand changes. For instance, a finding that education employment is nonresponsive to the cycle may be irrelevant if educational demand moves noncyclically.

Columns 2 and 4 of table 8.11 provide some very simple correlations between aggregate economic cyclicality and changes in sectoral employment and wages. These columns report the regression coefficient on changes in real per capita disposable income, regressed against changes in log employment (column 2) or changes in the log of real wages (column 4). The results in these columns provide a very simple measure of the contemporaneous correlations between aggregate demand movements and changes in sectoral labor markets.[25] In the United States, changes in private sector employment are strongly positively correlated with contemporaneous movements in real per capita disposable income. Changes in public sector employment are also positively correlated with change in disposable income, but the effects are much smaller in magnitude. In the United Kingdom, the correlation of changes in employment to changes in per capita disposable income is weak and insignificant in both the private and the public sectors of the economy.

U.S. wages are consistently procyclical in all sectors but are somewhat more cyclically correlated in the private sector than in the public sector. Federal wages appear to be more responsive to changes in per capita disposable income, while state and local wages (particularly in education) are relatively unaffected by these changes. U.K. wages are available for a much shorter time period and are less well measured by sector, as discussed above. Private sector wages show stronger cyclical correlation than public sector wages. For both countries, there is little evidence that local wages move with changes in per capita disposable income. Wages in the U.K. National Health Service appear rather strongly countercyclical.

The results in table 8.11 indicate that contemporaneous employment and wage changes in the private sector are generally more correlated with cyclical movements in the economy than are such changes in the public sector, although employment in the United Kingdom is not very cyclical in either sector. Changes in per capita disposable income, however, do not provide a good measure of demand for many government functions. For instance, health or education employment should move with the demand for those services, which may or may not be cyclical. In fact, certain federal functions in both countries are explicitly designed to grow countercyclically. In addition, table 8.11 presents only contemporaneous correlations. Employment and wage responses to demand changes may occur over time rather than instantaneously.

In order to more fully understand the relationship between changes in aggregate demand and changes in employment, an obvious approach is to turn to vector autoregressions. With annual data on only a small number of years, the usefulness of time series analysis may be limited, but it can provide some indication of how employment is related to demand changes over time.

I have run a variety of vector autoregression models. The specification reported in this paper for U.S. data is a four-equation system with two lags. The four equations estimated are (in sequence):

(1) $UR_t = f(UR_{t-1}, UR_{t-2}, DispY_{t-1}, DispY_{t-2}, PubW/PrivW_{t-1,j},$
$PubW/PrivW_{t-2,j}, Employ_{t-1,j}, Employ_{t-2,j})$;

25. These results are quite sensitive to specification. Using level values rather than changes, the results change markedly with different specification of the time trend. The first-difference estimates are somewhat more stable across specifications but—as is typical with first differences—show less significant results.

(2) $DispY_t = f(UR_t, UR_{t-1}, UR_{t-2}, DispY_{t-1}, DispY_{t-2},$
        $PubW/PrivW_{t-1,j}, PubW/PrivW_{t-2,j}, Employ_{t-1,j}, Employ_{t-2,j});$

(3) $PubW/PrivW_{t,j} = f(UR_t, UR_{t-1}, UR_{t-2}, DispY_t, DispY_{t-1},$
        $DispY_{t-2}, PubW/PrivW_{t-1,j}, PubW/PrivW_{t-2,j}, Employ_{t-1,j},$
        $Employ_{t-2,j});$

(4) $Employ_{t,j} = f(UR_t, UR_{t-1}, UR_{t-2}, DispY_t, DispY_{t-1}, DispY_{t-2},$
        $PubW/PrivW_{t,j}, PubW/PrivW_{t-1,j}, PubW/PrivW_{t-2,j}, Employ_{t-1,j},$
        $Employ_{t-2,j});$

where UR is the national unemployment rate, DispY is real disposable per capita income, $PubW/PrivW_j$ is the log difference between public sector wages in the jth branch of the public sector and private sector wages, and $Employ_j$ is the per capita employment in the jth branch of the public sector.[26] I will interpret changes in real disposable per capita income as an approximate measure of changes in aggregate private sector demand.

To measure the effects of changes in government demand in branch j on government employment in branch j, I estimated a second system of equations, replacing real disposable per capita income with total government expenditures on goods and services on the jth branch of the public sector. For instance, this meant that one system of equations was run using unemployment rates, real state and local expenditures on goods and services in education, log differences between public sector wages in education and aggregate private sector wages, and state and local employment in education. While I could potentially include both government expenditures and disposable income per capita in the same system of equations, they are highly intercorrelated (their contemporaneous correlation coefficient is .987). Because I think that increases in government demand (government expenditures on goods and services) are conceptually somewhat different from increases in overall aggregate macroeconomic demand (per capita disposable income), I chose to estimate two separate systems of equations.

Within the United Kingdom, I used an identical specification, with two differences. First, I used the vacancy rate rather than the unemployment rate in the United Kingdom. Empirically, this made little difference, and the vacancy rate is probably a better measure of economic cyclicality. Second, I omitted the third equation and all data on public/private wage ratios from the U.K. estimates. I did this because the U.K. wage data was only available from the early 1970s, which seriously limited the usefulness of time series estimation. In addition, as noted above, these data are not a very accurate measure of sectoral wage levels.

The results from these vector autoregressions can only be viewed as indica-

26. I experimented with using GDP rather than disposable income, and it made no difference. Reordering unemployment and disposable income or reordering the wage ratio and employment in the system of equations also did not make a substantial difference.

tive. With annual data, the number of observations is limited and the model extremely simple. In addition, disposable per capita income and government expenditures on goods and services are uncomfortably endogenous measures of private and public sector demand. At best, these models provide only an approximate indication of the employment elasticity response to changes in private or public demand, although they probably provide superior estimates to the older cross-section literature that investigates this question.[27]

The estimation results from running these systems of equations for all sectors and subsectors for which I have employment data produce a host of coefficients. In order to summarize the results of these estimates, I estimated a series of impulse-response models. Essentially, these use the coefficients in the estimated system to calculate the effect of a 1 standard deviation exogenous shock to one of the variables on the succeeding variables in the model. I am interesting in looking first at the effect of an exogenous increase in per capita disposable income (interpreted as an exogenous increase in macroeconomic growth) on employment in the jth branch of the public sector, as estimated by the first system of equations. The second system of equations gives me impulse-response estimates of the effect of an exogenous increase in government expenditures in the jth branch of the public sector on employment in the jth branch of the public sector.

The results from these impulse-response models are shown in table 8.12. What I show is the contemporaneous effect of the shock on employment and the cumulative effect one year and three years after the shock occurs. I am primarily interested in the cumulative long-term effects, but these three effects together indicate the path of the response. In a number of cases, as we shall see, initial negative responses turn into substantial positive responses over time and vice versa. Columns 1 to 3 show the employment response in each category to shocks in government spending on goods and services in that category. Columns 4 to 6 show the employment response to shocks in real per capita disposable income. The coefficients in table 8.12 can be interpreted as the proportional change in the relevant employment variable resulting from a 1 standard deviation change in the relevant exogenous variable. For instance, the first row indicates that a 1 standard deviation increase in per capita disposable income produces a contemporaneous 0.13 percent increase in private sector employment, a 0.39 percent increase in private sector employment one year later, and a cumulative 1.04 percent increase three years out.

Look first at columns 1 through 3. The private sector coefficients indicate whether or not an increase in government spending on goods and services has any expansionary or contractionary effect on private sector employment. Within the United Kingdom, increases in government spending on goods and

27. An earlier public finance literature attempts to measure these elasticities by regressing aggregate employment against contemporaneous measures of expenditure and other variables (e.g., Ashenfelter 1977).

Table 8.12   **Impulse Response Effects in Log (Employment) One Year After a 1 Standard Deviation Shock in Real Public Expenditure or in Real Disposable Income per Capita (standard deviations in parentheses)**

| | Percentage change after shock in: | | | | | |
| | Log (Appropriate Government Expenditure Category) | | | Log (Real per Capita Disposable Income) | | |
Employment Category	Contempor-aneous (1)	1 yr. out (2)	3 yrs. out (3)	Contempor-aneous (4)	1 yr. out (5)	3 yrs. out (6)
United Kingdom						
Private sector	−0.42*	−0.63	−0.83	0.13	0.39	1.04*
	(0.30)	(0.60)	(1.25)	(0.26)	(0.42)	(0.70)
Public sector	0.18	0.26	−0.26	0.05	−0.14	−0.94*
	(0.27)	(0.43)	(0.73)	(0.31)	(0.33)	(0.49)
Central—all	0.55**	1.06**	1.16*	0.52**	0.50	0.85
	(0.21)	(0.38)	(0.79)	(0.21)	(0.40)	(0.75)
Central—NHS	0.76**	2.14**	2.90**	0.47*	0.64	0.84
	(0.29)	(0.60)	(1.13)	(0.34)	(0.63)	(1.19)
Central—civilian (except NHS)	0.17	0.18	−0.25	0.31	−0.21	−0.72
	(0.37)	(0.62)	(1.05)	(0.36)	(0.58)	(0.82)
Local—all	1.08**	0.99*	0.65	0.21	0.17	−0.33
	(0.34)	(0.50)	(0.54)	(0.32)	(0.50)	(0.48)
Local—education	0.77**	0.85*	0.05	0.05	−0.09	0.75
	(0.32)	(0.48)	(0.64)	(0.29)	(0.45)	(0.63)
Public enterprise	2.49**	2.93**	2.55*	0.13	0.002	−0.92
	(0.74)	(1.01)	(1.82)	(0.94)	(1.15)	(1.57)
United States						
Private sector	−0.51**	−0.58*	−0.37	0.39**	1.34**	0.71**
	(0.12)	(0.36)	(0.44)	(0.13)	(0.35)	(0.28)
Public sector	1.61**	0.49	−0.68	−0.40	1.32**	1.53*
	(0.26)	(0.54)	(0.73)	(0.34)	(0.54)	(0.67)
Federal—all	3.02**	1.14*	−0.32	−1.45**	1.58*	1.74*
	(0.53)	(0.85)	(1.02)	(0.59)	(0.89)	(0.93)
Federal—civilian	0.64*	−0.12	1.46**	−0.62*	1.31**	1.28**
	(0.34)	(0.45)	(0.38)	(0.34)	(0.51)	(0.45)
State/local—all	0.22*	0.48*	1.06*	0.10	0.12	0.42
	(0.13)	(0.24)	(0.48)	(0.14)	(0.25)	(0.41)
State/local—education	0.28*	0.45*	0.74*	−0.06	0.05	0.25
	(0.18)	(0.25)	(0.54)	(0.16)	(0.29)	(0.47)
Public enterprise	0.57*	0.66*	0.23	−0.06	0.40	0.71*
	(0.25)	(0.33)	(0.48)	(0.26)	(0.33)	(0.41)

Note: See text for description of VAR models underlying these impulse-response coefficients.
*Significant at 10 percent.
**Significant at 1 percent.

services seem to come at the expense of the private sector. Three years out, private employment has declined by slightly less than one percent (-0.83). Strikingly, while the initial effect of an increase in government spending on public employment is positive, its longer-run effect is essentially zero. This implies that in the United Kingdom, government spending does not have any long-run employment-increasing effects in either the public or the private sectors.

The employment response in the United States to government spending on goods and services is only slightly different. As in the United Kingdom, government spending reduces private sector employment, although by a smaller amount (-0.37) over three years. The initial effect on public sector employment is very strong (a 1.61 percent rise), but the long-term effect is relatively large and negative, with a large standard error. Thus, increases in overall government spending on goods and services appear to have few employment-enhancing effects in the long run in either country.

Different subsectors within the public sector respond quite differently to expansions in expenditures on goods and services within their own subsector. Within the United Kingdom, a 1 standard deviation increase in expenditure on goods and services within the National Health Service produces close to a 3 percent increase in NHS employment over three years. Central civilian expenditures, however, have small effects on civilian central employment. Increases in local expenditures produce about a 0.65 percent increase in local government employment, although the elasticity of education employment to education expenditures is substantially lower. Public enterprise expenditures have large employment effects.

Within the United States, federal civilian spending appears to produce substantial increases in federal civilian employment. A 1 standard deviation increase in state and local government spending results in a 1.06 percent increase in state and local employment after three years; education spending also produces long-run employment growth. Public enterprise spending has a very low employment elasticity in the United States.

Changes in aggregate public demand (as measured by per capita disposable income) produce different effects. A 1 standard deviation increase in disposable income translates into between a 0.71 (U.S.) and a 1.04 (U.K.) percent increase in private sector employment three years out. In the United Kingdom we again see a trade-off between public and private sector employment. Disposable income increases actually have a long-term negative effect on overall public sector employment. There is little evidence of employment trickle-down from the macroeconomy to the public sector. There are differences in the extent to which subsectors are affected by disposable income growth, but in general the public sector in the United Kingdom is far less affected (or even negatively affected) by overall demand expansions than the private sector is.

The U.S. results are strikingly different. Growth in disposable income actually produces larger long-term increases in public sector than in private sector employment, primarily due to large employment elasticities at the federal level. In general, the U.S. economy appears to have a very different relationship between its public and private sectors, as measured by these estimates. While expansions in public sector demand have few employment effects outside of a few subsectors of government, expansions in private demand spill over into both sectors and expand employment in the long run. The United Kingdom appears to be much more balkanized between the sectors. Expansion in private disposable income has a net negative effect on public sector employment, while growth in public sector expenditures causes employment contractions over the long term in both sectors. These results are striking, given many of the similarities in the characteristics of the U.S. and U.K. public sectors that we observed earlier in this paper. In general, even though the public sectors in the two countries appear to attract a similar mix of workers and to repay them in somewhat similar ways, the larger macroeconomic relationships between these two sectors seem quite different, perhaps reflecting differences in unionization, government behavior, the openness of the economy to international competition, and macroeconomic structure.

8.7 Conclusions

This paper has investigated the relative differences in the public and private sectors in the United States and the United Kingdom, with particular attention to the question of how expansions in these two sectors affect the labor market. There are some striking similarities between the two countries: Both countries hire public sector workers who are more skilled, older, and more likely to be in professional or service occupations. Both countries show evidence of paying higher wages to certain groups of public sector workers, particularly women. Both countries have seen these wage differentials erode over the 1980s, particularly among senior public managers, and both have seen a widening of both public and private sector wage distributions.

The differences between the countries are also striking. The aggregate relationships between public and private sector spending and public and private sector employment in the two countries is quite different, with the United States showing much greater feed-through between the sectors and generally greater employment responsiveness to demand changes. The exact reasons underlying this difference are hard to judge with the data available here. In addition, the United States shows smaller public/private wage differentials in general and has seen a greater divergence in the distribution of wages in the public versus the private sector over the last decade.

The results also indicate that different groups within the public sector exhibit very different wage and employment behavior. It is hard to infer the expected effect of changes in public sector demand without specifying the exact nature of any particular change. Decreased government spending on education will have a very different effect than decreased government spending on public enterprises. There is enormous variance in the employment and wage outcomes in different subsectors of the public sector and in their changes over time.

My general conclusion is that on the basis of the data in this paper, which admittedly provide only a partial picture of the public sector, there is little evidence within the United States of substantial inflexibilities emerging from the public sector. There is evidence over the 1980s that the wage-setting process has responded to attempts to align public and private wages more closely. Public sector wages and employment demonstrate substantial variability over time. The response of public and private sector employment to changes in public and private sector expenditures is generally similar. The most striking evidence of less flexibility in the public and private sectors is that the most-skilled and the least-skilled workers in the public sector have not seen their wages adjust as rapidly as in the private sector, while real wage changes for both of these groups have occurred over the 1980s. This is to the disadvantage of more-skilled workers, whose wages seem to be unduly low at this point relative to their private sector counterparts. But it is to the advantage of less-skilled workers, whose public sector wages appear not to have fallen as rapidly as their private sector counterparts.

Within the United Kingdom, there is also substantial evidence of labor market flexibility in the public sector. Public/private wage differentials are larger than within the United States, but they have also declined more rapidly over the 1980s. Wage distributions in the public sector have moved closer to private sector distributions. The primary evidence of inflexibility in U.K. public sector labor markets is that public sector employment does not appear to respond substantially to changes in overall demand. The very different relationship between demand changes and employment elasticities in the United Kingdom compared to the United States clearly deserves more research.

Overall, this paper provides little evidence that major contractions in the size of the public sector will produce substantially more flexible aggregate labor market outcomes. Contractions in the public sector, however, will clearly disadvantage certain workers and advantage others. In addition, the specific effects of any change in public sector size will depend heavily upon which particular subsectors within the public sector are shrinking and will vary by size of establishment and level of government.

Appendix A
Data Sources

National Income and Product Accounts (NIPA)

United States

Annual employment and annual wage data for full-time equivalent workers by public and private sector and by various subsectors of the public sector are available for the years 1948–90. Source: *Survey of Current Business,* U.S. Department of Commerce, Bureau of Economic Analysis.

United Kingdom

Employment data by public and private sector and by various subsectors of the public sector are available for the years 1961–90. Full-time equivalent employment is available only in more recent years. Source: *Economic Trends,* Central Statistical Office.

New Earnings Survey (NES): United Kingdom

Average weekly earnings, excluding those whose pay was affected by absence, for full-time male and female workers by occupational category, industry category, and for various national bargaining units, are available for the years 1970–91. Source: *New Earnings Survey,* Department of Employment, Government Statistical Service. (Annual publication.)

For the years 1978–91, average weekly earnings are available for private sector, public sector, central government, local government, and public enterprise workers. In order to obtain wages over a longer time period for the calculations reported in section 8.6, I used the NES data from 1970 to 1991, approximating the different sectors with the following wage series. (In all cases, I created a total wage series with a weighted average of wages among male and female workers in each category, using the share of observations among men and women in the category for weights.)

Private Sector. Wage series for all workers.

Public Sector. Wages for nonmanual workers in the public administration industry.

Central Government. Wages for civil service, executive-grade workers covered by national wage agreements.

National Health Service (Central Subsector). Wages for female nurses and midwives, National Health Service, covered by national wage agreements.

Local Government. Wages for local authorities, administrative, professional, and technical grades, covered by national wage agreements.

Education (Local Subsector). Wages for workers in the elementary and secondary occupation.

Police (Local Subsector). Wages for male workers in the police occupation.

Current Population Survey (CPS): United States

Collected monthly in the United States by the U.S. Bureau of the Census. Each March a special supplement asks about income and employment experiences of workers over the previous year. Available on tape from the Bureau of the Census.

General Household Survey (GHS): United Kingdom

Collected annually in the United Kingdom by the Social Survey Division of the Office of Population, Censuses, and Surveys (OPCS). Contains information on earnings, income, and demographic characteristics over the last pay period. Available on tape from the ESRC data archive at Essex University.

Appendix B
Occupational Categories for the United States and United Kingdom

Occupational classification codes from the CPS for the United States and key occupational statistics (KOS) from the GHS for the United Kingdom are used in this paper. There are two types of comparability problems with this data. First, within the United States, occupational codes change between the 1980 and 1990 CPS surveys and can only be matched approximately in some cases. Second, the U.S. and U.K. occupational categories are not identical. Although the GHS (U.K.) data provide a very detailed KOS breakdown in 1987 that can be generally although not precisely matched with the U.S. occupational classification codes, this detailed breakdown is not available in the U.K. data in 1983. Thus, this report uses relatively aggregate occupational comparisons between the United States and the United Kingdom that are only approximately comparable.

The four occupational categories used in tables 8.6 and 8.7 can be defined as follows:

United Kingdom

Senior Managers and Professionals. KOS category 1. Includes senior managers in professional and related occupations (excluding managers in health, education, and welfare–related professions) and senior supporting management; also senior national and local government managers.

Health, Education, and Welfare Professionals. KOS category 2. Professional and related occupations in education, welfare, and health.

Clerical Workers. KOS category 6. Clerical and related occupations.

Manual Workers. Semiskilled manual workers, tallied in compact socioeconomic group category 13.

United States

Senior Managers and Professionals. 1990: Senior executive, administrative, and managerial occupations (code numbers 3–19). 1980: A matched group of 1980 occupational categories, designed to mimic the 1990 category.

Health, Education, and Welfare Professionals. 1990: Health occupations, teachers, social scientists and urban planners, and social, recreation, and religious workers (code numbers 84–177). 1980: A matched group of 1980 occupational categories, designed to mimic the 1990 category.

Clerical Workers. 1990 and 1980: Secretaries, stenographers, and typists.

Manual Workers. 1990: Cleaning and building service occupations, except household (code numbers 448–55). 1980: Cleaning service workers.

Note that these last two occupational categories for the United States are more narrowly defined than are their U.K. equivalents.

References

Ashenfelter, O. C. 1977. Demand and supply functions for state and local government employment: The effect of federal grants on nonfederal governmental wages and employment. In *Essays in labor market analysis,* ed. O. C. Ashenfelter and W. Oates. New York: John Wiley & Sons.
Auld, D. A. L., L. N. Christofides, R. Swidinsky, and D. A. Wilton. 1980. A microeconomic analysis of wage determination in the Canadian public sector. *Journal of Public Economics* 13:369–87.

Baumol, W. J. 1967. The macroeconomics of unbalanced growth: The anatomy of the urban crisis. *American Economic Review* 57:415–26.

Beaumont, P. B. 1981. *Government as an employer: Setting an example.* London: Royal Institute of Public Administration.

Blank, R. M. 1985. An analysis of workers' choice between employment in the public and private sectors. *Industrial and Labor Relations Review* 38:211–24.

Cappelli, P. 1983. Comparability and the British civil service. *British Journal of Industrial Relations* 21:33–45.

Coleman, J. S. 1991. Earnings-tenure profiles in the public and private sectors. Working paper. Economics Department, University of Stirling, U.K.

Danziger, S., and P. Gottschalk. 1993. *Uneven tides: Rising inequality in America.* New York: Russell Sage Foundation.

Dickerson, A. P., and M. B. Stewart. 1992. Is the public sector strike prone? Working paper.

Ehrenberg, R. G., and J. L. Schwarz. 1986. Public sector labor markets. In *Handbook of labor economics.* Volume 2, ed. O. C. Ashenfelter and R. Layard. Amsterdam: Elsevier Science Publishers.

Freeman, R. B. 1987. How do public sector wages and employment respond to economic conditions? In *Public sector payrolls,* ed. D. A. Wise. Chicago: University of Chicago Press.

Freeman, R. B., and C. Ichniowski. 1988. Introduction: the public sector look of American unionism. In *When public sector workers unionize,* ed. R. B. Freeman and C. Ichniowski. Chicago: University of Chicago Press.

Gramlich, E. M. 1982. Models of excessive government spending: Do the facts support the theories? In *Public finance and public employment,* ed. R. H. Haveman. Detroit: Wayne State University Press.

Green, F., S. Machin, and A. Manning. 1992. The employer size-wage effect: Is monopsony the explanation? Working Paper.

Gregory, M. B. 1990. Public-sector pay. In *A portrait of pay, 1970–1982,* ed. M. B. Gregory and A. W. J. Thomson. London: Clarendon Press.

Gyourko, J., and J. Tracy. 1988. An analysis of public- and private-sector wages allowing for endogenous choices of both government and union status. *Journal of Labor Economics* 6:229–53.

Heller, P. S., and A. A. Tait. 1983. *Government employment and pay: Some international comparisons.* Occasional Paper no. 24, Washington, D.C.: International Monetary Fund.

Ichniowski, C., R. B. Freeman, and H. Lauer. 1989. Collective bargaining laws, threat effects, and the determination of police compensation. *Journal of Labor Economics* 7:191–209.

Katz, L. F., and A. B. Krueger. 1991. Changes in the structure of wages in the public and private sectors. In *Research in labor economics.* Volume 12, ed. R. G. Ehrenberg. Greenwich, Conn: JAI Press.

Kay, J. A., C. Mayer, and D. J. Thompson. 1986. *Privatisation and regulation: The UK experience.* Oxford: Clarendon Press.

Kay, J. A., and D. J. Thompson. 1986. Privatisation: A policy in search of a rationale. *Economic Journal* 96:18–32.

Keller, W. J. 1981. Public sector employment and the distribution of income. *Journal of Public Economics* 15:235–49.

Kessler, I. 1990. Flexibility and comparability in pay determination for professional civil servants. *Industrial Relations Journal* 21:194–208.

Kessler, S. 1983. Comparability. *Oxford Bulletin of Economics and Statistics* 45:85–104.

Krueger, A. B. 1988a. Are public sector workers paid more than their alternative wage? Evidence from longitudinal data and job queues. In *When public sector workers unionize,* ed. R. B. Freeman and C. Ichniowski. Chicago: University of Chicago Press.

————. 1988b. The determinants of queues for federal jobs. *Industrial and Labor Relations Review* 41:567–81.

Levitt, M. S., and M. A. S. Joyce. 1987. *The growth and efficiency of public spending.* Cambridge: Cambridge University Press.

Organization for Economic Cooperation and Development (OECD). 1982. *Employment in the public sector.* Paris: OECD.

Pederson, P. J., J. B. Schmidt-Sorensen, N. Smith, and N. Westergard-Nielsen. 1990. Wage differentials between the public and private sectors. *Journal of Public Economics* 41:125–45.

Rose, R. 1985. *Public employment in western nations.* Cambridge: Cambridge University Press.

Saran, R., and J. Sheldrake. 1988. *Public sector bargaining in the 1980s.* Aldershot, U.K.: Avebury.

Schmitt, J. 1992. The changing structure of male earnings in Britain, 1974–88. Working Paper no. 223. Centre for Economic Performance, London School of Economics.

Smith, S. P. 1977. *Equal pay in the public sector: Fact or fantasy?* Princeton, N.J.: Industrial Relations Section. Monograph.

Towers, B. 1989. Running the gauntlet: British trade unions under Thatcher, 1979–1988. *Industrial and Labor Relations Review* 42:163–88.

Trejo, S. J. 1991. Public sector unions and municipal employment. *Industrial and Labor Relations Review* 45:166–80.

Venti, S. F. 1987. Wages in the federal and private sectors. In *Public sector payrolls,* ed. D. A. Wise. Chicago: University of Chicago Press.

Vickers, J., and G. Yarrow. 1988. *Privatization: An economic analysis.* Cambridge: MIT Press.

Zax, J. 1989. Employment and local public sector unions. *Industrial Relations* 28:21–31.

Zetterberg, J. 1990. *Essays on inter-sectoral wage differentials.* Ph.D. thesis, Department of Economics, Uppsala University, Sweden.

9 Does Public Health Insurance Reduce Labor Market Flexibility or Encourage the Underground Economy? Evidence from Spain and the United States

Sara de la Rica and Thomas Lemieux

The basic postulate that there is a trade-off between social protection and economic flexibility crucially relies on the premise that legislation aimed at enhancing social protection imposes real constraints on the behavior of economic agents. This legislation must be enforced, however, for these constraints to be binding. In the realistic case where enforcement is imperfect, the presence of underground markets (or parts of the economy that avoid legislated requirements) may significantly alter the trade-off between social protection and economic flexibility. Underground markets are known to be important in countries such as Spain, where they account for more than 10 percent of the work force.[1]

Ideally, to look at the flexibility and adjustment question, one would like to have data on a country's underground and regular sector at different points in time. One would then see whether some firms adjust over time by simply not complying with the new legislation. The impact of legislations on economic flexibility would depend on the proportion of firms not complying with the legislations. We are fortunate to have one good survey of underground sector activities in Spain, but repeated surveys of underground sector activities are virtually never available. So although we cannot observe adjustments over time as new legislation is introduced, we can still use cross-national variation in

Sara de la Rica is assistant professor of economics at the Universidad del País Vasco and a research associate of the Instituto de Economía Pública. Thomas Lemieux is assistant professor of economics at the Université de Montréal, a research associate of the Centre de Recherche et Développement en Économique, and a faculty research fellow of the National Bureau of Economic Research.

The authors are grateful to the Industrial Relations Section of Princeton University and to the Ford Foundation for financial support and to Luis Toharia for providing some of the data used in this paper. Sara de la Rica also acknowledges financial support from the Spanish Ministry of Education and Science.

1. These estimates are based on the ECVT data that we use in this paper. See also Muro and Toharia (1986).

social legislation to identify the impact of such legislation on the fraction of firms that decide to operate in the underground sector.

More specifically, to investigate the effects of the parameters of the public health insurance system in Spain on the decision of firms to operate in the underground sector, we compare Spanish firms to similar firms in the United States. We also investigate the comparative effect of the Spanish system on social protection, in this case on the percentage of workers covered by health insurance. These comparisons crucially rely on institutional differences in the financing and provision of health insurance in Spain and in the United States that need to be examined in detail. The U.S. system is often viewed as very flexible and economically efficient because the provision of health insurance to workers is based on private decisions of workers and firms.[2] By contrast, the same health care package is imposed on all workers and firms in Spain irrespective of their needs and/or capacity to pay for these services. The Spanish system is financed by a payroll (social security) tax and covers both workers and nonworkers.[3] Workers and their dependents are covered either under the social security card of the head of the family or, in the case of families with more than one worker, under their own card. Cardholders and their employers must in turn pay a social security tax of 25 percent of wages.

In a simple demand and supply framework, the payroll tax used to finance health care in Spain should have adverse employment effects on all the firms that decide to comply with the tax.[4] A closer analysis suggests, however, that summarizing the Spanish system in terms of a simple payroll tax may overstate the differences between the two systems. The point is that the incidence of a payroll tax that entitles taxpayers to some benefits is very different from the incidence of a tax that does not directly entitle the taxpayer to these benefits. For example, many Spanish workers who must pay the social security tax to get health insurance coverage would also prefer to pay an insurance premium under a privately provided insurance scheme. To some extent, the tax they pay is thus a mere relabeling of the insurance premium they would have to pay in a privately provided insurance scheme.[5] For these workers, the estimated im-

---

2. By efficiency we mean efficient provision of health insurance conditional on the insurance packages sold in the private market. We make no claims that the U.S. health care industry is efficient as a whole. For example, private provision of health insurance might create a "job lock" problem and thus an inefficiently low level of turnover (See Holtz-Eakin, ch. 6 in this volume).

3. The public health care system in Spain provides comprehensive health care to the whole population. Essentially all health care is provided by the public sector. By contrast, publicly provided health care is primarily available for only the elderly and families below the poverty line in the United States. The uninsured population typically consists of families in which the head is working but not earning enough to afford private health insurance.

4. Examples of empirical studies of the incidence of payroll taxes on employment include Hamermesh (1979) and Gruber and Krueger (1990).

5. One important difference between the two systems is that, since the payroll tax is proportional to wages up to a very high cap, high-wage workers pay more for the same service than low-wage workers do. Under the U.S. system, the health insurance premium is unrelated to wages, holding other characteristics of workers constant.

pact of a Spanish-type health insurance program on labor market outcomes such as wages, employment, and the decision to join the underground sector may thus be small. By contrast, the effects of a Spanish-type health insurance program may be large among workers who would not receive health insurance in the absence of a universal health insurance program.

This suggests comparing the characteristics of workers who do not receive health insurance in the United States to the characteristics of workers who do not comply with social security in Spain. If these characteristics were found to be similar, this would suggest that some of the adverse effects of a Spanish-type system on economic performance would be reduced by the decisions of firms and workers to join the underground sector. We investigate this issue by comparing the pattern and extent of the private provision of health care in the United States to the pattern and extent of compliance with the social security tax in Spain.

The paper is divided as follows. In section 9.1, we compare the structure of the labor market in Spain and in the United States, with a special emphasis on the provision of employee benefits. We then propose, in section 9.2, a simple framework to analyze the decision of firms to provide benefits to their employees. This section also analyzes the decision of Spanish firms to comply with the social security tax. In section 9.3, we compare empirically the pattern of compliance with social security taxes in Spain to the pattern of provision of health insurance by employers in the United States. The comparison is done along both demographic lines (age/gender/marital status) and industry affiliations of workers. We conclude by discussing the implication of our findings on well-being under the two systems of health insurance.

9.1 Institutional Background

This section describes the set of institutional constraints in which firms operate in Spain and in the United States. In particular, we discuss the characteristics of employee benefits in the two countries, how they are provided, and how they are financed. We also discuss the role of government economic policies and regulations in the growth of the underground sector in Spain and briefly describe the Spanish government policies aimed at enforcing compliance with social security taxes.

9.1.1 Employee Benefits in the United States

In monetary terms, the two most important components of employee benefits in the United States are health insurance and pensions. Most workers who have a health insurance plan get it through their employer. The employer usually pays most of the cost of the plan. Medicare and Medicaid, two government-sponsored programs, cover most health care needs of the poor and the elderly, but they are available to only a small fraction of workers. Most of the health insurance coverage of workers is thus privately provided in the

United States. By contrast, the government is a major provider of retirement benefits, via Social Security. Similarly, compensation for injuries is administered by state governments. Additional sickness and accident insurance may also be provided by the employer. Sickness leaves are either paid directly by employers or indirectly via private insurance, while permanent-disability pensions are provided by both Social Security and private insurance funded by the employer. Other wage benefits, such as overtime premium and vacation pay, are often counted as benefits, but we consider them as part of wage and salaries for the purpose of this paper.[6]

Separate statistics are available for three major categories of employee benefits that are often provided by employers in the United States. These three categories are insurance (mostly health and life), sick leaves (excluding those paid by private insurance), and private pensions. The firms' shares of expenditures on these three categories of benefits are presented in table 9.1, where these expenditures are also presented as fractions of the gross domestic product. Table 9.1 clearly indicates that insurance (mostly health insurance) accounts for the bulk of privately provided employee benefits in the United States, followed by pensions.

As mentioned above, a substantial fraction of employee benefits are publicly provided in the United States. Table 9.2 nevertheless indicates that, on average, the contribution rate of U.S. employers to privately provided benefits is larger (12.1 percent of wages) than their contribution rate to publicly provided benefits (10.7 percent of wages). Overall, the cost of benefits to employers and employees represents 30 percent of wage payments. This number would be even larger if employees' contributions to privately provided benefits were taken into account.

9.1.2   Employee Benefits in Spain

In Spain, the state, through social security, provides three major types of benefits to workers: health care, sick leave, and pensions.[7] These benefits are financed by a social security tax shared between employers and employees. We describe the three types of benefits in detail and discuss their financing below.

Health Care

This provision consists of any public health assistance, as well as a fraction of the cost of medications. This fraction depends on the medical condition of the worker. The beneficiaries of this provision are the worker (either employed,

---

6. See Morke and Morton (1990) for more details on the composition of employee benefits in the United States.
7. Unemployment benefits were a component of social security provisions until 1979, when they were transferred to the National Institute of Employment (INEM). Other minor provisions, such as temporal and permanent disability provisions, widow's and orphan's pensions, or family help are also provided by social security, but we will not analyze them in detail as they constitute a very small fraction of social security expenditures.

Table 9.1   **Shares of Expenditures on Employee Benefits**

	% of Total Expenditures	% of GDP
U.S. firms (private worker benefits)		
Insurance[a]	57.8%	4.3%
Sick leaves	8.9	0.7
Pensions	33.3	2.5
Spanish social security		
Health care	26.6	3.3
Sick leave	5.5	0.7
Pensions	61.0	7.6

Sources: United States: Employment Cost Indexes and Levels, 1975–1990, and *Statistical Abstract of the United States* (1990). Spain: Ministerio de Trabajo y Seguridad Social (1986).
[a]Includes life insurance

Table 9.2   **Contribution Rates to Publicly and Privately Provided Employee Benefits in 1988**

	Spain (public)[a]		U.S. Public[b]		U.S. Private:[b]
	Employer	Employee	Employer	Employee	Employer
Social security[c]	24.0%	4.8%	9.4%	7.2%	12.1%
Unemployment insurance[d]	5.2	1.1	1.3	0	0
Total	29.2	5.9	10.7	7.2	12.1

Sources: United States: *Statistical Abstract of the United States* (1990) and the Annual Statistical Supplement to the *Social Security Bulletin* (1990). Spain: Ministerio de Trabajo y Seguridad Social (1993).
[a]Administrative social security (and unemployment insurance) tax rates that apply to earnings between a minimum base and a maximum base.
[b]Average contribution of employers to the indicated item, divided by wages and salaries including supplemental pay such as bonuses, paid vacations, and holidays.
[c]The following benefits are included under social security: pensions, health insurance, sickness leaves, and workers' compensation for workplace injuries.
[d]Unemployment insurance in Spain is financed by employer and employee in a proportion of 60 percent. The rest is provided by the state, through the public treasury. The contribution rates are for 1985.

retired, or unemployed), the spouse, and any close relatives who live with the worker and depend economically on him or her.[8] Health care provisions can also be extended to Spanish residents who do not work and who lack economic resources. To access these provisions, workers must be affiliated with social security and pay the taxes. The affiliation with social security is legally com-

8. Note that in dual-earner households, both spouses must pay the social security tax. Since the second earner is already covered under the social security card of the first earner, he or she does not get any additional health care benefits in return for paying the tax.

pulsory. It is the responsibility of the employer to affiliate the worker in the five days following the beginning of an employment contract. From that date onward, the employer deducts taxes from the wages of the employee and periodically pays both employee and employer taxes to the social security system.

Sick Leave

This benefit provides pay to workers when they temporarily cannot work because of sickness. For ordinary sickness, workers receive 60 percent of their regular wages from the fourth day to the twenty-first day of sickness.[9] They then receive 75 percent of their regular wages from the twenty-first day onward.[10] In cases of maternity leaves or leaves for workplace injuries, the replacement rate is 75 percent from the fourth day onward. This provision is available for twelve months and can be extended six more months. Workers can use this provision only if they have been affiliated with social security and paid their taxes for at least 180 days before the start of the sick leave.

Pensions

This provision offers pay to retired workers (the age of retirement in Spain is 65). The amount the worker receives varies with the number of years that the worker has contributed to social security. It ranges from 50 percent of the wage (or the maximum or minimum base, if the wage is not within these limits) for workers who have contributed ten years, to 100 percent for workers who have contributed for thirty-five years. This provision lasts until the death of the pensioner. Workers can access this provision when they have paid social security taxes for at least ten years and have contributed to social security for at least two of the eight most recent years.

Table 9.1 shows the share of each of these three major components in total social security expenditures. These three components are also shown as fractions of the gross domestic product. Pensions are the largest component of social security expenditures in Spain, followed by health care. Pensions in Spain also represent a larger fraction of the gross domestic product (7.6 percent) than do privately provided pensions in the United States (2.5 percent). The relative importance of pensions in Spain and in the United States is much more comparable when publicly provided pensions are taken into account in the United States.

9.1.3   Social Security Taxes in Spain

As mentioned before, workers can only gain access to social security provisions when they are affiliated with social security and when they and their em-

---

9. Although on many occasions the whole wage is the monetary base, minimum and maximum bases exist that vary by occupation. For workers who earn more (less) than the maximum (minimum) base, the maximum (minimum) base is considered instead of the whole wage.

10. From the first day to the fourth, the employer must pay the worker. This disposition was modified in April 1992, so now the employer must pay the worker from the first to the fifteenth day, and from then onward, the social security offers the provision.

ployers pay their taxes to the system. These taxes are unequally shared by employers and employees. Table 9.2 shows that the tax rate paid by employers is 24 percent, while the tax rate paid by employees is about 5 percent. The sum of social security and unemployment insurance taxes amounts to almost 30 percent of wages for the employer. This large payroll tax may explain why employers can feel tempted to avoid this indirect cost by hiring workers off the books—that is, by not affiliating them with social security and hence not paying the taxes. Workers who are not affiliated with social security or do not pay the taxes or both are said to be working in the informal, or underground, sector. As we will see below, hiring workers off the books has not been a rare practice in Spain during the past two decades. In the remainder of this section, we explain the reasons for this resurgence of the underground sector in Spain.

9.1.4   Underground Sector in Spain

In order to understand the patterns of the underground economy in Spain during the 1980s, it is important to know which factors contributed to its development. It seems fair to say that the division between the formal and the informal (or underground) economy dates back to the early 1970s. Under Franco's dictatorship, the state set wage increases and thus managed to keep real wages very low until the 1970s. Strikes were illegal, and any kind of organized labor was suppressed. However, the consolidation of workers' opposition to the regime in the early 1970s started to put an upward pressure on real wages. In an effort to keep wages down and to quiet workers' opposition, the state decided to increase the amount of workers' benefits in 1972. Unemployment benefits were expanded and employer taxes were increased.

After Franco's death in 1975, Spain started a quick political transition to democracy. In 1977, unions were legalized as representatives of workers in collective bargaining. Their first aim was to increase the level of real wages of workers. Over the period 1973–79, real wages increased at an average annual rate of 8.2 percent. The combination of increases in direct labor costs with rapid increases in indirect labor costs was considered by some people to be the main cause of the resurgence of the underground economy. But what seems to be the key in understanding the spread of the underground sector in Spain is the state of the Spanish economy when these measures were implemented. The average inflation for the 1973–79 period was 18.3 percent, while the growth rate of real gross domestic product per capita was only 1.4 percent (it was 5.8 percent in the 1968–73 period). The deep recession led to massive plant closures, which increased the rate of unemployment from 5.8 percent in the 1974–79 period to 17.4 percent in the 1980–85 period. Workers who had been displaced from the formal sector became an attractive labor force either for firms already operating in the underground sector or for those who, in spite of operating in the formal sector, wanted to employ some workers off the books. In doing so, firms reduced labor costs greatly by not paying social security taxes. Employing workers off the books also gave firms the freedom to fire these workers when they were no longer needed, which solved a serious problem for employers, as firing workers who had permanent contracts necessitated costly severance payments. Although most displaced workers would have preferred to work in the formal sector to enjoy social security provisions, working in the underground sector was typically the only way for them to find a job.

In addition to the weak state of the Spanish economy and of the Spanish labor market, some institutional factors also encouraged the growth of the underground economy. First, the legal framework lacked (and still lacks) any criminal disposition for fraud against social security. The penalty in most cases was only administrative, consisting of a fine on employers who did not pay social security taxes.[11] Besides, the possibility of being caught was very small, especially for small firms. Furthermore, to explain how the Spanish authorities felt about the underground economy, we should mention a comment on the underground economy made by Joaquin Almunia, minister of labor, in November 1984. He stated that it was "necessary to try to accept the underground economy because it reflects the inadequacy of the laws." He characterized the underground economy as a "lesser evil" and explained that the government's approach would be to facilitate the legalization of clandestine enterprises "through the reduction of social security payments, and other measures" (*El Pais,* 3 November 1984).

Unions could not do much to force employers to pay social security taxes, given the weak state of the labor market in the 80s. As a result of other union efforts, the Spanish labor market had very little flexibility because of the very high cost of firing workers with indefinite contracts. Had unions tried to force employers to hire workers in the formal sector, even fewer workers would have been employed, and unions would have been blamed for increasing unemployment, which was already very high. In that sense, for unions as well as for the government, the underground economy was a lesser evil than an even higher rate of unemployment.

By the mid-1980s, there was a widespread belief that the underground sector was important enough to be considered as part of the Spanish system. Even the government believed that the official statistics overestimated the unemployment rate in Spain because people who worked in the underground sector were counted as unemployed. In order to measure a more accurate unemployment rate, the government carried out a survey, called the 1985 Survey of Living and Working Conditions (ECVT), which is the survey used in this paper. As we will discuss later, the survey did establish the existence of a large underground sector but was less successful in showing that the measured unemployment rate was too high.[12]

---

11. When a worker was caught working off the books, the employer had to reimburse to the state all the unpaid social security and unemployment insurance taxes plus a 20 percent penalty for the whole period the worker had been employed.

12. The explanation for this puzzle is that most underground workers report themselves as working in the regular labor force survey. A similar phenomenon was observed by Ramos (1988) in Puerto Rico.

9.2   The Economics of Employee Benefits and Tax Compliance

Given the institutional environments in which firms operate in Spain and in the United States, we turn to the question of how profit-maximizing firms react to the different constraints being imposed on them by these two environments. We first examine the determinants of employers' decision to provide benefits to their workers in a simple demand and supply framework, focusing on the case of health insurance. This is more or less representative of the U.S. system, in which health insurance is privately provided to workers. We then focus on the case in which, as in Spain, the employer is forced to provide these benefits through the social security system. On the one hand, forcing the provision of employee benefits through social security should not affect the behavior of employers who would have provided benefits to their employees in the absence of social security. For these employers, the Spanish system is merely a relabeling of the U.S. system. On the other hand, employers who would not otherwise provide benefits to their workers have to either adjust their employment and production choices or avoid paying social security taxes.

9.2.1   A Model for the Private Provision of Employee Benefits

Consider a model in which firms offer wage-benefit packages (W,B) to their workers. For simplicity, consider the case in which only a given benefit package (health insurance) is available to workers. B is an indicator variable equal to one when workers are getting this benefit package from their employers and equal to zero otherwise. This model is quite similar to the basic model of equalizing differences for job amenities considered by Rosen (1986). As in models of equalizing differences, we want to solve for the hedonic equilibrium in the market for labor and for benefits.

Assume that preferences of worker i are characterized by the following utility function that is separable in a composite consumption good C and in B:

$$(1) \qquad U_i(C,B) = u(C) + \theta_i B .$$

For simplicity, assume that consumption of the composite good C is equal to labor earnings W. Also assume that workers have a reservation wage W^r and that they can only obtain health insurance from their employers.[13] The reservation wage W^r varies across workers, depending on their skill level. Consider the wage-benefit packages $(W,0)$ and $(W - \Delta W,1)$. The worker prefers the package that offers health insurance when the following inequality is satisfied:

$$(2) \qquad \theta_i > u(W) - u(W - \Delta W) .$$

This inequality is satisfied whenever the utility a worker attaches to health insurance, θ_i, is larger than the value, in utility terms, of the income that has to

---

13. More generally, it may be that the cost of benefits such as health insurance is prohibitive for workers who want to buy them on their own, perhaps because of adverse selection.

be sacrificed to obtain health insurance (ΔW). The utility that workers attach to health insurance, θ_i, depends on a series of household and demographic characteristics. Clearly, workers already covered under the health insurance plan of another household member do not benefit from having their own health insurance plan. For these workers, θ_i is thus equal to zero. The effect on θ_i of health insurance coverage under the policy of another household member is particularly important for married women and teenagers. More generally, the utility of health insurance coverage also depends on the number and the health status of household members covered by the plan. Taken together, these considerations imply that health insurance is typically the most valuable for married men and the least valuable for youth and married women.[14]

In the standard case where the marginal utility $u'(W)$ declines in consumption, the loss of utility $u(W) - u(W - \Delta W)$ is inversely related to earnings W. This is due to a standard income effect that makes health insurance relatively more valuable (compared to money) when earnings increase.[15] Increases in either θ_i or W thus increase the probability that the inequality in equation (2) is satisfied and that workers will want to receive health insurance coverage from their employers.

We now turn to the supply side of the market, where firms must decide which wage-benefit package should be offered to each worker. Consider a profit-maximizing firm that has access to a production technology with decreasing marginal product of labor. The firm also has access to a pool of workers characterized by utility functions such as the one in equation (1) and by a fixed reservation wage W^r. The cost to the firm of offering health insurance coverage to worker i is equal to BC_i. For now, assume that BC_i is the same (BC) for all workers. It is straightforward to show that in the efficient hedonic equilibrium, all workers whose willingness to pay for the benefits exceed the cost, BC, of providing these benefits will receive the benefits. The willingness to pay for the benefit, WP_i, is the amount of money such that

$$\theta_i = u(W) - u(W - WP_i) .$$

Workers will thus receive benefits whenever the following inequality is satisfied:

$$(3) \qquad \theta_i > \theta^* = u(W^r) - u(W^r - BC) .$$

In the most interesting case to consider, inequality (3) is only satisfied for a fraction of the work force. Workers who receive the benefits are paid a wage rate $W^r - BC$, while workers who do not receive benefits are paid W^r. The

---

14. Demographic and household variables can be thought of as proxies for whether a person would be covered by some health insurance plan if that person were not covered under a plan offered by his or her current employer (this is not observed in standard data sets such as the Current Population Survey).

15. This income effect may explain the positive relationship between wages and benefits across industries. It may also explain some of the cross-country differences in the share of health care expenditures in the gross national product.

relevant marginal workers for employment determination are those who do not receive benefits. Employment is thus determined by the condition

$$(4) \qquad\qquad VMPL(L^*) = W^r,$$

where $VMPL(L)$ is the value of the marginal product of labor evaluated at L.

In this simple case where BC_i is the same for all workers, supply factors thus have only an indirect role on the provision of health insurance through the income effect. The idea is that high-skill workers, because their reservation wage is higher, command a better compensation package than low-skill workers. Everything else being equal, their compensation package is thus more likely to include health insurance because of income effects. Supply factors play a richer role in the provision of health insurance benefits when the assumption that BC_i is constant is relaxed. It is well known that, in the United States, supply factors such as the size of the firm have a big effect on the cost of providing health insurance. Since θ^* is positively related to BC in equation (3), the critical value θ^* must be larger for small firms than for large firms. As a result, relatively fewer workers will be covered by a health insurance plan in small firms than in large firms. Differences in the cost of supplying health insurance among industries may also explain differences in health insurance coverage among firms in the same industries. Furthermore, the cost of providing health insurance may depend on the fraction of workers in the firm that are covered. As a result, the distribution of all workers' preferences will affect the probability of coverage of a given worker through the preferences' effect on BC and θ^*. For example, it may be harder to obtain coverage in a firm employing mostly youths who are already covered under their parents' health insurance plan than in a similar firm employing mostly heads of households. The average characteristics of workers employed in a given firm or industry may thus be an important supply factor.

Other supply factors may also be important once the assumption of perfectly competitive markets is relaxed. For instance, it is well known (Freeman and Medoff 1984) that wages are higher and benefits packages more generous in unionized than in nonunionized environments. More generally, some labor market rents may be dissipated in the form of both wages and benefits. Health insurance coverage rates are thus likely to be higher in high-rent than in low-rent industries.

What is the effect of mandating benefits in this simple model? If employers comply, all workers will receive the benefits, but employment will be reduced. Clearly, all workers who were receiving benefits in the absence of mandatory provision will remain employed, since it is efficient to employ them and to provide them with benefits. The employment of workers who were not receiving benefits in the absence of mandatory provision will, however, decrease until the following condition is satisfied:

$$(5) \qquad\qquad VMPL(L^{**}) = W^r - WP(L^{**}) + BC,$$

where $WP(L)$ is the willingness to pay of the Lth worker (ranked in decreasing order). $WP(L^{**})$ must be lower than BC since the marginal worker was not receiving benefits in the absence of mandatory provisions. Since the function $VMPL(L)$ is decreasing in L, the new employment level, L^{**}, must be lower than employment in the absence of mandatory provisions, L^*. Mandatory benefits thus reduce the employment of workers who would not otherwise receive benefits, but do not affect the employment of workers who would receive benefits in the absence of mandatory provisions.[16]

9.2.2   The Economics of Compliance with the Social Security Tax

The model of private provision of benefits of section 9.2.1 was a stylized representation of the U.S. system. This model, however, is clearly not an accurate representation of the Spanish system. The key difference between the two systems is that all Spanish firms have to contribute to the financing of the public health insurance system by paying social security taxes, while U.S. firms pay for health insurance on a voluntary basis. Since Spanish workers need a social security card to have access to public health care, the same system could be implemented by mandating employers to provide health insurance to their workers at a cost BC equal to the corresponding social security tax.[17] With perfect enforcement of social security provisions, we can use the terms "mandating benefits" and "paying the social security tax" interchangeably.

As discussed earlier, an important feature of the Spanish system is that many firms adjust to the constraints imposed by the social security system by simply not complying with the social security tax. In Spain, when employers do not comply with social security, employees do not hold social security cards, which prevents them, in principle, from gaining access to public health care services. As we said before, however, workers who do not hold a social security card may still be covered under the social security card of another household member. This situation is thus qualitatively similar to the situation of U.S. workers who do not get health insurance from their employers but are covered under the health insurance plan of another household member.

Formally, compliance can be treated as a problem of profit maximization under uncertainty.[18] The uncertainty arises because enforcement of government regulations is costly and thus imperfect unless very large resources are devoted to the detection of noncompliers.[19] Noncompliers thus face a probability λ, which is smaller than one, of being detected. In the event they are caught cheat-

16. See Summers (1989) and Danzon (1989) for related points on the labor market effects of mandating benefits.

17. We implicitly assume that the quality of care—that is, the value of the benefits in utility terms—is the same under the two systems.

18. There is a vast theoretical literature on the economics of tax compliance (see Cowell 1990, and the studies mentioned therein). By contrast, the empirical literature is still in its infancy, partly because of data limitations.

19. This is the basic postulate of the economic approach to criminal behavior (see Stigler and Becker 1977).

ing, they have to repay the social security tax plus a penalty P. A risk-neutral firm decides to comply (or not comply) by comparing profits when complying to the expected value of profits when not complying.

While the expected profits of employing an Lth worker and paying social security is given by

$$E\pi^c = VMPL(L) - (W^r - WP) - BC,$$

the expected profits of employing this worker but not paying social security is given by[20]

$$E\pi^{nc} = VMPL(L) - W^r - \lambda(BC + P).$$

Note that BC is now equal to the social security tax. The new hedonic equilibrium with a social security tax BC and the possibility of noncompliance is easily derived by comparing the expected profits $E\pi^c$ and $E\pi^{nc}$ to the expected profits when the firms does not employ the worker (zero). Comparing $E\pi^c$ and $E\pi^{nc}$ indicates that social security will be paid for all workers whose willingness to pay for health insurance, WP, exceeds $BC - \lambda(BC + P)$. Social security is thus paid for all workers whose θ_i satisfies the following inequality:

(3') $\theta_i > \theta^* = u(W^r) - u[W^r - BC + \lambda(P + BC)]$.

The total employment of a firm not paying social security for some of its workers is the value of L such that $E\pi^{nc}$ is equal to zero. Total employment must thus satisfy the following condition:

(5') $VMPL(L) = W^r + \lambda(P + BC)$.

Employment is thus lower than in the case of private provision with incomplete coverage (equation [4]) but higher than in the case of mandatory benefits when enforcement is perfect (equation [5]). Except for the term $\lambda(B + P)$, the inequality (3') is the same as the inequality (3). Thus, the impact that supply and demand factors listed in section 9.2.1 should have on the decision to privately provide health insurance should be similar to their impact on the decision to comply with the social security tax. In addition, the decision to comply with the tax is affected by the probability of detection λ and the penalty P. Both λ and P reduce the expected profits of not complying and thus increase the chances the firm will comply with the social security tax.

It is also important to point out an important difference between the cost of providing benefits in a U.S.-type system and the amount of payroll taxes paid in a Spanish-type system. While the cost of providing private health insurance is more or less fixed for workers with similar health conditions, the social security tax is proportional to wages and salaries up to a very high exclusion cap.

---

20. The profits of a firm that does not comply and does not get caught are equal to $VMPL(L) - W^r$. However, these profits are reduced to $VMPL(L) - W^r - BC - P$ when the firm gets caught. The expression for $E\pi^{nc}$ is obtained by taking the expected value of these two profit levels (the probability of detection is equal to λ).

In Spain, the variable BC is thus proportional to wages. The income effect in the demand for coverage should thus be smaller in Spain than in the United States, since higher wages increase the marginal utility of benefits but also increase the costs (taxes) of obtaining coverage through social security.

9.2.3 Empirical Implications

The model proposed above is not aimed at generating precise, testable implications on the extent and pattern of provision of health insurance benefits in the United States and of compliance with the social security tax in Spain. Rather, it tries to establish that these patterns should be similar in the two countries. Supply-side considerations suggest that firms in industries that are the most likely to provide health benefits in the United States should also be the most likely to comply with the social security tax in Spain, assuming the characteristics of workers and industries are similar in Spain and in the United States. Demand-side considerations also suggest similarities in the incidence of health insurance coverage in the United States and compliance in Spain along age/gender/marital status lines.

Our empirical model is obtained by treating the inequalities (3) and (3') as participation conditions in discrete-choice models for the private provision of health insurance and the decision to comply with social security. Consider the following stochastic specifications for the preference variable θ_i and the supply cost variable BC_i:

$$(6) \qquad\qquad \theta_i = \beta_x' x_i + u_i ,$$

$$(7) \qquad\qquad BC_i = \beta_z' z_i + v_i ,$$

where x_i is a vector of demand-side (or preference) variables, z_i is a vector of supply-side variables, and u_i and v_i are two normally distributed error terms. Furthermore, consider the first-order approximation of $u(W^r) - u(W^r - BC)$:

$$(8) \qquad u(W^r) - u(W^r - BC) = \gamma_0 + \gamma_1 W^r + \gamma_2 BC ,$$

where $\gamma_1 < 0$ and $\gamma_2 > 0$. Substituting equations (6), (7), and (8) into the participation condition (3) yields the following threshold equation:

$$(9) \qquad \varepsilon_i = (u_i - \gamma_2 v_i) > \gamma_0 + \gamma_1 W^r + \gamma_2 \beta_z' z_i - \beta_x' x_i .$$

Benefits are thus provided whenever ε_i is larger than the right-hand side of equation (9); benefits are not provided otherwise. Under the assumption that u_i and v_i are normally distributed, it is straightforward to estimate this model using maximum-likelihood probit methods. The same probit model can be estimated for the decision to comply with social security taxes when $P\lambda$ is a given constant for all jobs. Differences in $P\lambda$ across industries would be captured by a set of industry effects included in the vector z_i.

On the one hand, this empirical model focuses on the behavior of an individual. The reservation wage of the individual is one of the important determinants of the decision to provide health insurance or to comply with social security taxes. On the other hand, health insurance policies often cover all household members, which suggests looking at a model of household behavior instead of individual behavior. Estimating such a model is beyond the scope of this paper, however, because of data limitations.[21] It may nevertheless be preferable to capture income effects by looking at the effects of family income, as opposed to the income of the individual, on the probability of holding a health insurance plan. We will thus replace W^r by a measure of family income in the empirical specification of the probit model.[22]

A related point is that many family members may be covered under a health insurance plan in the name of another household member. It is thus important to distinguish whether an individual is covered by a plan from whether the individual holds a plan under his or her name. The empirical analysis seeks to explain the probability of the latter.

9.3   Results

In this section, we first describe the data sets used and present comparative statistics on the composition of the labor force and the structure of wages in Spain and in the United States. We then analyze the decision to comply with social security (Spain) and the decision to provide health insurance (United States), using maximum-likelihood probit techniques.

9.3.1   Data Sources

The Spanish data are taken from the Survey of Living and Working Conditions (henceforth ECVT). This survey was carried out in the last quarter of 1985. Its main purpose was to measure the magnitude of the underground economy. More than sixty thousand people were interviewed. People were asked questions about their socioeconomic characteristics and job experiences. Workers were also asked whether they had a social security card. People who answered yes to this question were also asked whether they paid social security taxes, as it is possible but unlikely to be affiliated but not pay the taxes. Answers to these two questions were used to identify those workers who were working off the books, either because they did not have a social security card or because in spite of having one they did not pay taxes. Furthermore, the workers who did not have a social security card were asked whether they were

---

21. Only one household member was interviewed in each household surveyed in the Spanish survey used in this paper. As a result, we cannot jointly model wages and compliance with social security taxes for all household members. The best we can do is to include measures of family income and family composition in the probit model.

22. If family income were exogenous, its effect should be positive because of income effects. Family income may, however, fail to be exogenous to the extent that unobserved preferences for benefits, u_i, are negatively correlated with labor income. A person with a large u_i prefers to trade off more benefits for less income. Estimates of the effect of family income may thus be biased downward.

covered by some relative's card. As will be shown later in the paper, a typical underground worker is a married woman covered by her husband's social security card.[23]

Estimates of the size of the underground sector based on self-reports of illegal activities may certainly understate the importance of the phenomenon. It is thus important to keep in mind that many of the estimates reported in this paper may be lower bounds to the true effects.[24] One weakness of the ECVT data set is that it does not contain direct measures of wage rates but offers only seven brackets for monthly earnings. The income measure we use for the empirical analysis consists of the midpoints of these brackets.[25]

For the United States, we use the May 1988 Current Population Survey (CPS), which includes an employee benefits supplement. The May CPS has been matched to the March demographic file, which includes additional information on benefits coverage in 1987. We select comparable samples of workers aged 16 to 70 from the ECVT and the May 1988 CPS. More details on the construction of the U.S. and Spanish samples are provided in the data appendix.

9.3.2 Wages and Employment in Spain and the United States

The sample means of several socioeconomic variables are reported for Spain and the United States in table 9.3. These means suggest important differences in the composition of the labor force in the two countries. Women account for close to half of the labor force in the United States but only 28 percent of the labor force in Spain. In addition, the U.S. work force is more educated. In Spain, 25 percent of workers have completed only primary school, as opposed to 13 percent in the United States. Furthermore, 23 percent of workers in the United States hold a college degree, compared to 13 percent in Spain. These differences partly reflect the fact that it takes more years to complete a similar degree in Spain than it takes in the United States.[26] This explains why the number of years of education completed are similar in Spain and in the United States. Another important difference between the labor markets in the two countries is that the duration of jobs is longer in Spain than in the United States. For example, 40 percent of U.S. workers have more than five years of

---

23. Alternatively, some dual jobholders may pay social security taxes on their primary job but not on their secondary job. Information on this particular type of underground sector work is not available, however, in the ECVT data.

24. Evidence based on a comparison of reported income and expenditures in the underground economy in Canada suggests that approximately 70 percent of underground sector income (excluding income from criminal activities) is self-reported in survey data. See Fortin, Lemieux, and Fréchette (1990) for more details on the survey data used for these calculations.

25. The midpoints for the upper (more than 200,000 pesetas) and lower (less than 25,000 pesetas) brackets are calculated by assuming that income follows a lognormal distribution. See the data appendix for more details and evidence that this imputation scheme has little effect on the parameter estimates.

26. For instance, it usually takes eighteen years to complete a university degree in Spain, compared to sixteen years in the United States.

Table 9.3   **Sample Means of the Variables**

	Spain		United States	
	Mean	Standard Deviation	Mean	Standard Deviation
Weekly earnings[a]	179.915	106.040	449.120	310.120
Sex (1 = female)	0.280	0.450	0.460	0.248
Married (1 = married)	0.680	0.470	0.620	0.235
Age	38.870	12.970	36.890	12.318
Education (years)	12.890	3.620	13.030	2.669
Primary	0.250	0.430	0.130	0.113
High school	0.410	0.490	0.400	0.240
Vocational	0.080	0.270	0.200	0.640
College	0.130	0.340	0.230	0.177
Tenure (< 1 year)	0.110	0.320	0.300	0.490
Tenure (1–5 years)	0.210	0.400	0.305	0.211
Tenure (> 5 years)	0.660	0.470	0.395	0.239

Sources: Based on 17,463 observations from the 1985 ECVT (Spain) and 23,402 observations from the 1988 May CPS (United States).

[a]The earnings variable in Spain is monthly earnings (after taxes) divided by four, while it is weekly earnings (before taxes) in the United States. Both earnings variables are expressed in 1990 U.S. dollars. The original earnings numbers were first converted in 1990 pesetas and 1990 U.S. dollars, using the gross domestic product (GDP) deflators for Spain and the United States. The 1990 pesetas were then converted in 1990 U.S. dollars, using OECD Purchasing Power Parity numbers for 1990 (113.08 pesetas/dollar).

tenure, compared to 66 percent in Spain. Finally, real weekly earnings are much higher in the United States (449.1 in 1990 U.S. dollars, before taxes) than in Spain (179.9 in 1990 U.S. dollars, after taxes).

The industrial composition of employment in Spain and in the United States is shown in Figure 9.1. The key difference between the two countries is that agriculture accounts for a much larger share of employment in Spain (14.3 percent) than in the United States (1.8 percent). The United States compensates by having a larger share of employment than Spain in trade and services.

We compare the structure of wages in Spain and in the United States by fitting standard log earnings equations, using ordinary least squares (OLS). The results are reported in table 9.4. All the specifications include a set of region dummies (four in the United States, sixteen in Spain); dummies for gender, marital status, and their interaction; potential experience and its square interacted with gender; and the highest grade completed. The specifications reported in columns 2 and 4 also include twenty-four industry dummies, seven occupation dummies, two dummies for tenure, and a dummy variable for part-time status. The specification for the United States also includes dummy variables for race and coverage by a collective bargaining agreement.

The estimated effects of gender and marital status on earnings are compara-

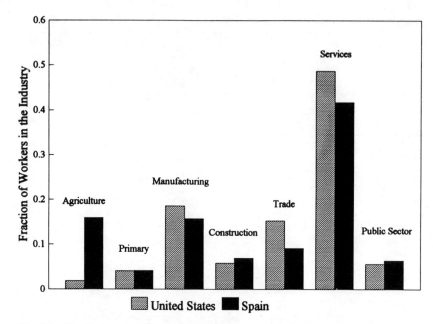

Fig. 9.1 Employment shares by major industries, Spain and the United States
Sources: Calculations of the authors, using the 1985 ECVT (Spain) and the May 1988 Current
Population Survey (United States).

ble in the two countries, while the estimated returns to education and to experience are higher in the United States than in Spain. These estimated returns are reduced when job characteristics are included in columns 2 and 4, but their pattern does not change. The estimated returns to tenure reported at the bottom of table 9.4 are much larger in the United States than in Spain. For instance, workers with more than five years of tenure are estimated to make 25 percent more than workers with less than one year of tenure in the United States, but only 10 percent more in Spain. Finally, the estimated interindustry wage premiums are large and significant in both countries. The weighted standard deviation of the estimated industry wage premiums is .165 in the United States and .161 in Spain. The weighted correlation between the estimated premiums in the two countries is .688. This positive correlation can also be observed in figure 9.2, which presents a plot of the industry wage premiums in Spain as a function of the wage premiums in the United States. The fitted regression line depicted in figure 9.2 has a slope of .527.

9.3.3 Determinants of Compliance with Social Security and Private Provision of Health Insurance

The probabilities of compliance with social security taxes (Spain) and of receiving an employer-provided health insurance plan (United States) are pre-

Table 9.4 **OLS Estimates of Earnings Equations for Spain and the United States[a] (dependent variable: log of earnings)[b]**

	Spain		United States	
Intercept	5.119	5.523	4.030	4.720
	(0.025)	(0.032)	(0.027)	(0.039)
Female	−0.141	−0.132	−0.128	−0.097
	(0.019)	(0.017)	(0.021)	(0.016)
Married	0.219	0.151	0.216	0.096
	(0.012)	(0.011)	(0.014)	(0.011)
Married*female	−0.239	−0.135	−0.270	−0.121
	(0.019)	(0.017)	(0.019)	(0.015)
Experience	0.028	0.017	0.064	0.028
	(0.001)	(0.001)	(0.001)	(0.001)
Experience^2	−0.053	−0.033	−0.112	−0.052
	(0.027)	(0.002)	(0.003)	(0.002)
Experience*female	−0.005	−0.005	−0.015	−0.009
	(0.002)	(0.001)	(0.002)	(0.001)
Experience^2*female	0.008	0.011	0.020	0.015
	(0.004)	(0.003)	(0.005)	(0.003)
Education	0.075	0.043	0.106	0.063
	(0.021)	(0.001)	(0.001)	(0.001)
Agriculture		−0.140		−0.061
		(0.033)		(0.048)
Energy, gas, water		0.186		0.304
		(0.031)		(0.039)
Mining and chemicals		0.239		0.283
		(0.031)		(0.038)
Metal industries		0.146		0.238
		(0.025)		(0.033)
Food, beverage, tobacco		0.056		0.127
		(0.025)		(0.040)
Textiles		−0.024		0.089
		(0.029)		(0.046)
Leather		0.159		−0.006
		(0.083)		(0.134)
Footwear		−0.014		−0.154
		(0.039)		(0.090)
Wood and furniture		−0.052		0.136
		(0.030)		(0.041)
Paper, printing, publishing		0.115		0.125
		(0.037)		(0.037)
Other manufacturing		0.065		0.138
		(0.033)		(0.042)
Construction		0.083		0.211
		(0.023)		(0.034)
Trade		−0.076		0.029
		(0.023)		(0.032)
Hotels, restaurants, cafes		0.003		−0.266
		(0.025)		(0.035)

(continued)

Table 9.4   (continued)

	Spain		United States	
Repairs		0.016		−0.030
		(0.030)		(0.043)
Transportation		0.086		0.259
		(0.027)		(0.035)
Communication		0.211		0.277
		(0.036)		(0.040)
Insurance, finance		0.297		0.181
		(0.034)		(0.034)
Firm services		0.101		0.123
		(0.026)		(0.035)
Public administration, armed forces[c]		0.287		0.111
		(0.025)		(0.034)
Education and research		0.253		−0.139
		(0.026)		(0.034)
Private services		−0.218		−0.144
		(0.034)		(0.049)
Household services		−0.382		−0.641
		(0.026)		(0.050)
Other services		0.133		0.018
		(0.022)		(0.033)
Tenure (1–5 years)		0.022		0.106
		(0.013)		(0.008)
Tenure (> 5 years)		0.097		0.256
		(0.013)		(0.009)
Part-time		−0.288		−0.759
		(0.012)		(0.009)
Occupation dummies	No	Yes	No	Yes
Number of observations	14,898	14,898	23,402	23,402
Mean of dependent variable	6.397	6.397	5.942	5.942
R^2	0.358	0.518	0.377	0.623

Note: Standard errors are in parentheses.

[a]The model for Spain also includes fifteen region dummies and one dummy for temporary workers. The U.S. model also contains three region dummies, eight occupation dummies, one dummy for race, and one dummy for the union effect. The base group consists of skilled blue-collar single male workers, working full time in the apparel industry.

[b]The dependent variable is monthly earnings (after taxes) for Spain and weekly earnings (before taxes) for the United States in 1990 U.S. dollars (OECD purchasing power parity numbers for 1990 have been used to convert pesetas into U.S. dollars).

[c]Armed forces are included in this category only for Spain.

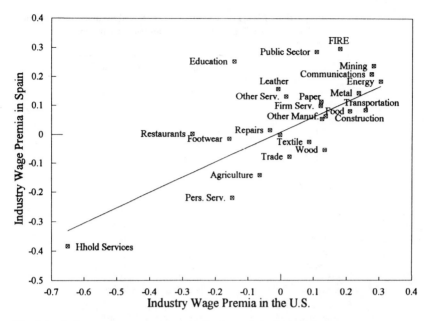

Fig. 9.2   Industry wage premiums in Spain and the United States
Source: Estimates of the industry wage effects reported in columns 2 and 4 of table 9.4.
Note: Base industry is apparel. The slope of the fitted regression line is equal to 0.527.

sented for several socioeconomic groups in table 9.5. Eighty-eight percent of Spanish workers comply with social security, while 68 percent of U.S. workers receive a health insurance plan from their employer. Both probabilities increase with age until age 30, are then stable until age 60, and decline after age 60. Both probabilities are also higher than average for married men, lower than average for single men and women, and much lower than average for married women. On the one hand, the fraction of U.S. workers who do not receive employer-provided health insurance (32 percent) is two to three times larger than the fraction of Spanish workers who are not affiliated with social security (12 percent). On the other hand, more than 99 percent of married men in Spain are affiliated with social security, while 20 percent of married men in the United States do not get health insurance from their employers. Essentially, these figures show all families have access to health insurance in Spain, while an important fraction of families in the United States do not. For example, 28 percent of employed married women in Spain are not affiliated with social security, but they are virtually all covered under the cards of their husbands. By contrast, 43 percent of employed married women in the United States do not get health insurance from their employer. While 78 percent of these women are covered under the plan of their husband or of another family member, 22

Table 9.5   Proportion of Workers Complying with Social Security Taxes (Spain) and Receiving a Health Insurance Plan from Their Employer (United States)

	Spain	United States
All workers	0.882	0.678
By age		
16–20	0.430	0.151
21–30	0.842	0.619
31–50	0.913	0.730
51–60	0.940	0.739
61–70	0.863	0.612
By education		
Primary	0.895	0.471
High school	0.844	0.655
Vocational	0.886	0.665
College	0.917	0.809
By tenure		
< 1 year	0.759	0.436
1–5 years	0.837	0.664
> 5 years	0.945	0.850
By gender and marital status		
Single male	0.857	0.603
Single female	0.832	0.614
Married male	0.996	0.802
Married female	0.720	0.569

percent (or 12.6 percent of all employed married women) are not covered.[27] So although compliance with social security in Spain and the provision of health insurance in the United States are driven by similar demand factors, it is important to recognize that the two systems have very different effects on the well-being of workers. We next control for all demand and supply factors simultaneously by estimating a series of probit models.

The estimates of probit models for the decision to comply with social security in Spain are reported in the first two columns of table 9.6. Similarly, probit estimates for whether a worker receives an employer-provided health insurance plan in the United States are reported in columns 3 and 4. The base group in all these models consists of skilled blue-collar, single male workers, working full time in the apparel industry.

The results for Spain show that single women are significantly more likely to comply with social security than single males (coefficient of .146 in column 1). Married men, however, are estimated to be much more likely to comply than single men (coefficient of .787). The situation is reversed for married

27. These percentages are calculated using responses to questions on health insurance coverage in the March 1987 CPS that have been matched to the May 1988 CPS. It is necessary to use the March 1987 data since, although the May 1988 CPS asks many question on the plan received from the employer, it does not ask any direct questions on health insurance coverage.

Table 9.6 **Maximum-Likelihood Probit Estimates of the Probability of Complying with Social Security Taxes (Spain) and Receiving Health Insurance from Their Employer (United States)**

Dependent variable:	Spain		United States	
	Complies with social security		Holds employer-provided health insurance plan	
Independent variables				
Intercept	−1.386	−0.914	−1.736	−0.580
	(0.116)	(0.166)	(0.065)	(0.123)
Female	0.146	0.145	0.150	0.157
	(0.064)	(0.073)	(0.047)	(0.055)
Married	0.787	0.701	0.246	0.050
	(0.093)	(0.101)	(0.033)	(0.038)
Married*female	−1.606	−1.472	−0.586	−0.428
	(0.107)	(0.117)	(0.044)	(0.050)
Experience	0.153	0.132	0.082	0.023
	(0.008)	(0.009)	(0.004)	(0.005)
Experience²	−0.219	−0.177	−0.143	−0.051
	(0.019)	(0.021)	(0.008)	(0.009)
Experience*female	−0.093	−0.081	−0.027	−0.019
	(0.010)	(0.010)	(0.005)	(0.006)
Experience²*female	0.164	0.140	0.046	0.036
	(0.022)	(0.023)	(0.011)	(0.013)
Education	0.094	0.061	0.100	0.055
	(0.007)	(0.008)	(0.004)	(0.006)
Family income (÷ 10,000)	0.051	0.018	0.035	−0.006
	(0.005)	(0.005)	(0.005)	(0.005)
Agriculture		−0.201		−0.764
		(0.174)		(0.151)
Energy, gas, water		0.750		0.444
		(0.327)		(0.141)
Mining and chemicals		0.893		0.389
		(0.293)		(0.132)
Metal industries		0.879		0.467
		(0.211)		(0.106)
Food, beverage, tobacco		0.178		0.243
		(0.120)		(0.132)
Textiles		0.220		0.583
		(0.137)		(0.154)
Leather		0.069		0.997
		(0.435)		(0.567)
Footwear		−0.184		−0.026
		(0.174)		(0.276)
Wood and furniture		0.146		0.107
		(0.184)		(0.130)
Paper, printing, publishing		0.016		0.091
		(0.230)		(0.120)
Other manufacturing		0.232		0.241
		(0.219)		(0.137)

(continued)

Table 9.6   (continued)

	Spain		United States	
		Complies with social security		Holds employer-provided health insurance plan
Construction		0.501		−0.547
		(0.156)		(0.106)
Trade		−0.081		−0.297
		(0.102)		(0.101)
Hotels, restaurants, cafes		0.027		−0.784
		(0.114)		(0.108)
Repairs		0.187		−0.462
		(0.207)		(0.131)
Transportation		0.216		−0.110
		(0.199)		(0.110)
Communication		0.591		0.341
		(0.256)		(0.145)
Insurance, finance		0.863		0.072
		(0.317)		(0.107)
Firm services		0.474		−0.391
		(0.140)		(0.109)
Public administration, armed forces[a]		0.948		−0.023
		(0.179)		(0.109)
Education and research		0.508		−0.268
		(0.135)		(0.105)
Private services		0.132		−0.892
		(0.146)		(0.152)
Household services		−0.272		−1.990
		(0.107)		(0.276)
Other services		0.624		−0.203
		(0.116)		(0.102)
Tenure (1–5 years)		0.221		0.502
		(0.057)		(0.027)
Tenure (> 5 years)		0.337		0.935
		(0.061)		(0.031)
Part-time		−0.778		−1.180
		(0.048)		(0.032)
Covered by a collective agreement				0.548
				(0.034)
Occupation dummies	No	Yes	No	Yes
Number of observations	14,727	14,727	19,908	19,908
Log-likelihood	−2,845.4	−2,483.3	−11,162.4	−8,559.8
Percentage of successes	0.883	0.883	0.678	0.678
Pseudo-R^2	0.357	0.437	0.108	0.316

Notes: The model for Spain also includes fifteen region dummies and one dummy for temporary workers. The U.S. model also contains three region dummies and one dummy variable for race. The base group consists of skilled blue-collar single male workers, working full time in the apparel industry. Standard errors are in parentheses.

[a]Armed forces are included in this category for Spain only.

women, who are much less likely to comply with social security than single women (coefficient of −.819, which is the sum of .787 and −1.606). The results also indicate that family income increases the probability of compliance with social security. This result can be interpreted as an income effect. The estimated effects of demographic variables are not significantly changed when a series of job characteristics variables is included in the probit model reported in column 2. The estimated magnitude of the coefficients is nevertheless reduced. This is particularly true for the effect of family income.

The results are thus consistent with demand factors playing a major role in the decision to comply with social security. In most cases, married women already have access to health care under their husband's social security card. They thus receive few benefits from complying with the social security tax. By contrast, a married man whose wife does not work gains a lot by complying with social security because all his dependents are covered under his card. The estimated effect of potential experience on the probability to comply with social security is also positive. This finding is not surprising, since young workers are already covered under their parents' cards. More-educated workers are also more likely to comply with social security.

Estimates of a probit model for whether or not a worker has an employer-provided health insurance plan in the United States, as a function of demographic characteristics only, are reported in column 3. The estimated probit coefficients follow a pattern similar to the estimated coefficients for Spain. In particular, married men are more likely to be covered by such a plan than single men, while married women are less likely to be covered than single women. The probability of coverage by such a plan also increases with potential experience and with years of education. Finally, family income has a positive effect on the probability of coverage by an employer-provided health insurance plan.

The estimated effects change substantially when job characteristics are included as regressors in column 4. For example, the effect of the marriage dummy is no longer significant, and the effect of potential experience is reduced by a factor of four. In addition, the effect of family income is now negative and not significant, although married women remain less likely than single women to be covered. Overall, job characteristics (supply factors) explain an important part of the variation in the probability of coverage by a employer-provided health insurance plan.[28]

The estimated coefficients reported in columns 2 and 4 for the job characteristics are similar in the two countries. Both the probability of compliance with social security and the probability of coverage by a health insurance plan increase with tenure and are lower for part-time than for full-time jobs. The

28. Demand factors may be less important in the United States than in Spain because an important fraction of the population has no health insurance coverage. For example, when a married man in the United States does not have a health insurance plan, his wife will have a strong demand for health insurance. This is not the case in Spain, since virtually all married men have health insurance.

weighted correlation coefficient between the estimated industry effects in the two countries is positive (.666) and significant. These estimated industry coefficients are plotted in figure 9.3. The figure clearly shows the positive association between the estimated effects in the two countries (the slope of the fitted regression line is .262). This is consistent with supply factors being a key determinant of both the probability of compliance with social security and the probability of coverage by a health insurance plan. The industry wage effects are also positively correlated to the industry effects on the probability of compliance (.885) and the industry effects on the probability of holding a health insurance plan (.752). These correlations are consistent with the existence of labor market rents at the industry level that are dissipated in the form of both wages and employee benefits.

In table 9.7, by running several second-stage regressions, we further analyze the determinants of the industry propensities to comply with social security and to provide health insurance plans. More precisely, we run weighted regressions of the estimated industry effects on a series of industry characteristics.[29] The estimated industry effects are the estimated probit coefficients renormalized in term of marginal impacts on probabilities. One problem with this approach is that the set of available industry characteristics for Spain is quite limited. For instance, we do not have direct measures of industry concentration rates or of shares of unionization.[30] We proxy these variables with value added per worker and the numbers of workdays lost because of strikes (per employee). We also include the industry unemployment rate as a measure of labor market tightness, and the fraction of women in the industry as a measure of "feminization" of the industry. The results reported in the first column of table 9.7 indicate that log value added per worker has a positive and significant effect on the industry propensity to comply with social security. The other estimates indicate that workdays lost because of strikes also have a positive but not statistically significant effect on the probability of compliance with social security.[31] The presence of strong and militant unions may thus help enforce compliance with social security taxes. Perhaps surprisingly, the effect of the unemployment rate is not statistically significant. The fraction of women in the industry has a negative and significant (at the 90 percent level) effect on the probability of compliance. Firms in industries with a high concentration of women are thus

29. The explanatory variables used in the second step cannot be included in the original probit models (table 9.6, columns 2 and 4) since they are perfectly colinear with the industry dummies. The weights used in the regressions are industry employment.

30. In Spain, the share of unionization is not representative of the strength of the union in each industry. The percentage of unionization in Spain is very low, but every agreement reached between unions and employers covers every worker, independent of their union status. Besides this, many agreements are reached at the industry level instead of at the firm level.

31. To approximate union strength, variables such as number of collective agreements, workers covered by collective agreements, and wage increase agreed with unions were also included in this regression, but none of them was significant.

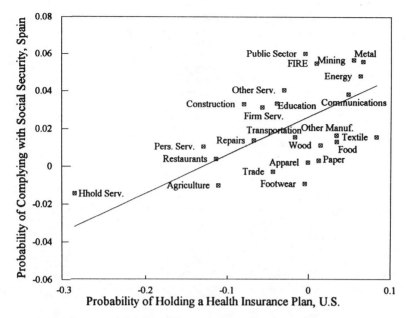

Fig. 9.3   Probability of compliance with social security in Spain, versus probability of holding an employer-provided health insurance plan in the United States

Source: Estimates of the industry wage effects reported in columns 2 and 4 of table 9.6 renormalized in terms of marginal impacts on probabilities.

Note: Base industry is apparel. The slope of the fitted regression line is equal to 0.262. The leather industry (it only employs .06 percent of workers in the United States) lies outside the bounds of this figure; its coordinated are (.143,.005).

less likely to comply with social security than firms with a low concentration of women.

The second-stage estimates for the United States are reported in the second column of table 9.7. The explanatory variables are similar to the ones used in Spain except that we now use the fraction of workers covered by collective agreements as a measure of union power.[32] The estimated effects of log value added per worker and of fraction of workers covered by collective agreements are positive and statistically significant, while the estimated effects of the unemployment rate and of the fraction of women in the industry are negative but not statistically significant. Interestingly, the estimated effect of log value added per worker on industry propensities is comparable in Spain and in the

---

32. For the sake of comparability with Spain, the probit coefficients used to construct the right-side variable were estimated without including a dummy variable for union coverage in the original probit model. These estimated industry effects are nevertheless very similar to the ones reported in column 4 of table 9.6.

Table 9.7   Second-Step Estimates of the Effects of Industry Characteristics on
the Propensity to Comply with Social Security (Spain) and to Receive
Health Insurance (United States)

	Spain	United States
Dependent variable:	Estimated industry effect on probability of complying with social security	Estimated industry effect on probability of holding a health insurance plan
Log of value added per worker	0.061 (0.020)	0.104 (0.031)
Unemployment rate	0.015 (0.110)	−0.011 (0.008)
Workdays lost because of strikes (per employee)	0.042 (0.030)	
Fraction of workers covered by collective bargaining agreements		0.358 (0.124)
Fraction of workers who are women	−0.097 (0.056)	−0.016 (0.099)
Adjusted R^2	0.451	0.544
Number of observations	22	23

Note: The right-hand side variables in the second-step regressions are the estimated industry effects in probit models (like those reported in table 9.6) renormalized in terms of marginal effects on the probability. The renormalization is done by multiplying the probit estimated coefficients by the standard normal density evaluated at the sample participation rate. The probit coefficients for Spain are from column 2 in table 9.6, while the probit coefficients for the United States are from a model similar to the one reported in column 4 of table 9.6 but in which the dummy variable for union contract coverage has been excluded (see text).

United States. This suggests once again that similar supply factors, such as rent-sharing considerations, are at work in the two countries.

In summary, the empirical results are consistent with the model presented in section 9.2. Demand and supply factors seem to be key determinants of both the probability of compliance with social security in Spain and the probability of coverage by an employer-provided health insurance plan in the United States.

9.4   Conclusions and Welfare Implications of the Results

The main finding of this paper is that although financing of health insurance in Spain and in the United States imposes very different constraints on each country's workers and firms, the two systems produce markedly similar outcomes in the two countries because of widespread noncompliance with social security taxes in Spain. This conclusion is based on the empirical finding that the same supply and demand factors seem to explain the private decision to provide health insurance in the United States and the decision to comply with social security taxes in Spain. In Spain, the extra costs of financing the social security system are high for firms that employ the kind of workers for whom health insurance is not provided in the United States. These firms prefer going underground, and facing the risk of being detected and penalized, to paying the tax. Our theoretical analysis clearly shows that forcing these firms to comply with social security would have adverse employment effects. These adverse employment effects were socially unacceptable in Spain in 1985, when the unemployment rate was almost 20 percent. This explains why the government did not more strictly enforce the payment of social security taxes.

It is unlikely, however, that such widespread noncompliance would be tolerated in the United States if health insurance coverage was mandated for all workers or if a tax was imposed to finance a government-administered program covering all otherwise uninsured workers. The Spanish experience nevertheless suggests some important lessons. First, noncompliance is more likely to happen in specific industries employing specific types of workers, such as married women. Enforcement efforts should thus target these industries if the goal is to enforce mandatory contributions to social security. In addition, U.S. firms not currently providing health insurance to their workers would have to adjust their behavior to the new institutional constraints that would be imposed on them. Without the option of not complying, employment in these firms would probably be reduced. The resulting labor market distortions would also cause social welfare to be reduced. It should be clear, however, that other factors not explicitly discussed here could also have important effects on social welfare. In particular, private provision of health insurance is bound to be inefficient because of adverse selection. Under some circumstances, mandating health insurance coverage could thus be a second-best equilibrium. Labor market distortions could be the price the United States has pay to improve the overall efficiency of its health care system.[33]

More important, even if the Spanish system cannot be directly implemented in the United States, it works in the sense that (1) essentially all workers have comprehensive health insurance coverage and (2) employment distortions are smaller than in a rigid system in which noncompliance would not be tolerated. The big difference between the two countries is that essentially all married males have a social security card in Spain, while many heads of households do not have health insurance coverage in the United States. It thus seems relatively easy for Spanish workers to get covered under social security if they really need it. By contrast, many U.S. workers and their dependents do not have any health insurance coverage. Although the proportion of U.S. workers who are covered by health insurance policies (85.7 percent in the March 1987 CPS) is larger than the proportion of workers who hold an employer-provided health insurance plan under their name (67.8 percent), an important fraction of work-

33. See, for example, Aaron (1991) and Diamond (1992) for a discussion of health insurance reform in the United States.

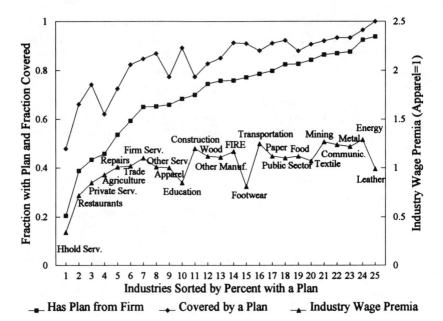

Fig. 9.4   Relationship among health insurance provision, health insurance coverage, and wages by industry in the United States

Sources: Industry wage premiums are from column 4 of table 9.4; the fraction of workers holding a health insurance plan was computed using the May 1988 CPS; the fraction of workers covered by health insurance was computed using the March 1987 CPS.

ers is still uncovered. A parallel figure for Spain would indicate that virtually everybody is covered under social security. Figure 9.4 indicates that, in the United States, the overall coverage rate follows the same cross-industry pattern as the proportion of workers holding a plan under their name and that the coverage rate is positively correlated with industry wages. This means the industry effects estimated in table 9.6 do not simply reflect the fact that workers in low-wage industries are less likely to hold a plan in their name because they are already covered by the plan of another household member. Rather, it means that all workers in these industries, whether they are teenagers or heads of families with children, are less likely to have health insurance coverage.[34]

In practice, the Spanish system thus works through a cross-subsidization from the employers of married males in high-wage industries to the employers of women and youth who are more likely not to pay taxes. One straightforward interpretation of this pattern of cross-subsidization is that married men tend to work in high-rent jobs (or industries) and that it is efficient to finance the whole health care system out of these labor market rents. The second-step estimates

---

34. Figure 9.6 suggests a positive correlation between spouses' health insurance coverage, as is found by Holtz-Eakin (ch. 6 in this volume) using data from the PSID.

of the effects of value added per worker on industry propensities are consistent with this interpretation. These facts suggest that cross-subsidization from high-rent to low-rent industries may have efficiency aspects that should not be ignored in current discussions of health insurance reform in the United States.

Data Appendix

Spain

Data from the Survey of Living and Working Conditions

The microdata for Spain were obtained from the Survey of Living and Working Conditions (ECVT), carried out by the Spanish government in the last quarter of 1985 (see Muro, Toharia, and Toharia 1986, for more details). The authors will make the ECVT data set available to other researchers on request.

Wage. Direct measures of wages are not available. The wage measure available is seven brackets of net monthly earnings: less than 25,000 pesetas, 25,001–50,000 pesetas, 50,001–75,000 pesetas, 75,001–100,000 pesetas, 100,001–150,000 pesetas, 150,001–200,000 pesetas, and more than 200,000 pesetas. As mentioned in the text, the earnings variable used in the empirical analysis is defined as the corresponding midpoint of the income bracket. To assess the impact of this imputation scheme on the estimated coefficients reported in columns 1 and 2 of table 9.4, we used a similar imputation scheme for the U.S. earnings variable. To do so, we defined seven income brackets similar to the ones described above that were such that the same fraction of workers was in the upper and in the lower bracket in Spain and in the United States. We then compared the U.S. estimates obtained using this imputed earnings measure to the estimates obtained using actual earnings. The results of these experiments are reported in table 9A.1. Columns 1 and 2 report the estimates for Spain, while columns 3 and 4 report the U.S. estimates obtained using the imputed earnings variable. The results reported in columns 3 and 4 of table 9A.1 are very similar to the results reported in columns 3 and 4 of table 9.4, suggesting that the estimates for Spain are not significantly biased because only seven brackets of earnings are available in the data.

We have also verified that using weekly wages as opposed to the hourly wage did not have a big impact on the estimated coefficients.

Tenure. The measure of tenure in the job is also bracketed. There are six brackets: less than one month, one–six months, between six months and one year, one–two years, two–five years, and more than five years.

Table 9A.1   **OLS Estimates of Earnings Equations (Imputed Income)[a] (dependent variable: log of earnings)[b]**

	Spain		United States	
Intercept	9.508	9.912	4.082	4.537
	(0.025)	(0.032)	(0.024)	(0.037)
Female	−0.141	−0.132	−0.066	−0.057
	(0.019)	(0.017)	(0.018)	(0.016)
Married	0.219	0.151	0.191	0.091
	(0.012)	(0.011)	(0.012)	(0.010)
Married*female	−0.239	−0.135	−0.254	−0.131
	(0.019)	(0.017)	(0.017)	(0.014)
Experience	0.028	0.017	0.056	0.026
	(0.001)	(0.001)	(0.001)	(0.001)
Experience^2	−0.053	−0.033	−0.097	−0.048
	(0.027)	(0.002)	(0.003)	(0.002)
Experience*female	−0.005	−0.005	−0.020	−0.014
	(0.002)	(0.001)	(0.002)	(0.001)
Experience^2*female	0.008	0.011	0.031	0.024
	(0.004)	(0.003)	(0.004)	(0.003)
Education	0.075	0.043	0.095	0.056
	(0.021)	(0.001)	(0.001)	(0.001)
Tenure (1–5 years)		0.022		0.093
		(0.013)		(0.008)
Tenure (> 5 years)		0.097		0.261
		(0.013)		(0.009)
Part-time		−0.288		−0.506
		(0.012)		(0.009)
Industry and Occupation dummies	No	Yes	No	Yes
Number of observations	14,898	14,898	20,566	20,566
Mean of dependent variable	10.786	10.789	5.761	5.761
R^2	0.358	0.518	0.376	0.576

[a]The model for Spain also includes 15 region dummies and 1 dummy for temporary workers. The U.S. model contains additionally 3 region dummies, 8 occupation dummies, 1 dummy for race and 1 dummy for the union effect. The base group consists of skilled blue-collar single male workers, working full time in the apparel industry. Standard errors are in parentheses.

[b]Earnings are defined as monthly earnings (after taxes) for Spain and weekly earnings (before taxes) for United States. Both income measures are based on the same imputation scheme that uses mid-points of seven income brackets.

Family Income. This variable is bracketed in exactly the same way as monthly wage brackets. The imputed variable that consists of midpoints of the brackets is used in the empirical analysis.

Education. The education system in Spain differs slightly from the one in the United States. The relevant question asked in the survey is the following:

"What is the highest level of education that you have completed?" The possible answers were:

- Less than primary (less than six years)
- Primary studies (six years)
- "O"-level studies (eight years)
- "A"-level studies (twelve years)
- Vocational studies (eleven years)
- College degree (fifteen or seventeen years, depending on the degree type)

We have used the number of years of education indicated in parentheses in our empirical analysis.

Married. This variable equals one if the individual answers to being married, as opposed to being single, divorced, or widowed.

Experience. There is no exact measure of labor market experience in the survey. The variable used is potential experience (age − education − 6).

Part-time. This variable equals one if the individual works less than two-thirds of the ordinary working week.

Other Spanish Data

Value Added. This variable was obtained from the National Accounts. It is defined as value added before taxes at market prices, disaggregated by industry.

Total Employment. This variable is defined as total number of occupied workers, disaggregated by industry. Data comes from the National Institute of Employment (INEM).

Value Added per Worker. As defined, this is value added by industry, divided by total employment by industry.

Number of Workdays Lost because of Strikes (per Employee). This is the number of workdays lost because of strikes in the industry in 1985, divided by industry employment. Data source is INEM.

Unemployment Rate. The unemployment rate is defined as the total number of unemployed, divided by total employment plus total unemployment. The total number of unemployed workers is disaggregated by industry. Data source is INEM.

United States

Data from the Current Population Survey

As mentioned in the text, we use microdata from the May 1988 *Employee Benefits Supplement* of the CPS. These data were obtained from the U.S. Bureau of the Census. The earnings data are obtained from the usual outgoing rotation group earnings supplement to the CPS. Most variables we used are very standard and will not be described here. One exception is the total family income variable, which is reported in fourteen income brackets ranging from less than $5,000 to $75,000 and more. We use the corresponding midpoints of each income bracket in the empirical analysis.

Data for the Second-Step Regressions

Industry Unemployment Rate and Employment. These data are based on CPS data as tabulated by the U.S. Bureau of Labor Statistics (source: *Statistical Abstract of the United States* 1989).

Value Added in the Industry. These data were obtained from the National Accounts (source: *Statistical Abstract of the United States* 1989).

Percentage of Workers Covered by Collective Agreement. Statistic are based on calculations of the authors, using May 1988 CPS data.

References

Aaron, H. J. 1991. *Serious and unstable condition: financing America's health care.* Washington, D.C.: Brookings Institution.
Benton, L. 1990. *Invisible factories: The informal economy and industrial development in Spain.* Albany: State University of New York Press.
Cowell, F. 1990. *Cheating the government.* Cambridge: MIT Press.
De Vicente, R. 1991. *Delitos contra la Seguridad Social.* Barcelona: Praxis.
Danzon, P. 1989. Mandated employment-based health insurance: Incidence and efficiency effects. Philadelphia: University of Pennsylvania. Mimeograph.
Diamond, P. 1992. Organizing the health insurance market. *Econometrica* 60:1233–54.
Fortin, B., T. Lemieux, and P. Fréchette. 1990. An empirical model of labor supply in the underground economy. NBER Working Paper no. 3392. Cambridge, Mass.: National Bureau of Economic Research.
Freeman, R. B., and J. Medoff. 1984. *What do unions do?* New York: Basic Books.
Gruber, J., and A. Krueger. 1990. The incidence of mandated employer-provided insurance: Lessons from workers' compensation insurance. NBER Working Paper no. 3557. Cambridge, Mass.: National Bureau of Economic Research.
Hamermesh, D. 1979. New estimates of the incidence of payroll tax. *Southern Economic Journal* 45:1208–19.

Ministerio de Trabajo y Seguridad Social. 1986. *Análisis económico-financiero del sistema español de Seguridad Social, 1964–1985.* Madrid: Colección informes, Ministerio de Trabajo y Seguridad Social, servicio de Publicaciones.

———. 1990. *Acción protectora del Régimen General de la Seguridad Social,* ed. Secretaría General de la Seguridad Social. Madrid.

———. 1993. *Proyección económico-actuarial de los gastos e ingresos de la Seguridad Social, 1985–1992.* Madrid: Colección informes, Ministerio de Trabajo y Seguridad Social, servicio publicaciones.

Morke, T. P., and J. D. Morton. 1990. How firm size and industry affect employee benefits. *Monthly Labor Review* 113 (12): 35–43.

Muro, J. R., J. L. Toharia, and L. Toharia. 1986. *Análisis de las condiciones de Vida y Trabajo España,* ed. Ezequiel Uriel. Madrid: Secretaría General de Economía y Planificación.

Ramos, F. 1988. The concealed labor market in Puerto Rico. Cambridge: Harvard University. Mimeograph.

Rosen, S. 1986. The theory of equalizing differences. In *Handbook of labor economics,* ed. O. Ashenfelter and R. Layard, 641–92. Amsterdam: Elsevier–North Holland.

Stigler, G. J., and G. S. Becker. 1977. De gustibus non est disputantum. *American Economic Review* 67:76–90.

Summers, L. 1989. Some simple economics of mandated benefits. *American Economic Review* 79:177–83.

10 Social Welfare Programs for Women and Children: The United States versus France

Maria J. Hanratty

One of the central dilemmas in social welfare policy is how to protect families from financial hardship without causing them to become too reliant upon social assistance. The United States' approach to this dilemma has been to restrict cash assistance to the least "employable" segments of the population (single parents or families with a disabled adult) and to provide means-tested aid to these groups on an extended basis. This approach guarantees that certain segments of the population receive minimal income support, while preserving work incentives for the remainder of the population.

The French have taken a different tack to resolve this dilemma. First, rather than target aid only to the unemployable, France provides assistance to nearly all families with children. Second, rather than encouraging some segments of the population to remain permanently out of the labor force, France encourages all women with children to work. Thus, while France provides generous transfer assistance to families when their children are young, it sharply reduces transfer payments when the youngest child reaches age 3. In addition, other French policies (e.g., universal public nursery school, universal medical insurance, and mandatory maternity leave) make it easier for women to enter the labor force when their children reach age 3.

This paper will examine the impact of two time-limited transfer programs in France on the employment rates of women with children. The first, the Single-Parent Allowance (API) program, is a means-tested program for single parents. Much like the U.S. Aid to Families with Dependent Children (AFDC) program, this program offers means-tested assistance to single parents under a

Maria J. Hanratty is assistant professor of economics at Princeton University and a faculty research fellow of the National Bureau of Economic Research.

The author is grateful for comments from Rebecca Blank, John Abowd, Timothy Smeeding, and conference attendees. Support from the Ford Foundation is gratefully acknowledged.

high implicit tax rate. However, unlike the AFDC program, this program is provided only until the youngest child reaches age three or for one year after divorce/separation from or death of a spouse. The second program, the Parental Education Allowance, provides a payment to women who have three or more children and who take an employment leave following the birth of a child. Like the API, this program continues until the youngest child reaches age 3.

The French experience with time-limited benefits is relevant to the current U.S. debate over welfare reform, since many analysts in the United States have argued for a limit on the length of time that a single parent may receive welfare. They argue that this policy would prevent families from permanently relying on welfare as a means of support and thus would promote the economic sufficiency of single-parent families (Ellwood 1988). Currently, little is known about the impact of time-limited benefits; while there is a time limit on the unemployment insurance program, the United States has not experimented with placing a limit on welfare benefits for single-parent families. Thus, an examination of the French experience may be an important first step in determining how such a policy might affect the United States.

The French experience is also relevant to our understanding of the trade-offs between economic protection and economic flexibility. One of the classic complaints about the U.S. welfare system is that it creates an "underclass" of families with little attachment to the labor force.[1] The French system of time-limited benefits may avert this problem if it is more successful in integrating women into the labor force. Placing a time limit on welfare benefits may increase work efforts of single parents in the short run, since it will decrease the returns to remaining out of the labor force. In addition, it may have important long-run effects: women may invest more in education and training if they anticipate that they cannot permanently rely on welfare for support. Finally, this policy may have important spillover effects if reducing welfare use by one family decreases the incentive for other families in the community to use welfare.[2]

A second component of the social protection–economic flexibility debate is the extent to which investments in children affect the future productivity of the work force. For younger children, France provides greater assistance in the form of both cash transfers and medical insurance coverage than does the United States. For older children (age 3–5), France provides less direct income support to some groups of families than the United States does, but it also more invests heavily in education through its high-quality universal public nursery school system.[3] Finally, the French system clearly provides greater in-

---

1. See Murray (1984) for a recent exposition of this view.
2. See Wilson (1987) for an exposition of this view.
3. Kamerman (1991) argues that attendance at public nursery school in France is important to later school performance.

ducement for single mothers with children over age 3 to work. This in turn may have important effects on their children's development.[4]

This paper adds to excellent descriptions of social welfare institutions in France for women and children by Starzec and David (1991), Jenson and Kantrow (1990), and Lefaucheur (1991). For a review of the extensive U.S. literature on poverty and social welfare programs, see Sawhill (1989) or Moffit (1992). Finally, Ray, Jeandidier, and Carvoyeur (1988) present an analysis of family allowances for a sample of women in Luxembourg and Lorraine. The chief contribution of this paper is the explicit comparison of programs and their impact on women's work effort in France and the United States.

10.1   Social Welfare Institutions in the United States and France

10.1.1   Cash Assistance Programs

This section provides information on social welfare programs in France and the United States in 1987 for families with children. These programs are summarized in appendix A.[5] All dollar amounts are in units of 1990 U.S. dollars.[6]

France

France offers cash assistance to families with children through a complex set of child and family allowance programs administered by the federal government. These programs are designed to serve multiple objectives: targeting assistance to families with children, increasing the French birth rate, and protecting economically vulnerable families (single parents and families with three or more children).

France offers assistance on a demogrant basis through its *Family Allowance Program.* This program offers assistance to all families with two or more children. Monthly payments increase with both the number and the age of children in the family: a family with two children ages 10–14 would receive a monthly

---

4. The desirability of encouraging mothers to work is controversial. On the one hand, a working mother may have less time to devote to her children; on the other hand, she may become a better role model if she is able to find a fulfilling job. See Blau and Grossberg (1990) for recent empirical research on this topic.

5. This analysis ignores the impact of differences in nonrefundable income tax subsidies to families with children. Under the French *Quotient Familial,* the marginal income tax rate declines with family size. Families compute their total tax liability by dividing taxable income by an index that varies by family size; they then compute their income tax liability on the basis of each share. In the United States, the federal income tax system allows families to claim a tax deduction for each dependent child.

6. To convert from French to U.S. dollars, this paper uses an estimate of the purchasing power parity for consumption of French relative to U.S. dollars in 1990 (OECD 1992). It adjusts this index for the relative inflation rates in each country from 1987 to 1990, using the gross domestic product deflators reported in International Monetary Fund (1992).

payment of $105, while a family with three children in the same age range would receive $257.

France offers three programs to assist economically vulnerable families on a time-limited basis. The first program is the Allowance for Young Children, which provides a monthly payment of $119 to families with a child under age 3. The "short form" of this program is provided on a non-means-tested basis from the fourth month after conception to the third month after pregnancy. The "long form" of this program continues for low-income families until the youngest child reaches age 3. To qualify for assistance, both the mother and child must complete a federally mandated schedule of medical care visits.

A second time-limited program is the Parental Education Allowance.[7] This program provides a monthly payment of $367 to parents who take a leave from their job following the adoption or birth of a child. Unlike the Young Child Allowance, this program is only available to families with three or more children. To qualify, the parent must have worked two of the preceding ten years. If they remain out of the labor force, parents may continue to receive the full benefit until their youngest child reaches age 3. After the third year, parents may receive a half-payment of $183 per month if they work part-time or enter a vocational education program.

A final program that assists families on a time-limited basis is the Single-Parent Allowance (API). This program assists low-income single parents who recently have had a child or experienced a divorce/separation from or death of a spouse. The maximum payment for a mother with two children is $730 per month. Like the U.S. AFDC program, this program is intended to temporarily assist single parents in times of crisis. Unlike the AFDC program, the API program tightly limits the duration of benefits. While a single parent in the United States may receive AFDC until her youngest child reaches age 18, a single parent in France may receive the API until her youngest child reaches age three or for up to twelve consecutive months within the eighteen months following the loss of a spouse.

France provides further cash assistance to vulnerable families through its Family Support Allowance, a small monthly payment provided on a non-means-tested basis to single-parent families. In addition, the Large-Family Supplement provides a monthly payment of $107 to low-income families with three or more children all over age 3. Finally, the Return to School Allowance provides a small payment to low-income families to defray the costs of school supplies at the beginning of the academic year.

France provides in-kind assistance to low-income families through its Housing Allowance program. This program provides cash payments to low-income families to help cover the costs of rent or mortgage payments. Both families

---

7. Despite the title of this program, the parent is *not* required to enter an education or training program to receive this benefit.

with a dependent child and newly married couples under age 40 may qualify for this program.

According to Starzec and David (1991), these programs provide assistance to a large number of families in France. By far the largest assistance program is the Family Allowance program, which served 3.6 million families in 1988, followed by the Return to School Allowance program (2 million children), the Young Child Allowance program (1.6 million families), and the Housing Allowance program (1.1 million households). The two time-limited programs were less extensive, with the Single-Parent Allowance serving 130,000 families and the Parental Education Allowance serving 160,000 families.[8]

United States

The U.S. transfer system differs from the French transfer system on a number of dimensions. First, while France provides assistance to all families with children, the U.S. system assists only low-income families. Second, the United States targets assistance more directly toward single-parent families. Finally, while the French programs provide greater assistance to families with young children, U.S. programs do not vary by age of children.

The main cash assistance program in the United States is Aid to Families with Dependent Children (AFDC). This joint federal-state program provides cash assistance primarily to low-income single-parent families with children. In 1987, some states also allowed two-parent households to receive AFDC under stricter eligibility requirements; however, two-parent families represented only 6 percent of all AFDC recipients in these states.[9] Monthly benefits vary substantially across states. In 1987, the maximum monthly benefit for a family of three ranged from $133 to $845 per month, with a median of $400 per month. This program served 3.8 million families, or approximately 64 percent of all poor single-parent families in 1987.

A second U.S. program that assists the low-income population is the Food Stamps program. This federal program provides low-income families and individuals with coupons that can be used to purchase food. In 1987, the maximum coupon amount for a family of three was $242, reduced by 30 cents for every

---

8. These programs appear to reach a large share of their target population. In 1987, there were 365,000 families in France with three or more children and a child under age 3 (author's calculations from the 1987 Enquête sur l'Emploi). Thus, the Parental Education Allowance reached an estimated 44 percent of all categorically eligible women. It is more difficult to compute the number of families eligible for the API. While the data available make it possible to identify single parents who are eligible for this program because they have a child under age 3 (84,000 in 1987), it is not possible to identify single parents who qualify because they have recently lost a spouse due to divorce/separation or death.

9. The Family Support Act of 1988 requires all states to provide assistance to families with two-parent families in which the principal earner is unemployed. However, partly due to more stringent eligibility requirements for this group, two-parent families remain a very small part (7 percent) of the AFDC population in 1991.

dollar of countable income. This program served 19.1 million individuals, or approximately 59 percent of all poor individuals in 1987.

Finally, the United States provides assistance to working poor families with children through the earned income tax credit. This program provides a refundable income tax credit equal to 14 percent of earnings, to a maximum of $900; it then decreases by 10 cents for every $1 of earnings above $7,300. This program served 7.5 million families in 1987; of these, 2.9 million received a cash refund.

The combined effect of these programs is illustrated in table 10.1, which

Table 10.1   Transfers for Families with Children: the United States versus France, 1987 (1990 U.S. dollars)

| Number of Children/Age of Youngest Child (in years) | United States[a] | | France[b] | | | |
| | Single-Parent Family Maximum | Two-Parent Family Maximum | Single-Parent Family | | Two-Parent Family | |
			Maximum	Minimum	Maximum	Minimum
1 child						
0	$5,701	$2,899	$ 7,439	$1,195	$ 4,613	$ 404
1	5,701	2,899	7,035	791	4,613	0
2	5,701	2,899	7,035	791	4,613	0
3+	5,701	2,899	3,685	791	2,997	0
2 children						
0	7,264	3,672	9,256	2,321	6,181	1,530
1	7,264	3,672	8,852	1,917	6,181	1,126
2	7,264	3,672	8,852	1,917	6,181	1,126
3+	7,264	3,672	4,973	1,917	4,565	1,126
3 children						
0	8,615	4,362	12,505	4,396	11,817	3,605
1	8,615	4,362	12,505	3,992	10,379	3,201
2	8,615	4,362	12,505	3,992	10,379	3,201
3+	8,615	4,362	8,955	3,992	7,261	3,201
4 children						
0	9,998	5,243	14,672	6,401	13,984	5,610
1	9,998	5,243	14,672	5,997	13,984	5,206
2	9,998	5,243	14,672	5,997	13,984	5,206
3+	9,998	5,243	11,122	5,997	10,434	5,206

Note: "Maximum" indicates maximum transfer payments for a family with no other income; "minimum" indicates transfer payments for a high-income family (over $24,000 for a family with one child, $27,000 for a family with two children, and $32,000 for a family with three children).

[a]U.S. transfers include food stamp and median AFDC benefits. Calculations assume that single-parent family is eligible for AFDC and that two-parent family receives food stamps only.

[b]French transfers include Family Allowances, Family Support Allowance, Parental Education Allowance, Allowance to Young Children, Large-Family Supplement, Return to School Allowance, Single-Parent Allowance, and Housing Allowance, as described in appendix A. Calculations assume that two-child family has one child age 10–14, that three-child family has two children ages 10–14, and that four-child family has two children ages 10–14 and one child age 15–16. Calculations also assume that family receives maximum housing allowance.

indicates the total transfer income available to families in each country. The first two columns indicate maximum transfer payments to single- and two-parent families in the United States. The next four columns indicate both maximum and minimum payments to single- and two-parent families in France.

This table highlights several differences between the two systems. First, maximum transfer payments are much more generous in France than in the United States. For example, a single parent with two children under age 3 would receive $8,850 in France and $7,260 in the United States, while a married couple with two children age 3 would receive $6,200 in France and $3,700 in the United States. Second, while the United States offers virtually no non-means-tested assistance, French demogrant payments can be quite substantial: the minimum income for a family with three children ranges from $3,000 to $4,000 in France, while the minimum income for a family with four children ranges from $5,000 to $6,000.

Third, while both countries provide higher transfer payments to single parents than to two-parent families, French payments also provide relatively high levels of support to families with three or more children. For example, the maximum payment for a married couple increases from $6,180 to $10,400 as the number of children increases from one to three, whereas they would increase from $3,700 to $4,400 in the United States. This reflects both the French goal of increasing the birth rate and the view in France that large families are economically vulnerable and need additional income support.[10]

Finally, transfer payments decrease substantially in France when the youngest child reaches age 3, reflecting the termination of French time-limited benefits. This decline is particularly large for economically vulnerable groups in France: single parents and families with three or more children. For example, the maximum payment to a single parent with two children declines from $8,852 to $4,973 when the youngest child reaches age three, while the payment to a couple with three children declines from $10,400 to $7,300. In the United States, transfers remain constant until the youngest child reaches age 18.

10.1.2 Medical Assistance Programs

In addition to providing more extensive income support than the United States does, France offers greater access to medical care through its universal health insurance program. This program covers nearly 100 percent of the population; it is administered through the social security system and financed through a payroll tax. Families must pay a coinsurance rate of 25 percent of physician fees, 20 percent of hospital charges, and 30 percent to 60 percent of pharmaceutical costs (Rosa and Lanois 1990). In addition, both private insurance and municipal assistance to low-income families may defray costs not covered by the federal program.

---

10. For example, Centre d'Étude des Revenus et des Coûts (1987) identifies both of these two groups as economically vulnerable.

The U.S. provides medical care to low-income families with children through its Medicaid program. This joint federal and state program offers comprehensive, first-dollar coverage of most medical services to low-income families with children. However, due to tight financial and categorical eligibility criteria, this program reaches just a fraction of the poor: only 53 percent of poor children were covered by the Medicaid program in 1987.

10.1.3   Day Care

France provides access to day care for a much broader segment of the population than does the United States. For children above age 3, France has made day care universally available through its public nursery school system. For children under age 3, France, like the United States, uses a combination of limited public provision and subsidies to increase access to care.

The key program in France that provides day care to families with children over age 3 is the French public nursery schools (*écoles maternelles*). This system is open at no cost to all children from the age that they are first toilet trained until the age of school entry (age 6). In 1989, 36 percent of children age 2, 98 percent of children age 3, and nearly 100 percent of children ages 4–5 attended nursery school. While the nursery school is viewed as a necessary component of a child's education, it also plays an important custodial role, since it is open for the majority of the working day: 8:30 A.M. to 4:30 P.M. daily except Wednesday, and one-half day on Saturday.[11]

For children under age 3, France offers a combination of publicly provided care and subsidies to help parents obtain day care. Subsidized day care is provided through its public daycare centers (*crèches*). While the most common form of the crèche is the public day nursery, the French are now experimenting with daycare centers operating on a smaller scale, in family homes or through parent cooperatives. While these centers are an attractive daycare option, there are far too few slots currently available to meet the demand for daycare services (Bergmann 1992).

France also subsidizes the purchase of day care from mother's helpers (*assistantes maternelles*)—federally certified childcare workers who care for children in their homes. These workers are exempted from both the employer's and employee's social security tax contributions, which together amount to over 40 percent of wages.[12] In addition, the federal government allows families to deduct up to 10,000 francs per year from their taxable income for childcare expenses.

In 1986, 12 percent of all children under 3 with two parents working outside of the home received day care through public daycare centers, 26 percent re-

---

11. Schools are closed on Wednesday afternoon to allow children to attend religious education classes. Parents may purchase day care for times when the nursery school is not in session on a fee-paying basis (Kamerman 1991).

12. The employee's contribution is exempted from taxation, while the parent receives a rebate of any payments made for the employer's contribution.

ceived assistance through certified mother's helpers, and 6 percent received day care through family daycare centers. The remaining 56 percent received day care from other sources, such as nonregulated day care or from friends and other family members (Starzec and David 1991).

The U.S. system is more fragmented than the French system, with both federal and state governments playing a role in providing child care. While the federal government operates over forty programs to expand daycare availability, over 80 percent of all federal spending in 1988 was devoted to the four programs described below (U.S. General Accounting Office 1989).[13]

The federal government subsidizes public childcare centers through its Title XX Social Services Block Grant program, an unrestricted grant that states may use to pay for child care and other social services. Total spending for this program in 1987 was $2.7 billion, of which approximately $660 million were allocated to daycare services.[14]

The federal government directly sponsors childcare services through its Head Start program. This enriched education program prepares disadvantaged children ages 3–5 for primary school. Unlike the French nursery school, most Head Start programs operate for half a day: only one-fifth of all program participants in 1987 attended Head Start for a full six-hour day. In 1987, this program served 450,000 children, or 17 percent of poor children ages 3–5. Total expenditures on the program for 1987 were $1.1 billion.

Finally, the federal government supports child care through its dependent care tax credit. This is a nonrefundable income tax credit of up to 30 percent of employment-related expenses on dependent care, up to a limit of $2,400 per child and $4,800 per family. Total tax expenditures for this item were $3.8 billion in 1987.

In 1987, 17 percent of all U.S. children under age 3 with a working mother were cared for in public daycare centers: 33 percent were cared for by nonrelatives in informal settings; the remaining 50 percent were cared for by relatives. Of children ages 3–4 with a working mother, 36 percent were cared for in organized childcare or education facilities, 22 percent were cared for by nonrelatives, and 42 percent were cared for by relatives (U.S. Department of Commerce 1990).

10.1.4 Maternity Leave

France has a legally mandated maternity leave policy that requires all employers to provide a job-protected leave at the time of the birth or adoption of a child. The length of the required leave varies with the number of children in the family: it begins six–eight weeks prior to expected date of delivery and ends ten–eighteen weeks after childbirth. During this period, the parent may

---

13. See Robins (1991) for an excellent overview of the U.S. childcare system.

14. Unless otherwise noted, all estimates of expenditures and recipiency rates presented in this section are from U.S. House of Representatives (1988, 1989).

also qualify for maternity insurance, which replaces 84 percent of average earnings.

In addition to standard maternity leave, parents may also qualify for an extended leave under the Parental Education Leave program.[15] This program allows parents to claim a two-year job-protected leave at the end of the standard maternity leave. Firms with fewer than 100 employees may be exempted from this requirement if they can demonstrate that this leave is harmful to their company. Parents may combine this leave with the Parental Education Allowance, described above.

As of 1987, the U.S. policy regarding family leave was much more limited than that of France. At the federal level, the Pregnancy Discrimination Act of 1980 required all employers who operate disability insurance programs to cover pregnancy-related disabilities. This legislation is very short term in nature, since it applies only to the period during which a mother cannot work due to pregnancy-related disabilities (Trzcinski and Alpert 1994).[16] In addition, in 1987, thirteen states (twenty-five states by 1991) had enacted legislation requiring employer-provided parental leave. These laws require employers to provide an unpaid job-protected leave of from six to twenty-four weeks for the birth, adoption, or serious illness of a child (Finn-Stevenson and Trzcinski 1991).[17]

10.2 Predictions and Estimation Approach

This section will examine the impact of the termination of two time-limited transfer programs in France. The first is a means-tested program for single parents, the API program described above. The second, Parental Education Leave, is a program for families with three or more children.

10.2.1 Single-Parent Family Programs

Figure 10.1 illustrates the income-earnings frontier for single parents in France and the United States. As shown, both U.S. single parents and French single parents with a child under age 3 have income-earnings frontiers that exhibit a flat "notch" around zero earnings, reflecting the presence of a means-tested welfare program with a high tax rate on earnings. However, while the U.S. income-earnings frontier remains constant, the French income-earnings frontier changes substantially when the youngest child reaches age 3.

As shown, there are two important changes in the income-earnings frontier

---

15. As before (see note 7 above), the parent does not need to participate in an education or training program to qualify.

16. In 1980, when this legislation was enacted, pregnant women who were covered by disability programs were covered for an average of six weeks of benefits.

17. The U.S. government recently passed the Family and Medical Leave Act of 1993. The act requires employers who have at least fifty employees to guarantee an unpaid job-protected leave of twelve weeks per year for family and medical emergencies.

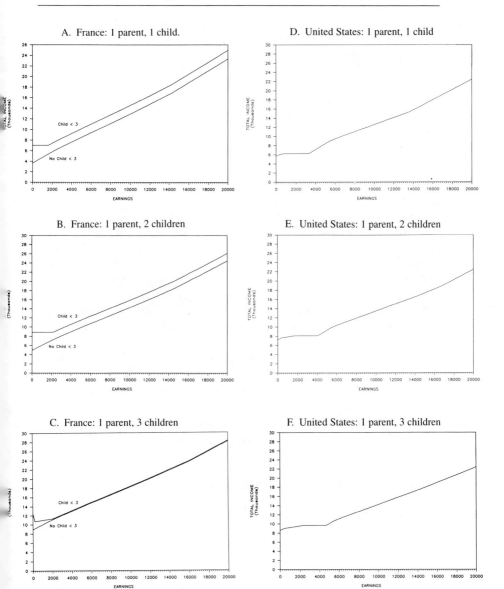

Fig. 10.1   Income-earnings frontier for single parents in the United States and France

in France that should increase the employment rate of single parents when their youngest child reaches age 3. First, the income-earnings frontier shifts downward, reflecting a decline in total nonlabor income available to French single parents. Second, the flat notch around zero earnings is eliminated, reflecting a decline from 100 percent to 6 percent in the tax rate on earnings.

Both of these changes should increase the incentive to work: since single mothers have less nonlabor income, they will find it harder to forgo market work. In addition, since they realize a larger gain in total income as their earnings increase, they will be more likely to substitute market for nonmarket work.

One way to estimate the impact of the termination of French time-limited transfer benefits is to compute the difference between the employment rate of French single parents with a youngest child age 3–5 and those with a child age 0–2:

$$(1) \qquad \Delta E_{fs} = h(\Delta G_{fs}, \Delta t_{fs}) + \theta_f + \Phi_s,$$

where f indicates France, s indicates single parent, ΔE_{fs} represents the difference in employment rates of women with a youngest child age 3–5 versus age 0–2, $h(\Delta G, \Delta t)$ represents the impact of the change in implicit tax rate and income guarantee under the transfer system when the youngest child changes from age 0–2 to age 3–5, θ_f represents factors common to France, and Φ_s represents factors that are common to single parents and could change the employment rate of French women when their youngest child reaches age 3.

The estimator shown in equation (1) is likely to overestimate the impact of terminating time-limited transfers, because it ignores other important factors common to France, such as the dramatic expansion in public day care or the termination of government-mandated maternity leave, which occurs when the youngest child reaches age 3. Failure to account for these factors, designated θ_f in equation (1), could clearly lead to a biased estimate of the impact of time-limited benefits.

One way to deal with this problem is to compute the difference between the change in employment of single parents and the change in employment of two-parent families when the youngest child reaches age 3:

$$(2) \qquad \Delta E_{fs} - \Delta E_{fm} = h(\Delta t_{fs}, \Delta G_{fs}) + \Phi_s - \Phi_m,$$

where m designates married and the remaining terms are as defined above. As shown, this "difference in difference" estimator eliminates the θ_f term in equation (1), thus eliminating factors common to France that may affect the employment rates of women with children.[18] However, this estimator may still be biased because it does not control for other underlying differences between single and married women, designated $\Phi_s - \Phi_m$ above, which may affect the relative change in employment. For example, differences in the availability of informal daycare services, family income, or alternative costs of time all may cause women in single-parent and two-parent families to have different rates

18. Note that equation (2) assumes there is *no* change in transfers for two-parent families in France. However, as shown in figure 10.2, there is a slight decline in the income guarantee for this group when their youngest child reaches age 3, which in turn may cause their employment rate to increase. Thus, the estimates presented here may underestimate the impact of the termination of the API.

at which their employment increases when their youngest child reaches age three.

To control for these factors, one can compute a "difference in difference in difference" estimator, which computes the difference between France and the United States in the difference between single- and two-parent families in the change in employment when the youngest child changes from age 0–2 to age 3–5:

$$(3) \qquad (\Delta E_{fs} - \Delta E_{fm}) - (\Delta E_{us} - \Delta E_{um}) = h(\Delta t_{fs}, \Delta G_{fs}) ,$$

where u indexes United States and all remaining terms are defined above. To the extent that the United States is a valid control group for France (i.e., the underlying difference $\Phi_s - \Phi_m$ is the same in both countries) this estimator will produce an unbiased estimate of the impact of the termination of time-limited transfer programs for single parents in France.

10.2.2   Programs for Large Families (Parental Education Allowance)

As noted earlier, the French system provides supplemental assistance on a time-limited basis to families with three or more children through its Parental Education Allowance (PEA). Panel C of figure 10.2 illustrates how this program changes the incentive for married women with three or more children to work when their youngest child reaches age 3. As shown, when the youngest child reaches age three, the income guarantee available to this group declines markedly, reflecting the elimination of the PEA payment. In addition, the implicit tax rate on earnings decreases substantially: before the youngest child reaches age three, members of this group effectively face an infinite tax rate on earnings since they must remain out of the labor force to qualify for the PEA, whereas afterward the implicit tax rate is near zero (6 percent). Both of these changes should increase the incentive of women in large families to work, since they imply a decrease in nonlabor income available to "spend" on nonmarket activities, and an increase in the return to market work.

To isolate the impact of the Parental Education Allowance from that of the API program, this analysis will focus on married women only. As before, there are three possible methods of estimating the impact of the Parental Education Allowance. First, for women with large families (three-plus children), one could compute the difference between the employment rates of those with a youngest child age zero–two and those with a child age three–five. As before, this estimator does not control for other factors that change at the time the youngest child reaches age three, such as the increase in publicly provided day care. Second, one could compute a difference-in-difference estimator, which would compute the difference between large families (three-plus children) and small families (one–two children) in the difference between the employment rates of women with a youngest child age 3–5 versus age 0–2. While this would eliminate the potentially contaminating impact of factors that do not vary by family size, it still would not control for factors that affect the underlying

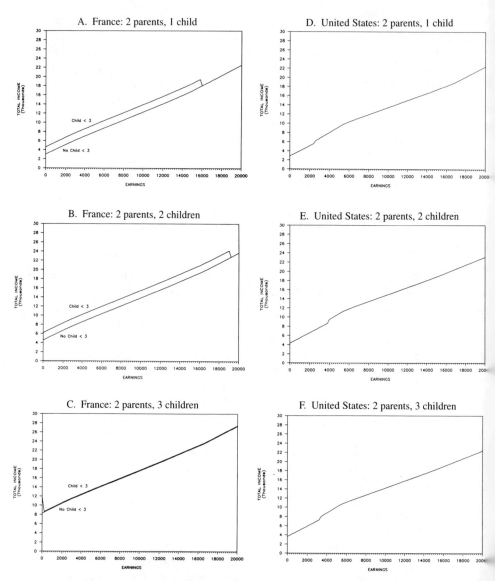

Figure 10.2   Income-earnings frontier for two-parent families in the United States and France

change in employment of small versus large families.[19] Third, one could compute a difference-in-difference-in-difference estimator, which computes the difference between the United States and France in the difference between large and small families in the change in employment when the youngest child reaches age 3:

(4) $(\Delta E_{fb} - \Delta E_{fs}) - (\Delta E_{ub} - \Delta E_{us}) = h(\Delta t_{fs}, \Delta G_{fs})$,

where f indicates France, u indicates United States, b indicates "big" family (three or more children), s indicates "small" family (two or fewer children), and the other terms are defined above.

10.3   Estimated Impacts

10.3.1   Data

The primary data source used for France is the French Enquête sur l'Emploi for 1987. This annual survey of 68,000 households in France asks detailed questions about labor force activity and family demographic characteristics. Given its large size and its focus on labor force measures, this survey is well suited for an analysis of the impact of time-limited transfer programs on employment. Unfortunately, this survey contains limited information on family income and thus does not make it possible to analyze the impact of these programs on economic well-being.

The primary data source used for the United States is the March Current Population Survey. This annual survey of over 60,000 households in the United States contains detailed information on family demographic characteristics, labor force activity, and family income sources.

In France, cohabiting couples with children represent a relatively large share of all families with children (4.5 percent), whereas they represent a relatively small share of families with children in the United States (1.4 percent). For purposes of this analysis, cohabiting couples are included with married couples. There are two reasons for this classification. First, in both countries, cohabiting couples are not legally eligible for transfer programs targeted toward single-parent families. Second, the women in this group exhibit employment patterns more similar to those of women in two-parent families than to women in single-parent families.[20]

Table 10.2 presents estimates of the employment rates of women with children, by age of youngest child in the family. The first three columns present estimates for France; the second three columns present estimates for the United States. This table classifies the patterns of employment in the preceding week by total employment (one or more hours), full-time work (thirty-five or more hours), and part-time work (one to thirty-four hours).

---

19. For example, women with three or more children may be more likely to remain out of the labor force altogether and thus show a smaller increase in employment than do women with one or two children.

20. One obtains very similar results if one drops cohabiting couples or if one treats them as a separate group in the analysis. However, if cohabitors are treated as a part of the single-parent family group, the estimated effects become much weaker.

Table 10.2   **Employment Rates of Women in the United States and France (standard errors in parentheses)**

Employment Measure/ Age of Youngest Child (in years)	France			United States		
	Single Parent, < 3 Kids	Two Parents, < 3 Kids	Two Parents, 3+ Kids	Single Parent, < 3 Kids	Two Parents, < 3 Kids	Two Parents, 3+ Kids
Total employment						
0–2	0.430	0.479	0.172	0.502	0.504	0.399
	(0.024)	(0.011)	(0.018)	(0.028)	(0.009)	(0.014)
3–5	0.657	0.561	0.292	0.612	0.593	0.487
	(0.027)	(0.010)	(0.019)	(0.023)	(0.011)	(0.016)
6–17	0.683	0.574	0.345	0.696	0.659	0.594
	(0.014)	(0.005)	(0.015)	(0.010)	(0.006)	(0.014)
Full-time employment						
0–2	0.340	0.335	0.082	0.378	0.293	0.199
	(0.023)	(0.011)	(0.015)	(0.028)	(0.008)	(0.012)
3–5	0.496	0.380	0.151	0.443	0.366	0.271
	(0.028)	(0.010)	(0.019)	(0.023)	(0.011)	(0.014)
6–17	0.530	0.391	0.189	0.550	0.442	0.347
	(0.015)	(0.005)	(0.016)	(0.011)	(0.006)	(0.014)
Part-time employment						
0–2	0.090	0.144	0.090	0.124	0.211	0.200
	(0.014)	(0.008)	(0.014)	(0.019)	(0.007)	(0.012)
3–5	0.161	0.181	0.141	0.169	0.227	0.216
	(0.021)	(0.008)	(0.018)	(0.017)	(0.009)	(0.013)
6–17	0.153	0.182	0.156	0.145	0.217	0.247
	(0.011)	(0.004)	(0.015)	(0.008)	(0.005)	(0.012)
Sample size	1,779	15,635	3,948	2,888	12,593	3,524

Sources: U.S. data from Current Population Survey (March 1987); French data from Enquête sur l'Emploi (1987).

Note: Sample includes women ages 23–58 who are heads of a single-parent family or are wives in a two-parent family with one or two children under age 18. Two-parent family includes cohabiting couples. "Full-time employment" indicates 35 or more hours of work last week; "part-time employment" indicates 1–34 hours. Estimates are computed using sample weights; unweighted estimates are very similar to weighted estimates presented here.

As shown, France's more generous assistance to single parents with young children does not appear to have permanently depressed the relative employment rate of single parents: while the employment rate of single parents with children under age 3 is lower in France than in the United States (43 percent versus 50 percent), the employment rate of single parents with a child age 3–5 is higher (66 percent versus 61 percent). By contrast, two-parent families with three or more children have consistently lower employment rates in France (17 percent versus 40 percent for a family with a youngest child age 0–2 and 29 percent versus 49 percent for a family with a youngest child age 3–5). Finally, two-parent families with one or two children have similar employment rates in both countries, despite the higher transfer payments in France.[21]

To isolate the impact of each of the time-limited programs addressed here, this paper will repeat the analysis for two different subsets of the population. To estimate the impact of the API program, it will focus on women with one or two children. To estimate the impact of the Parental Education Allowance, it will focus on married women with children. These estimates are provided below.

10.3.2   Single-Parent Family Programs (API)

Table 10.3 presents estimates of the difference between the employment rates of women with a youngest child age 3–5 versus age 0–2 for single- and two-parent families in each country. These estimates can be used to compute the estimators of the API program impact outlined in equations (1) through (3) above.

As shown, the employment rate of French single parents is 22.7 points higher for women with a youngest child age 0–2 than for those with one age 3–5, compared to a difference of 8.2 points for two-parent families. This yields a difference-in-difference estimate of the API program impact of 14.5 points (equation [2]). Part of this difference may reflect unmeasured factors unrelated to transfer benefits, since U.S. single parents also experienced a 2.1-point gain in employment relative to two-parent families when their youngest child reached age 3–5. Thus, the net effect attributable purely to the termination of French time-limited transfers is 12.4 points, the difference-in-difference-in-difference estimator of equation (3).

As shown in table 10.3, the impact of the API appears to operate exclusively through an increase in full-time employment: while the net increase in full-time employment for single parents was 11.9 points, part-time employment increased by 0.5 points. The estimates for both full-time and total employment are significantly different from zero at a 5 percent confidence level.

One problem with this analysis is that it does not control for differences in demographic characteristics that may affect the trend in employment rates of single parents in each country. As shown in table 10.4, there are substantial differences in the characteristics of single parents relative to two-parent families in each country. Single parents in the United States have both a higher relative concentration in minority groups and lower relative educational attainment than do single parents in France. These factors could influence the comparison of trends in employment in each country.

---

21. These comparisons may understate the extent of labor market attachment in France relative to the United States, since a larger share of nonemployed women in France have ties to a job through maternity or sick leave.

Table 10.3   Difference-in-Difference-in-Difference Estimates: Women with 1 or 2
Children (standard errors in parentheses)

	Single Parent	Two Parents	Difference[a]
Total employment			
France (3–5 minus 0–2)	0.227	0.082	0.145
	(0.036)	(0.015)	(0.039)
United States (3–5 minus 0–2)	0.110	0.089	0.021
	(0.036)	(0.014)	(0.039)
Net change	0.117	−0.007	0.124
	(0.051)	(0.021)	(0.055)
Full-time employment			
France (3–5 minus 0–2)	0.156	0.045	0.111
	(0.036)	(0.015)	(0.039)
United States (3–5 minus 0–2)	0.065	0.073	−0.008
	(0.036)	(0.014)	(0.039)
Change	0.091	−0.028	0.119
	(0.051)	(0.020)	(0.055)
Part-time employment			
France (3–5 minus 0–2)	0.071	0.037	0.034
	(0.025)	(0.011)	(0.027)
United States (3–5 minus 0–2)	0.045	0.016	0.029
	(0.025)	(0.011)	(0.028)
Change	0.026	0.021	0.005
	(0.036)	(0.016)	(0.039)

Sources: See table 10.2.
Note: See table 10.2.
[a]One-parent family minus two-parent family.

Table 10.5 presents probit estimates of the probability of employment, which control for demographic characteristics of families in each country. It presents estimates of the impact on total employment (columns 1–2), full-time employment (columns 3–4), and part-time employment (columns 5–6).

As shown, the demographic controls perform in the United States roughly as expected: employment rates are higher for more-educated women, for women ages 29–39, and for minorities (full-time employment measure only). In France, the results for age and education have the same sign as those for the United States, although the impact of education is smaller and the impact of age larger in magnitude. In addition, unlike in the United States, minority status appears to decrease rather than increase employment in France.

The key variable of interest is the interaction variable, France*single parent*kid35, which corresponds to the difference-in-difference-in-difference estimate shown in equation (3).[22] As shown, this coefficient is positive and sig-

22. The estimated regression is equivalent to the following equation:

$$(5) \qquad E = \delta_0 + \delta_1 Kid35 + \delta_2 Single + \delta_3 Single * Kid35 + \delta_4 France +$$
$$\delta_5 France * Kid35 + \delta_6 France * Single + \delta_7 France * Single * Kid35 ,$$

Table 10.4   **Mean Characteristics of Women with Children, France versus the United States (standard errors in parentheses)**

	France			United States		
	Single Parent, < 3 Kids	Two Parents, < 3 Kids	Two Parents, 3+ Kids	Single parent, < 3 Kids	Two Parents, < 3 Kids	Two Parents, 3+ Kids
Age < 28	0.111	0.153	0.082	0.161	0.172	0.164
	(0.008)	(0.003)	(0.004)	(0.003)	(0.007)	(0.014)
Age > 40	0.287	0.254	0.114	0.259	0.279	0.116
	(0.011)	(0.003)	(0.005)	(0.005)	(0.007)	(0.012)
One child	0.666	0.524		0.584	0.503	
	(0.011)	(0.004)		(0.009)	(0.004)	
Two children	0.334	0.476		0.416	0.497	
	(0.011)	(0.004)		(0.009)	(0.004)	
Three children			0.726			0.723
			(0.005)			(0.007)
Four or more children			0.274			0.277
			(0.007)			(0.007)
Minority	0.034	0.024	0.144	0.316	0.117	0.138
	(0.004)	(0.001)	(0.006)	(0.009)	(0.003)	(0.006)
Size < 100,000	0.437	0.577	0.612	0.212	0.263	0.288
	(0.012)	(0.004)	(0.008)	(0.009)	(0.004)	(0.007)
Size 100,000–199,000	0.104	0.076	0.069	0.067	0.064	0.063
	(0.007)	(0.002)	(0.004)	(0.005)	(0.002)	(0.004)
Size 200,000–1.999 million	0.244	0.190	0.176	0.384	0.366	0.332
	(0.010)	(0.003)	(0.006)	(0.009)	(0.004)	(0.008)
Size 2 million+	0.214	0.156	0.142	0.338	0.306	0.318
	(0.010)	(0.003)	(0.006)	(0.009)	(0.004)	(0.008)
< High school	0.761	0.740	0.803	0.222	0.123	0.209
	(0.010)	(0.002)	(0.006)	(0.008)	(0.004)	(0.007)
High school	0.089	0.099	0.061	0.410	0.438	0.418
	(0.007)	(0.003)	(0.004)	(0.009)	(0.004)	(0.008)
College	0.127	0.143	0.114	0.368	0.439	0.373
	(0.008)	(0.003)	(0.005)	(0.009)	(0.004)	(0.008)
Youngest child age 0–2	0.121	0.242	0.360	0.113	0.263	0.345
	(0.008)	(0.003)	(0.008)	(0.000)	(0.004)	(0.008)
Youngest child age 3–5	0.155	0.174	0.283	0.173	0.165	0.285
	(0.009)	(0.003)	(0.007)	(0.007)	(0.003)	(0.007)
Youngest child age 6–17	0.724	0.583	0.357	0.714	0.572	0.370
	(0.011)	(0.004)	(0.008)	(0.008)	(0.004)	(0.008)

Sources: See table 10.2.

Note: Sample includes women ages 23–58 who are heads of a single-parent family or are wives in a two-parent family with one or two children uner age 18. Two-parent family includes cohabiting couples. "Full-time employment" indicates 35 or more hours of work last week: "part-time employment" indicates 1–34 hours. Other variables are defined in appendix B. Estimates are computed using sample weights; unweighted estimates are very similar to weighted estimates presented here.

Table 10.5   **Probit Estimates of Employment Determinants, All Women with Less than Three Children**

	Total Employment		Full-Time		Part-Time	
	Beta	S.E.	Beta	S.E.	Beta	S.E.
Intercept	−0.541**	0.042	−1.058**	0.044	−0.904**	0.048
France	0.524**	0.051	0.670**	0.052	−0.160**	0.059
France*single parent	−0.120	0.117	−0.194*	0.119	0.059	0.155
France*single*kid35	0.285*	0.157	0.274*	0.157	0.050	0.196
France*Single*Kid617	0.221*	0.127	0.256*	0.129	0.006	0.166
Single parent	0.038	0.075	0.227**	0.077	−0.295**	0.095
Single*kid35	0.095	0.099	0.006	0.100	0.150	0.120
Single*kid617	0.146	0.082	0.047	0.083	0.126	0.102
France*kid35	−0.091*	0.049	−0.113*	0.050	0.040	0.056
France*kid617	−0.183**	0.044	−0.241	0.045	0.095*	0.050
Kid35	0.259**	0.036	0.215**	0.037	0.074	0.040
Kid617	0.511**	0.032	0.494**	0.032	0.025	0.035
Age < 28	−0.042	0.032	−0.049	0.033	0.002	0.036
Age > 40	−0.132**	0.027	−0.106**	0.026	−0.026	0.029
Minority	0.038	0.031	0.218**	0.030	−0.266**	0.037
High school	0.556**	0.031	0.445**	0.033	0.200**	0.037
College	0.753**	0.032	0.629**	0.033	0.201**	0.037
France*age < 28	−0.146**	0.045	−0.048	0.046	−0.169**	0.053
France*age > 40	−0.236**	0.036	−0.284**	0.036	0.044	0.041
France*minority	−1.029**	0.078	−1.092**	0.084	−0.184*	0.102
France*high school	−0.322**	0.046	−0.366**	0.047	0.030	0.053
France*college	−0.558**	0.043	−0.714**	0.044	0.183**	0.049
Log likelihood	−21323		−21318		−15629	

Sources: See table 10.2.

Note: Sample includes women ages 23–58 who are single parents or wives of a two-parent family with less than three children. Two-parent family includes cohabiting couples. "Part-time employment" indicates 1–34 hours of work last week; "full-time employment" indicates 35 or more hours. Regression includes controls for population size (100,000–199,000, 200,000–1.999 million, or 2 million−+); these controls enter separately and are interacted with France dummy. $N = 32,827$.

*Significant at 10 percent confidence level.

**Significant at 1 percent confidence level.

nificant in both the total employment and the full-time employment equations but is not significant in the part-time employment. These estimates suggest that the termination of time-limited benefits was associated with an increase in

---

while the difference-in-difference-in-difference estimator is equivalent to:

$$(6) \qquad (\Delta E_{fs} - \Delta E_{fm}) - (\Delta E_{us} - \Delta E_{uf}),$$

where δE is the difference in employment rates of women with a youngest child age 3–5 versus age 0–2, f = France, u = United States, s = single, and m = married. Substituting in terms from equation (5), the second term in equation (6) is equal to $[(\delta_0 + \delta_1 + \delta_2 + \delta_3) - (\delta_0 + \delta_2)] - [(\delta_0 + \delta_1) - \delta_0] = \delta_3$. Using similar logic, one can show that the first term in equation (5) is equal to $\delta_3 + \delta_7$. Thus, the difference between these two numbers is δ_7, the coefficient on France*single*kid35 in equation (5).

employment, which was driven primarily by an increase in full-time employment.

The top four rows of table 10.6 present simulations of the implied magnitude of the estimated impact of time-limited transfers shown in table 10.5. It presents estimates for both single- and two-parent families in each country who have a child age 0–2 and who have fewer than three children. For each group shown, this table uses the parameter estimates of table 10.5 to compute the average change in predicted employment before and after adding in a term equal to the coefficient on the interaction variable France*single parent*kid35. As noted above, this term is intended to capture the impact of time-limited transfers for single parents in France.

Table 10.6   **Simulated Impact of Time-Limited Benefits**

	Employment Rate		
	Total	Full-time	Part-time
Single-parent family benefits (table 10.5)			
Single parent, 1–2 children, youngest child 0–2			
France	11.0	10.2	0.8
United States	10.9	10.2	1.1
Two parents, 1–2 children, youngest child 0–2			
France	10.8	10.3	1.0
United States	10.9	9.9	1.5
Large-family benefits (table 10.9)			
Two parents, 1–2 children, youngest child 0–2			
France	8.9	7.8	4.5
United States	6.1	3.6	2.4
Two parents, 1–2 children, youngest child 0–2			
France	9.0	7.6	4.5
United States	8.9	6.3	4.3

Sources: See table 10.2.

Note: Sample includes women ages 23–58 who are heads of a single-parent family or are wives in a two-parent family with one or two children under age 18. Two-parent family includes cohabiting couples. "Full-time employment" indicates 35 or more hours of work last week; "part-time employment" indicates 1–34 hours. The top five rows of this table present simulations of the average impact of time-limited transfer programs for single-parent families on the employment rates of women with young children in each country; the bottom five rows present simulations of the impact of time-limited transfers for families with three or more children. For each group, it computes the average over all individuals of the function $\phi(XB + \delta) - \phi(XB)$, where XB is the cross-product of the vector of personal characteristics and the vector of estimated parameters from table 10.5 (top four rows) or table 10.8 (bottom four rows), and δ is the estimated impact of time-limited transfer programs. This table assumes that the impact of time-limited transfers is captured by the coefficient on the interaction variable France*single*kid35 in table 10.5 and the coefficient on France*3 children*kid35 in table 10.8 (see text note 22).

As shown in table 10.6, probit estimates imply an increase in the total employment rate of 10.8 to 11.0 points for each group, slightly less than the estimate from table 10.3 of 12.4 points. As before, this change largely reflects changes in full-time (9.9 to 10.3 points) rather than part-time employment (0.8 to 1.5 points).

10.3.3   Programs for Large Families (Parental Education Leave)

Table 10.7 presents estimates of the difference in employment between women with a youngest child 3–5 versus 0–2 years for married women with children, by number of children in the family (1–2 versus three-plus children). Following the approach outlined in equation (4), these estimates can be used to identify the impact of time-limited programs for large families.

As shown, French women with three or more children had an increase in employment of 3.8 points relative to women with one or two children when their youngest child reached age 3, compared to a relative decrease for the United States of 0.1 points. Thus, the difference-in-difference-in-difference

Table 10.7   Difference-in-Difference-in-Difference Estimates, Married Women with Children

	3+ Children	< 3 Children	Difference
Total employment			
France (3–5 minus 0–2)	0.120	0.082	0.038
	(0.017)	(0.015)	(0.023)
United States (3–5 minus 0–2)	0.088	0.089	−0.001
	(0.021)	(0.014)	(0.026)
Net change	0.032	−0.007	0.039
	(0.027)	(0.021)	(0.034)
Full-time employment			
France (3–5 minus 0–2)	0.069	0.045	0.024
	(0.013)	(0.015)	(0.020)
United States (3–5 minus 0–2)	0.071	0.073	−0.002
	(0.018)	(0.014)	(0.023)
Net change	−0.002	−0.028	0.026
	(0.023)	(0.020)	(0.030)
Part-time employment			
France (3–5 minus 0–2)	0.051	0.037	0.014
	(0.013)	(0.011)	(0.017)
United States (3–5 minus 0–2)	0.017	0.016	0.001
	(0.018)	(0.011)	(0.021)
Net change	0.034	0.021	0.013
	(0.022)	(0.016)	(0.027)

Sources: See table 10.2.

Note: Sample includes women ages 23–58 who are wives in a two-parent family with one or two children under age 18. Two-parent family includes cohabiting couples. "Full-time employment" indicates 35 or more hours of work last week; "part-time employment" indicates 1–34 hours. Estimates are computed using sample weights; unweighted estimates are very similar to weighted estimates presented here.

estimator is equal to a 3.9-point increase in employment. As shown, most of this increase reflects a net increase in full-time employment (2.6 points), compared to an increase in part-time employment (1.3 points). None of the estimates presented here is statistically significant at a 5 percent confidence level.

Table 10.8 presents probit estimates of the difference-in-difference-in-difference estimator, which include demographic controls for age, education, minority status, and population density. As before, estimates are presented for total employment (columns 1–2), full-time employment (columns 3–4), and part-time employment (columns 5–6).

Table 10.8   **Probit Estimates of Employment Determinants, Married Women with Children**

	Total		Full-time		Part-time	
	Beta (1)	S.E. (2)	Beta (3)	S.E. (4)	Beta (5)	S.E. (6)
Intercept	−0.473**	0.042	−0.927**	0.044	−1.004**	0.048
France	0.468**	0.050	0.548**	0.052	−0.049	0.058
France*3 children	−0.625**	0.064	−0.630**	0.073	−0.238**	0.074
France*3 children*kid35	0.233**	0.093	0.214*	0.103	0.147	0.106
France*3 children*kid617	0.177*	0.084	0.255*	0.092	0.020	0.096
3 children	−0.229**	0.043	−0.278**	0.048	−0.024	0.049
3 children*kid35	0.017	0.065	0.039	0.070	0.021	0.072
3 children*kid617	0.073	0.058	0.019	0.062	0.161**	0.064
France*kid35	−0.100*	0.049	−0.112*	0.050	0.020	0.056
France*kid617	−0.235**	0.044	−0.270**	0.045	0.066	0.050
Kid35	0.258**	0.036	0.210**	0.037	0.084*	0.040
Kid617	0.532**	0.032	0.504**	0.033	0.045	0.035
Age < 28	0.005	0.032	−0.009	0.033	0.012	0.035
Age > 40	−0.179**	0.027	−0.146**	0.027	−0.036	0.030
Minority	0.169**	0.033	0.406**	0.032	−0.344**	0.039
High school	0.474**	0.031	0.316**	0.033	0.275**	0.036
College	0.636**	0.032	0.448**	0.033	0.311**	0.036
France*age < 28	−0.228**	0.045	−0.102*	0.047	−0.227**	0.053
France*age > 40	−0.145**	0.037	−0.205**	0.037	0.042	0.041
France*minority	−1.167**	0.069	−1.258**	0.076	−0.298**	0.088
France*high school	−0.228**	0.045	−0.250**	0.047	−0.002	0.051
France*college	−0.387**	0.042	−0.487**	0.044	0.088*	0.047
Log likelihood	−22,980		−21,760		−16909	

Sources: See table 10.2.

Note: Sample includes married women ages 23–58 with children under age 18. Two-parent family includes cohabiting couples. "Full-time" indicates 35 or more hours of work last week; "part-time" indicates 1–34 hours. Regression includes controls for population size (100,000–199,000, 200,000–1.999 million, or 2 million–+); these controls enter separately and are interacted with France dummy. $N = 22,178$.

*Significantly different from zero at 10 percent confidence interval.

**Significant at 1 percent level.

As shown, the impact of demographic controls is roughly the same as before. Older women (over age 40) have lower total and full-time employment rates. Women with higher education levels have higher full-, part-time, and total employment rates. Minorities appear to work more full time and less part time in the United States, whereas they have lower rates of employment on all three employment measures in France.

The variable that corresponds to the difference-in-difference-in-difference estimator is the interaction variable France*3 children*kid35. This variable is positive and statistically significant in the total employment and the full-time employment equation, while it is insignificant in the part-time employment equation.

The bottom four rows of table 10.6 present estimates of the simulated impact of this program for two-parent families with a child under age 3 in each country, disaggregated by number of children (1–2 versus three-plus children). As shown, these estimates imply a much larger impact of time-limited benefits than the estimates presented in table 10.7: time-limited benefits increase the employment rate of French families with three or more children by 6.1 points, compared to the estimate from table 10.7 of 3.9 points. This reflects an increase in both full-time (3.6 points) and part-time employment (2.4 points).

Calculations not presented here suggest that the primary reason that the results are much stronger in the probit specification than in the simple tabulations of table 10.7 is that each approach assumes a different functional form.[23] In particular, table 10.7 assumes that time-limited benefits have the same absolute effect on the probability of employment on all groups within the population, whereas tables 10.6 and 10.8 allow the impact to vary with the initial employment rate of each group. These estimates may be more sensitive to functional form than the estimates presented for single parents, because there is a greater divergence between the employment rates of large and small families than there is between single- and two-parent families.

10.4   Conclusion

The French model offers a unique resolution to the conflict between social protection and economic flexibility. France offers extensive social protection to families when their children are young and then, by cutting back cash transfers and increasing publicly subsidized day care, promotes the work effort of women when their youngest child reaches age 3. By contrast, the United States provides cash assistance to single parents until their youngest child reaches age 18, thus encouraging them to rely on welfare on a long-term basis.

---

23. A probit estimate with no demographic controls produces estimates similar to those presented in table 10.8, suggesting that the difference is not driven by the addition of demographic controls. In addition, a linear regression model with the same controls shown in table 10.8 yielded estimates similar to those found in table 10.7, further confirming that differences in functional form are causing the estimates to differ.

This paper suggests that the French policy of placing a time limit on transfer payments can provide a powerful incentive for women to enter the labor force. Simulations suggest that the 40 percent to 44 percent reduction in transfers to single parents when their youngest child reaches age 3 results in an increase in their employment rate of 11 points, while the 26 percent to 30 percent reduction in transfers to families with three or more children increases the employment rate of large families in France by 6 points. These estimates imply an elasticity of employment with respect to transfer maximums of 0.55 to 0.59 for single parents and of 1.17 to 1.40 for large families.[24]

It is not possible at this point to assess whether such a policy would be advantageous for the United States. To do so, one would want to know more about how time-limited transfers affect the economic well-being of families and children. In addition, one would want to know how these policies affect broader measures of economic flexibility such as entry onto welfare, investment in education or training, and the educational development of children.

It is clear, however, that the United States would be unlikely to reduce total short-run expenditures if it adopted the French system of cutting back welfare and expanding public day care when the youngest child reaches age 3. Assuming the same per child daycare cost and the same dollar reduction in transfers as found in France, the United States would realize a reduction in expenditures of $400 per family if it could precisely target daycare subsidies toward the current AFDC recipient pool.[25] However, if as in France the United States were to make day care broadly available to families with children, its short-run expenditures on families with children would increase substantially.

Finally, it is important to stress that one reason that the French system of time-limited transfer payments may be effective in integrating women into the labor force is that France provides extensive support to working families through its systems of universal public day care, universal medical insurance, universal family allowances, and federally mandated maternity leave. If these programs were not also in place, it is not clear that time-limited welfare programs would have the same impact in the United States as they have had in France.

24. The much larger elasticity for large families is due to the very low initial employment rate for this group.
25. This estimate assumes reductions in transfer payments equal to those shown in table 10.1, a family size distribution equal to that found in the U.S. Current Population Survey (1987), and a per child cost of public nursery school of $2,100, as documented in Bergmann (1992).

Appendix A

Transfer Programs for Women with Children (nonelderly, non–health related)

French Programs as of 1 January 1987

The source of the information in this section is Lefebvre (1987). In France, all family benefits are calculated with respect to a monthly base salary. This monthly base amount in 1987 was equal to $292 (1990 U.S. dollars).

Family Allowance

The Family Allowance program provides non-means-tested monthly payments to families with two or more children. Monthly payment varies by number of children: 32 percent of base amount if two children, 73 percent if three children, and 114 percent if four children. In addition, the payment is increased by 9 percent of the monthly base for each child age 10–14 and by 16 percent for each child age 15 or more, except when the child is the eldest of a family with fewer than three children.

Family Support Allowance

Non-means-tested monthly payments to children with an absent parent are provided by the Family Support Allowance. Monthly payment is equal to 30 percent of monthly base if two parents are missing, 22.5 percent if one parent is missing.

Parental Education Allowance

Parents of three or more children who take leave from employment following the birth of a child receive a monthly Parental Education Allowance of 142.57 percent of the monthly base. To qualify, the parent must have worked at least two years in the ten years preceding the birth of the child and must completely stop working after the child is born. The allowance is paid until the youngest child reaches age 3 or the parent reenters the labor force. In the year before the youngest child reaches age 3, the parent may receive half of the allowance if he or she works or enters a training program on a part-time basis. Families may claim only one allowance per family. This allowance may not be combined with the Young Child Allowance or unemployment insurance; however, families may combine this payment with Family Allowances.

Allowance to Young Children

The Allowance to Young Children program provides monthly cash payments of 45.95 percent of the monthly base to families with children under age 3. The "short form" of this program is not means-tested and lasts from the fourth month of pregnancy until the third month after childbirth. The "long form" of this program continues until the youngest child reaches age 3 if families meet an income test: gross family income must fall below $23,700 for a single parent with one child or a two-parent family with one child in which both parents are working, and below $18,000 for a two-parent family with one child in which only one parent is working. The income eligibility cutoff increases by $2,600 if the family has a second child and by an additional $3,100 for the third and any subsequent child.

Large-Family Supplement

Through the Large-Family Supplement program, a monthly payment of 41.65 percent of the monthly base is available to families who have three or more children all over the age of 3. To qualify for assistance, the family must meet an income test (described above, under "Allowance to Young Children").

Return to School Allowance

Low-income families with school-aged children are entitled to the Return to School Allowance, an annual payment equal to 20 percent of the monthly base for each child age 6–16 who is registered in school. To qualify for assistance, a family with one child must have total income below $12,600. This income cutoff is increased by $2,900 for each additional child.

Single-Parent Allowance

The Single-Parent Allowance provides payment to single-parent families with children under age 3 or to women who have children of any age and have recently experienced a divorce/separation from or death of spouse. Payments may be made for twelve consecutive months within eighteen months following date of divorce, separation, or spouse's death or until youngest child reaches age 3. Maximum monthly benefit amount for a single parent with one child is equal to 200 percent of monthly base (150 percent for a pregnant woman) and is increased by 50 percent of the monthly base for each additional child. The total benefit is reduced by one dollar for every dollar of countable income. Countable income does not include the Allowance to Young Children (short form) or the Return to School Allowance.

Housing Allowance

The Housing Allowance program provides a monthly payment to low-income households with a dependent child or a dependent elderly or handicapped adult. In addition, newly married young (under age 40) couples without children may qualify for up to five years. Housing must meet minimum quality standards. The total allowance is determined by the formula:

Housing allowance $= K * (L + C - L^0)$, where

$K =$ $.90$ $-$ Resources $/$ $\{\$24,900 * [1 + (.4 * \text{Number of children})]\}$

$L =$ Actual rent up to a ceiling that varies by family size and location. Maximum monthly rent is $186 for single individual living alone, $220 for a family with one or two dependents, and $246 for family with three dependents.

$C =$ $55 for a family size of two, with an increment of $9.60 for each additional family member. This is intended to adjust for utility costs.

$L^0 =$ Minimum annual rent contribution of family. This is equal to 0 percent of first $1,650 of annual income, 15 percent of income between $1,650 and $2,400, 26 percent of income between $2,400 and $4,800, and 36 percent of income greater than $4,800. This amount is then increased by $70.

U.S. Transfer Programs as of 1 January 1987

The source of the information in this section is U.S. House of Representatives, Committee on Ways and Means (1987).

Aid to Families with Dependent Children (AFDC)

AFDC is a joint federal-state program that provides cash payments to low-income families with children, primarily to single-parent families. Some states allow two-parent households to receive AFDC under stricter eligibility rules; however, in 1987, two-parent families represented only 6 percent of all AFDC families. A 66 percent tax rate on earnings applies for the first four months of recipiency and rises to 100 percent thereafter. The median state maximum benefit for a family of three is $400 per month (lowest state $133, highest state $845; the latter is an outlier, as the next highest state pays $696 per month).

Food Stamps

The Food Stamp Program provides low-income families and individuals with coupons that can be used to purchase food. The federal government establishes both eligibility and benefit levels. Maximum food stamps benefit is $91 for an individual, $168 for a family of two, $242 for a family of three, $306 for a family of four, and $363 for a family of five. The food stamp benefit is reduced by $0.30 for every dollar of net income after deductions. Deductions include (1) a standard deduction of $110, (2) 20 percent of earnings, (3) a deduction of up to $168 for expenditures on shelter over 50 percent of countable income, and (4) a dependent childcare deduction of up to $180.

Earned Income Tax Credit (EITC)

The EITC is available to low-income families with children under age 18. It does not vary with family size. Credit is 14 percent of earnings to a maximum of $900. The amount of the credit is decreased by $0.10 for every $1 of earnings above $7,300. Credit is refundable to those without tax liabilities.

Appendix B
Data Sources

Current Population Survey (CPS)

The March Current Population Survey is an annual survey of over 60,000 households conducted by the U.S. Bureau of the Census. It contains detailed information on family demographic characteristics, income, and employment over the previous year. It is available on tape from the U.S. Bureau of the Census.

Enquête sur l'Emploi

The Enquête sur l'Emploi is an annual survey of 68,000 households in France conducted by the Institut National de la Statistique et des Études Economiques (INSEE). It contains detailed information on labor force activity and family demographic characteristics. Unfortunately, it contains limited information on family income or income sources. It is available on tape from the French Observatoire Economique de Paris (OEP).

Sample Construction

The sample includes women ages 23–58 who are heads of a single-parent family or are wives in a two-parent family with at least one child under age 18. Since the French data do not make it possible to readily identify subfamilies, this analysis only includes the primary family in each household.

This analysis defines nonmarried couples living together in the same household to be equivalent to married couples. In the French data, cohabiting couples are readily identifiable; in the U.S. data, they must be imputed. Thus, this analysis assumes that any male and female who live together in the same household who differ in age by less than ten years are a cohabiting couple. This process identified as cohabiting couples 4.5 percent of families with children in France and 1.4 percent of families with children in the United States.

Variable Definitions

The definitions of the variables used in the regression analysis are as follows:

Employed	= 1 if worked one or more hours in last week
Employed full time	= 1 if worked thirty-five or more hours in last week
Single parent	= 1 if single-parent family

Kid35	= 1 if youngest child in family is age 3–5
Kid617	= 1 if youngest child in family is age 6–17
Age < 28	= 1 if age of mother is less than 28 years
Age > 40	= 1 if age of mother is greater than 40 years
Minority	= 1 if mother is nonwhite in the United States and non-European in France
Size 100,000–199,000	= 1 if city size is 100,000–199,000
Size 200,000–1.999 million	= 1 if city size is 200,000–1.999 million
Size 2 million +	= 1 if city size is 2 million–plus
High school	= 1 if twelve years of school in United States or baccaulauréat in France
Post–high school	= 1 if thirteen or more years school in United States, degree beyond baccaulauréat in France

All variables equal zero if they do not satisfy the criteria specified above.

References

Bergmann, B. 1992. Can we afford to save our children? Cost and structure of government programs for children in the U.S. and France. American University Mimeograph.

Blau, F., and A. Grossberg. 1990. Maternal labor supply and children's cognitive development. NBER Working Paper no. 3536. Cambridge, Mass.: National Bureau of Economic Research.

Centre d'Étude des Revenus et des Coûts. 1987. Familles Nombreuses, Mères Isolées, Situation Économique et Vulnérabilité. Documents du Centre d'Étude des Revenus et des Coûts no. 85. Paris.

Ellwood, D. 1988. Poor support: Poverty in the American family. New York: Basic Books.

Finn-Stevenson, M., and E. Trzcinski. 1991. Mandated leave: An analysis of federal and state legislation. American Journal of Orthopsychiatry 61 (4): 567–75.

International Monetary Fund. 1992. International financial statistics yearbook. Washington D.C.: International Monetary Fund.

Jenson, J., and R. Kantrow. 1990. Labor market and family policy in France: An intersecting complex for dealing with poverty. In The feminization of poverty: Only in America? ed. G. Schaffner Goldberg and E. Kremen. New York: Greenwood Press.

Kamerman, S. 1991. Child care policies and programs: An international overview. Journal of Social Issues 47 (2): 179–96.

Lefaucheur, N. 1991. Policies towards lone parents: Social categories and social policies. Centre National de la Recherche Scientifique. Mimeograph.

Lefebvre, F. 1987. *Memento pratique Francis Lefebvre—social 1987.* Paris: Francis Lefebvre.

Moffit, R. 1992. Incentive effects of the U.S. welfare system: A review. *Journal of Economic Literature* 30 (1): 1–61.

Murray, C. 1984. *Losing ground: American social policy 1950–1980.* New York: Basic Books.

Organization for Economic Cooperation and Development (OECD). 1987. *Purchasing power parities and real expenditures, 1985.* Paris: OECD.

Ray, J. C., B. Jeandidier, and L. S. Carvoyeur. 1988. *Activité Féminine, Isolement et Prestations Familiales: Une Comparaison International.* Faculté de Droit, University of Nancy.

Robins, P. 1991. Child care policy and research: An economist's perspective. In *The economics of child care,* ed. David Blau. New York: Russell Sage Foundation.

Rosa, J.-J., and R. Launois. 1990. France. *Advances in health economics and health services research* 11, supplement 1.

Sawhill, I. 1988. Poverty in the U.S.: Why is it so persistent? *Journal of Economic Literature* 26:1073–119.

Starzec, C., and M.-G. David. 1991. France: A diversity of policy options. In *Child care, parental leave, and the under 3s: Policy innovation in Europe,* ed. S. Kamerman and A. Kahn. New York: Auburn House.

Trzcinski, E., and W. Alpert. 1994. Changes in pregnancy and parental leave benefits in the U.S. and Canada: Judicial decisions and legislation. *Journal of Human Resources.* Forthcoming.

U.S. Department of Commerce, Bureau of the Census. 1990. Who's minding the kids? Child care arrangements, winter 1986–7. Current Population Reports Series P-70, no. 20. Washington D.C.: U.S. Government Printing Office.

U.S. General Accounting Office. 1989. Child care funding sources coordination and service availability. Washington, D.C.: U.S. Government Printing Office.

U.S. House of Representatives, Committee on Ways and Means. 1987 and selected years. *Background material and data on programs within the jurisdiction of the Committee on Ways and Means.* Washington D.C.: U.S. Government Printing Office.

Wilson, W. J. 1987. *The truly disadvantaged: The inner city, the underclass, and public policy.* Chicago: University of Chicago Press.

11 Three Regimes of Child Care: The United States, the Netherlands, and Sweden

Siv Gustafsson and Frank P. Stafford

Differences in social protection across countries have received greater attention as national economies have become more interconnected through trade and finance. It has been shown that different levels of social protection are factors shaping the competitive position of national partners in an economic union (Abraham 1991). The long-term productivity of a nation's export sectors may be influenced favorably or unfavorably by social protection. To illustrate, well-designed income insurance (Friedman 1953; Stafford 1977; Varian 1980; Milgrom and Roberts 1992) can encourage productive division of labor and improve the market performance of an economy. On the other hand, some policymakers see a minimal level of social protection and insurance as a way to realize gains in competition with countries having more-generous systems. This has created concern in European countries over England's perceived move toward reduced social insurance.

Recent work has emphasized the idea that a country's wage growth will depend on the difference between the rate of growth of its own export sector productivity and productivity growth in the corresponding sectors of its competitors (Krugman 1979; Johnson and Stafford 1992, 1993). In the basic Johnson-Stafford model of world trade (with unitary price and income elasticities of demand), the real wage can be expressed as an increasing function of the country's own productivity in its exportables and its nontraded goods sector and as a decreasing function of the productivity of its competitors in its exportables. If the social protection system acts either as a force improving the productivity of the different sectors of an economy on the one hand or as a costly burden on the other (e.g., U.S. health insurance), the system will affect a country's position in world trade and thereby its standard of living.

Siv Gustafsson is professor of economics at the University of Amsterdam. Frank P. Stafford is professor of economics at the University of Michigan.

Childcare arrangements shape the payoff to educational quality, a particular interest in the advanced industrial economies. Preschool experiences are of major significance for cognitive function in children, so childcare arrangements have an important impact on long-term growth and competitiveness, even if the links are difficult to measure. At the same time, childcare arrangements enable women to realize the market payoff from their formal schooling.

There is an emerging view that advanced industrial economies need a well-trained career work force in order to compete in world markets and that women will constitute a growing share of such workers. But for women with children to have lifetime labor market careers, they need to obtain child care to permit the career development and on-the-job training emphasized in life-cycle theories of human capital formation. Otherwise, they can be expected to have a shallow labor market profile: attenuated skill formation, fewer market hours, and early retirement (Ryder, Stafford, and Stephan 1976, 666). A paucity of resources for child care could be consistent with career development but would have long-term costs for the well-being of the children and their development. On the other hand, child care uses both market and nonmarket resources, and some extensive programs and family sacrifices to attain better child well-being may facilitate added market work that is just not worth the cost.

In this paper, we study the nature and functioning of the childcare market and childcare policies in Sweden, the Netherlands and the United States. These three countries, despite being at what might be regarded as similar levels of industrialization, have dramatically different regimes under which families secure child care to facilitate labor market activity of young women. Perceived economic pressures and wage slowdowns in all three countries will undoubtedly shape the debate on the expansion or reduction of the public policy role in these and other areas of social protection.

Our thesis is that to understand both the context and features of these specific programs, one needs a broader framework to understand the historical and conceptual origins of the welfare concept in each country. As outlined in section 11.1, the welfare concept, in turn, shapes the system of social protection and its modification in light of emerging economic forces. From this outline, section 11.2 provides a historical interpretation of the welfare regime concept developed in each of the three countries and then describes the salient features of current childcare, leave, and related policies.

Section 11.3 presents the basic descriptive differences in the use of public programs and market and informal arrangements that constitute the childcare subsystem of the larger social welfare system in the three countries. In this section, we summarize some of the existing research findings on the use of the systems and, utilizing three separate microdata sets (one for each country), provide some comparative differences in earnings growth and behavioral responses in terms of labor force participation and price sensitivity. In section 11.4, we offer a brief conclusion.

11.1   Different Welfare Regimes

In simplest form, the three social protection, or welfare, regimes that apply to these three countries are residual, institutional (or consensus), and corporate (Esping-Andersen 1990).

11.1.1   Residual

In the residual welfare state conception of the United States, the state is involved only when the family or market fails, and this is presumed to apply to a small share, or residual, of the population. Programs such as Head Start and the Family Support Act of 1988 are centered on the idea that intervention is needed to encourage "positive effects of preschool on disadvantaged children" and that the "needs of employed mothers [be met] while providing developmentally appropriate experiences for children" (Hofferth et al. 1991, 8). While there is some public support for child care extending beyond lower-middle income groups, this support is in the form of tax credits. Tax credits as a policy allow minimum government involvement and facilitate a wide range of choice in the market. Guarantees of unpaid leave have been opposed on the grounds that the firm and its employees can form private agreements on an individualized market basis.

11.1.2   Institutional, or Consensus

The virtual opposite of the residualist approach is the case of an institutional welfare state such as Sweden and other Scandinavian countries. There programs such as parental leave and child care are regarded as being available for everyone—in principle, although in practice the more educated are more likely to avoid being rationed from spaces (Gustafsson and Stafford 1992). The service provided is regarded as essential and universal; the belief is that if it were not available, some parents and children would be denied a basic component of the standard of living.

11.1.3   Corporate

The corporate welfare state is seen as one in which the social policy is shaped by the interplay of powerful political interest groups. In the case of the Netherlands, the rather modest public daycare program and features of related policies affecting women in the job market are seen as the result of conflicting, historical interests of the church. Both Catholics and Protestants feared that a high birthrate of the rival religion would undermine their political power; for this reason, both interests had a family perspective and supported policies to increase fertility.

Based on the distinction between residual and institutional welfare states (Titmuss 1958), we might expect different responses to emerging economic pressures. Under the market approach, a political minority dependent on public benefits may lose out when economic pressure redirects attention to the well-being of the majority. Witness the 1992 U.S. presidential campaign proposals to enact "tax cuts for the middle class." In the consensus case, with slow economic growth, pressure to cut back spending to balance the budget may be more than offset by pressure to expand the program coverage and serve more broadly, even if per user benefits are reduced somewhat.

Our empirical work verifies that the Netherlands as a corporate-style regime is more than just an "in-between" case. In the context of encouraging the family, the church saw market work as inhibiting the size and character of the traditional family, so policies to encourage women's market work were not developed in the Netherlands.[1] Research indicates that even today the small public daycare program in the Netherlands is used about equally by labor market participants and by nonparticipants (Groot and Maassen van den Brink 1992) and that a woman's religious orientation has a measurable impact on labor force participation in the Netherlands but not in the United States (section 11.3.3). In contrast, the extensive Swedish parental leave and daycare programs are for the nearly exclusive use of labor market participants, and religion plays a minor role.

Comparing across the three countries, there is a type of consistency among the set of policies in each country. The result of the corporatist interplay in Holland was not just the shaping of a given policy but the character of a *set* of related policies: marriage bars on women's market work (historically), the limited extent of parental leave benefits, and public day care. The Swedish parental leave and childcare and related programs (including taxes) fit together and are part of the country's overall system.

The great social policy differences across what one might assume to be countries with rather similar levels of industrialization can be seen in the overview comparisons of the three countries and other industrialized nations from a recent study (Sundström and Stafford 1992, presented as table 11.1). We feel that understanding some of the reasons for these broad intercountry differences is essential. The approach of simply assessing the traditional responses to policy parameters, which is common in the literature of economic evaluation, is not sufficient.

11.2   Childcare Policies: Origins and Differences

Public childcare programs in the United States are very rare and are operated at the local level. The main policies supporting child care are tax deductibility of childcare expenses on federal tax schedules and some modest state supplements (Michalopoulos, Robins, and Garfinkel 1992). Only recently has very

---

1. This is quite apart from the validity of the implicit hypothesis that market work need limit fertility over the range observed across industrialized economies. Both Ireland and Sweden currently have very high total fertility rates, over 2.0, but the labor force participation of women is more than twice as high in Sweden. See table 11.1.

Table 11.1 Total Fertility Rate (TFR), Female Labor Force Participation Rate (FLFPR), and Statutory Parental Leave Benefits in Selected OECD Countries

	TFR 1988	FLFPR 1988 (%)	Maximum Weeks of Maternity Leave[a] 1989/90	Benefit Rate 1989/90 weeks (w), %, money	Employer or Tax Financed[b]	Separate or Joint Taxation	Substantial Day Care or Not	Public Consumption as Share of GNP 1988 (%)
Australia	1.9[c]	59.0	52	0	—	Separate	No	17.4
Austria	1.44	53.7	60	16w 100% + 44w S 4, 524–6,725	Tax	Separate	No	18.4
Belgium	1.57	51.4	14	4.5w 100% + 8.5w 80%	Tax	Joint	No	15.3
Canada	1.7[d]	66.6	17–18[e]	60% up to a ceiling	Tax	Separate	No	18.8
Denmark	1.56	78.3	28	90%	Both	Separate	Yes	26.0
Finland	1.7	73.0	52	80%	Tax	Separate	Yes	20.2
France	1.82	55.7	16–28[g]	84%	Tax	Separate	Yes	18.6
West Germany	1.42	54.4	14	100%	Both	Joint	No	19.5
Greece	1.52	43.4	14	100%	Tax	Joint	No	20.6
Ireland	2.17	37.6	14	75%	Tax	Joint	No	16.7
Italy	1.34	43.9	47	22w 80% + 25w 30%	Tax	Separate	No	17.2
Japan	1.66	58.4	14	60%	Employer	Joint	No	9.3
Luxembourg	1.51	47.6	16	100%	Tax	Joint	No	17.0
Netherlands	1.55	51.6	16	100%	Tax	Separate	No	15.7
New Zealand	1.5[c]	62.0	14	0	—	Separate	No	17.5
Norway	1.84	72.8	22	100%	Tax	Joint	No	20.6

(continued)

Table 11.1 (continued)

	TFR 1988	FLFPR 1988 (%)	Maximum Weeks of Maternity Leave[a] 1989/90	Benefit Rate 1989/90, %, money weeks (w), %, money	Employer or Tax Financed[b]	Separate or Joint Taxation	Substantial Day Care or Not	Public Consumption as Share of GNP 1988 (%)
Portugal	1.53	59.1	13	100%	Tax	Joint	No	16.0
Spain	1.38	39.4	14	75%	Tax	Joint	No	14.3
Sweden	1.96	80.1	65	52w 90% + 13w SKr 60/day	Tax	Separate	Yes	26.0
United Kingdom	1.84	63.5	18	6w 90% + 12w £36.25	Tax	Separate	No	19.9
United States	1.8[c]	66.9	0	0	—	Joint	No	18.3

Sources: TFR: Eurostat (1991); OECD (1988), 204. FLFPR: OECD (1990), 144. Leave benefits: OECD (1990), 200. FLFPR: OECD (1990), 144; Stein (1989); Badelt (1991); David and Starzec (1991); Nordisk statistisk sekretariat (1990). Separate taxation: OECD (1990), 166, updated.

[a]In Denmark and Ireland four weeks must be used prior to birth; in France six–ten weeks; in Germany, Greece, the Netherlands, and Japan six weeks; in Italy and Austria eight weeks.

[b]Employers' and employees' mandatory social insurance contributions are here considered a form of tax.

[c]1986.

[d]1981.

[e]In some provinces seventeen weeks, in others eighteen.

[f]Benefits are 90 percent of earnings up to a ceiling of DKr 2,397 per week. However, some white-collar workers (e.g., civil servants) get negotiated benefits equal to their full wage from their employer.

[g]Sixteen weeks for the first and second child, twenty-eight weeks for third or higher.

limited legislation allowing women to take unpaid leave from an employer been proposed and enacted (Family Leave Act). Until the 1950s it was common for there to be marriage and maternity bars on women's employment (Goldin 1990). In contrast, the right to unpaid maternal leave at childbirth dates back to 1939 in Sweden (Sundström and Stafford 1992; Gustafsson 1984), and paid leave dates back to 1962 (Gustafsson 1984).

From the perspective of most U.S. economists, even those in the field of human resources, the rationale for public provision of childcare services is seen as very weak. The usual justification for government intervention is to correct market failures arising from public goods or externalities. In addition, there is sometimes a case made for social insurance on the grounds of adverse selection and contract compliance in private markets. This is the implicit and sometimes explicit logic for unemployment insurance. Perhaps the closest justification for public child care would be as a merit good or to correct an externality arising from insufficient resources devoted to child care under choices made by individual parents or families.

This contemporary U.S. perspective on child care is consistent with the view of Nassau Senior, who was responsible for reforming the Poor Laws, and later Manchester liberals who emphasized individual choice and argued that social protection be offered in terms of cash payments (Esping-Andersen 1990, 10). In terms of the residualist approach discussed by Titmuss (1958), the market and family are regarded as the main and preponderant sources of such services; only those who cannot use the market or who have family problems are seen as needing public services.

It has been argued that the extent to which economic goods are provided through the public sector will depend on the variance in consumption preferences of voters. If there is a great deal of variance, consensus about what and how much to consume via public provision, even of purely public goods, will be difficult to achieve, and a greater reliance will be placed on the market (Buchanan and Tullock 1965).

Given a lack of consensus about the appropriate form and level of resources for preschool children, public child care in the United States is often discussed solely as an antipoverty program for lower-income groups to ensure child development and/or to enable women on welfare to become self-sufficient via labor market skills. Virtually all U.S. programs with this concept have small benefit levels, are applicable only to a narrowly defined eligible population, and are often proposed to be converted to a cash basis (Rainwater, Rein, and Schwartz 1986).

Contributory social insurance programs in the United States provide a sharp contrast to such programs for the poor. Social Security is close to universally applicable (with some anomalous exceptions such as federal civil servants) and is close to being politically sacred. The level of revenues from Social Security and other payroll taxes to fund social insurance (including unemployment and disability insurance) are almost as large as those from personal income taxes.

Yet there has been little in the way of calls to scale back these social insurance programs. The reason appears to be that benefits are based on contributions, and though some receive actuarial present values of benefits in excess of contributions, there is a sufficient element of insurance that the system is not regarded as an income transfer program.

The potential relevance of the Social Security experience for public child care is that public child care is unlikely to get much support as a policy in the United States unless it is relatively universal. Possibly, public child care could be offered on a contributory basis if those who used it would face a *future tax surcharge rate* to pay off the cost for their children. Another design element that could be attractive from the U.S. perspective is to make child care a cash benefit via the tax system, and much of what has been done is along these lines, via tax deductibility of childcare expenses. Without design elements emphasizing private choice and a contributory connection to benefits received, public child care or parental leave is unlikely to get much support as a policy in the United States.

While the United States was historically a leader in developing free public education,[2] the family and market orientation seems to have been a continuing factor shaping policy toward very young children. Care of preschool children was regarded as a public obligation only in cases of poverty, widowhood, or family abandonment of children. The main dialogue was over the question of whether aid should be outside the home (in orphanages or the poorhouse) or within the home.

A major change was the shift toward an in-home approach during the Progressive era (1900–17) (Garfinkel and McLanahan 1986, 97) with mother-only families receiving cash benefits on the condition that the child be living in a "suitable home," defined diversely to include religious training, school performance of the child, and absence of male boarders. Very seldom did black families receive benefits, and there were usually restrictions on benefits to never-married women. That only a small share of the population received any benefits is consistent with the residualist hypothesis about the nature of U.S. welfare programs. Market work of the mother was not a major objective of these early programs of aid to dependent children.

Contemporary U.S. policy discussion has focused on market-based expansions of child care with emphasis on family need. The Child Care and Development Block Grant passed by the 101st Congress in October 1990 authorized new grants to states to fund childcare assistance to low- and moderate-income families (Hofferth and Wissoker 1992), an expansion of existing tax credits for low-income parents, and added funding for Head Start (Golonka and Ooms 1991). This set of new initiatives can be classified into price reductions, in-

2. As of 1803, the state of Ohio had begun the movement toward free public education in the United States. By 1848 virtually all of the United States had mandatory, free public education, well ahead of most European countries (Garfinkel and McLanahan 1986).

come increases, and subsidies for quality of child care. Consistent with long-standing traditions, these initiatives are seen as only for the use of the segment of the population with limited income, and the actual services are purchased through the market and not from government providers.

The current U.S. childcare system is, for most parents, a market- and family-based system and one that is very diverse in terms of the methods used for child care. Of employed women with preschool-age children, 30 percent are cared for primarily by a parent, 26 percent in centers, (childcare centers, nursery schools) 19 percent in family day care, 18 percent by other relatives, 4 percent by an in-home provider, and the balance (3 percent) by other forms of care (Hofferth et al. 1991). The use of centers and family day care is much higher for women working full time (54 percent) than for those working part time (31 percent), which in turn is higher than for those not employed (17 percent).

In sharp contrast to the United States and the Netherlands, Sweden has a very extensive program of day care and parental leave. Some influences of distant history have shaped today's policy, but the large-scale expansion of public day care and parental leave dates from more recent times, primarily 1974 on. Here we will offer some brief remarks on the social history of the Netherlands and Sweden that has shaped the context for modern policy in these countries.

Our view is that much of the difference in the current-day systems is historical-cultural and connects to the Esping-Andersen thesis of distinct regimes of social protection. This thesis contrasts with the usual functional approach of most economic thinking, which emphasizes system design as the result of solving a problem: if all three countries have industrial market economies, one would expect similarity in the problems and therefore in the solutions. However, there may not be a strong uniqueness to the solution of common problems; in addition, path dependence in the form of history can be important even if there is some "best" way.

In this historical, or path-dependent, context the difference between Sweden and the Netherlands is fascinating. At the time of the Reformation, the Swedish political leader, Gustav Wasa, believed that he could consolidate his power by creating a uniformly Protestant country. This he accomplished over the period 1526–41, shortly after Martin Luther began the Reformation in 1517 in Wittenberg, Germany. In the Netherlands there was a protracted standoff between Protestants and Catholics that persisted for centuries and that divided, or "columnized," all aspects of economic and social life with separate banks, universities (the "free" in the Free University of Amsterdam meant free to pursue instruction according to the principles of the Dutch Reformed Church), companies, unions, neighborhoods, and social clubs. For fear of losing political control, both factions resisted anything perceived as reducing their constituency, and this persisted after World War II.

In this setting, a whole collection of policies evolved predicated on preserving a strong traditional family and, it was believed, high fertility. The labor market activity of Dutch married women was regarded as competing with these family values, and this contributed to enactment of overt restrictions on women's employment. For example, married female schoolteachers were dismissed under a 1934 provision (van Kessel, Kuperus, and Pott-Buter 1986). The Netherlands did, in fact, have higher fertility until quite recently. As of the late 1960s, the total fertility rate was above 2.5 in the Netherlands and below 2.0 in Sweden (Gustafsson 1992b).

Since the 1970s, religion has had reduced scope in Dutch politics, and fertility has declined (see table 11.1). Market work of younger women has risen dramatically in the 1980s. As of 1990, 82 percent of married women under age 40 without children were labor market participants, compared to 28 percent of those aged 40 to 66 (OSA 1991). Yet certain traditional elements remain. Women with young children are not supported extensively by special public policies, and market participation and hours of these women are very low.

A modern watershed in Swedish labor market policy for women dates back to the 1930s. Just as in the Netherlands (but for other reasons, such as migration to the United States and persistently weak performance in the agricultural sector), there was concern over possible depopulation. The Great Depression accentuated these depopulation fears and fueled the belief that women's employment was at the expense of men's jobs. What is surprising is the turn of events in which Alva Myrdal was able to argue for labor market programs for women. As head of a committee on women's labor market policy, she advanced the principle that mothers should have the right to participate in the labor market and that policies to accomplish this were needed (Gustafsson 1992a). What in fact has evolved from this conception is a system of benefit for the *joint* condition of market work and fertility.

This belief is implicit in the design of the current Swedish system: simply working without children means that one loses out on extensive benefits, and simply having children without labor market attachment implies a low standard of living. In addition to providing a maximum monetary payoff to joint work and fertility, the benefits are unrelated to family structure: unmarried women and married women receive the same benefits so long as they work in the market and have children.

The personal income tax is based on the separate earnings of the husband and wife. Given separate taxation combined with strong progressivity, there are general incentives for market work (Gustafsson 1992b). Combining the influence of the tax system with child-dependent benefits, the full effect of the Swedish system is to encourage fertility and a career or lifetime commitment to the labor market by women. While the system is often criticized on the grounds that it discourages the traditional, two-parent family, at least for preschool children there does not appear to be a problem: as of 1984 over 90 percent of preschoolers lived with both biological parents (Gustafsson and Stafford 1992).

We find the regimes approach useful in gaining an initial understanding of the dramatic system differences across the three countries. As with any classification, however, this approach brings with it some danger of overcategorizing or stereotyping the system differences. Clearly there are pressures to reconsider the scope and design of the Swedish system in light of arguments concerning allocative efficiency. To illustrate, it has been argued that for a given total daycare subsidy, it would be better to reduce the per child subsidy, raise the parents' copayment, and end the extensive rationing (Gustafsson and Stafford 1992, 214–15). On the other side of the spectrum, there has been rising concern over the developmental well-being of young children of low-income, single-parent families in the United States. Early development is seen as shaping subsequent school performance and grade completed, and there is a remarkably strong relationship between crime and school completion for young people (U.S. Department of Labor 1992).

Because of its distinctive features, we will discuss the contemporary Swedish system and its policy elements in some detail. The existing parental leave program dates from 1974, when parental leave was extended to fathers and the benefit level was raised to 90 percent of gross earnings up to a ceiling.[3] As can be seen in table 11.1, parental leave benefits are for fifty-two weeks at 90 percent of one's prior labor earnings, and another thirteen weeks of benefits are available at SKr 60 per day (about $10). The system allows either parent to draw benefits; to encourage greater use by men, starting in 1980 it has had a small special portion available for fathers only ("daddy days"). The program is strongly tied to labor market hours and therefore to labor earnings. For this reason, it is not sensible to think of the leave program as needs based. In fact, those with no earnings history receive a small "flat payment" (SKr 60 per day as of 1990), which has not kept pace with inflation since 1974 when it was introduced (at SKr 25 per day).

Figure 11.1 presents the time line of parenting leave benefit policy provisions from 1974 to 1990. The modifications in 1980 were the most significant in terms of scope and coverage of the program. The level of benefits is based on past earnings over an eligibility interval. The eligibility period was extended to twenty-four months in 1980 and then to thirty months in 1986, and this had a major impact on program use. The time extension makes it possible realistically to plan the birth of two children in succession. During this protracted period out of the labor force, benefits will equal 90 percent of pay rather than the modest amount received under the flat payment. The parental leave program extensions combined with the daycare system are regarded as having created a fertility boom in Sweden; as can be seen in table 11.1, Swedish fertility was on the same order as Irish fertility in 1988, and by 1992 the Swedish

---

3. The ceiling was applicable to only about 1 percent of women and 10 percent of men as of 1985 (Sundström and Stafford 1992). Contact days are those allowed for arranging schedules with employers, daycare centers, or schools.

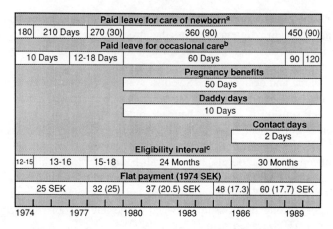

Figure 11.1   Developments in parental leave benefits in Sweden, 1974–1990

Source: National Insurance Board, various publications. Figure adapted from Sunstrom and Stafford (1992).

Note: SEK = SKr (Swedish crowns).

[a]Total number of paid leave days (days at the flat rate are in parentheses). On 1 January, 1980, days with full pay were increased to 270; On 1 July, 90 days at the flat rate were added.

[b]Before 1980, benefit days were counted per family with children under age 10; since 1980, benefit days are counted per child under age 12.

[c]Maximum number of months between births for mother to remain at least at the benefit level of the previous birth.

fertility rate had edged up still further, with added births concentrated among older and more-educated women.

The contemporary daycare system in Sweden also was established in the 1960s and expanded from the mid-1970s on. It is primarily available to mothers of preschool children after parental leave and prior to the start of grade school at age 6–7. Eligibility is based on "substantial" market work (commonly twenty or more hours per week), and in most local communities the fee paid is partly needs or income based. As can be seen in table 11.2, the system is very expensive per child (about SKr 60,000 per year, or $10,000), and the copayment by the family averages only about 10 percent of the cost, or less than $100 per month, for very high quality day care.

The number of spaces available in community childcare centers or community-sponsored homes has risen from about 15 percent of the children ages 0–6 to 47 percent in 1987, where it has stayed (approximately) since. In 1977 there was a shift toward central (state) matched funding, and until 1984 the matching formula to the local community was a combined 50 percent from the central government. From 1984 the central government funding formula was modified to SKr 22,000 per child and SKr 30,000 per childcare worker. With a ratio of one worker per four children, the per-child subsidy to the community is currently on the order of SKr 30,000, which is still 50 percent.

Table 11.2   **Characteristics of Public Child Care in Swedish Communities, 1974–1987**

Year	Ratio of Spaces to Children	Cost per Space SKr (1986 SKr)[a]	Percentage of Cost Paid by		
			Family	Community	State
1975	.15	20,675 (54,566)	12	50	38
1976	.18	23,540 (56,289)	10	56	34
1977	.20	26,960 (57,902)	10	38	52
1978	.23	31,460 (61,373)	10	40	50
1979	.27	34,505 (62,812)	10	38	52
1980	.31	39,590 (63,436)	9	40	51
1981	.34	42,700 (61,026)	8	42	50
1982	.37	44,200 (58,196)	9	41	50
1983	.40	47,800 (57,770)	10	40	50
1984	.42	54,100 (60,539)	10	38	52
1985	.45	58,100 (60,557)	10	41	49
1986	.45	62,050 (62,050)	10	44	46
1987	.47	62,400	10	43	47

Source: Arbete och Löner. S. Gustaffson and P. Lantz, (1985), (Stockholm: Industrial Institute for Economic and Social Research and Arbetslivscentrum).

[a] The figures in parentheses are conversion of the nominal SKr to common 1986 prices.

The share paid by the local community is on the order of 40 percent, and the fee paid by the parents, while averaging 10 percent, varies across communities and among families with different incomes, as illustrated for four communities in Figure 11.2. Other communities are simply represented by the two endpoints (minimum and maximum) of their income-based fee schedules. In communities with a sliding scale, families at the lowest income levels will commonly pay only 3 percent or 4 percent of the total cost, while the highest-income families will be paying about 40 percent of the cost per space. Under the sliding scale (as with the four communities illustrated, with the exception of Danderyd), the parents' share rises with income up to a ceiling, beyond which there is no added copayment. Rationing of spaces is common: at the set price in the local community, a higher share of the eligible population would like to use the system than there are spaces available. Studies indicate

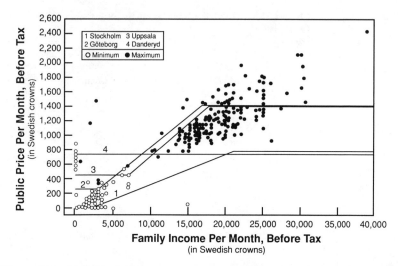

Figure 11.2   Monthly public daycare price in Swedish communities for families of differing monthly incomes.

that parents with professional occupations are far more likely to surmount the rationing barrier than are blue-collar parents (Gustafsson and Stafford 1992, 215).

A fascinating aspect of the daycare system in Sweden is its broad political support. The extent of the daycare program and the rate of parental copayment are subject to control by the 285 local communities, which (as has been noted) pay an approximate average of 40 percent of the cost. What is surprising is that in local communities not under majority control of the Social Democrats (who have championed the program), there are on average only two fewer spaces per one hundred children (Gustafsson and Stafford 1992, table 2). Evidently, there is a broad consensus that public day care should be available, and this applies to parental leave as well.

11.3   Patterns of Childcare Arrangements in the Three Countries

11.3.1   Research Findings

Research on the childcare arrangements in the three countries shows major differences in its availability and use in conjunction with labor force participation. Distinctive features of child care in the United States and the Netherlands include use of multiple modes or, particularly in the United States, arranging parental schedules to allow parental presence throughout the day (Ribar 1992, 145; Groot and Maasen van den Brink 1992, table 3; U.S. Department of Labor 1992a, table 2). In Sweden, families with a space in the public daycare system generally use this as the primary childcare arrangement (Gustafsson and Stafford 1992). For women with children under 18 months of age, paid parental leave with the mother providing the primary child care is the dominant option used (Sundström and Stafford 1992).

In contrast to the use of mothers' own time for very young children in Sweden, mothers in the United States are likely to return to the job market very soon after the birth of a child. Data from the female youth sample of the National Longitudinal Survey for 1988 (at which time the women in the sample were ages 23–30) show that close to half of the women with a child under the age of 2 were employed and that over half of these women were working thirty-five hours a week or more. This pattern has been highlighted recently (Leibowitz, Klerman, and Waite 1992, 127, table 3) and raises concerns over possible stresses on the family and the child. As we recall from section 11.2, a parent or other family member is the primary care provider for 30 percent of preschoolers even when the mother is employed full time. For those employed part time, 61 percent have the parent or other family member as the primary care provider. This has been discussed in the United States, particularly by the popular press, under the general heading of "time squeeze."

Studies based on U.S. time diaries show that educated women are likely simultaneously to work substantially in the job market, to devote a great deal of time to direct child care, and to take on added housework associated with preschool children. The net result is an obvious decline in sleep and free time (Hill and Stafford 1985). Specifically, married women college graduates with a preschooler under age 2 devoted about ten hours a week to child care and another seven hours per week to added housework. Yet market time was reduced only about seven hours a week (as of 1976). Given the fundamental time constraint, there have to be some other time use reductions. About seven hours of the ten-hour deficit $(10 + 7 - 7 = 10)$ were made up for by a reduction in passive leisure and sleep, implying a time squeeze and presumed stress for these women. The rest of the time was "financed" from a variety of alternative time uses.

While generally similar patterns are observed for educated women in Israel, (Gronau 1992), there has not been, overall, a postwar trend toward a time squeeze for women in the United States or Israel. A possible reversal of this may now be taking place, as the average real wage in the United States has stagnated and declined since the mid-1970s (Bound and Johnson 1992). Moreover, the growth of single-parent, female-headed households has raised many questions about the well-being of these mothers and children (Garfinkel and McLanahan 1986, 14 and 48), given that the poverty rate for mother-only families is on the order of 50 percent and their earnings capacity is typically very low. Is it the case that both married women and single mothers return quickly to the job market in the United States, with educated women seeking to ensure better career earnings and the single mothers with low education simply trying to make ends meet?

11.3.2   Descriptive Differences in Labor Supply of Women with Young
Children

For the purpose of comparing the three countries, we constructed tables of
labor force participation and hours for young women, by age of preschool
child. For the United States, where there is special concern over the economic
status of mother-only families, the data are presented for single women separately.

From comparisons across tables 11.3–11.6, some of the intercountry differences and program impacts can be seen.[4] In contrast to the United States,
where a high percentage of women are at work soon after giving birth, the level
of participation and work hours of Swedish women with children under age 2
is far lower, almost 40 percent lower than for women with older preschoolers.
In contrast to U.S. women, time diary data for Sweden show a fifteen-hour
decline in market work per week and an increase in free-time activities of
women with babies in the household (Klevmarken and Flood 1989). Rest and
personal care consume three hours more per week for Swedish mothers when
there are preschoolers under age 2—in contrast to the decline in personal care
and sleep of U.S. mothers. This suggests much less time pressure on Swedish
women with young preschoolers (Klevmarken and Flood 1990).

On the other hand, comparing tables 11.3 and 11.6, by the time the youngest
preschooler is age 2 many Swedish women have secured a place for the child
in the public daycare system, and the participation rate of these women is much
higher than in the United States. Given the sharply progressive tax rates that
prevailed in Sweden as of 1984, as well as the legal right to work shorter hours
(to a six-hour workday) with job protection, we see far fewer Swedish women
working thirty-five or more hours per week in the labor market when preschool
children are present. Although Swedish women with 2- and 3-year-olds average somewhat higher market hours than comparable U.S. women, the U.S.
women are more than twice as likely to work thirty-four hours per week or
more.

As of 1985 the overall Dutch female labor force participation rate for women
with preschoolers was only 27 percent, well below the rate in the Scandinavian
countries and the United States (Pott-Buter 1993). In addition, hours of work
for those working were low, and there was the continuation of a long tradition
of volunteer work by married women. It is possible that the low correlation
between use of formal day care and market work is the consequence of the
prevailing view (as in Germany; see Braun, Scott, and Alwin 1992) that full-
time parenting was the best lifestyle for women. As its corresponding embodi-

---

4. Assessing data from the Netherlands requires that careful attention be given to the age of the
women and time period of any sample used. This is because there has been a dramatic increase in
participation among younger women in recent years (OSA 1991). For example, a new sample of
six thousand families in the Dutch population shows the following labor force participation rates
for mothers with children in specified age ranges: under age 1, 39.7 percent; age 1, 41.7 percent;
age 2, 42.6 percent; age 3, 43.0 percent; and age 4, 43.2 percent (Maassen van den Brink 1993).

Table 11.3   **Market Work of Mothers according to Age of Child: United States**

Age of Youngest Child (in years)	Hours per Week of Market Work						
	None	1–9	10–19	20–29	30–34	35 or More	
Under 1	57.6%	3.2%	5.3%	5.0%	3.5%	25.4%	100.0% (1,052)
1–1.99	45.1	4.2	6.4	6.2	4.7	33.3	100.0 (450)
2–3	44.5	2.6	3.2	5.6	5.6	38.6	100.0 (663)
4–5	36.9	3.3	6.4	7.6	4.5	41.2	100.0 (485)
0–5.99	48.4	3.2	5.1	5.8	4.4	32.9	100.00 (2,650)

Source: National Longitudinal Surveys, Young Women Age 23–30 as of 1988.

Table 11.4   **Market Work of Not-Married Mothers according to Age of Child: United States**

Age of Youngest Child (in years)	Hours per Week of Market Work						
	None	1–9	10–19	20–29	30–34	35 or More	
Under 1	64.5%	1.9%	2.3%	2.3%	2.3%	26.6%	100.0% (259)
1–1.99	50.7	0.7	6.7	5.3	5.3	31.3	100.0 (150)
2–3	51.8	2.8	1.6	4.9	4.1	34.8	100.0 (247)
4–5	48.3	1.1	4.6	8.1	5.8	32.2	100.0 (87)
0–5.99	55.6	1.9	3.2	4.4	3.9	31.0	100.00 (743)

Source: National Longitudinal Surveys, Young Women Age 23–30 as of 1988.

ment in public policy, this view has elements ranging from eligibility for the small public day care for women not in the labor market to tax deductions for dependent children (until 1990).

Table 11.5 shows the very low participation rates for women with preschoolers under age 2. While the U.S. participation rate is 46 percent, in the Netherlands it is 26 percent for those with children under age 1 and 22 percent for those with a child age 1–1.99 years. These participation rates, about half the corresponding U.S. rates, occur despite fairly similar public policies (with the possible exception of paid child leave for sixteen weeks in the Netherlands (see table 11.1). Even among mothers with older preschool children, the participa-

Table 11.5   **Market Work of Mothers according to Age of Child: The Netherlands**

Age of Youngest Child (in years)	Hours per Week of Market Work						
	None	1–9	10–19	20–29	30–34	35 or More	
Under 1	74.4%	4.9%	13.3%	3.0%	1.0%	3.5%	100.0% (203)
1–1.99	78.0	7.6	8.5	3.4	0.9	1.7	100.0 (118)
2–3	73.2	8.5	12.7	.7	0.7	4.2	100.0 (142)
4–5	62.1	15.5	12.6	2.9	0.0	6.8	100.0 (103)
0–5	72.6	8.3	12.0	2.5	0.7	5.8	99.9 (566)
6 or older	65.2	8.2	13.1	5.6	1.8	6.3	100.0 (1,079)

Source: OSA Survey, Women Age 16–65 as of 1988.

Table 11.6   **Market Work of Mothers, according to Age of Child: Sweden**

Age of Youngest Child (in years)	Hours per Week of Market Work						
	None	1–9	10–19	20–29	30–34	35 or More	
Under 1	58.8%	0.0%	1.5%	16.2%	1.5%	22.1%	100.0% (68)
1–1.99	20.4	0.0	26.5	32.7	10.2	10.2	100.0 (49)
2–3	23.9	2.7	16.8	31.9	8.0	16.8	100.0 (113)
4–5	25.0	0.0	13.3	25.0	10.0	26.7	100.0 (60)
0–5	31.7	1.0	14.4	27.0	7.2	18.7	100.0 (290)
6–18	16.6	2.1	18.7	20.6	7.7	34.3	100.0 (379)

Source: HUS Survey, Women Age 18–64 as of 1984.

tion rate remains below 40 percent, and hours of market work of those who work are rarely in excess of thirty-five hours in the Netherlands. Only about 6 percent of Dutch women with children under age 6 work more than thirty-five hours per week in the market. This labor supply pattern is consistent with the finding that the Netherlands and Japan had a similar near-constancy in housework hours of women over the period 1960–80, while in other industrialized countries there was a strong movement away from housework and toward market work (Juster and Stafford 1991, table 6).

The three countries differ dramatically in the percentage of preschoolers in mother-only families. In the Netherlands 4.6 percent of our sample was mother-only cases; in Sweden special census tabulations place this at 11.0 percent; in the U.S. National Longitudinal Survey (NLS) sample, 28.0 percent of the mothers were not married or living in a consensual union.

11.3.3   Econometric Analysis of Labor Force Participation

Wage Regressions

Based on our three microdata samples of women with young children, we have sought to portray some of the salient differences in women's labor market payoffs to work and education and how wage opportunities, family status, and childcare costs influence market participation. Given that most Dutch women have to arrange child care without much in the way of public policy, we estimated a simple model of responsiveness of daycare use to market price. What we find is that simple models of labor market behavior show many differences across the countries.

To begin, we examined the market payoff to education and work experience. Table 11.7 displays wage regressions for the three countries. The wage variable in the U.S. data is before-tax wage, whereas the Dutch data provide information only on after-tax monthly earnings. In the Swedish data there is information on before-tax wage, and use of previous work (Gustafsson 1992b) allows us to compute the after-tax wage in order to make comparisons with the Dutch data. In both the Swedish and Dutch data, we included women age 45 and younger. A limitation in comparing those results with the U.S. results is that the age range in the NLS only went up to age 30. The Swedish sample size is quite small, and limiting the sample size to include only women 33 years of age and younger would have been too restrictive.

The wage regressions are standard Mincer (1974) earnings functions; we expect education and labor market experience to be the most important explanatory variables. The Dutch data do not include information on years of labor market experience; after some experimentation with ages of the children as an indicator of experience, we opted for age of the woman and number of family members as explanatory variables in the Dutch wage regression. The results of the wage regressions show that there is much more wage variation in the United States than in the Netherlands or Sweden.

Both high school and college education carry a higher wage premium in the United States than in the other two countries. Also, work experience carries a much higher wage premium in the United States than in Sweden, but this may partly reflect the higher payoff to experience early in one's career, since the U.S. sample is younger and less experienced. The average length of labor force experience in the United States is less than a year, compared to thirteen years in Sweden.

In appendix table 11A.1, the means of variables are given. It turns out that the distribution over educational groups between the three countries is very

Table 11.7   **Wage Regressions (OLS), All Women (dependent variable Ln(w);**
                    t-values in parentheses)

	United States[a]	Netherlands[b]	Sweden[c] I	Sweden[c] II
Year	1988	1988	1984	1984
Constant	1.63	−.473	1.97	3.03
	(58.4)	(−1.99)	(32.0)	(29.1)
Education (compulsory = reference category)				
High school	.235	.070	.167	.135
	(8.7)	(2.5)	(5.7)	(5.1)
College	.573	.319	.271	.181
	(18.3)	(10.0)	(5.9)	(4.4)
Experience				
Age		.141		
		(8.8)		
(Age)[b]		−.002		
		(7.8)		
Number of family members		−.022		
		(7.8)		
Experience	.288		.0256	.0238
	(9.3)		(2.7)	(2.7)
(Experience)[b]	−.062		−.0006	−.0006
	(−3.8)		(−1.9)	(−1.9)
n	3145	532	382	366
R^2	.14	.34	.15	.12

Sources: United States: NLS/4; The Netherlands: OSA; Sweden: HUS.
Note: Ln (w) = Natural logarithm of wage.
[a]Wage variable is before-tax wage.
[b]Wage variable is net after taxes.
[c]I = Before-tax wage; II = Net after tax.

unequal. In the United States, almost everyone has completed high school. In Sweden and the Netherlands, about one-third fall into this group. In both the United States and the Netherlands, about 22 percent have completed college. It is difficult to say if these differences are real or an effect of definitions of education used in the different samples (see appendix A). However, given that college completion is more selective in Sweden than in the United States, it is of note that the payoff to college education of women in the United States *exceeds* the payoff in Sweden.

Participation Regressions

The sample means of labor force participation of young married women in the three countries are 72 percent in the United States, 49 percent in the Netherlands, and 82 percent in Sweden (see table 11.8). In all three countries,

Table 11.8   **Participation Equations (Logit): Married Women under 45 Years of Age (dependent variable: labor force participation; *t*-values in parentheses)**

	United States[a]	Netherlands[b]	Sweden[c] I	Sweden[c] II
Year	1988	1988	1984	1984
Constant	1.303	−.413	1.202	1.227
	(5.0)	(−1.2)	(1.6)	(1.4)
Husband's monthly income				
(× 1,000)	−1.90	−.396	−.1603	−.893
	(−2.5)	(−2.5)	(−1.1)	(−2.2)
Own wage	.044	.257	.0921	.255
	(1.9)	(4.9)	(1.4)	(2.3)
Child age 0–2 (= 1)	−.436	−.789	−1.099	−1.15
	(−2.5)	(−3.5)	(−3.2)	(−3.3)
Child age 3–5 (= 1)	.011	−.318	−.449	−.475
	(−.06)	(−1.2)	(−1.3)	(−1.4)
Number of children 0–12	−.055	−.501	.103	.088
	(−.7)	(−4.8)	(.69)	(.59)
Husband unemployed (= 1)	−.383	−.707		
	(−1.6)	(−2.3)		
Goes to church (= 1)	.006	−.332	n.a.	n.a.
	(.05)	(−1.9)		
Index of day care				
availability	—	—	.004	.006
			(.18)	(.27)
N	1,252	872	357	371
Log likelihood	−732	−536	−163	−163

Sources: United States: NLS/Y; The Netherlands: OSA; Sweden: HUS.
Note: Labor force participation = At least one hour paid work per week.
[a]Women ages 23–30 in 1988.
[b]OSA data net after taxes.
[c]I = Before-tax wage; II = Net after tax.

husband's income has a negative effect and wife's wage a positive effect on participation, as we would expect.[5] The Swedish after-tax regression performs better than the before-tax regression. Theoretically, people should be making decisions on the basis of their after-tax wage and income, and Swedish income tax rates in 1984 were both high and progressive. On the other hand, net wages are endogenous to the hours-of-work decision. Yet, since our dependent variable is to work at least one hour for pay in the survey week, this endogenity is less of a problem.

In all three countries, the impact of children under age 3 is to significantly lower labor force participation; this effect is most pronounced in Sweden,

5. The Dutch earnings data are after tax, and the equation should be compared to the second Swedish wage regression.

where the generous parental leave program has its impact. Children ages 3 to 5 have a far smaller impact on participation, and only in the Netherlands does the number of children under 13 years of age decrease mothers' labor force participation significantly. We believe this to be fairly strong support for the hypothesis that long-standing beliefs about the mother's obligation to a full-time childcare commitment holds sway over labor market behavior of Dutch women. The most telling comparison is with U.S. women, since the parental leave policy in the Netherlands is among the United States husbands 10.5 percent were unemployed according to this definition. In the Swedish data there are fourteen husbands who received unemployment benefits. All of them have working wives, and the variable could not therefore be included.

Finally, for Sweden we included an index of availability of community day care in the community where the mother lives. The variable is not significant, but controlling for this variable increases the t-values of the wage and income variables.

Price Sensitivity of Daycare Use and Mother's Work

In table 11.9, for Dutch women, we present an ordered probit regression on whether the respondent would increase the use of day care if the price were lower. The higher the husband's income, the less likely the mother is to be price sensitive in the use of day care. If she is religious, she is also less likely to respond to lower daycare price, although the coefficient is not quite significant. Family resources, represented by husband's income, and religious outlook, represented by church attendance, have an apparent and jointly discouraging effect on market work of Dutch women limited to fourteen weeks (in contrast to sixty-five weeks in Sweden).

The view that historical and cultural influences matter is supported further by the impact of religious activity on labor force participation of Dutch women. In the Netherlands, women who attend church are less likely to participate in the labor market. The definition of the variable is "goes to church at least once a month," and 26 percent of the Dutch mothers do so. There is an NLS/y variable based on an identically phrased question, and 52 percent of the women in our sample go to church at least once a month. There is no apparent relation between church attendance and labor market participation in the United States.

In the Netherlands, unemployment benefits are dependent on family income, and the participation equation shows that Dutch women whose husbands are unemployed (7 percent of the sample) participate significantly less in the labor market than other women. This is consistent with the hypothesis of a "poverty trap" in the Dutch tax and social security system (Gustafsson and Bruyn-Hundt 1991), which is also present in the British social security system. In England, the husband's unemployment has similarly strong negative effects on wife's labor force participation.

A "husband unemployed" variable in the U.S. regression shows a negative

Table 11.9   **Price Sensitivity for Day Care in the Netherlands: Women with Children under 12 (asymptotic *t*-values in parentheses)**

Price query: Would you use more day care if the price were lower?

Response	Percentage Observed
No (= 1)	81.2%
Do not know (=2)	9.9
Yes (=3)	8.9
	100.0

Ordered Probit Estimates		Means
Constant 1	.403	
Constant 2	.887	
Own wage	−.008	12.0
	(−.33)	
Husband's monthly income (× 1,000)	−.217	2.39
	(−2.3)	
Labor force participation (hours > 0)	.086	.34
	(.57)	
Child age 0–2 (= 1)	.199	.41
	(1.5)	
Uses child care (= 1)	.345	.17
	(2.0)	
Goes to church (= 1)[a]	−.270	.26
	(−1.75)	
N	494	
Log likelihood	−293	

[a]At least once a week.

but not statistically significant effect on wife's labor force participation. The unemployment definition was "husband has no earnings," and insofar as these variables would lower the willingness to utilize day care even if the price were lower. On the other hand, for those who do use child care, a lower price would lead to more use. This parallels the well-established result for the U.S. childcare market (Ribar 1992; Michalopoulos, Robins, and Garfinkel 1992) and for user response to the variation in copayment rate in the Swedish public childcare system (Gustafsson and Stafford 1992). Further, using an approach similar to that of Ribar (1992) for U.S. data, the substantial price sensitivity of daycare use and mother's work is observed in a recent study of the Netherlands (Groot and Maassen van den Brink 1992).

11.4   Conclusion

Comparisons have shown that among these three advanced industrialized countries, the policies and practices of child care and labor supply of women with young children differ dramatically. Partly, these differences arise from historical differences in broad social institutions (Stafford and Robinson 1990). These differences have shaped contemporary differences not just in isolated features of the childcare or tax laws but in major, complementary elements of a system shaping the choices of families with young children.

The impact of these historical and policy variables (other than tax rates, which influence the wage rate and family income) may help explain the puzzle in multinational comparisons of labor supply conducted in the mid-1980s (Layard and Mincer 1985). Within countries, labor supply of married women seems to be explained by some of the same variables: wages and income variations, tax incentives, and family responsibilities. Yet across countries the differences in such variables seem to have far less power. A possible resolution of this result is that there are major long-term institutional and social protection policy differences that cause differences in labor supply.

Appendix
Data

The Netherlands

The Organisatie voor Strategisch Arbeidsmarktonderzoek (OSA) data are organized as a panel (OSA 1991) (see table 11A.1). To utilize the OSA data,

Table 11A.1   Means of Variables

	United States	Netherlands	Sweden	
In wage regression				
Compulsory education	.15	.44	.57	
High school	.63	.34	.32	
College	.22	.22	.11	
Experience	.8		13.0	
Age		30.1		
Number of family members		2.9		
In participation logits			I	II
Participation	.72	.49	.82	
Husband's income	1,633	2,335	8,689	4,799
Own wage	7.4	11.7	39.7	26.9
Child age 0–2	.52	.24	.18	
Child age 3–5	.28	.12	.24	
Number of children < 12	1.74	.97	.65	
Husband unemployed	.105	.07	.039	
Goes to church	.52	.23	n.a.	
Index of daycare possibility			11.1	11.2

one can contact OSA, Van Stolkweg 14,2585 JR The Hague, The Netherlands. For the first wave of April 1985, a random sample of two thousand households was selected. In all households, all members between ages 16 and 65 years of age were interviewed if they were not full-time students or military draftees.

The second and third waves took place in fall 1986 and 1988, respectively. This study uses the 1988 wave. All respondents interviewed in the first wave were asked to participate, and household members who had moved were included in the sample. To counter the loss of households by nonresponse, new households were added by the "random walk" method (i.e., a new household from the same neighborhood was chosen). The total number of observations in 1988 were 4,464, and the number of respondents among these who were interviewed also in 1985 was 1,868, less than half of the respondents (OSA 1991, B15).

The wage and income variables are constructed from a question on net earnings. The respondent could choose between answering net income per week, net income per four weeks, or net income per month. To get wage per hour we used the variable average number of hours, excluding overtime, worked per week. The education variable is highest education completed. The Dutch education system is derived from the "columnized" society, so there are many parallel schools of different kinds covering the same age groups of students but with different profiles (e.g., degree of academic achievement). We have grouped the different educations into three groups covering as closely as possible the division into compulsory school (BO, LBO, MAVO), high school (MBO, HAVO, VWO), and college (HBO, WO). The Dutch data do not have any information on years of labor market experience. It turned out that the number of family members in addition to age and age square predicts the wages fairly well for married women (legally married plus women living in consensual unions).

For the participation equation, we predicted net own wage for nonworkers and used actual net wage for workers. The variable husband unemployed was asked: Do you currently receive unemployment benefits? If the husband answered this question affirmatively, the variable is equal to one and he also answered the question, How many hours do you currently work (by zero)? A person was considered religious if she answered that she went to church every week or at least once a month. For child care, the person was asked, Do you currently use child care (yes or no)?

United States

In the analysis of child care and female labor supply, we use the National Longitudinal Youth panel (NLS/y) (see table 11A.1). The National Longitudinal Survey of Youth was designed by the Center for Human Resource Research, Ohio State University, and fielded by the National Opinion Research Center (NORC) at the University of Chicago. The NLS/y began in 1979 with a national probability sample of subjects aged 14–21 on 1 January 1979. The original sample was 12,686 persons living in the United States. The respondents have been reinterviewed annually.

We selected 1988 for our basis year because there was more child documentation up to and including 1988 and the Dutch data also are for 1988. In order to create our file for the wage equation and the participation equation, we had to use variables from the following files: Keyvar 1988, Marriage 1988, Schools for all years, CPS 1988, Common file, and Family Background 1982. The data include women aged 23–30 in 1988. The hours variable is number of hours worked during the survey week (R2518800). The question was phrased, How many hours did you work last week at all jobs? The wage variable we used is hourly rate of pay of current or most recent job (R2526010). Religious activity is once a month or more frequent (R6556). Whether the husband is unemployed is defined in the NLS/y data as husband having zero earnings. The definition of completing high school is to have completed the twelfth grade; the definition of college is to have completed the sixteenth grade.

Sweden

The Hushallens Ekonomiska Levnadsforhallanden (HUS) data are organized as a panel (see table 11A.1). The director of the HUS data is Prof. Anders Klevmarken. People interested in analyzing the data should contact Professor Anders Klevmarken, Department of Economics, University of Gothenburg, Viktoriagatan 30, S-41125 Gothenburg, Sweden.

The first wave was collected in 1984. The original data include 1,184 women and 1,114 men. In the 1984 HUS data all adult members of a select household are interviewed if they are not in an institution. Split households are followed in subsequent panels, and young people are added to make the cross section representative. The second wave was collected in 1986. In 1988 the University of Gothenburg mailed a small survey without external fundings with the most important variables. In 1991 there was a new small survey, and for 1993 a larger survey is again funded. The number of respondents who are in all three panels (1984, 1986, and 1988) are 656 women and 602 men. Data from the HUS panel have been used for analysis of separate taxation in Gustafsson (1992c) and on childcare subsidies and labor supply in Sweden (Gustafsson and Stafford 1992). We choose to use the 1984 HUS data because thereby we can make use of the auxiliary data on child care and taxes that were constructed for the two previous papers. The HUS data have very many more variables than the more limited OSA survey.

In this paper, we attempted regressions that were as similar as possible across the three countries. The wage variable we defined in the same way as the Dutch variable—namely, net after tax wage at actual hours worked—and net wage was predicted in the same way. The variable in the HUS data is before-tax monthly income if the person receives monthly pay and before-tax hourly wage if the person receives hourly pay. The variable was converted into net wage by use of a tax simulation worked out for Gustafsson. The whole tax program is published (Gustafsson and Bruyn-Hundt 1991). Husband's income after tax was calculated by the same procedure. There is a variable on whether the person was unemployed. Among the 445 women who were younger than age forty-five, there were fourteen unemployed husbands. There is no information on religiosity in the Swedish data because practically no religious groups remain in Sweden.

References

Abraham, F. 1992. Social protection and regional convergence in an EMU. International Economics Research Paper no. 83. *OER.* Forthcoming.

Bound, J., and G. E. Johnson. 1992. Changes in the structure of wages during the 1980's: An evaluation of alternative explanations. *American Economic Review* 82, June, 371–92.

Braun, M., J. Scott, and D. F. Alwin. 1992. Economic necessity of self-actualization? Attitudes toward women's labor force participation in the East and West. Occasional Paper no. 9. Essex: University of Essex, ESRC Centre on Micro-social Change.

Buchanan, J., and G. Tullock. 1965. *The calculus of consent.* Ann Arbor: University of Michigan Press.

Esping-Andersen, G. 1990. *The three worlds of welfare capitalism.* Princeton, N.J.: Princeton University Press.

Friedman, M. 1953. Choice, chance, and the personal distribution of income. *Journal of Political Economy* 61, August, 277–90.

Garfinkel, I., and S. McLanahan. 1986. *Single mothers and their children: A new American dilemma.* Washington, D.C.: Urban Institute Press.

Goldin, C. 1990. *Understanding the gender gap: An economic history of American women.* New York: Oxford University Press.

Golonka and Ooms. 1991. Paper presented at the Family Impact Seminar. Cited in Hofferth and Wissoker, (1992).

Gronau, R. 1992. Private communication on research.

Groot, W., and H. Maassen van den Brink. 1992. Labor supply, child care, and consumption. Research manuscript. University of Amsterdam, Department of Economics, May.

Gustafsson, S. 1984. Equal opportunity policies in Sweden. In *Sex, discrimination, and equal opportunity: The labor market and employment policy,* ed. G. Schmid and R. Weitzel. London: Gower.

———. 1992a. Female labor supply and pronatalism: An economic history of Swedish family policies. Research memorandum. Department of Economics, University of Amsterdam.

———. 1992b. Public policies and women's labor force participation: A comparison between Sweden, the Netherlands, and Germany. Paper presented at the Conference on Women's Human Capital and Development, Bellagio, Italy, 18–22 May.

———. 1992c. Separate taxation and married women's labor supply. A comparison of West Germany and Sweden. *Journal of Population Economics* 5(7): 61–85.

Gustafsson, S., and M. Bruyn-Hundt. 1991. Incentives for women to work: A comparison between the Netherlands, Sweden, and West Germany. *Journal of Economic Studies* 18, no. 5/6: 30–65.

Gustafsson, S., and F. P. Stafford. 1992. Childcare subsidies and labor supply in Sweden. *Journal of Human Resources* 27, winter, 204–30.

Hill, C. R., and F. P. Stafford. 1985. Parental care of children: Predictability and variety. In *Time, goods, and well-being*, ed. F. T. Juster and F. P. Stafford, 415–38. Ann Arbor: Survey Research Center, University of Michigan.

Hofferth, S., A. Brayfield, S. Deich, and P. Holcomb. 1991. *National child care survey, 1990*. Urban Institute Report 91–5. Washington, D.C.: Urban Institute Press.

Hofferth, S., and D. Wissoker. 1992. Price, quality, and income in child care choice. *Journal of Human Resources* 27, winter, 70–111.

Johnson, G. E., and F. P. Stafford. 1992. Models of international competition and real wages. Discussion Paper no. 314, Research Forum on International Economics, Institute of Public Policy Studies. Ann Arbor: Department of Economics, University of Michigan, July 1992.

―――. 1993. International competition and real wages. *American Economic Review Papers* and *Proceedings* 83 (May) 2: 127–30.

Juster, F. T., and F. P. Stafford. 1991. The allocation of time: Empirical findings, behavioral models, and problems of measurement. *Journal of Economic Literature* 29 (June):471–522.

Klevmarken, A., and L. Flood. 1989. *Tidsänvandningen i Sverige i 1984* (Time use in Sweden in 1984). Research Memorandum 127. Gothenburg: University of Gothenburg, Department of Economics.

―――. 1990. Arbete och fritid: Svenska hushålls tidsanvändning. In *Tid och Råd: Om Hushållens Ekonomi*, ed. Klevmarken, 177–233. Stockholm: Industriens Utredningsinstitut.

Krugman, P. 1979. A model of innovation, technology transfer, and the world distribution of income. *Journal of Political Economy* 87, April, 253–66.

Layard, R., and J. Mincer, eds. 1985. Trends in women's work, education, and family building. Conference proceedings. Chelwood Gate, 31 May–3 June 1983. *Journal of Labor Economics* 3, Supplement.

Leibowitz, A., J. A. Klerman, and L. J. Waite. 1992. Employment of new mothers and child care choice. *Journal of Human Resources* 27 (winter): 127.

Maassen van den Brink, H. 1993. Female labor supply, child care, and marital conflict. Dissertation research. Amsterdam: University of Amsterdam, Department of Economics.

Michalopoulos, C., P. K. Robins, and I. Garfinkel. 1992. A structural model of labor supply and child care demand. *Journal of Human Resources* 27, winter, 166–203.

Milgrom, P., and J. Roberts. 1992. *Economics, organization, and management.* Englewood Cliffs, N.J.: Prentice Hall.

Mincer, J. 1974. Schooling, experience and earnings. New York: Columbia University Press.

Organisatie voor Strategisch Arbeidsmarktonderzoek (OSA). 1991. *Trendrapport aanbood van arbeid,* 12. The Hague: OSA.

Pott-Buter, H. 1993. Facts and fairy tales about female labor, family and fertility. A seven-country comparison, 1850–1990. Amsterdam: Amsterdam University Press.

Rainwater, L., M. Rein, and J. Schwartz. 1986. *Income packaging in the welfare state: A comparative study of family income.* Oxford: Clarendon Press.

Ribar, D. C. 1992. Child care and the labor supply of married women: Reduced form evidence. *Journal of Human Resources* 27 (winter): 134–65.

Ryder, H., F. P. Stafford, and P. E. Stephan. 1976. Labor, leisure, and training over the life cycle. *International Economic Review* 17 (October) 3:651–74.

Stafford, F. P. 1977. More on unemployment insurance as insurance. *Industrial and Labor Relations Review* 30 (July):526–31.

Stafford, F. P., and M. Robinson. 1990. Industrial growth and social institutions. In

Institutions in American society: Essays in market, political, and social organiza-tions, ed. J. E. Jackson. Ann Arbor: University of Michigan Press.
Sundstrom, M., and F. P. Stafford. 1992. Female labor force participation, fertility, and public policy in Sweden. *European Journal of Population* 8:199–215.
Titmuss, R. 1958. *Essays on the welfare state.* London: Allen and Unwin.
U.S. Department of Labor, Bureau of Labor Statistics. 1992a. Childcare arrangements of young working mothers, table 2. Research Note.
———. 1992b. National Longitudinal Surveys. Research memorandum. Unpublished.
van Kessel, E., M. Kuperus, and H. Pott-Buter. 1986. *Hoezo gelijk belast?* Amsterdam: De Populier/Amazone.
Varian, H. R. 1980. Redistributive taxes as social insurance. *Journal of Public Finance* 14, August, 49–68.

Contributors

Katharine G. Abraham
Department of Economics
University of Maryland
Room 3105, Tydings Hall
College Park, MD 20742

Rebecca M. Blank
Department of Economics
Northwestern University
2003 Sheridan Rd.
Evanston, IL 60208

Axel Börsch-Supan
Department of Economics
University of Mannheim
D-68131 Mannheim, Germany

Sara de la Rica
Departamento de Fundamentos del
    Analisis Economico
Universidad del País Vasco
Avenida Lehendakari Aguirre, No 83
48015 Bilbao, Spain

Richard B. Freeman
National Bureau of Economic Research
1050 Massachusetts Ave.
Cambridge, MA 02138

Siv Gustafsson
Economics Department
University of Amsterdam
Roetersstraat 11
1018 WB Amsterdam, Netherlands

Maria J. Hanratty
Industrial Relations Section A-19-G3
Firestone Library
Princeton University
Princeton, NJ 08544

Douglas Holtz-Eakin
Metropolitan Studies Program
Syracuse University
Room 400, Maxwell Hall
Syracuse, NY 13244

Susan N. Houseman
W. E. Upjohn Institute for Employment
    Research
300 South Westnedge Ave.
Kalamazoo, MI 49007

Thomas Lemieux
Department of Economics
University of Montréal
P.O. Box 6128, Station A
Montréal, Quèbec, Canada H3C 3J7

Edward B. Montgomery
Department of Economics
University of Maryland
Room 3115, Tydings Hall
College Park, MD 20742

Marcus E. Rebick
New York State School of Industrial and
   Labor Relations
Cornell University
265 Ives Hall
Ithaca, NY 14853

Peter Scherer
Social Affairs and Industrial Relations
   Division
Organisation for Economic Co-operation
   and Development
2, rue André Pascal
75775 Paris cedex 16, France

Frank P. Stafford
Department of Economics
University of Michigan
611 Tappan Street
Ann Arbor, MI 48109

Author Index

Subject Index